SECOND EDITION

# America's Teachers

## AN INTRODUCTION TO EDUCATION

## JOSEPH W. NEWMAN

*University of South Alabama*

**Longman**

New York & London

**AMERICA'S TEACHERS, Second Edition**

Longman, 10 Bank Street, White Plains, N.Y. 10606

Associated companies:
Longman Group Ltd., London
Longman Cheshire Pty., Melbourne
Longman Paul Pty., Auckland
Copp Clark Pitman, Toronto

Acquisitions editor: Stuart B. Miller
Development editor: Virginia L. Blanford
Production editor: Linda S. Moser
Cover design: Bob Crimi Studio
Production supervisor: Anne Armeny

 This book is printed on recycled paper.

**Library of Congress Cataloging-in-Publication Data**

Newman, Joseph W.
    America's teachers : an introduction to education / Joseph W.
Newman. — 2nd ed.
        p.   cm.
    Includes bibliographical references.
    ISBN 0-8013-0843-7
    1. Education—United States—History.  2. Teachers—Vocational
guidance—United States.  I. Title.
LA217.2.N5   1993
370'.973—dc20                        93-16924
                                             CIP

1 2 3 4 5 6 7 8 9 10-MA-9796959493

# Contents

*Preface    xi*


**PART I    TEACHING AS AN OCCUPATION**                                         **1**


CHAPTER 1    **DECIDING TO TEACH AND FINDING A JOB**      **3**

Motives for Teaching    *3*
   *Perceived Advantages of Teaching 5, Teachers Who Love, Teachers*
   *Who Care 5, Teachers and Culturally Diverse Students 6,*
   *Teaching as Academic Work 7*
Satisfaction with Teaching     *8*
   *Burnouts, Dropouts, and the Promise of School Reform 10, The*
   *Critical Years Ahead 12*
The Teacher Job Market     *13*
   *Baby Boom, "Generation X," and Baby Boom: The Demand for*
   *Teachers 13, A Complex Guessing Game: The Supply of*
   *Teachers 16, The Politics of Teacher Supply and Demand 18,*
   *Bending Standards, Changing Standards 19, Trends in the Job*
   *Market, Field by Field 20*
*Activities    22*
*Recommended Readings    23*
*Notes    23*

CHAPTER 2 **EARNING A LIVING AND LIVING WITH EVALUATION** **27**

Teacher Salaries, State by State *28*
A Profile of America's Teachers *31*
Comparing Salaries in Teaching and Other Occupations *33*
Teacher Salary Schedules *35*
Merit Pay: The Birth of "Sound and Cheap" *40*
The Accountability Movement: Merit Pay Reborn *42*
   *The Factory Model of Schooling 43, Accountability-Based Merit Pay on Trial 43*
Behavioral Evaluation of Teachers *44*
Portfolios and Assessment Centers: Multifaceted Teacher Evaluation *46*
Merit Pay, Latest Versions *47*
   *Two Recent Experiments 47, Merit Pay Plans that Last 48, State and Local Career Ladders 48*
A National Career Ladder *51*
*Activities 53*
*Recommended Readings 53*
*Notes 53*

CHAPTER 3 **LEARNING TO TEACH AND PROVING YOUR COMPETENCE** **57**

Multiple Routes into Teaching *59*
   *The Traditional Route: Undergraduate Teacher Education 59, Nontraditional Routes 63*
Raising Standards in Teacher Education *69*
   *Nostalgia for a Golden Age of Teaching 69, Teacher Competency Today 71*
Literacy Tests *72*
   *Why Such Low Cutoff Scores? 72, Why Not Just Raise the Cutoffs? 73*
Teacher Certification Tests *73*
   *General Knowledge 74, The Teaching Field 75, Professional Education 75, The Successor to the National Teacher Examinations 76, The National Board for Professional Teaching Standards 77*
Teacher Testing and Minority Teachers *78*
   *A Precarious Situation 78, A Way Out? 79, Cautious Optimism 80*
The Positive Vision of John Goodlad *80*
*Activities 82*
*Recommended Readings 82*
*Notes 83*

CHAPTER 4    **JOINING A TEACHER ORGANIZATION AND EMPOWERING A PROFESSION    89**

NEA and AFT    *90*
  *Four Key Differences 91, Labor, Management, and Gender 93, What Membership Means 94*
Collective Bargaining    *95*
  *AFT Points the Way 95, How Bargaining Works 96, What Bargaining Covers 97*
Teacher Strikes    *98*
Political Action    *99*
  *PACs 100, Who Gets Endorsed 100, Grassroots Politics and Teacher Power 101*
A Teaching Profession?    *102*
  *A Unique, Essential Social Service 103, A Defined, Respected Knowledge Base 104, Autonomy 105*
Pressing toward Professionalism    *107*
  *State Professional Standards Boards: A Case Study of NEA Strategy 107, Restructuring in Rochester: A Case Study of AFT Strategy 109, Professionalism, Feminism, and Unionism 112*
*Activities    113*
*Recommended Readings    113*
*Notes    114*

CHAPTER 5    **EXERCISING YOUR RIGHTS AND FULFILLING YOUR RESPONSIBILITIES    119**

Employment    *120*
  *Contracts 120, Tenure 120, Dismissal 121, Due Process 123*
Liability    *124*
  *Injuries to Students 124, Reporting Child Abuse and Neglect 125, The Teacher and AIDS 126, Educational Malpractice 128*
Expression    *129*
  *Academic Freedom 129, Right of Public Dissent 131, Other Forms of Expression 133*
*Activities    134*
*Recommended Readings    134*
*Notes    135*

**PART II    SCHOOLS AND SOCIETY    137**

CHAPTER 6    **HISTORY OF AMERICAN EDUCATION    139**

Debates and Patterns    *139*
Historical Interpretation    *140*

Common School Reform in Historical Context    *141*
   *District Schools, Academies, and Other Schools  142, The Impact of*
   *Modernization  144*
Debates over Common School Reform    *147*
   *Politics  148, Morality and Religion  149*
The Triumph of Common Schools    *151*
Progressive School Reform in Historical Context    *152*
   *Modernization Accelerates  153, Liberal and Conservative School*
   *Reformers  154, Ordinary People: Students, Parents, Teachers, and*
   *Others  154*
Debates over Progressive School Reform    *155*
   *Assimilation for Immigrant Children  155, The Middle Course of*
   *Pluralism  156, Separation for African-American Children  158*
Progressive School Reform in Perspective    *162*
Twentieth-Century Patterns of Education    *163*
   *Competition for Control of the Schools  163, The*
   *Local/State/Federal Balance  165, The Quest for Equal Educational*
   *Opportunities  166, Trends in the Curriculum  167*
*Activities    169*
*Recommended Readings    169*
*Notes    170*


CHAPTER 7   **PHILOSOPHIES AND THEORIES**
            **OF EDUCATION        175**

"Why" Questions    *175*
Four Philosophies    *176*
   *Idealism  176, Realism  177, Pragmatism  177, Existentialism  178*
Theories of Education: An Overview    *179*
Perennialism    *180*
   *The Great Books  181,* The Paideia Proposal *181*
Essentialism    *184*
   *William C. Bagley and the 1930s  185, The Academic Critics of the*
   *1950s  186, Back to Basics through Behavioral Essentialism: The*
   *1970s, 1980s, and 1990s  187, Contemporary Essentialists  189*
Progressivism    *191*
   *Children, Society, and Their Problems  193, Progressivism in the*
   *Classroom  194, Social Reconstructionism  196, Life*
   *Adjustment  197, Blame It on Progressivism: Bashing the 1960s*
   *and 1970s  198, Critical Theory and Postmodernism  199, A*
   *Progressive Revival?  200*
*Activities    204*
*Recommended Readings    205*
*Notes    205*

CHAPTER 8 **SOCIOLOGY OF EDUCATION** **209**

Social Class   *210*
   *The American Social Structure 210, Sorting and Selecting in
   School 211, Families, Peer Groups, and Schools 213, Gangs:
   Working-Class Resistance in the Extreme 215, Ability Grouping
   and Tracking 215, Creating a Culture of Detracking 217*
Race and Ethnicity   *218*
   *Defining a "Sense of Peoplehood" in a Multicultural Nation 218,
   African-American Students 219, Hispanic-American Students 221,
   Asian-American Students 222, Native American Students 223*
Desegregation or Resegregation?   *223*
   *Historical Perspective 223, De Facto versus De Jure 225,
   Academic, Social, and Economic Effects of Desegregation 226,
   Busing 227, Magnet Schools 228, Neo-Plessy Thinking? 229,
   "Acting White" 230, African Identity Schools 231*
Bilingual Education   *232*
   *Washing Culture Out, Ironing Culture In 232, Models of Bilingual
   Education 233, Bilingual Politics and Academic Research 234*
Gender   *235*
   *Shortchanging Girls 235, Gender-Role Socialization 236, Gender
   Bias in Textbooks 236, Unequal Treatment in the Classroom 237,
   Title IX 238, Cognitive Differences between Females and
   Males 239, Toward the Future: Feminism and Education 240*
*Activities   241*
*Recommended Readings   241*
*Notes   242*


CHAPTER 9 **POLITICS OF EDUCATION** **249**

Local Politics of Education   *250*
   *Regulations from Above, Pressure from Below 250, Local Boards
   and Local Superintendents 251, Reinventing Local Control: The
   Changing Politics of School Districts 252, Local Board Members:
   Demographics and Representation 253, Local Board Elections: At
   Large or by Subdistricts? 255*
State Politics of Education   *256*
   *Legislatures, Governors, Boards, Superintendents, and
   Departments 257, Excellence and Accountability: State Politicians
   Discover School Reform 258, The Politics of More of the
   Same 260, School Reform on Hold: State Politics in the 1990s 261*
Federal Politics of Education   *262*
   *Federal Money and Federal Influence 262, The Cold War, the
   Poverty War, and Other Battles 264, Mr. Reagan Goes to
   Washington 265, Educational Advocacy:* A Nation at Risk

*and Bill Bennett 267, George Bush, National Goals, and America 2000 268, Bill Clinton: An Education Governor as President 271*
Educational Finance    273
*Local Property Taxes: Some Districts Are More Equal Than Others 273, State Funds: Reducing the Inequalities 275, Lawsuits, Reform, and the Economy: Educational Finance in the 1990s 277*
*Activities    279*
*Recommended Readings    279*
*Notes    280*


**PART III   ISSUES FOR THE 1990S**                                    **285**


**CHAPTER 10   TEACHERS AND THE CURRICULUM    287**

Back to Basics and Testing, Testing, Testing    *288*
*Outputs and Inputs 288, What's Wrong with the Schools? 289, The Measurement-Driven Curriculum 291, The National Assessment of Educational Progress: A National Curriculum Driver? 293, The Children of Lake Wobegon 294, Curriculum Alignment 295, Pausing to Reconsider Testing, Testing, Testing 296*
National Standards Plus National Assessments Equals National Curriculum?    *296*
*The New Standards Project 297, Getting Reform Right 298, Student Portfolios and Other Performance Assessments 299, The Promise and Peril of National Reform 300*
What Do Americans Need to Know?    *300*
*Essentialists, Progressives, and the New Basics 300, The Great Literacy Debate 302, Is Literacy Slipping Away? 303, Cultural Literacy 304, The Critics Respond: Multicultural Literacy and a Better Future 307, A Message for Essentialists: Take the Blame along with the Credit 308*
*Activities    309*
*Recommended Readings    309*
*Notes    309*


**CHAPTER 11   PRIVATE SCHOOLS VERSUS PUBLIC SCHOOLS    315**

Three Sectors of Private Elementary and Secondary Education    *316*
A Profile of Private Schools and Their Students    *317*
*New Patterns within the Three Sectors 318, Who Goes to Private School? 319*

Roman Catholic Schools    *320*
  *James Coleman and the Issue of Academic Achievement 320,*
  *Private School Superiority? 322, Functional Communities and*
  *Value Communities 323, Human Capital and Social Capital 323*
Fundamentalist Christian Schools    *324*
  *Inside Christian Schools 325, The Struggle against Secular*
  *Humanism 326, Home Schooling 328*
Government Regulation of Private Schools    *329*
Educational Choice    *331*
  Politics, Markets, and America's Schools *331, The Critics*
  *Respond 333, Tuition Tax Credits and Vouchers 334, Experiments*
  *with Choice 336*
*Activities    339*
*Recommended Readings    339*
*Notes    339*


*Index    345*

# Preface

I wrote the first edition of *America's Teachers* to help prospective teachers see what they're getting into. Having taught Introduction to Education and Foundations of Education courses since the late 1970s, I felt ready by the late 1980s to put down on paper what I had said to several thousand future teachers.

I put *their* words into the first edition, too, hoping the book would come across as a conversation rather than a lecture. I wanted to capture the give and take of a good class discussion—those moments of candor when people take risks and speak their minds. When the discussion subject is American education and when the participants are prospective teachers and a professor who is a former teacher, the exchanges can range from encouraging to upsetting.

I am grateful for the favorable reactions to the first edition. Students and colleagues across the nation have commented on its readability and honesty. I tried to write clearly, and I refused to pass out rose-colored glasses with each copy because I wanted to help prospective teachers see the challenges as well as the rewards of the work they are considering.

As I began work on this second edition, I set out to improve it in several ways. I tried to listen even more carefully to the voices of teachers and future teachers. I tried to pay even more attention to school reform, especially the movements of the 1990s. And I tried to make the book even more sensitive to multicultural issues, a reflection of America's increasing diversity. This new edition combines the organizational scheme of the first with thoroughly revised and updated contents.

Part I consists of five chapters with a depth and frankness that, I hope, will continue to distinguish the book. Every chapter contains new material. Chapter 1 surveys teachers' feelings about school reform and presents the latest information on the job market. Chapter 2 highlights recent trends in teacher salaries and evaluation, including the portfolios and evaluation centers the

National Board for Professional Teaching Standards is developing as a step toward a national career ladder. Chapter 3 maps the multiple routes opening into the occupation and analyzes new developments in teacher assessment, including the successor to the National Teacher Examinations. Chapter 4 on teacher organizations and professionalism features a case study of school restructuring in Rochester, New York. New material on academic freedom, particularly the selection of textbooks, highlights chapter 5 on school law.

The four chapters in part II explore the relationship between schools and society in greater depth and with greater emphasis on diversity. Chapter 6 on the history of American education expands the discussion of assimilation, separation, and pluralism with more attention to the roles of ordinary people. Chapter 7 brings philosophies and theories of education to life with examples of current thought, such as Jonathon Kozol's *Savage Inequalities*—a book that is taking critical theory to a popular audience. Recent trends in ability grouping and tracking, desegregation, bilingual education, and gender equity highlight chapter 8 on the sociology of education. Chapter 9 analyzes the local, state, and federal politics of education, now more fascinating than ever with former education governor Bill Clinton in the White House.

Part III focuses on trends that will shape American education well into the next century. Chapter 10 on the curriculum follows the ongoing debate over literacy, including cultural literacy, and tracks the movement toward national standards and national assessments. Chapter 11 brings the book to a conclusion with a discussion of private schools versus public schools, featuring a new section on educational choice.

I hope the second edition of *America's Teachers,* like the first, provokes critical thought and good conversation. I present this new edition to my Rose. I dedicate it to teachers who can transform teaching from the occupation it is into the profession it should be.

## ACKNOWLEDGMENTS

I thank the following professors who reviewed the manuscript of *America's Teachers,* second edition, and provided many helpful suggestions, which I have incorporated into the text:

Joseph C. Bronars, Jr., Queens College, City University of New York
Harry J. Hadley, Fairmont State College
Susan Mintz, University of Virginia
Gary A. Negin, California State University
Franklin Parker, Western Carolina University
Vince Peterson, Indiana University, South Bend
Robert L. K. Richardson, University of Wisconsin, La Crosse
Peter A. Soderbergh, Louisiana State University, Baton Rouge
Jack Stewart, Columbus College

# Teaching as an Occupation

# CHAPTER 1

# Deciding to Teach and Finding a Job

*Teaching is not a job. Teaching is a privilege. Teachers should be more dedicated to their task—directing and educating the youth of America. We must set examples for young people to follow. . . . I am* PROUD *to be a teacher.*

—South Carolina teacher

*We're expected not only to teach but to help with the total ills of society. . . . We're overworked, often trying to care so damn much about those we teach and yet see the incredible destruction of their lives due to alcohol and drugs. We're underpaid for our services yet we're still under the shadow of the "3 month" vacation idea. In short we're burning out.*

—Washington State teacher[1]

## MOTIVES FOR TEACHING

Talking with prospective teachers about why they want to teach is an excellent way to begin a discussion of teaching as an occupation. For more than 15 years, I have asked the students in my Introduction to Education classes to write down their major motive for teaching. Comparing their responses with the results of similiar surveys conducted around the nation, I see several clear patterns.

Why do *you* want to be a teacher? Almost certainly you can give several reasons, but try to narrow them to your major motive for wanting to teach. Now compare your response with those in Table 1.1. If your motivation centers on *students,* you have plenty of company. With remarkable consistency, about half the prospective teachers in my classes link their desire to teach directly to young people. If *academics*—the love of a particular subject or of learning in general— prompts you to teach, you are also in good company. Approximately one-fifth

**TABLE 1.1**   Why do you want to be a teacher? Motives of prospective teachers.

1. Students
   "I love children."
   "I like working with young people."
   "I want to help students."
2. Academics
   "I enjoy [a particular subject]."
   "I love learning."
3. Job advantages
   "I like having my summers off."
   "My hours as a teacher will match my children's hours in school."
   "Teaching is a good job for people on their way to something else."
4. Social value
   "Teaching is society's most important job."
   "I can improve society by teaching."
5. Influence of other teachers
   "Some of my teachers helped me so much, they made me want to teach."
   "Some of my teachers hurt me so much, they made me want to teach."

SOURCES:   This profile is based on my ongoing survey of prospective teachers at the University of South Alabama and on the National Education Association's *Status of the American Public School Teacher, 1990–1991* (Washington, D.C.: NEA, 1992), pp. 62–64; Cassandra L. Book and Donald J. Freeman's "Differences in Entry Characteristics of Elementary and Secondary Teacher Candidates," *Journal of Teacher Education* 37 (March–April 1986): 47–51; and J. Marc Jantzen's "Why College Students Choose to Teach: A Longitudinal Study," *Journal of Teacher Education* 32 (March–April 1981): 45–48.

of the future teachers in my survey give academic reasons as their major motive. Surveys conducted throughout the nation show the same patterns: Student-centered motives top the list, with academic motives running a distant second or third.[2]

Other motives for teaching (and the rounded percentages of my prospective teachers who put them in first place) include *job advantages* (10 percent), the *social value* of teaching (10 percent), and the *influence of other teachers* (5 percent). These patterns, too, are consistent with the results of other surveys. The brief statements quoted in Table 1.1 are representative of the ways future teachers summarize their motives.

Considered as a whole, studies of motivation pay future teachers genuine compliments. Teachers are altruistic; they want to help. Most of them enter the occupation with the welfare of others in mind, believing they can make a difference in their students' lives. Some prospective teachers have been helped— or, in a few cases, hurt—so much by their own teachers that they feel motivated to teach. Some extend their concern for others to society as a whole. Now notice what the surveys do *not* say. People do not go into teaching for the money— with good reason, as we will see in the next chapter. Nor do people choose teaching for the prestige. Americans respect teachers, but it is a peculiar respect—the kind accorded to outsiders, to people set apart from the mainstream of society.[3]

## Perceived Advantages of Teaching

Can we take at face value what prospective teachers say about their motives? Aren't some of their statements too good to be true? Based on my work with future teachers, I am convinced that their altruism and idealism are real. But because of what they say outside of class, informally and off the record, I am also convinced the perceived advantages of the occupation pull more people into teaching than the surveys indicate.

Notice the job advantages listed in Table 1.1. Teacher education students often joke, "Teaching has three main benefits: June, July, and August." Of course the summer vacation is attractive, but should it be someone's major reason for wanting to teach? Prospective teachers who admit that it is, along with others who are reluctant to confess, should consider that some school districts have already adopted a year-round schedule, and the summer break is closer to 10 weeks than to 12 in most districts. Taking graduate and inservice courses during the summer further reduces time off. So does "moonlighting." Twenty-nine percent of America's teachers work a second job: Twelve percent hold an evening or weekend job outside their school systems during the school year, and 17 percent find outside summer employment.[4]

Another perceived advantage of teaching is the daily schedule. As more nontraditional students (25 and older), many of them women, go to college to pursue the degrees they did not obtain when they were younger, more students talk frankly about choosing a career that will allow them to spend time with their own children. As a parent, I can appreciate this motive, but should it be first on a prospective teacher's list? Although the nontraditional students in my classes have generally realistic expectations of the occupation, they often underestimate the time demands teaching will make on their evenings and weekends.[5]

Finally, there is the perception that teaching is a good temporary job for people who have other career and life plans in mind. As one student told me recently, "I want to be a lawyer, but I think I'll teach for a while. After all, teaching is easy to get into and easy to get out of." Actually this is an old notion. Historical studies going back to the colonial era show how some teachers (mostly males) have used the occupation as a stepping stone to other careers, while others (most of them females) have used it as a way station en route to marriage and family.[6]

## Teachers Who Love, Teachers Who Care

Americans view teaching as women's work. The feminization of the occupation began in the mid-1800s when school boards turned increasingly to women to fill teaching positions. Females had two advantages over the males who had dominated the occupation: The character and personality of women were regarded as better suited to working with young children, and women constituted a cheap, reliable labor force. These nineteenth-century perceptions are with us still. Today 72 percent of all teachers and 88 percent of elementary school teachers are women, and the percentages are even higher in areas of the nation where highly traditional views of sex roles prevail.[7]

Prospective teachers often choose these words to express their motivation for teaching: "I love children." Thus we would expect employed teachers to reflect the same sentiment. The evidence, however, is curiously mixed.

Contemporary and historical studies of teachers' letters and diaries reveal few discourses on loving children. Instead, teachers discuss how demanding teaching is or focus on matters unrelated to their work. In these letters and diaries, teaching comes across as a job, something people do for economic survival. Yet for a century and a half, society has been sending women the message that they should teach because they love children. They should *want* to be teachers—obviously not for the money but for the children. It is almost as if women, trying hard to please by saying what society expects, have repeated "I'm going to teach because I love children" so often they have come to believe it.[8]

Perhaps this discussion is too harsh. Teachers *should* care about students, and the evidence suggests most of them do. When asked why they stick with their demanding jobs, most teachers answer, "The students." What gives teachers their greatest intrinsic satisfaction? They reply, "Reaching the students."[9]

For convincing evidence of how student-centered teachers are, read almost any issue of *NEA Today,* a newspaper for members of the National Education Association (NEA). "If I touch kids' hearts in some way," says an Arizona teacher, "then I'm doing what I'm supposed to. And they in their turn will do something similar for someone else." A Michigan teacher with 28 years of experience puts it this way: "I want to make students feel better about themselves when they leave my class than they did when the semester began . . . . Humans are fragile creatures whose egos need stroking and bolstering." A Tennessee teacher explains why she was willing to leave a marketing job with an excellent salary and fringe benefits: "No other profession offers the opportunity to mold dreams and mend broken destinies. I suppose there are just some things an expense account can't begin to cover." A California teacher whose career spans six decades, a veteran with "no qualms about using the word *love,*" says the best teachers "exult when children succeed—and bleed when they hurt."[10] As a teacher educator, I only wish the public understood how much teachers care.

Admittedly, teaching is no job for people who do not care about young people, but personal concern is not the only quality teachers need. A logician would say caring about students is a necessary but not sufficient qualification for teaching. The job involves an entire range of interpersonal skills, plus much more. Teachers who enter the occupation motivated solely by their good feelings can be bitterly disappointed when students do not return their affection. A survey sponsored by the Metropolitan Life Insurance Company suggests the toll the first year of teaching takes on the idealism of new teachers: After spending a year in the classroom, teachers express less faith in their ability to reach students and make a difference in their lives.[11]

Let me be blunt. Some students do not want your love. Think twice about becoming a teacher just because you care.

## Teachers and Culturally Diverse Students

Also reconsider your choice if you believe you will be teaching students whose socioeconomic backgrounds are similar to yours. A demographic profile of prospective teachers shows they are overwhelmingly middle-class white females.

More than 80 percent grew up in suburbs or rural areas and want to return to teach students like themselves. Only 9 percent—and the percentage is shrinking—want to teach in big cities, where teacher shortages are often acute. The demographic profile of America's public school students is strikingly different. Twenty percent are in large school districts with enrollments of more than 40,000. As we will see in chapter 8, one in five students is from a family living in poverty. Thirty percent of students are African, Hispanic, Asian, or Native American, and nearly 40 percent will be minorities by the turn of the century. By contrast, only 13 percent of public school teachers are now minorities, and some studies show that the percentage of minorities among newly hired teachers is even smaller. As chapter 3 points out, America's schools will enter the twenty-first century with a student body more culturally diverse than ever before and a teaching force whiter than at any time since the nineteenth century.[12]

These trends suggest a serious and increasing mismatch between teachers and students. Future teachers are increasingly unlikely to find jobs teaching Dick-and-Jane kids. Instead, more teachers may find themselves identifying with "Here I Was, a New Teacher," a moving account of one teacher's difficult first year in the New York City public schools, published in the June 22, 1988, issue of *Education Week*. Hoping to help make your entry into the occupation more positive, I will highlight the influence of cultural diversity throughout this textbook.

## Teaching as Academic Work

Future teachers not only need to consider the kind of students they will be working with but also need to think seriously about the kind of work they will be doing. Some prospective teachers, not particularly fond of any academic subject, may gravitate toward elementary, early childhood, or special education, where they believe the emphasis will be on "getting along with the kids." Much of the school day will be filled with games and activities, they feel sure. The human side of teaching will be fun and rewarding. As for the academic side, surely they will know more than their students. Besides, a number of people—including some teachers and administrators—have told them you don't have to be very smart to be a teacher. They may even have heard that being too bright can hurt.

Let me dispel several myths about teaching. In spite of all the publicity about teacher burnout, some people cling to the belief that teaching is a fun job. It is not. Getting through to students can certainly be rewarding, but reaching them takes hour after hour of effort. *Fun* is not the right word. Listen to the counsel of a Florida teacher: "Teaching is work. It is the hardest job there is. Learning is work. We try to make it enjoyable, interesting, exciting, motivating, relevant, palatable, etc. But any way you slice it, it's work."[13]

Notwithstanding the pubic outcry over academically incompetent teachers, some people believe another myth: Rudimentary literacy is the only academic qualification teachers of the youngest or least able students must have. It is not. This myth, another holdover from the past, finds no support in the research on teacher effectiveness; nevertheless, it dies hard.

Perhaps such myths appeal to a basic anti-intellectual streak in the American character. When taken to the extreme of "the smarter you are, the worse you will do as a teacher," the mindset has disastrous effects on the occupation. On college campuses, it crops up in the guise of professors who steer bright students away from elementary teaching and toward secondary teaching, or toward college teaching, or out of teaching entirely. In school districts, it appears in the form of administrators and personnel officers who are wary of teacher applicants with excellent grades and test scores because they believe such people will not be patient with slower students. Despite the lack of evidence to support this myth, some school systems search diligently for teachers whose academic abilities are mediocre. After all, they reason, these people will probably be less likely to leave teaching for another career.[14]

Yes, this discussion is harsh. To put things more positively, the best teachers strike a balance between their concern for academics and their concern for students. They do not emphasize one to the exclusion of the other. But today the scales of the occupation are out of balance, tipped heavily toward the concern for students. When recruiting teachers, society in effect asks college students who care about young people to step forward. After academic requirements screen out a few candidates, many of the remainder become teachers.

Suppose society sends a different message: Will people with excellent academic skills please step forward? Of these, the candidates who care about students *and* are able to help them learn can become teachers. To balance the scales in this way will require top-to-bottom reform of teaching as an occupation—major improvements in teacher salaries and working conditions no less than in teacher education and certification. Make no mistake about it, these are radical changes. As we will see in the following chapters, however, the odds they will occur are better today than in previous years. Despite the many problems we will discuss in the next section and throughout this book, there are good reasons to be cautiously optimistic about teaching as an occupation.[15]

## SATISFACTION WITH TEACHING

Ask currently employed teachers how they feel about their jobs. Listen carefully to their answers, for they are speaking volumes about teaching as an occupation. Since 1961, the NEA, the nation's largest teacher organization, has asked teachers the ultimate question about job satisfaction: If you could make your decision again, would you teach? The trends in their answers, collected by the NEA at five-year intervals, are reported in Table 1.2.

Throughout the 1960s and into the early 1970s, at least three-fourths of teachers responded they would teach again, with fewer than 15 percent saying they would not. As late as the mid-1970s, more than 60 percent said they would enter the occupation again, while fewer than 20 percent said they would not.

These changes in job satisfaction, though, were an early sign something was going wrong with teaching. The survey conducted in 1980–1981 left no doubt:

**TABLE 1.2**  If you could make your decision again, would you teach? Teachers' responses.

| Response | Percentage of Teachers | | | | | | |
|---|---|---|---|---|---|---|---|
| | *1961* | *1966* | *1971* | *1976* | *1981* | *1986* | *1991* |
| Certainly/probably would | 76 | 77 | 74 | 64 | 46 | 49 | 59 |
| Chances are about even | 13 | 13 | 13 | 18 | 18 | 20 | 19 |
| Certainly/probably would not | 11 | 9 | 13 | 19 | 36 | 31 | 22 |

SOURCE:  National Education Association, *Status of the American Public School Teacher, 1990–1991* (Washington, D.C.: NEA, 1992). Reprinted by permission.

Only 46 percent of teachers gave their occupation a vote of confidence, while more than a third said they would choose another career.

Some of the most encouraging news in years about teaching is that the two latest NEA surveys have shown rising levels of satisfaction. Although votes of confidence in the occupation have not returned to the levels of the 1960s and early 1970s, the 15-year downward spiral has been reversed. The 1986 survey marked the beginning of the turnaround, and the 1991 survey shows 59 percent of teachers affirming they would teach again.

More than 20 percent, though, insist they would not teach again—a level of dissatisfaction roughly twice as high as during the 1960s and early 1970s. When teachers speak out on the reasons for their dissatisfaction, they highlight several qualities that have become scarce in the public schools, where almost 90 percent of them work. According to Gallup Polls, teachers report the top four things the schools lack are parental interest and support, public financial support, student interest, and student discipline. Adding insult to injury, from the teachers' point of view, is the fact that the general public sees the problems of schools differently. While Gallup Polls at least show a public consensus that discipline and money are lacking, most citizens seem unaware of—perhaps even unconcerned with—the problems caused by the lack of parental support and student interest. That hurts.[16]

These problems sting teachers all the more because they are who they are. Most of them, as we have seen, go into teaching because they want to work with students, to help them. Other teachers are attracted to a subject or to the learning process. These teachers, along with others whose motives are equally idealistic, enter the occupation only to discover their work always demands much and often returns little. Teachers care, but they say too few of their students do. It upsets teachers even more that so few parents care.

What keeps teachers in the occupation then? To put the situation in the most positive and complimentary light possible, many teachers are so strongly committed to their work they are able to overcome the problems they face. This perseverance is all the more admirable because they rarely receive the praise and recognition they deserve. Another positive but seldom-mentioned factor is that some teachers work in schools with the healthy vital signs other schools lack: supportive parents, adequate financial resources, and interested, well-behaved students.

### Burnouts, Dropouts, and the
### Promise of School Reform

We must also acknowledge a far less pleasant reality: The economic risks of changing careers, combined with teachers' doubts about their ability to succeed in other lines of work, keep many of them on the job. Teachers who remain in spite of their desire to leave are candidates for *burnout.* Typically, they begin by missing a few days of class; then their absences increase. When they report to school, they go through the motions of teaching, but their commitment has gone. They may want to care, they may try to care, yet they cannot. The very quality that brought most of them into teaching, their concern for others, has dissipated. They are physically, mentally, and emotionally exhausted.[17]

Teachers are not the only workers who must cope with burnout, of course. People who work in the helping occupations—which include medicine, nursing, social work, psychology, and child care as well as teaching—are all highly susceptible. Helpers have jobs that are stressful by their very nature, with working conditions that often aggravate the stress. Fortunately, the workers in some helping occupations are able to manage stress by controlling their jobs, and some helpers have jobs with incentives that encourage people to cope. Other helping occupations, by contrast, leave their workers feeling demoralized and powerless, almost as if the jobs were perversely designed to burn people out.[18]

Compare two occupations within the field of health care. Both physicians and nurses help the sick, but their jobs differ in several important ways. First, physicians have more *autonomy,* more control over their work. As we will see in chapter 4, autonomy is the right to make decisions and use judgment. Physicians have a great deal of autonomy—more, in fact, than the members of any other occupation. Being in control helps them manage the stress of their work. But while physicians are in a position to give orders, nurses must take orders. Serving as the buffers between those in control and those who need medical help, nurses experience the frustration that comes from knowing what to do but lacking the authority to do it.[19]

Second, physicians have a greater sense of *self-esteem.* As members of America's most prestigious occupation, they receive a great deal of respect and admiration. Society regards physicians as full professionals but nurses as *semi*professionals. Several steps lower in the heath care hierarchy, nurses feel their work is underrated and underappreciated. They go home feeling far less positive than physicians about their contributions to their patients.[20]

Finally, as everyone knows, physicians earn substantially more than nurses. We do not have to be crass to understand how the *extrinisic rewards* of income go a long way toward encouraging workers to cope with occupational demands. Physicians work hard and receive high monetary rewards; nurses feel they work just as hard, but their incomes are only a fraction as high.

Teachers have more in common with nurses than with physicians. It may sound flattering to call teaching "a noble profession," but teaching, like nursing, is a semiprofession. In fact, teachers have recently become even less like physicians and more like nurses. Teachers have never had the autonomy accorded to full professionals, but beginning in the late 1970s teachers watched their informal control of the classroom slip away. As American education went back to basics by way of standardized testing, teachers lost control over how to teach, how to test, and how to grade. Today, school board members and school administrators hand down these policies, and teachers have to carry them out whether or not they believe they are in the best interest of students. A barrage of public criticism has wounded the self-esteem of teachers. Their salaries are often not high enough to make coping with job stress seem worthwhile. So why try?[21]

The picture does have a brighter side. Chapter 4 points out encouraging signs the tide may be turning, that teachers themselves are trying to take charge of their occupation and move toward professionalism. Empowering teachers, restructuring schools, and reorganizing workplaces—these are the watchwords of school reform. The spotlight of reform is on the individual school as a job site and on teachers as the workers with the greatest responsibility for helping students learn. At last, some teachers are saying, reformers are asking the right question: How can schools change to give teachers the power and support they need to help students?[22]

In some schools, in some school districts, and perhaps throughout some states, reform has moved past the talking stage to produce real improvements. *The Condition of Teaching: A State-by-State Analysis, 1990*—a teacher survey conducted by the Carnegie Foundation for the Advancement of Teaching—confirms there are indeed bright spots throughout the nation. Teachers in Connecticut, South Carolina, Iowa, Minnesota, Mississippi, New Jersey, and Wisconsin seem most positive about the success of recent reform efforts in their respective states. Local teacher organizations throughout the nation, inspired by the success of American Federation of Teacher (AFT) locals in Rochester, Dade County, Toledo, Cincinnati, and other urban school districts, are jointly involved with administrators and school board members in experiments that could empower teachers as never before. We will examine these efforts in chapter 4.[23]

Yet many teachers say they feel bypassed by school reform. The overall tone of the voices in *The Condition of Teaching* is skeptical. Listen to a teacher in Connecticut, a state where reform appears to be going well: "I would like my words to make a difference, but I have learned from experience that the public, boards of education, and superintendents will not listen." A teacher in Indiana: "Education takes place in the classroom. Teachers are education. There are too many people making decisions for teachers who *never* see a student." A Nevada teacher has this to say: "The respect for teachers and education has declined each year I (have been) involved in the education system." An Oklahoma teacher: "If we are to be professional and act professional, we cannot have a salary that is almost at the poverty line."[24] When the public asks why, after more than a decade of school reform, many teachers are still unhappy with their jobs, teachers can point to their lack of autonomy, self-esteem, and extrinsic rewards.

People who have left teaching for greener pastures emphasize the importance of these three factors again and again. A survey of "teacher dropouts" conducted for the Metropolitan Life Insurance Company gives straight answers to the public's questions. Why do people leave teaching? Sixty percent of the former teachers say their main reason was low pay. Thirty-six percent fault working conditions, criticizing such things as excessive paperwork, nonteaching duties (cafeteria and hall supervision, bus duty, and so forth), and a lack of involvement in making decisions. The latter complaint is especially significant. The former teachers had definite ideas about how to improve the schools, but they lacked the autonomy to put their ideas into practice.[25]

What about stress? Fifty-seven percent say they were under "great stress" as teachers; only 22 percent find the stress as great in their new careers. Self-esteem? Sixty-four percent say the respect they received as teachers was less than they had expected. Do they miss teaching? Fifty-eight percent say they do, but 83 percent doubt they will ever return to the classroom, for almost all the dropouts are satisfied with their new careers.[26]

When currently employed teachers are polled about their work, their answers are much the same. Sadly, teachers who have stuck with the occupation echo the complaints of their colleagues who have quit. Metropolitan Life surveys show about one-fifth of teachers saying they are "very likely" or "fairly likely" to leave within the next five years. The good news, though, is that the percentage of teachers who say they are likely to leave has decreased since the late 1980s, as salaries have improved for most teachers (see chapter 2) and working conditions have improved for some.[27]

## The Critical Years Ahead

For your sake as a prospective teacher, I am trying to paint a realistic picture of the career you are considering. I prefer to call it realistic rather than negative, for there certainly are positive aspects. In the chapters that follow, we will see that teaching may indeed be on the verge of real progress. The next few years will be critical.

A major reason is that America's teaching force is graying. The median age of teachers is now 42, up from 33 in the mid-1970s, and the median length of teaching experience is 15 years, almost double the 8 years of the mid-1970s. Given the fact that 6 percent of teachers are retiring or resigning each year—a rate that will increase as the teaching force grays—we can predict that about two-thirds of the teachers who were in the occupation in 1990 will be gone by the year 2000. The women and men who will take their places will be in an excellent position to shape the future of teaching.[28]

What happens to American education during these critical years may depend on whether parents and other citizens listen to teachers and make long-needed changes in teaching as an occupation. Keith Geiger, president of the NEA, constantly reminds politicians and the general public that they can no longer afford to ignore teachers' voices. Mary Futrell, Geiger's predecessor, put it this way: "I think what the teachers are saying and what they are crying out for is that they want to be treated like professionals and want to be paid like professionals." Albert Shanker, often at odds with the NEA as president of the rival AFT, in this case heartily agrees: "We have to quit treating teachers like they are hired hands in a factory and start treating them more like partners in a law firm." Otherwise, these leaders caution, the nation will be forced to replace a large number of its teachers with "illiterate baby sitters."[29] Fair warning.

## THE TEACHER JOB MARKET

Your main interest in the job market understandably revolves around your own prospects of employment. Articles in academic journals as well as the popular press offer contradictory views of the odds you face: "Teacher Shortage Looms." "Teacher Shortage Vanishes." "No One Wants To Be a Teacher." "College Students Show More Interest in Teaching." Whom do you believe?

Always consider the source. Keep in mind that many people have a vested interest in shaping public opinion of the job market. Teacher organizations have been trying their best to convince the nation a major shortage of teachers is just around the corner. The NEA and AFT hope that, with teachers in short supply, school systems will compete for their services by raising salaries (which *have* gotten better) and improving working conditions. Taxpayers will have to cooperate, of course, and teacher organizations want them to believe better salaries and working conditions offer the only hope for easing the shortage. Obviously, currently employed teachers stand to profit, but if these improvements attract more capable people into the occupation, as the NEA and AFT promise, the entire nation will benefit.

Representing a different point of view are politicians committed to holding down taxes and social spending. They insist that throwing money at educational problems will not solve them, adding teachers are better paid and more satisfied than their unions admit. These politicians say the way to attract more *and* better teachers is to open the occupation to college graduates who have not been trained in traditional teacher education programs. Obviously the politicians have a sharp eye on the bottom line—they want to ease the teacher shortage without raising the taxpayers' ante for public education—but their desire to improve the academic quality of the teaching force seems sincere.

I will organize my discussion of the job market around the *demand* for teachers and the *supply* of teachers. In both areas, I will rely heavily on demography, the study of population characteristics and population trends.

### The Baby Boom, "Generation X," and Baby Boomlet: The Demand for Teachers

Every discussion of the teacher job market must take account of the *baby boom.* Often called the postwar baby boom because it began when World War II ended, this demographic bulge of more than 70,000,000 people continues to throw its weight around in American schools and society. Actually the word *postwar* is misleading, for although the number of births in the United States started to climb in 1946, the peak year for births was 1957, and the number of births remained high through the mid-1960s. Thus the baby boom was a phenomenon that lasted about 20 years. The early baby boomers, the children born from the mid-1940s through the mid-1950s, took American education by surprise. The young people who would come of age in the era of Vietnam, civil rights, and social change strained their schools at the seams. Many of them attended elementary school on double sessions and found high schools and colleges unprepared for their arrival.[30]

The children of the late baby boom, those born from the mid-1950s through the mid-1960s, those who would become young adults during the malaise of the 1970s, found American education in a better state of physical if not academic readiness. These students strained the schools in other ways. Academic standards fell as drug use and discipline problems increased. School officials breathed a sigh of relief as the last baby boomers graduated from high school.

Now paying more attention to demography, officials knew the number of births had fallen throughout most of the period between the mid-1960s and the mid-1970s. As the students born during this era made their way through the schools, their much smaller age cohort picked up the unfortunate label *baby bust.* Understandably, they hope the label will not stick. So far no name has stuck to this cohort, not even "Generation X," a term the media sometimes use to suggest the group's small numbers and hazy identity. Whatever we call these students, they saw their schools go back to basics as the national mood grew more conservative in the late 1970s and 1980s. The oldest students in this group became adults during the Reagan era; their youngest peers graduated from high school in the early 1990s. Today, members of Generation X constitute the largest group of college students reading this textbook.[31]

The demand for teachers rose and fell in response to these trends in student enrollment. As the baby boomers entered school and enrollment went through the ceiling, the demand for teachers outstripped the supply. Teacher shortages developed, hitting elementary schools (K–8) during the 1950s and spreading to secondary schools (9–12) during the 1960s. Prospective teachers found excellent employment opportunities throughout this era.[32]

But the favorable job market did not last into the 1970s. As Table 1.3 indicates, elementary school enrollment peaked in 1969, then decreased with the baby bust until 1984—15 years of virtually unbroken decline. Enrollment in secondary schools reached a peak in 1976, then decreased until 1990—14 years of decline. The total number of students in grades K through 12 decreased from 1972 through 1984. As enrollment dropped, the demand for teachers fell, and the job market turned sour.

Fortunately, the outlook for prospective teachers is better today. In 1976, the United States entered the era of the *baby boomlet,* a phenomenon also dubbed the "echo" of the baby boom. At first, the nation greated the echo with little fanfare, but demographers now recognize it as a major trend. The number of births rose during most of the period from 1976 through 1988, not because of a significant increase in the *fertility rate* (which demographers define as the number of children born per year per 1,000 women) but simply because the baby boomers had entered their prime childbearing years and started families. Their families are small, but there are so many of them.[33]

**TABLE 1.3** Enrollment in elementary and secondary schools, 1965–2002 (in millions).

| Year | Elementary (K–8) | Secondary (9–12) | Total (K–12) |
|---|---|---|---|
| 1965 | 35.5 | 13.0 | 48.5 |
| 1966 | 35.9 | 13.3 | 49.2 |
| 1967 | 36.2 | 13.7 | 49.9 |
| 1968 | 36.6 | 14.1 | 50.7 |
| 1969 | 36.8 | 14.3 | 51.1 |
| 1970 | 36.6 | 14.6 | 51.3 |
| 1971 | 36.2 | 15.1 | 51.3 |
| 1972 | 35.5 | 15.2 | 50.7 |
| 1973 | 35.1 | 15.4 | 50.4 |
| 1974 | 34.6 | 15.4 | 50.1 |
| 1975 | 34.2 | 15.6 | 49.8 |
| 1976 | 33.8 | 15.7 | 49.5 |
| 1977 | 33.1 | 15.6 | 48.7 |
| 1978 | 32.1 | 15.6 | 47.6 |
| 1979 | 31.6 | 15.0 | 46.6 |
| 1980 | 31.7 | 14.6 | 46.2 |
| 1981 | 31.4 | 14.2 | 45.5 |
| 1982 | 31.4 | 13.8 | 45.2 |
| 1983 | 31.3 | 13.7 | 45.0 |
| 1984 | 31.2 | 13.7 | 44.9 |
| 1985 | 31.2 | 13.8 | 45.0 |
| 1986 | 31.5 | 13.7 | 45.2 |
| 1987 | 32.2 | 13.3 | 45.5 |
| 1988 | 32.5 | 12.9 | 45.4 |
| 1989 | 33.3 | 12.6 | 45.9 |
| 1990 (estimated) | 33.8 | 12.4 | 46.2 |
| *Projected* | | | |
| 1991 | 34.3 | 12.5 | 46.8 |
| 1992 | 34.9 | 12.7 | 47.6 |
| 1993 | 35.3 | 13.1 | 48.4 |
| 1994 | 35.8 | 13.5 | 49.3 |
| 1995 | 36.1 | 13.9 | 50.1 |
| 1996 | 36.5 | 14.3 | 50.8 |
| 1997 | 36.8 | 14.6 | 51.3 |
| 1998 | 37.1 | 14.6 | 51.8 |
| 1999 | 37.3 | 14.8 | 52.1 |
| 2000 | 37.5 | 14.9 | 52.4 |
| 2001 | 37.7 | 15.0 | 52.7 |
| 2002 | 37.8 | 15.2 | 53.0 |

Note: Figures show combined enrollment in public and private schools in the fall of each year. Details may not add to totals due to rounding.

SOURCES: Figures for 1965–1979 are from U.S. Department of Education, Center for Education Statistics, *Digest of Education Statistics, 1987* (Washington, D.C.: U.S. Government Printing Office, 1987), p. 8. Figures for 1980–2002 are from U.S. Department of Education, National Center for Education Statistics, *Projections of Education Statistics to 2002* (Washington, D.C.: U.S. Department of Education, 1991), p. 9.

Because of the baby boomlet, enrollment in elementary schools began climbing in 1985 and will continue to rise into the twenty-first century (see Table 1.3). Enrollment in secondary schools started to grow in 1991 and will increase through the turn of the century and beyond. As the children of the boomlet move through the education system, the demand for teachers should remain strong.

The echo of the baby boom is loudest in the nation's Sunbelt. In general, school enrollment registers the greatest increases in the South, followed by the West, the Northeast, and the Midwest. In fact, demographers predict that between 1980 and 2000, almost three-fourths of the nation's increase in children under 14 will be concentrated in five Sunbelt states: California, Florida, Texas, Arizona, and North Carolina. High birthrates among African and Hispanic Americans are accentuating this trend.[34]

Factors other than birthrates and school enrollment affect the demand for teachers. We have already discussed the occupation's 6 percent attrition rate, which will increase as the teaching force ages. Pupil/teacher ratios also have an effect on teacher demand. Overall, the ratios have fallen in both elementary and secondary schools since the 1960s. But the state budget crises of the 1990s (see chapter 9) are threatening to reverse several decades of progress toward smaller classes. Some local school districts, facing bankruptcy as a result of state funding cutbacks, are desperately trying to balance their budgets by raising class sizes to levels unheard of in districts with more financial support. Many public school teachers in my community, to cite a personal example, are struggling to teach classes of 40 to 50 students.[35]

On balance, though, the news about the need for teachers is good. The indicators point to strong, steady demand. Now we turn our attention to the supply side of the ledger.

## A Complex Guessing Game: The Supply of Teachers

The information about teacher supply is far more speculative than that about teacher demand. While demographers can confidently project elementary and secondary school enrollment into the twenty-first century by counting children who have already been born, there are no comparable sources of demographic information on the supply of teachers. A large number of hard-to-estimate variables enter the equation. First, how many people will *want* to teach between now and the turn of the century? The answer hinges on a wide range of social, political, and economic factors, forces at work both inside and outside the occupation. We simply do not know how high teacher salaries will be in 2001, for example, nor how attractive those salaries will be in the economy of the new century. Second, how many people will society *allow* to teach? That answer depends in part on trends in teacher education and certification, and social, political, and economic variables once again make it impossible to answer precisely.

We can try to answer, though, for we have reliable information on the past answers to such questions. We know that as the baby boom swelled elementary and secondary school enrollments, the news that teaching jobs were available traveled fast. College students responded by preparing to teach in larger numbers. Teacher education, long the most popular program at many colleges and universities, did even bigger business from the mid-1950s through the early 1970s. Teacher educators swung the gates open wide in an effort to meet the demand for new teachers, with little concern for standards and selectivity. The public wanted teachers in those classrooms, and teacher educators were more than happy to deliver.

As the early baby boomers reached college in the mid-1960s, the gap between teacher supply and demand began to close—with astonishing speed. "Major in education and you'll get a job," students were told, and many took the advice. The number of bachelor's degrees in education climbed steadily and peaked in 1972–1973 at 194,000. Education majors earned 21 percent of all the baccalaureate degrees awarded that year. But recall how elementary school enrollment turned down after 1969 and secondary school enrollment declined after 1976. As these supply and demand trends came together, the unhappy result was the teacher surplus of the 1970s. Teacher educators helped close one gap—now the nation had enough teachers—but they opened another. Many prospective teachers could not find jobs. Almost overnight, or so it seemed, the job market was flooded with applicants in search of teaching positions that simply were not there.[36]

College students responded by turning away from teacher education. After 1972–1973, the number of bachelor's degrees awarded in education fell by roughly 10,000 per year through the rest of the decade. Given the size of the teacher surplus, though, the numbers did not fall nearly fast enough. In 1986–1987, the number of bachelor's degrees awarded in education bottomed out at 87,000—less than 9 percent of all the baccalaureate degrees awarded that year and less than half the number of bachelor's degrees in education awarded 15 years earlier.[37]

Then the situation changed, once again so rapidly it caught many people off guard. The National Commission on Excellence in Education's *A Nation at Risk* (1983) and the flood of reports that followed called attention to problems in the schools. Suddenly education was in the news almost every day. School reform became one of the hottest political issues of the 1980s. In state after state, governors and legislators put together reform packages that included pay raises for teachers. At the same time, as we have seen, the echo of the baby boom sent more students to school, pushing up the demand for teachers. In the fall of 1983, teacher educators returned to campus to find more freshmen interested in teaching—the first signs of a trend that continued into the 1990s.[38]

In spite of efforts to track such trends, predicting the supply of America's teachers remains a complex guessing game. Increasingly, the occupation is drawing people from sources other than the pool of recent college graduates. School districts fill about half their job openings with transfer teachers who move from one school to another (whether within the same district, within the same state, or from state to state). Former teachers returning to the occupation take another 25 percent of the available jobs. That leaves only 25 percent for first-time teachers.[39]

Of these new recruits, most come into the occupation through traditional bachelor's degree programs, and many graduates of these programs are 25 and older. A growing number of first-time teachers are entering through master's degree programs and a variety of other nontraditional routes, which we will examine in chapter 3. As we will see in the next section, politicians have been eyeing every available source of supply—especially candidates entering via nontraditional routes—hoping to attract enough teachers to avoid or at least to minimize a shortage.

## The Politics of Teacher Supply and Demand

According to the conventional wisdom of the mid-1980s, the nation should now be grappling with a massive shortage of teachers. During the eighties, when report after report told Americans their schools were in trouble, respected commissions such as the Carnegie Forum on Education and the Economy issued dire warnings of an impending shortage. The Carnegie Forum's *A Nation Prepared: Teachers for the 21st Century* (1986) calculated 23 percent of each college graduating class would have to enter teaching to avoid a major shortage by the early 1990s.[40] Officials of the NEA and AFT dramatized these warnings for the news media. In 1986, AFT President Shanker predicted the demand for teachers would soon far exceed the supply, creating an "enormous gap." According to Shanker, the nation's schools would soon be searching for "hundreds of thousands of missing teachers."[41]

Officials of former President Ronald Reagan's Department of Education tried to downplay such predictions, even though the department's own reports actually supported them. In 1985, the National Center of Education Statistics made three alternative projections of the balance between teacher supply and demand. Under all three, the nation faced a teacher shortage. The only question was how severe it would be. Consider the three forecasts for the 1993–1994 school year: Under the high projection, teacher supply would satisfy 90 percent of the demand; under the intermediate projection, the supply would fill 63 percent of the demand; and under the low projection, only 45 percent of the demand would be met—a massive shortage indeed.[42]

With our 1990s hindsight, we can now see the high projection of teacher supply was most accurate. America does have a teacher shortage to contend with, but only a mild one. In the nation as a whole, the supply is sufficient to fill about 90 percent of the demand for new teachers each year. Most shortages of the mid-1990s are "spot" shortages in particular teaching fields, particular regions of the nation, or particular school districts.

What happened to the massive teacher shortage predicted for the 1990s? The answer involves a fascinating case study in the politics of education.

The views of former President George Bush and former Secretary of Education Lamar Alexander represent one end of the spectrum of opinion on the teacher job market. America 2000, the education strategy developed by Bush and Alexander, called for alternative certification programs to allow people to teach without completing a traditional teacher education program.[43] As Bush saw the situation, "Teachers-by-training aren't the only ones who can teach. I'm not saying you don't need some education courses, but I urge the state and local school systems to . . . open up our schools to those with a lifetime of experience outside the classroom."[44] William Bennett helped pave the way for alternative certification while he was Secretary of Education during the second Reagan administration.

At the other end of the spectrum of opinion are teacher educators who defend traditional education and certification standards and ask if society would allow "capable" people who happen to lack the "paper credential" called a medical school diploma to practice medicine. Of course not, most Americans answer, not even if such people have a "lifetime of experience" as pharmacists or biologists. Shouldn't we be just as careful, then, about the people we allow to teach? As we will see in chapters 3 and 4, teacher educators beg the question, and society hedges the answer.

Meanwhile, actors in the politics of education take stands at different points along the spectrum of opinion. The NEA and AFT position themselves toward the teacher educators' end of the spectrum. Many governors and state legislators are at the other end. State education officials move back and forth in response to trends in supply and demand. And President Bill Clinton, although elected with the support of the NEA and AFT, favors opening up the occupation by allowing people to repay their college tuition by performing "public service" work as teachers.[45]

## Bending Standards, Changing Standards

It is important to place these issues in a larger context. Teacher shortages have been the rule rather than the exception in this century. Politicians and school officials have been willing to bend teacher education and certification standards to help alleviate the shortages. The plain truth is that academic standards have taken a back seat to market demands. During the 1950s and 1960s, state legislators and state boards of education opened the occupation to large numbers of people with little or no formal training in education. When local school boards exhausted the supply of certified teachers, state officials simply issued emergency certificates.[46]

What else could we have done? politicians and school officials ask. Raising salaries and improving working conditions would have made the occupation more attractive, and salaries did rise gradually during the 1960s. But the main response of the states was putting uncertified people into classrooms. State officials also called on certified teachers to teach out of field—that is, to teach academic subjects outside their areas of expertise—when local school boards ran short of personnel certified in particular subjects, most frequently science and math.[47]

In some respects, we are now witnessing a replay of the 1950s and 1960s. Faced with spot shortages in certain regions, school districts, and teaching fields, state officials are once again dusting off their emergency certificates. In many states, officials have dressed up this once-unmarked back door into teaching with a freshly painted "alternate route" sign (see chapter 3). Likewise, about 16 percent of teachers spend at least part of their time teaching out of field. The news media and popular press sometimes call these make-do practices "education's dirty little secret." The unpublicized but time-honored practice of *bending* standards, then, is one force working to manage the teacher shortage.[48]

Another force is the political strategy of *changing* standards to open up alternate routes into the occupation. Making an end run around teacher educators and teacher organizations, politicians have eased the shortage of teachers by easing entry into teaching. Former New Jersey Governor Thomas Kean and State Education Commissioner Saul Cooperman led the way in 1985, arguing that many people with bachelor's degrees in fields other than education, especially the arts and sciences disciplines, can make excellent teachers. The New Jersey plan allows people with such credentials to bypass traditional teacher education and move directly into elementary and secondary classrooms as provisional teachers. About 25 percent of New Jersey's teacher recruits are now entering the occupation by the alternate route.[49]

At least 39 states have opened a wide variety of alternate routes into teaching. Several states have simply renamed their old emergency certificates. Some seem to be competing for the "Easiest Entry into Teaching" award, requiring as few as nine credit hours in education beyond an arts and sciences bachelor's degree for full certification. Other states, by contrast, require as many as 45 credit hours in education as part of a complete master's degree program.[50]

Here is another reason the teacher shortage has been mild: Politicians have managed the shortage by opening up the occupation, a force that is still gathering strength as the 1990s unfold. Inspired by the idea of openness and eased entry, an independent group called Teach for America is encouraging graduates of top-rung public and private colleges to try their hands at teaching, if only en route to careers as doctors or lawyers. School districts facing shortages, particularly of teachers for poor and minority students, are allowing Teach for America's recruits into the classroom after one summer of training. Whether alternative certification will eventually crowd out traditional certification remains to be seen. Constantly shifting political winds combined with social and economic changes make it difficult to forecast how many people will want to teach and how many society will allow to teach—and thus the job market.[51]

## Trends in the Job Market, Field by Field

One thing we can do is look at the success prospective teachers are having in their search for jobs. Table 1.4 is a status report on the job market based on research conducted by the Association for School, College and University Staffing (ASCUS). Every year, ASCUS surveys teacher placement officers throughout the United States and produces a rank-ordered list of teaching fields based on the balance between teacher supply and demand in each field. This table is a valuable guide to the job market in the nation as a whole.

To locate more specific information, talk with university faculty members and teacher placement officers, local and state school personnel officers, and others who are familiar with market conditions where you would like to teach. Even in the five fields with considerable shortages of teachers, the market varies from region to region. The same is true of fields whose rankings are low. The job market for elementary school teachers, for example, is most favorable in the south central, western, and southeastern states, where the baby boom is echoing loudly.[52]

**TABLE 1.4**   The job market for teachers: Outlook in 1992.

**Teaching Fields**

*Considerable Shortage of Teachers*
1. Special education—multiple handicaps
2. Special education—visual impairment
3. Speech and hearing therapy
4. Special education—learning disabilities
5. Special education—hearing impairment

*Some Shortage of Teachers*
6. Special education—mental retardation
7. Physics
8. Chemistry
9. Foreign languages other than Spanish, French, and German
10. Spanish
11. Mathematics
12. School psychologist
13. Computer education—secondary
14. Gifted education—elementary
15. Computer education—elementary
16. Gifted education—secondary
17. Guidance—elementary
18. Earth science

*Balanced Supply and Demand*
19. Library science—secondary
20. French
21. Library science—elementary
22. German
23. General science
24. Guidance—secondary
25. Biology
26. Reading—secondary
27. Reading—elementary
28. Industrial arts/technology
29. Instrumental music
30. Vocal music
31. Prekindergarten
32. Agriculture
33. English
34. Distributive education

*Some Surplus of Teachers*
35. Business education
36. Home economics
37. Speech
38. Art—secondary
39. Elementary education
40. Art—elementary
41. Physical education—elementary
42. Health
43. Social studies
44. Physical education—secondary (female)
45. Physical education—secondary (male)

Note: Rankings are based on reports from teacher placement officials.
SOURCE:   From Alex C. Moody and Dorothy Christoff, *A Study of U.S. Teacher Supply and Demand* (fifth in a series). Copyright © 1992 by ASCUS. Reprinted by permission.

As many prospective teachers view the job market, however, it is not national, regional, or statewide but local. Teachers tend to be less willing than, for instance, lawyers or accountants to move to obtain a job. The financial payoff from a move is less for teachers, and many have family and personal ties that make them reluctant to leave a given area. Teachers who *are* willing to relocate—even within their state—can improve their job prospects dramatically. New York State teachers, for example, can improve their chances if they are willing to teach in New York City or a rural upstate county rather than in a suburb. Teachers in most other states can follow the same guidelines. In general, the school systems with the greatest difficulty filling vacancies are in central cities and rural areas.[53]

Trying to make it easier for teachers to relocate within a wider geographical area, seven northeastern states—Connecticut, Maine, Massachusetts, New Hampshire, New York, Rhode Island, and Vermont—and four midwestern states—Iowa, Kansas, Missouri, and Nebraska—have established regional certification programs. These plans allow teachers certified in one state to teach in any other participating state within the region.[54]

Another strategy for broadening the job market is sponsoring job fairs for teachers. Florida led the way with an annual fair called "The Great Florida Teach-In," which draws large numbers of prospective teachers from the Southeast as well as other regions. In the words of one teacher who recently attended, "It's great to be wanted for a change. The Florida recruiters made me feel I have an important contribution to make to their state as a teacher." Other states, especially in the Sunbelt, have followed Florida's lead.[55]

Even Madison Avenue has gotten into the act. "Reach for the Power—Teach" is the slogan of a national advertising campaign sponsored by Recruiting Young Teachers, Inc. The toll-free number 800-45-TEACH flashes on television screens across the nation as viewers learn that no other occupation "has this power. The power to wake up young minds. The power to wake up the world. Teachers have that power. Reach for it. Teach." In its first three years of operation, Recruiting Young Teachers logged nearly 400,000 calls, one-fourth from minorities and almost one-half from men.[56]

Financial incentives also are effective. More than two-thirds of the states now offer teacher scholarship programs and loan forgiveness plans that erase part of a teacher's college loan for every year spent in the elementary or secondary classroom. Some local school systems encourage teachers to relocate by giving them recruitment bonuses, finding them apartments and paying the first month's rent, offering discounts on bank loans and credit cards, and trying in other ways to make teachers feel appreciated. This treatment is as welcome as it is overdue.[57]

Most teachers have yet to receive such treatment, though, for it is a product of the job market rather than of human kindness and goodwill. During the early 1990s, as Americans found themselves facing an economic recession rather than a massive teacher shortage, state and local recruiters scaled back their job fairs, recruitment bonuses, and other concessions. Teacher loan and scholarship programs are now in jeopardy in several states. Returning to a market flooded with job seekers would be a step backward, but a market in which candidates are sought after and highly prized helped move medicine, law, and other occupations down the road to professionalism. Optimistically, the same thing may happen to teaching.[58]

## ACTIVITIES

1. Conduct your own survey of teacher motivation. After talking with prospective teachers about their motives, ask currently employed teachers why they chose the occupation. Play the role of a friendly critic in your interviews.
2. Talk with principals and personnel officers about what they look for when they hire teachers. Ask about the relative importance of personal qualities versus academic skills.

3. Interview a variety of currently employed teachers—female and male, experienced and inexperienced, elementary and secondary, urban, suburban, and rural—about their job satisfaction. Conduct similar interviews with former teachers and make comparisons.
4. Use the information and suggestions in this chapter to begin your job search. Consider as wide a range of school systems as possible and take advantage of the services provided by your institution's placement office. If you have the chance to attend a job fair for teachers, by all means do so.

## RECOMMENDED READINGS

Association for School, College and University Staffing. *Teacher Supply and Demand in the United States* (Evanston, IL: ASCUS, updated annually).
This report is the best single source of information on the current job market.
Carnegie Foundation for the Advancement of Teaching. *The Condition of Teaching: A State-by-State Analysis, 1990* (Princeton, NJ: Princeton University Press, 1990).
The individual and collective voices of teachers speak out clearly on issues ranging from students to the status of the occupation.
Lortie, Dan C. *Schoolteacher: A Sociological Study* (Chicago: University of Chicago Press, 1975).
This is the modern classic on teachers, their work, and their world.
National Education Association. *Status of the American Public School Teacher 1990–1991* (Washington, D.C.: NEA, 1992).
This volume, the most recent in an ongoing study conducted at 5-year intervals since 1961, offers current information as well as a 30-year perspective on teaching.

## NOTES

1. Both quotes are from Carnegie Foundation for the Advancement of Teaching, *The Condition of Teaching: A State-by-State Analysis, 1990* (Princeton, NJ: Princeton University Press, 1990), pp. 9–10.
2. My ongoing study of teacher motivation, 1977 through the present, includes information on more than 3,000 prospective teachers at the University of South Alabama. Compare the other studies cited as sources for Table 1.1.
3. Linda Darling-Hammond and Arthur E. Wise, *A Conceptual Framework for Examining Teachers' Views of Teaching and Educational Policies* (Santa Monica, CA: Rand Corp., February 1981). Two landmark studies of teachers, their attitudes, and their status in American society are Willard Waller's *The Sociology of Teaching* (New York: Wiley, 1932) and Dan C. Lortie's *Schoolteacher: A Sociological Study* (Chicago: University of Chicago Press, 1975).
4. Lortie, *Schoolteacher*, pp. 30–37; National Education Association, *Status of the American Public School Teacher, 1990–1991* (Washington, D.C.: NEA, 1992), pp. 73–74.
5. Lortie, *Schoolteacher*, pp. 31–32.
6. To gain a historical perspective on teaching as an occupation, begin your reading with Willard S. Elsbree's classic, *The American Teacher: Evolution of a Profession in a Democracy* (New York: American Book Company, 1939), and continue with Donald R. Warren, ed., *American Teachers: Histories of a Profession at Work* (New York: Macmillan, 1989).

7. Elsbree, *The American Teacher,* chap. 17; National Education Association, *Status of the American Public School Teacher,* p. 80.

8. Dee Ann Spencer, *Contemporary Women Teachers Speak: Balancing School and Home* (White Plains, NY: Longman, 1986); Nancy Hoffman, *Woman's "True" Profession: Voices from the History of Teaching* (Old Westbury, NY: Feminist Press, 1981); Joseph W. Newman, "Reconstructing the World of Southern Teachers," *History of Education Quarterly* 24 (Winter 1984): 585–595.

9. Sylvia Mei-Ling Yee, *Careers in the Classroom: When Teaching Is More Than a Job* (New York: Teachers College Press, 1990); Robert B. Kottkamp, Eugene F. Provenzo, Jr., and Marilyn M. Cohn, "Stability and Change in a Profession: Two Decades of Teacher Attitudes, 1964–1984," *Phi Delta Kappan* 67 (April 1986): 559–567; Lortie, *Schoolteacher,* chap. 4.

10. See "Rachel Moreno: All in 'La Familia,' " *NEA Today* (March 1990), p. 19; Lynn Larson, "Is Self-esteem Oversold?" *NEA Today* (December 1990), p. 31; Rebecca K. Merriman, "What? Leave All This?" *NEA Today* (February 1992), p. 34; "Meet: Will Hayes," *NEA Today* (December 1987), p. 11.

11. Louis Harris and Associates, *The Metropolitan Life Survey of New Teachers* (New York: Metropolitan Life Insurance Co., 1991).

12. Blake Rodman, "Teacher–Training Enrollment Surging Upward, Poll Finds," *Education Week* (March 2, 1988), pp. 1, 26; National Education Association, *Status of the American Public School Teacher,* p. 78; Patricia Albjerg Graham, "Black Teachers: A Drastically Scarce Resource," *Phi Delta Kappan* 68 (April 1987): 598–605; Barbara J. Holmes, "A Closer Look at the Shortage of Minority Teachers," *Education Week* (May 17, 1989), p. 29.

13. Ray Rasmussen, "Teaching's Not Fun," *NEA Today* (November 1990), p. 30.

14. Arthur E. Wise, Linda Darling-Hammond, and Barnett Berry, *Effective Teacher Selection: From Recruitment to Retention* (Santa Monica, CA: Rand Corp., 1987), pp. 58–59; Phillip C. Schlechty and Victor S. Vance, "Do Academically Able Teachers Leave Education? The North Carolina Case," *Phi Delta Kappan* 63 (October 1981): 106–112.

15. See Richard J. Murnane, Judith D. Singer, John B. Willett, James J. Kemple, and Randall J. Olsen, *Who Will Teach? Policies that Matter* (Cambridge: Harvard University Press, 1991); and Susan Moore Johnson, *Teachers at Work: Achieving Excellence in Our Schools* (New York: Basic Books, 1990).

16. Alec Gallup, "The Gallup Poll of Teachers' Attitudes toward the Public Schools," *Phi Delta Kappan* 66 (October 1984): 104–105; Stanley M. Elam, Lowell C. Rose, and Alec M. Gallup, "The 23rd Annual Gallup Poll of the Public's Attitudes toward Public Schools," *Phi Delta Kappan* 73 (September 1991): 55.

17. Barry A. Farber and Julie Miller, "Teacher Burnout: A Psychoeducational Perspective," *Teachers College Record* 83 (Winter 1981): 235–243; Mark C. Shug, "Teacher Burnout and Professionalism," *Issues in Education* 1 (1983): 133–153.

18. Milbrey Wallin McLaughlin, R. Scott Pfeifer, Deborah Swanson-Owens, and Sylvia Yee, "Why Teachers Won't Teach," *Phi Delta Kappan* 67 (February 1986): 420–426; Shug, "Teacher Burnout," pp. 137–140.

19. See Joseph Benton Howell and David P. Schroeder, *Physician Stress: A Handbook for Coping* (Baltimore: University Park Press, 1984); and Marlene Kramer, *Reality Shock: Why Nurses Leave Nursing* (St. Louis: Mosby, 1974).

20. The classic study of the semiprofessions is Amitai Etzioni's *The Semiprofessions and Their Organizations: Teachers, Nurses, and Social Workers* (New York: Free Press, 1969).

21. Ibid.; Aruther E. Wise, "Legislated Learning Revisited," *Phi Delta Kappan* 69 (January 1988): 329–333; Linda Darling-Hammond, *Beyond the Commission Reports: The Coming Crisis in Teaching* (Santa Monica, CA: Rand Corp., July 1984), pp. 13–16; Wise, *Legislated Learning: The Bureaucratization of the American Classroom* (Berkeley: University of California Press, 1979).

22. Susan J. Rosenholtz, *Teachers' Workplace: The Social Organization of Schools* (White Plains, NY: Longman, 1989); Patricia Ashton and Rodman B. Webb, *Making a Difference: Teachers' Sense of Efficacy and Student Achievement* (White Plains, NY: Longman, 1986).

23. Carnegie Foundation for the Advancement of Teaching, *The Condition of Teaching*, p. ix.

24. Ibid., pp. 51, 60, 59.

25. Louis Harris and Associates, *The Metropolitan Life Survey of Former Teachers* (New York: Metropolitan Life Insurance Co., 1986); Nanci Hellmich, "Teachers Give Up on the Classroom," *USA Today* (March 14, 1986), p. 1.

26. Ibid.

27. Louis Harris and Associates, *The Metropolitan Life Survey of the American Teacher* (New York: Metropolitan Life Insurance Co., 1991).

28. National Education Association, *Status of the American Public School Teacher*, pp. 77, 27; U.S. Department of Education, National Center for Education Statistics, *Characteristics of Stayers, Movers, and Leavers: Results from the Teacher Followup Survey, 1988–1989* (Washington, D.C.: U.S. Department of Education, 1991), p. 6.

29. Quoted in Hellmich, "Teachers Give Up on the Classroom," p. 1.

30. U.S. Department of Education, National Center for Education Statistics, *Projections of Education Statistics to 2001: An Update* (Washington, D.C.: U.S. Department of Education, 1990), p. 118.

31. Ibid.

32. U.S. Department of Health, Education, and Welfare, National Center for Education Statistics, *Projections of Education Statistics to 1986–87* (Washington, D.C.: U.S. Government Printing Office, 1978), pp. 49–50, 55–60.

33. U.S. Department of Commerce, Bureau of the Census, *Fertility of American Women* (Washington, D.C.: U.S. Government Printing Office, 1985), pp. 1–7.

34. U.S. Department of Education, National Center for Education Statistics, *Projections of Education Statistics to 2002* (Washington, D.C.: U.S. Government Printing Office, 1991), pp. 113–114; Brad Edmondson, "The Education of Children," *American Demographics* 8 (February 1986): 26–29, 51–52, 54.

35. National Education Association, *Status of the American Public School Teacher*, pp. 40–41; Ann Bradley, "Recession Dampens Job Prospects for Teachers," *Education Week* (October 16, 1991), pp. 1, 12–13.

36. U.S. Department of Education, National Center for Education Statistics, *Digest of Education Statistics, 1991* (Washington, D.C.: U.S. Government Printing Office, 1991), pp. 276, 234.

37. Ibid.

38. National Commission on Excellence in Education, *A Nation at Risk: The Imperative for Educational Reform* (Washington, D.C.: U.S. Department of Education, 1983; "Interest in Teaching," *Education Week* (December 4, 1991), p. 7.

39. I base my estimates on U.S. Department of Education, National Center for Education Statistics, *The Condition of Education, 1992* (Washington, D.C.: U.S. Government Printing Office, 1992), pp. 148–149; American Federation of Teachers, *Survey and Analysis of Salary Trends, 1992* (Washington, D.C.: AFT, 1992), pp. 40–41; and

Ann Bradley, "Even as Gaps in Data Are Filled, Teacher-Supply Debate Lingers," *Education Week* (September 19, 1990), pp. 1, 14–15.

40. Carnegie Forum on Education and the Economy, *A Nation Prepared: Teachers for the 21st Century* (New York: Carnegie Forum, 1986), p. 31.
41. Albert Shanker, "Our Profession, Our Schools: The Case for Fundamental Reform," *American Educator* 10 (Fall 1986): 10–17, 44–45.
42. U.S. Department of Education, Center for Education Statistics, *The Condition of Education, 1986 Edition* (Washington, D.C.: U.S. Government Printing Office, 1986), pp. 62–65.
43. U.S. Department of Education, *America 2000: An Education Strategy Sourcebook* (Washington, D.C.: U.S. Government Printing Office, 1991), p. 24.
44. Quoted in "Bush: 'No' to Drugs; 'Yes' to Opening Up Teaching," *Education Week* (March 29, 1989), p. 16.
45. Beverly T. Watkins, "Rift over Teacher-Certification Rules Seen Impeding Reform Movement," *Chronicle of Higher Education* (October 18, 1989), pp. A19, 22, 23; Julie A. Miller, "Behind 'Love' of Clinton, Unease over Policy," *Education Week* (August 5, 1992), pp. 1, 46.
46. Michael W. Sedlak, " 'Let Us Go and Buy a School Master': Historical Perspectives on the Hiring of Teachers in the United States, 1750–1980," in Warren, ed., *American Teachers,* chap. 10; Donald R. Warren, "History and Teacher Education: Learning from Experience," *Educational Researcher* 14 (December 1985): 5–12.
47. U.S. Department of Education, National Center for Education Statistics, *The Condition of Education, 1992* (Washington, D.C.: U.S. Government Printing Office, 1992), pp. 144–145; National Education Association, *Status of the American Public School Teacher,* p. 70.
48. National Education Association, *Status of the American Public School Teacher,* p. 37.
49. Lynn Olson, "Cooperman Legacy: Gutsy Reforms, Unsolved Problems," *Education Week* (May 16, 1990), pp. 1, 10–11.
50. Emily Feistritzer and David Chester, *Alternative Teacher Certification: A State-by-State Analysis* (Washington, D.C.: National Center for Education Information, 1991), pp. 13–24. Arthur E. Wise and Linda Darling-Hammond, "Alternative Certification Is an Oxymoron," *Education Week* (September 4, 1991), p. 56.
51. Wendy Kopp, "Replace Certification with Recruitment," *Education Week* (October 9, 1991), p. 33.
52. Alex C. Moody and Dorothy Christoff, *A Study of U.S. Teacher Supply and Demand,* fifth in a series (Evanston, IL: Association for School, College and University Staffing, 1992), p. 7.
53. "Your Job Search: The Bigger Picture," *NEWS4U: A Special Publication for NEA Student Program Members* (May 1992), p. 1.
54. Meg Summerfield, "Regional Credential Found to Remove Job Barriers for Relocating Teachers," *Education Week* (August 5, 1992), p. 15.
55. Bradley, "Recession Dampens Job Prospects."
56. Ann Bradley, "Recruitment Ads Said to Uncover Teacher Source," *Education Week* (March 13, 1991), pp. 1, 25.
57. Ann Bradley, "Loan-Forgiveness Programs for Teaching Seen as Key Policy Tool," *Education Week* (February 28, 1990), pp. 1, 22.
58. Bradley, "Recession Dampens Job Prospects."

# CHAPTER 2

# Earning a Living and Living with Evaluation

*I absolutely cannot imagine going into business or something like that, just to make a lot of money. . . . I'm good at getting other people to think about things. And you have to go with what you're good at.*
—Prospective Midwestern teacher

*The first step is to convince teachers . . . to get out of this mindset that—yes, I went into teaching and I knew I wouldn't make much money. . . . That's a crock! . . . I believe in internal gratification, but I still contend that when my doctor cures somebody he gets internal gratification while he makes 120,000 dollars a year.*
—Southwestern teacher[1]

Can you make a decent living as a teacher? "It depends on what you call decent," the students in my Introduction to Education classes invariably respond. Although every prospective teacher's answer to this question will be personal and subjective, examining the facts and figures on teacher salaries will make your answer better informed.

This chapter surveys salaries as they are, have been, and may be, with the future contingent on the success of reforms promising teachers better wages. We will compare salaries of teachers to salaries of workers in other occupations. We will also look at the controversies over *merit pay, accountability,* and *evaluation*—issues that will directly affect your career. The chapter concludes with a discussion of reforms designed not only to raise teacher salaries but also to *restructure* teaching into an occupation with different levels of expertise and responsibility.

Reformers in the Carnegie Forum on Education and the Economy and the Holmes Group envision a national *career ladder* that would enable top-level teachers to earn salaries up to $90,000. As much as all teachers would welcome that kind of income, not everyone shares the vision of a highly *differentiated* occupation. Reflecting divisions within the teaching force, the NEA and AFT disagree on how to reward teachers and restructure teaching.

Still, the most recent news about salaries is encouraging. It may even change your mind about how well you can live as a teacher.

## TEACHER SALARIES, STATE BY STATE

In 1991–1992, the average salary of U.S. public school teachers was $34,148. As Table 2.1 indicates, teacher salaries vary considerably around the nation. In seven states, the average salary exceeds $40,000; in three states, the average falls below $25,000. Salaries tend to be highest in the Northeast, followed by the Midwest, the West, and the Southeast, but note the many exceptions to this pattern.

**TABLE 2.1**   Average salaries of public school teachers, 1991–1992.

| | | | |
|---|---|---|---|
| 1. Connecticut | $46,971 | 27. Florida | $31,070 |
| 2. Alaska | 44,718 | 28. Kentucky | 30,870 |
| 3. New York | 43,335 | 29. Kansas | 30,731 |
| 4. D. Columbia | 41,256 | 30. Wyoming | 30,425 |
| 5. Michigan | 41,149 | 31. Maine | 30,097 |
| 6. New Jersey | 41,027 | 32. Georgia | 29,509 |
| 7. California | 40,192 | 33. N. Carolina | 29,236 |
| 8. Maryland | 39,500 | 34. Iowa | 29,202 |
| 9. Pennsylvania | 38,715 | 35. Texas | 29,041 |
| 10. Massachusetts | 37,256 | 36. Missouri | 28,921 |
| 11. Illinois | 36,461 | 37. Tennessee | 28,621 |
| 12. Rhode Island | 36,047 | 38. S. Carolina | 28,340 |
| 13. Wisconsin | 35,227 | 39. Montana | 27,590 |
| 14. Indiana | 34,809 | 40. W. Virginia | 27,366 |
| 15. Washington | 34,800 | 41. Nebraska | 27,231 |
| 16. Delaware | 34,548 | 42. Louisiana | 27,037 |
| 17. Hawaii | 34,528 | 43. Alabama | 26,954 |
| 18. Oregon | 34,100 | 44. New Mexico | 26,653 |
| 19. Nevada | 33,857 | 45. Arkansas | 26,569 |
| 20. Minnesota | 33,700 | 46. Utah | 26,524 |
| 21. Vermont | 33,646 | 47. Idaho | 26,334 |
| 22. Ohio | 33,253 | 48. Oklahoma | 25,339 |
| 23. New Hampshire | 33,170 | 49. N. Dakota | 24,495 |
| 24. Colorado | 33,072 | 50. Mississippi | 24,368 |
| 25. Virginia | 31,921 | 51. S. Dakota | 23,291 |
| 26. Arizona | 31,176 | | |
| | U.S. Average   $34,148 | | |

SOURCE:   From National Education Association, *Rankings of the States, 1992* (Washington, D.C.: NEA, 1992), p. 21. Reprinted by permission.

Now examine Table 2.2, which shows how much teacher salaries have risen, in constant dollars, from the early 1980s through the early 1990s. Notice that when inflation is taken into account, teachers in the nation as a whole have increased their real earnings by 21 percent. As welcome as this news is, I must qualify it in two ways. First, most of the gains in real income since the early 1980s have simply restored purchasing power that was lost to inflation during the 1970s. Second, the sluggish economy of the early 1990s has applied the brakes to the drive for higher salaries. In the nation as a whole, teacher salaries have risen more slowly during the 1990s than they have since the mid-1960s.[2]

Now here is the best news: In real dollars, teacher salaries are the highest they have ever been. Much of the credit is due to the school reforms we will study throughout this book. With the release of *A Nation at Risk* in 1983, followed by a barrage of other reports on the schools, state legislatures and state boards

**TABLE 2.2**  Change in average salaries of public school teachers, 1981–1982 to 1991–1992 (constant dollars).

| | | | | |
|---|---|---|---|---|
| 1. Connecticut | 70% | | 27. Mississippi | 18% |
| 2. Vermont | 56 | | 28. D. Columbia | 16 |
| 3. New Hampshire | 52 | | 29. Nevada | 16 |
| 4. New Jersey | 41 | | 30. Michigan | 16 |
| 5. Maine | 36 | | 31. Minnesota | 16 |
| 6. Pennsylvania | 36 | | 32. Colorado | 16 |
| 7. Virginia | 28 | | 33. Oregon | 15 |
| 8. Maryland | 28 | | 34. Rhode Island | 14 |
| 9. Indiana | 28 | | 35. Texas | 13 |
| 10. Florida | 27 | | 36. Nebraska | 12 |
| 11. New York | 27 | | 37. Arizona | 11 |
| 12. Massachusetts | 26 | | 38. Idaho | 10 |
| 13. Kansas | 26 | | 39. Iowa | 9 |
| 14. Arkansas | 25 | | 40. W. Virginia | 9 |
| 15. Wisconsin | 24 | | 41. S. Dakota | 8 |
| 16. S. Carolina | 24 | | 42. Oklahoma | 7 |
| 17. Georgia | 23 | | 43. Montana | 6 |
| 18. Ohio | 23 | | 44. Hawaii | 5 |
| 19. Delaware | 23 | | 45. Washington | 4 |
| 20. Kentucky | 22 | | 46. Louisiana | 3 |
| 21. California | 21 | | 47. Utah | 0 |
| 22. Missouri | 21 | | 48. Wyoming | −2 |
| 23. Tennessee | 20 | | 49. New Mexico | −3 |
| 24. Illinois | 19 | | 50. N. Dakota | −4 |
| 25. Alabama | 18 | | 51. Alaska | −4 |
| 26. N. Carolina | 18 | | | |

U.S. Average  21%

SOURCE:  From National Education Association, *Rankings of the States, 1992* (Washington, D.C.: NEA, 1992), p. 22. Reprinted by permission.

of education went into action. The result was round after round of reform. Although teachers resent some reforms—the test-driven "cookbook" curriculum that takes classroom decisions out of their hands may be the most upsetting—they find it hard to fault the efforts of many states to recruit and retain better teachers through better salaries.

The NEA and AFT can claim part of the credit for higher salaries, as we will see in chapter 4, for they have lobbied hard in state capitols and negotiated impressive contracts with local school boards. Now that the enthusiasm for reform may be cooling off a bit, the two unions are trying to keep salaries from backsliding—a challenging goal in tough economic times.

Table 2.3 displays average starting salaries for teachers who enter the occupation with a bachelor's degree and no teaching experience. The national average is $22,171, but notice the variations. Four states start beginners at more than $25,000; five states pay them less than $18,000. Comparing Tables 2.1 and 2.3,

**TABLE 2.3**    Average starting salaries of public school teachers, 1991–1992.

| | | | |
|---|---|---|---|
| 1. Alaska | $30,429 | 27. Indiana | $21,081 |
| 2. New York | 27,166 | 28. Colorado | 20,906 |
| 3. Connecticut | 26,718 | 29. Vermont | 20,758 |
| 4. New Jersey | 26,162 | 30. Missouri | 20,652 |
| 5. California | 24,700 | 31. Kentucky | 20,559 |
| 6. Hawaii | 24,208 | 32. Tennessee | 20,371 |
| 7. Maryland | 24,069 | 33. Wyoming | 19,925 |
| 8. Pennsylvania | 23,750 | 34. Iowa | 19,873 |
| 9. D. Columbia | 23,325 | 35. N. Carolina | 19,810 |
| 10. Michigan | 23,250 | 36. S. Carolina | 19,706 |
| 11. Nevada | 23,228 | 37. Arkansas | 19,500 |
| 12. Virginia | 23,200 | 38. New Mexico | 19,499 |
| 13. Illinois | 22,899 | 39. Kansas | 19,438 |
| 14. Massachusetts | 22,889 | 40. Maine | 19,288 |
| 15. New Hampshire | 22,500 | 41. W. Virginia | 19,278 |
| 16. Wisconsin | 22,141 | 42. Nebraska | 18,779 |
| 17. Minnesota | 22,039 | 43. Ohio | 18,705 |
| 18. Arizona | 21,750 | 44. Mississippi | 18,664 |
| 19. Rhode Island | 21,692 | 45. Oklahoma | 18,660 |
| 20. Washington | 21,533 | 46. Montana | 18,407 |
| 21. Delaware | 21,532 | 47. Utah | 17,804 |
| 22. Alabama | 21,400 | 48. Louisiana | 17,686 |
| 23. Florida | 21,398 | 49. S. Dakota | 17,496 |
| 24. Oregon | 21,303 | 50. N. Dakota | 16,897 |
| 25. Georgia | 21,144 | 51. Idaho | 16,721 |
| 26. Texas | 21,100 | | |

U.S. Average    $22,171

SOURCE:    From F. Howard Nelson, *Survey and Analysis of Salary Trends, 1992* (Washington, D.C.: American Federation of Teachers, 1992), p. 43. Reprinted by permission.

you can see that several states rank much higher in beginners' salaries than in salaries of all teachers. New Hampshire, Virginia, Alabama, Texas, and Arizona are prime examples of states that are "front loading" teacher salaries, packing the greatest rewards (relatively speaking) into the first few years.

Because front-loaded salary schedules look good to new teachers, they may help these states avoid teacher shortages—or so their legislatures and boards of education hope. But such schedules quickly become discouraging as teachers gain experience. Once teachers are in the occupation, front loading gives them nowhere to go financially; front loading provides poor incentives to make teaching a career.

The patterns and trends in teacher salaries, like those in the teacher job market, are constantly changing. Just as you should investigate job opportunities in your teaching field in as wide a geographic area as possible, you owe it to yourself to conduct the same careful investigation of salaries.

The information in Tables 2.1, 2.2, and 2.3 should be only the beginning of your study, for variations in the cost of living make teacher salaries far more attractive in some places than in others. Housing is the most important cost-of-living variable. As a rule, the costs of buying or renting housing are higher in states ranked near the top of Table 2.1 than in states near the bottom, but variations *within* states are just as important. Housing tends to be more expensive in cities and suburbs than in small towns and rural areas, and the higher salaries in city and suburban school systems may not be enough to offset the difference. The "average" Illinois teacher whose salary is $36,461 may own a house and live comfortably in small-town Taylorville, while a teacher earning several thousand dollars more in an affluent Chicago suburb may be hard pressed to make ends meet, much less move out of a rented apartment and make payments on a house.[3]

## A PROFILE OF AMERICA'S TEACHERS

Who is the "average" teacher? The demographic profile in Table 2.4 offers some answers. In America as a whole, the average teacher is a white woman who is 42 years old and married, with two children. She holds a graduate degree and has been teaching for 15 years.

When you ask yourself whether you can make a decent living as a teacher, put yourself in this teacher's shoes—or at least put yourself well into your career. How would you like to earn $34,148 (or the average salary for the state where you would like to teach) after completing a graduate program and spending 15 years in the classroom?

You should consider that the average teacher has a spouse who contributes to the income of their family. In fact, in 1991 the average household income for all teachers was $55, 491. A household income of more than $55,491, 15 years into a teaching career, is certainly a more pleasant prospect than an individual salary of $34,148. With the sum of $55,491, enjoying a middle-class lifestyle, owning a home, and providing college tuition for the children all seem

**TABLE 2.4**   A profile of America's teachers.

| | |
|---|---|
| GENDER | |
| Female | 72% |
| Male | 28 |
| RACE AND ETHNICITY | |
| White | 87% |
| African American | 8 |
| Hispanic American | 3 |
| Asian American | 1 |
| Native American | 1 |
| AVERAGE AGE | 42 years |
| AGE DISTRIBUTION | |
| Under 30 | 11% |
| 30–39 | 27 |
| 40–49 | 39 |
| 50 and over | 23 |
| MARITAL STATUS | |
| Married | 76% |
| Single | 12 |
| Widowed, Divorced, Separated | 13 |
| TEACHERS WITH CHILDREN | 73% |
| AVERAGE NUMBER OF CHILDREN | 2 |
| TEACHERS WITH EMPLOYED SPOUSES | 62% |
| HIGHEST DEGREE | |
| Bachelor's | 46% |
| Master's or Specialist's | 53 |
| Doctor's | 1 |
| AVERAGE TEACHING EXPERIENCE | 15 years |

Note: Some columns do not total 100 due to rounding.
SOURCE:   National Education Association, *Status of the American Public School Teacher, 1990–1991* (Washington, D.C.: NEA, 1992), pp. 23, 27, 77–83, 176. Reprinted by permission.

within the realm of possibility. If we compare the average U.S. household income of $29,943 to the average teacher's household income of $55,491, teachers seem to be doing well indeed.[4]

The first time I discussed household income in my Introduction to Education classes, my students' reactions took me by surprise. I was being unfairly (and uncharacteristically) positive, they said. Students pointed out that household income also includes the moonlighting many teachers do outside the school system (see chapter 1), as well as the additional duties they take on at school—coaching and summer teaching, for instance. Yes, I admitted, more than half of all teachers find it necessary to supplement their household income in these ways.[5]

Several students also reminded me, referring to the profile in Table 2.4, that one of every four teachers is *not* married. It is small consolation to the single teacher who lives on one income that the average teacher has a household income of $55,491. Nor is that figure of much comfort to the divorced teacher who is trying to raise several children on one income, even with child support.

Thus I joined my students and concluded that although it may be helpful to know the average household income of an occupation's members, using household income to make individual salaries seem more acceptable can be deceptive. Prospective teachers who say "Teaching provides a good second income" or "I'll never earn much as a teacher, but if I get married I'll be OK financially," are apologizing for their occupation before they ever enter it. This defeatist attitude continues to hold teaching back. Teachers who regard their salaries as secondary may think of their work as secondary—as something less than a "real" career.

"We're teaching for a living, not a hobby," teacher organizations constantly remind politicians and the public. The facts about teaching support this view of the occupation. In the public school teaching force as a whole, the salaries of male teachers provide almost two-thirds of the income in their households, while the salaries of female teachers account for more than half their household income. In most teacher households, the income from teaching is primary, not secondary.[6]

Every chapter in Part I of this book stresses the point that teaching has the potential to become a full profession, evolving as medicine, law, and a few other occupations have during this century. For this change to occur, public attitudes toward teaching must change, with the attitudes of teachers themselves changing first.

## COMPARING SALARIES IN TEACHING AND OTHER OCCUPATIONS

Income is an important measure of worth in our society, one estimate of how much society values a particular kind of work. How do salaries of teachers compare to those of workers in other occupations?

To begin with the good news, I can report that since the early 1980s, public school teaching has outpaced virtually every other occupation in real income growth. Teachers have improved their economic position relative to all workers, to government workers, and to white-collar workers. Remember, though, that these gains for teachers came after steady losses during the 1970s. So far during the 1990s, the challenge for teachers and teacher organizations has been holding onto their gains in a stagnant economy.[7]

When considering the following occupational comparisons, remember that in 1991–1992 the average starting salary of public school teachers was $22,171, while the average salary of all teachers in the public schools was $34,148. (Private school teachers, who make up about 10 percent of the nation's teaching force, earn considerably less. As a rule, elite independent schools are the only private schools offering salaries comparable to those in public schools. See chapter 11 for more about private schools.)

The Labor Department's *Occupational Outlook Handbook, 1992–1993 Edition* provides information we can use to compare salaries. If we begin with *social work,* a female-dominated occupation that society views, like teaching, as semiprofessional, we see that teaching fares well. Starting salaries for social workers average $23,000. The average compensation for full-time social workers in private hospitals is $30,638, and for those employed by the federal government it is $38,195.[8]

Turning our attention to *nursing,* another female-dominated semiprofessional field, we find an occupation struggling with a shortage of trained workers. Hospitals, medical schools, and medical centers have been trying to cope with this shortage by raising the salary of beginning registered nurses, which has pushed their average starting pay up to $29,159. Full-time staff nurses in private hospitals earn an average of $33,696, with head nurses earning $41,246. Full-time clinical specialists and nurse practitioners command even higher salaries, averaging $43,722 and $44,990, respectively.[9]

Compared to business and management, fields in which women now receive almost half of the bachelor's and one-third of the master's degrees, teaching still looks competitive. *Accountants* with bachelor's degrees have starting offers averaging $26,600; with master's degrees, they receive offers of $31,100. Average earnings of nonsupervisory accountants are $37,000. Chief management accountants earn considerably more: an average of $55,700. *Financial managers* who work in banks, industry, and similar settings often start with salaries below $20,000, but their wages climb to an average of $35,800.[10]

Looking at salaries in scientific and technical occupations—fields in which women remain underrepresented—we can see clearly why there is a shortage of science and math teachers. Quite simply, people with such skills must be willing to make a financial sacrifice if they want to teach. *Engineers* with bachelor's degrees go to work in the private sector for starting salaries of $31,900; with master's degrees, their entry-level job offers average $36,200. Mid-level non-supervisory engineers have average earnings of $49,195, while their senior supervisors earn $93,514.[11]

*Mathematicians* have starting salaries of $27,000 and $30,100 with bachelor's and master's degrees, respectively. The average wages of all mathematicians in business and industry are $49,500.[12]

*Chemists* start at an average of only $23,000 with bachelor's degrees and $30,000 with master's degrees, but they can look forward to higher raises than teachers. With bachelor's degrees, chemists have average earnings of $39,000, and with master's degrees, $45,000.[13]

Turning finally to the two occupations Americans consider most professional, law and medicine, we can see the substantial financial rewards that accompany high occupational status. More women are reaping these rewards than ever before, for women now earn approximatley 30 percent of the nation's medical degrees and 40 percent of the law degrees.[14]

Beginning *attorneys* in private practice can anticipate earning about $47,000. Attorneys have average incomes of more than $60,000, while the most experienced attorneys in private practice earn more than $120,000.[15]

*Physicians* have greater earning potential than the workers in any other occupation. As residents, they receive stipends ranging from about $26,000 to $33,000, but on entering private practice their incomes climb steeply. General practitioners earn an average of $95,900; pediatricians, $104,700; specialists in internal medicine, $146,500; surgeons, $220,500; and all physicians, $155,800.[16]

Barring a drastic reordering of our nation's social and economic priorities, teachers will never command the average incomes of doctors or lawyers. Having said that, we should not despair of the possibility of major improvements in teacher salaries. The career ladders negotiated by unions and school boards in a few local districts now offer "lead teacher" salaries around $70,000. The Carnegie Forum on Education and the Economy and the Holmes Group would like to build a national career ladder for America's teachers. As we will see at the end of this chapter, the Carnegie-supported National Board for Professional Teaching Standards is developing a national certification system that may encourage school districts to pay their best teachers $50,000 to $90,000, depending on the wealth of the states and the districts where the teachers work.

Before analyzing the promises and pitfalls of these reforms, we can encourage ourselves with the fact that the most experienced, most highly educated teachers in some school districts are *already* earning $60,000 or more—on regular salary schedules. Or, we can just as easily discourage ourselves with the fact that, in other districts, teachers with graduate degrees and 30 years in the classroom make $30,000 or less—on regular salary schedules.

## TEACHER SALARY SCHEDULES

Tables 2.5, 2.6, and 2.7 illustrate the diversity in teacher pay throughout the United States. As different as the salaries on the three schedules are, they have several key features in common. These schedules, like most in the nation, are based on just two factors: experience and education. The schedules make no distinctions by subject or grade level, nor do they reward teachers according to their competence and performance. On each schedule, a teacher who has five years of classroom experience and a bachelor's degree earns exactly the same salary as every other teacher with five years and a bachelor's degree. Schedules like these bring a sense of security and predictability to teaching as an occupation.

For the first half of this century, teacher organizations fought for salary schedules with these features. School boards must treat all teachers alike, the organizations insisted; teacher salaries must be based strictly on experience and education. In district after district, state after state, teacher organizations won these battles, and gradually school boards stopped paying secondary teachers more than elementary, male teachers more than female, and, most recently, white teachers more than black. School boards adopted *single salary schedules* that put teachers with equal experience and education on equal footing.

Another battle the organizations won—or hoped they had won—was over merit pay, the practice of basing salaries on evaluations of competence and performance. Teacher organizations have consistently (and, for the most part, successfully) opposed merit pay, but this old battle keeps breaking out on new fronts.[17]

The operation of single salary schedules like those in Tables 2.5, 2.6, and 2.7 is easy to understand. New teachers with bachelor's degrees start at the first step on the bachelor's track and advance one step per year. When teachers qualify for another track by taking graduate work, they move laterally to the right— they do not return to the first step on the new track. On schedules like Table 2.5,

**TABLE 2.5** A teacher salary schedule with "perverse incentives."

| | Track | | |
| --- | --- | --- | --- |
| Step | Bachelor's | Master's | Specialist's |
| 1 | $19,000 | $21,000 | $23,000 |
| 2 | 19,200 | 21,200 | 23,200 |
| 3 | 19,400 | 21,400 | 23,400 |
| 4 | 21,000 | 23,000 | 25,000 |
| 5 | 21,200 | 23,200 | 25,200 |
| 6 | 21,400 | 23,400 | 25,400 |
| 7 | 21,600 | 23,600 | 25,600 |
| 8 | 21,800 | 23,800 | 25,800 |
| 9 | 22,000 | 24,000 | 26,000 |
| 10 | 22,200 | 24,200 | 26,200 |

teachers who move through all the tracks and take all the steps reach maximum salary well before retirement—a sad commentary on the way some school boards view teaching as a career. For teachers in this situation, an across-the-board raise granted by the state or local board offers the only hope for a higher salary. Schedules like Tables 2.6 and 2.7, however, provide longevity raises for career teachers, as the notes at the bottom of the schedules explain.

There are many other differences among the three salary schedules. The schedule in Table 2.5 is the kind that, to be blunt, offers discouragingly low salaries, bottom to top—to beginners with bachelor's degrees as well as to veterans with graduate degrees. This kind of schedule is standard in states that rank low in Tables 2.1 *and* 2.3. Pointing to one such state in each region as a prime example, we might single out Idaho, South Dakota, Mississippi, and Maine. But, as the salaries in Tables 2.1 and 2.3 suggest, these states are certainly not the only ones that allow this kind of salary schedule to dominate.

One bright spot is that even in the states ranked low in Tables 2.1 and 2.3, wealthier suburban and city districts may add enough local revenue to the minimum salary schedule established by the state board of education to offer teachers somewhat better wages. And, to be sure, the lower cost of living in some areas may make this schedule look fairly attractive to some prospective teachers.

Enough apologies and excuses. This schedule abounds with what economists call "perverse incentives." With its starting salary of $19,000, yearly step raises of $200, and top salary of $26,200, the schedule gives people strong incentives *not* to become teachers, and, even if they do, to leave the occupation after just a few years. Teachers can look forward to a raise exceeding $200 on just three occasions: when they become tenured, which occurs in most states after three years; when they receive a graduate degree; or when the school board or state legislature grants a cost-of-living raise to all teachers.

Imagine how veteran teachers must feel. After spending a large part of their adult lives in the classroom and going back to school for advanced degrees, they earn only a few thousand dollars more than the novice teachers down the hall.

What kind of people does this salary schedule attract? What kind does it keep in the occupation? To be complimentary for now, we can say truly dedicated people, but the next chapter balances this answer with a less flattering one.

The other two schedules offer a better outlook. Table 2.6 shows a schedule representative of districts paying average salaries to both beginning and experienced teachers. With its starting point of $22,500 and ratio of about 2 to 1 between its highest and lowest salaries, this schedule is fairly typical for America's teachers. Common in the Northeast, West, and Midwest, the schedule stands out as exceptional primarily in the Southeast and in a few states outside that region where top and bottom salaries are compressed into a narrower range.

Salary schedules like this one are often the products of collective bargaining between teacher unions and school boards, a practice we will discuss in chapter 4. Significantly, collective bargaining is relatively well established in every region but the Southeast. Where bargaining occurs, unions usually negotiate for less compressed schedules similar to this one, which offer relatively good salaries to the experienced teachers who make up most of the union's membership. The schedule gives teachers incentives to stick with the occupation and make it a career.[18]

Experienced teachers with graduate degrees can be expensive to school boards, though, and without the pressure of collective bargaining, boards often opt for front-loaded salary schedules. A cold, harsh fact of life makes front-loaded schedules more attractive to some board members than this schedule. Front

**TABLE 2.6**  A typical teacher salary schedule.

| | Track | | | | | |
|---|---|---|---|---|---|---|
| Step | Bachelor's | Bachelor's Plus 20 Hours | Master's | Master's Plus 20 Hours | Specialist's | Doctor's |
| 1 | $22,500 | $22,500 | $23,500 | $23,500 | $25,000 | $27,000 |
| 2 | 22,700 | 22,900 | 24,200 | 24,600 | 26,500 | 28,500 |
| 3 | 23,100 | 23,800 | 25,100 | 25,800 | 28,100 | 30,500 |
| 4 | 25,000 | 25,700 | 27,000 | 27,700 | 30,600 | 33,500 |
| 5 | 25,500 | 26,200 | 27,600 | 28,400 | 31,500 | 34,500 |
| 6 | 26,000 | 26,700 | 28,200 | 29,100 | 32,400 | 35,500 |
| 7 | 26,500 | 27,200 | 28,800 | 29,800 | 33,300 | 36,500 |
| 8 | 27,000 | 27,700 | 29,400 | 30,500 | 34,200 | 37,500 |
| 9 | 27,500 | 28,200 | 30,000 | 31,200 | 35,100 | 38,500 |
| 10 | 28,000 | 28,700 | 30,600 | 31,900 | 36,000 | 39,500 |
| 11 | | 29,200 | 31,300 | 32,700 | 37,000 | 40,600 |
| 12 | | | 32,000 | 33,500 | 38,000 | 41,700 |
| 13 | | | 32,700 | 34,300 | 39,000 | 42,800 |
| 14 | | | 33,400 | 35,100 | 40,000 | 43,900 |
| 15 | | | 34,100 | 35,900 | 41,000 | 45,000 |

Note: Teachers who reach the top of the master's, master's plus 20 hours, specialist's, and doctor's tracks qualify for longevity raises of 3 percent every two years.

loading produces higher rates of teacher turnover, driving out experienced teachers and attracting a steady stream of lower-paid recruits eager to fill the vacancies. What experienced teachers see as a perverse incentive, board members may see as good business.

Fortunately, the salary schedule in Table 2.6 has a fairly respectable high end of $45,000. Notice that this schedule contains more steps and more tracks than the first one we examined. As tenured teachers move down the tracks, they are encouraged to find that the later steps bring higher raises than the earlier steps. Notice, too, that the additional tracks provide more immediate incentives for teachers to pursue master's and specialist's degrees because they reward progress toward degrees.

This salary schedule acknowledges the fact that some classroom teachers are interested in and capable of obtaining doctoral degrees. School officials in districts with salary schedules similar to Table 2.5, by contrast, sometimes justify the lack of a doctoral track by asserting that anyone smart enough to earn a doctorate is too smart to be an elementary or secondary school teacher. Considering the salaries in Table 2.5, it seems the officials may have a point.

If all teachers worked in school districts with salary schedules like Table 2.7, this chapter—possibly this entire book—would have a different tone, for teaching

**TABLE 2.7**  An exceptionally good teacher salary schedule.

| | | | Track | | | |
|---|---|---|---|---|---|---|
| Step | Bachelor's | Bachelor's Plus 20 Hours | Master's | Master's Plus 20 Hours | Specialist's | Doctor's |
| 1 | $30,000 | $30,000 | $32,500 | $32,500 | $35,000 | $37,500 |
| 2 | 30,300 | 30,700 | 33,400 | 33,700 | 36,400 | 39,100 |
| 3 | 30,800 | 31,800 | 34,900 | 35,400 | 38,400 | 41,300 |
| 4 | 32,800 | 33,800 | 37,400 | 37,900 | 41,400 | 44,300 |
| 5 | 33,600 | 34,600 | 38,400 | 39.100 | 42,700 | 45,700 |
| 6 | 34,400 | 35,400 | 39,400 | 40,300 | 44,000 | 47,100 |
| 7 | 35,200 | 36,200 | 40,400 | 41,500 | 45,300 | 48,500 |
| 8 | 36,000 | 37,000 | 41,400 | 42,700 | 46,600 | 49,900 |
| 9 | 36,800 | 37,800 | 42,400 | 43,900 | 47,900 | 51,300 |
| 10 | 37,600 | 38,600 | 43,400 | 45,100 | 49,200 | 52,700 |
| 11 | | 39,400 | 44,500 | 46,400 | 50,600 | 54,200 |
| 12 | | | 45,600 | 47,700 | 52,000 | 55,700 |
| 13 | | | 46,700 | 49,000 | 53,400 | 57,200 |
| 14 | | | 47,800 | 50,300 | 54,800 | 58,700 |
| 15 | | | 48,900 | 51,600 | 56,200 | 60,200 |
| 16 | | | | 52,900 | 57,700 | 61,800 |
| 17 | | | | | 59,200 | 63,400 |
| 18 | | | | | 60,700 | 65,000 |
| 19 | | | | | 62,200 | 66,600 |
| 20 | | | | | 63,700 | 68,200 |

Note: Teachers who reach the top of the master's, master's plus 20 hours, specialist's, and doctor's tracks qualify for longevity raises of 3 percent every two years.

would be a different occupation. Without question, different would mean better, because we know that the small number of districts that actually pay top salaries in the neighborhood of $70,000 can afford to be more selective in hiring, more careful about granting tenure, and more supportive of people who make teaching their career.

Most such districts have collective bargaining between teacher and school board members, but the emphasis at the bargaining table is on cooperation rather than confrontation. Labor relations specialists call this a "win-win" approach to negotiations. Teachers win, the board wins, and, most important, students win, because all concerned can work together without having to fuss over money.[19]

A visit to a school district with such a salary schedule and the financial resources that make it possible—try Palo Alto, California; Winnetka, Illinois; or an affluent Washington, D.C. suburb—would convince most teachers that although money is not a panacea, it can certainly make a difference. The catch, of course, is that most of the districts paying top salaries of $70,000 are located in wealthy communities where local support for public education, financial and otherwise, is quite high. These districts are by no means typical. We will take a closer look at school finance in chapter 9, but obviously it would take quite a commitment from the federal, state, and local government to put all 2,429,967 of the nation's public school teachers on salary schedules resembling Table 2.7.[20]

Try to suspend disbelief for a moment. Giving America's teachers an across-the-board 50 percent raise would make the average salary more than $50,000. This reform would put the average teacher on a salary schedule similar to Table 2.7, and it would give teachers in such low-wage states as South Dakota and Mississippi salaries comparable to those in Indiana and Massachusetts in 1991–1992. The prospect of such a reform is exciting.

How much would it cost? The United States spends a total of about $210 billion on public elementary and secondary education every year, with about $85 billion going directly into teachers' paychecks. Considering such additional costs to school systems as retirement, insurance, and social security contributions, we can estimate that giving teachers a 50 percent raise would mean increasing the nation's annual spending for public schools by about $55 billion. Although this reform is too expensive to implement in a single year, it can still serve as a goal for teachers to work toward over several years.[21]

Albert Shanker, president of the AFT, believes this goal is out of reach and argues that the nation will never increase its real spending on public education by such a massive amount. As an alternative, Shanker and his union have been edging warily toward the concept of paying much better salaries to some teachers than to others.

Shanker understandably bridles at the words *merit pay* because they conjure up bitter memories of bias and favoritism, but he and the AFT are cautiously embracing an updated version as part of a plan to make teaching a *differentiated* occupation, one that would recognize different levels of expertise and responsibility. Shanker's ideas closely parallel the proposals of the Carnegie Forum and the Holmes Group, which we will examine in the last section of this chapter.

Why is the AFT, a teacher organization that has fought merit pay with do-or-die determination for most of this century, now softening its position? And why is the rival union Shanker refers to as the "other organization," the much larger NEA, trying to stick to its guns against merit pay?[22]

## MERIT PAY: THE BIRTH OF "SOUND AND CHEAP"

The answers lie in the organizations' differing views of the past, present, and future of merit pay. The NEA's position is that merit pay has failed miserably and that today's experiments are faring just as badly. To the NEA, merit pay for teachers is an inherently flawed concept. Opinion polls show more than 60 percent of America's teachers are opposed to merit pay. Why, the NEA asks, should teachers change their minds and support a bad idea?[23]

Even though the AFT agrees that merit pay has an unsavory past, it clings to the hope that the idea can be salvaged. Frankly, the AFT feels that with polls showing more than 60 percent of all Americans in favor of merit pay, pressure from the general public and especially the business community may force teachers to live with some version of the concept. Trying to cope with what it sees as a new political reality, the AFT wants to take the lead and develop the fairest merit pay plans possible.[24]

At least the two teacher organizations agree on the past. Educational historians have documented the record of merit pay, and a most unimpressive record it is. Forty to 50 percent of the nation's school districts tried merit pay in the World War I era and the 1920s. "Scientific efficiency" was all the rage in business management, and school boards jumped on the bandwagon with a variety of plans to base teachers' salaries on evaluations of their ability and performance. Scientific efficiency as applied to public education was, in theory, an attempt to make the schools "both sound and cheap." Teachers discovered that, in practice, the emphasis was on cheap.[25]

A typical merit pay plan entailed arranging a school district's teachers in a pyramidlike hierarchy based on their evaluations. For example, Rank 5 teachers were those judged to be the best; Rank 4 teachers were the next best; and so on down to Rank 1 teachers, who received the worst evaluations. Each rank carried a different salary schedule, with Rank 5 teachers earning the highest salaries and Rank 1 teachers the lowest.[26]

All well and good, some teachers thought. Then, as now, there was undeniable appeal in the principle that the better you are at a job, the greater your rewards should be. But then, as now, there were tremendous difficulties in defining what *better* meant and deciding which teachers fit the description. Relying on two techniques that were becoming fashionable in business management, school boards required administrators and supervisors to evaluate teachers in the classroom and required teachers to take tests. Neither technique was new in public education; what was different was that under merit pay plans, evaluations and test scores affected salaries.

Teachers fought back. School boards accustomed to quiet, complacent employees suddenly faced storms of teacher protest. Across the nation, teachers banded together and formed local organizations, sometimes taking the radical step of affiliating with the AFT, the national teacher organization that dared to call itself a union. The NEA and the state teacher associations, the "professional associations" dominated by administrators and college professors, also expressed reservations about merit pay, albeit more politely than the AFT. The major battles against merit pay, though, were fought by teachers in local school systems.

The complaints against classroom evaluations often centered on bias and favoritism. Teachers charged that administrators and supervisors used the evaluations to reward their friends and punish their enemies. Evaluators brought their political views, religious beliefs, and social preferences into the process, teachers claimed. Sometimes an especially controversial evaluation blew up into a newspaper sensation that had the entire community up in arms and taking sides: a Protestant principal's unfavorable evaluation of a Catholic or Jewish teacher, a Democrat's low ranking of a Republican teacher, or a male principal's alleged partiality toward the attractive woman who taught fourth grade. Merit pay could be the perfect topic for community gossip and debate.

The checklist evaluation instruments used during the 1910s and 1920s invited controversy because they were so subjective. Often the evaluator rated teachers on such items as "Teacher moves around frequently," "Teacher is neat and well groomed," and "Teacher has pleasant demeanor." Besides the room such items left for evaluators to inject their own biases, teachers complained that the items had no necessary connection to good teaching. It was just possible that students might be able to learn from rumpled, fussy teachers who seldom stirred from their desks as well as from teachers with the traits the checklists favored. The use of such evaluation instruments, slanted toward teachers who dotted their *i*'s and crossed their *t*'s, penalized those who were unconventional but nevertheless commanded the respect of students, parents, and peers.[27]

Teacher testing, which we will examine in greater detail in the next chapter, was also controversial. Although it alternately amuses and irritates the public that the people who give tests to students complain so much when they have to take tests themselves, the consistency of teachers' complaints over the years deserves our attention.

The essence of their criticism has been that many of the questions on teacher tests are irrelevant to the work they do. When school boards in the 1910s and 1920s mandated questions covering the *general knowledge* considered to be the mark of any well-educated person, teachers argued that translating passages from Latin or identifying capitals of foreign countries (yes, such items were frequently on the test) were things most teachers rarely, if ever, had to do. As for *pedagogy,* the art and science of teaching, the complaint was that questions about teaching could not measure the ability to teach. Questions covering the *subject matter* for which teachers were responsible—English or mathematics, for instance—were somewhat more acceptable, but teachers often criticized these questions, too, as unrepresentative of the knowledge they actually used in the classroom. There was also controversy over how much English or math or science the elementary teacher, a generalist, needed to know. Surely not as much as the specialized secondary teacher, but how much?[28]

Administrators and supervisors often joined the protest against merit pay since many of them were no more comfortable conducting the evaluations than teachers were being evaluated. Merit ratings proved to be divisive, pitting teachers against adminstrators and one teacher against another. Running a merit pay system was a bureaucratic nightmare, adminstrators complained, as a host of new responsibilities competed for time on their already-crowded schedules.

The last straw broke when it became clear that many school boards were using merit pay to reduce the budget for salaries. A favorite ploy was refusing to approve any teachers, regardless of their evaluations and test scores, for the highest rank. Sound and cheap? Transparently cheap.

The battles over merit pay were mercifully short in most school systems. Teachers took their case to the local communities, calling on newspaper editors and politicians to help win the sympathy of parents and other citizens. School boards, in the face of determined opposition, threw up their hands and decided that having a merit pay plan wasn't worth the trouble. Tried and rejected by almost half the nation's school systems, merit pay was a dead issue by the 1930s and 1940s.

## THE ACCOUNTABILITY MOVEMENT: MERIT PAY REBORN

If much of the above sounds familiar, it should, because in one sense the arguments over merit pay have changed very little. Merit pay has a habit of reappearing in slightly different incarnations, with each new-and-improved model promising to correct the defects of the older ones. Merit pay revived briefly during the 1950s, died again during the 1960s, and has been trying to come back to life since the 1970s as part of the accountability movement.

Accountability is a concept with a positive-sounding name and strong surface appeal. Who would dare argue that educators should *not* be accountable? Accountability is a response to the popular perception that the costs of public education have soared while the quality has plummeted. This movement promises taxpayers "more bang for the buck." No more vague promises—school boards have found new ways to measure student achievement, and now the pressure is on teachers to be accountable for how much their students learn.[29]

Accountability has changed the way Americans think about public education. As we will see in chapter 10, standardized achievement tests with their aura of scientific respectability have become the accepted means of measuring student achievement. Releasing news about test scores—preferably *rising* test scores— has become the accepted way for school boards to reassure the public that students are learning.[30]

A few school boards have tried to take accountability to the limit by using the concept as the latest twist in merit pay. Why not reward those teachers whose students have the highest achievement? In other words, why not base teacher salaries on student test scores?

## The Factory Model of Schooling

From a business management point of view, the above idea sounds great. Follow the logic of a school board member with a background in business. Just as the high-tech assembly-line worker who turns out better silicon chips than other workers deserves a financial pat on the back, so does the teacher who turns out better students. After all, the board member reasons, a school is like a factory; educated students are the products of the factory, and teachers, the workers in the factory, must be acountable for the quality of the products. If teachers complain about the subjectivity of classroom evaluations and the irrelevance of teacher tests, then surely they will have no objections to using student test scores as an index of how well they are doing their jobs. What could be more relevant and objective?[31]

Schools are most definitely not like factories, teachers respond—often angrily—because students are not like silicon chips or any other tangible "product." Students are human beings, not inanimate objects. The education of a human being is far more complex than the production of a silicon chip. High-tech workers, operating in a sterile environment, have almost complete control over their chips while teachers have no such environment and no such control. Teachers are responsible for teaching, to be sure, but students are responsible for learning. Countless factors, both inside and outside the school, influence the teaching-learning process.

Teachers have been fighting various versions of the factory model of schooling since before the Civil War, but the model has become more threatening than ever with the added feature of merit pay based on student test scores. Teacher organizations have drawn the line over the issue. School boards trying to implement acountability-based merit pay plans have faced determined opposition from teachers, with teacher organizations sometimes going to court to block the plans.[32]

## Accountability-Based Merit Pay on Trial

Picture a courtroom with a school district's director of testing on the stand. The director is using the example of a third-grade teacher and her class to explain accountability-based merit pay. "The district administers standardized tests to measure the achievement of the teacher's students at the start of the school year and again at the end of the year," the director testifies. "We attribute the difference between the two sets of test scores—an increase, we hope!—to the teacher, even though we know other factors also affect scores. To control some of the other factors, we compare the test scores of this teacher's students with the scores of other students from similar socioeconomic backgrounds.

"The teacher gets a merit raise if her students' scores have increased more than the scores of comparable third-grade students," the testing director concludes. "That's the essence of accountability-based merit pay."

Now listen as a witness for the teacher organization, a professor of educational measurement and evaluation, takes the stand. "The fundamental problem with such a plan," the professor begins, "is that the third-grade teacher is not the only influence on her students' test scores, as the previous witness admitted. We can divide the factors affecting test scores into two groups: school influences and nonschool influences. School influences include not just the one teacher but other teachers and also other students, administrators, textbooks, the classroom temperature, and countless other factors, many beyond the teacher's control. The list of nonschool influences is even longer, ranging from parents to peers, from exercise to diet, from magazines to television—virtually *all* beyond the teacher's control.

"The combined nonschool influences on achievement test scores are two to three times stronger, statistically speaking, than the combined school influences," the professor explains in conclusion. "Trying to isolate the influence of one teacher to use as the basis of merit pay is little more than a guessing game."

The opposition of teacher organizations to accountability-based merit pay—adamant opposition up through the mid-1980s—forced school boards to develop other strategies. The NEA remains adamant, while the AFT has indicated a willingness to accept the use of student test scores as *one* factor in experimental merit pay plans. Albert Shanker is hoping this gamble will pay off for his union and for teaching as an occupation.

## BEHAVIORAL EVALUATION OF TEACHERS

Meanwhile, another form of teacher evaluation has come to the fore in the merit pay controversy. It represents a return to the old idea of evaluating teacher performance in the classroom, with new emphasis on student achievement. This *behavioral* approach is the most important form of teacher evaluation in many of the career ladder plans we will examine in the last section of this chapter.

Developed by such researchers as Madeline Hunter and the team of Donald M. Medley, Homer Coker, and Robert S. Soar, the basic methodology of behavioral evaluation is disarmingly straighforward. It involves breaking down teaching into as many small, discrete behaviors as possible; deciding which behaviors are indicators of effective teaching; observing teachers to determine the degree to which they exhibit these behaviors; evaluating teachers on the basis of the observations; and rewarding teachers accordingly.[33]

Observers—who may be administrators, supervisors, or teachers themselves—are trained to look for the behaviors in the classroom and code them on computer-scanning sheets. As the observers watch a teacher in action during a period of 45 minutes or so, they repeatedly mark the scanning sheets, "bubbling in" the ovals that correspond to the behaviors they see. For instance, does the teacher "begin the lesson with a review of previous material"? "Conduct the lesson at a brisk pace"? "Provide students with immediate feedback"? "Summarize the main point(s) of the lesson at the end of the lesson"?[34]

These behaviors are 4 of the 25 "effective teaching skills" on the North Carolina Teacher Performance Appraisal Instrument (TPAI). The developers of such systems boast that their methodology is "noninferential," that it does not require the evaluator to pass judgment on a behavior, only to recognize the behavior and record the frequency with which it occurs. Moreover, the developers carefully use the term *observer* rather than *evaluator* in order to threaten teachers as little as possible. The actual evaluation comes later, when administrators review the observations and advise teachers how to improve their classroom work. To put things positively, helping teachers improve is the most important purpose of evaluation.[35]

But evaluation also involves the difficult and often unpleasant task of making decisions about salaries, promotions, and careers. Behavioral evaluation systems generate quantitative data; they produce averages, curves, standard deviations, and cutoffs. These systems make evaluation seem scientific and thus objective. From the administrator's point of view, they have the virtue of shifting the responsibility for tough decisions away from people and toward numbers. If a teacher barely misses the cutoff for a merit raise, the administrator can pinpoint the teacher's problems on the observation sheets: failing to conduct the lesson "briskly" enough, perhaps, or neglecting to "affirm a correct oral answer quickly, even tacitly."[36]

Teachers like the behavioral approach because it is specific, letting them know exactly what is expected of them and provides clear pointers on how to change. They dislike it because it is mechanical, pressuring them to teach in a certain way—at least while observers are present—and encouraging game playing.[37]

Teachers are asking critical questions about behavioral evaluation. Standing in front of a mirror at home on the night before an observation, practicing the approved repertoire of behaviors and trying to exhibit as many as possible in 45 minutes—is that the best way for a teacher to improve? Is it the best way for a teacher to qualify for a raise or promotion? Consider the goal of making teaching a profession. How would doctors or lawyers react to such an evaluation system? Would anyone dare define the competent practice of medicine or law as a set of 25 skills?

We can ask even more critical questions about the effects of behavioral evaluation on classroom instruction. Teachers often laugh off the effects and joke. "I'll flap my wings, walk in circles, touch my nose, do almost anything else to get a good evaluation," one teacher told me recently. "Then I'll teach like I want after the principal leaves." But behavioral evaluation may be shaping instruction more than teachers realize.

A study of North Carolina's TPAI suggests that as teachers conform to the style of instruction the instrument favors, behavioral evaluation is homogenizing teaching. The 25 skills on the TPAI reflect a view of teaching as didactic instruction in facts, principles, right answers, and best responses. Not surprisingly, researchers have found that teaching characterized by proposing, putting forth, and informing has increased in North Carolina classrooms since the 1985 adoption of the TPAI. Teaching that involves supposing, speculating, and conjecturing has sharply decreased. Both styles of instruction have their place, of course. But behavioral evaluation, harnessed to a "cookbook" curriculum that already pressures teachers to "teach the test," may be reducing teaching to an uncritical process of transmitting information.[38]

Some of the most effective teachers educational psychologist Jerome Bruner remembers are those who encouraged him to get beyond the facts—to question, hypothesize, think critically. Bruner recalls how Miss Orcutt, one of his elementary school teachers, made her students marvel at the way water freezes and

> extend[ed] my world of wonder to encompass hers. She was not just informing me! She was, rather, negotiating the world of wonder and possibility. Molecules, solids, liquids, movement were not facts; they were to be used in pondering and imagining. Miss Orcutt was the rarity. She was a human event, not a transmission device.[39]

Unfortunately, behavior evaluation may be putting teachers like Miss Orcutt on the endangered species list.

## PORTFOLIOS AND ASSESSMENT CENTERS: MULTIFACETED TEACHER EVALUATION

Multifaceted teacher evaluation draws on "multiple sources of evidence" to produce a composite portrait of a complex act—teaching. *Portfolios* allow teachers to document their actual work. *Assessment centers* put teachers through simulation exercises under the direction of experienced colleagues. Convinced that "cutting [teaching] into little pieces destroys its integrity," advocates of multifaceted teacher evaluation are trying to take a more holistic approach.[40]

Lee Shulman, who directs the Teacher Assessment Project (TAP) at Stanford University, admits that all teacher evaluation strategies are flawed. Having made that confession, Shulman is nevertheless trying to form a "union of insufficiencies"—a multifaceted evaluation plan capable of rising above the weaknesses of its individual components. Pencil-and-paper testing can provide valuable information about teachers, Shulman argues, and so can direct observation. Unfortunately, these methods of assessment offer, at best, narrow views of what teachers do. For evaluators who seek a more comprehensive picture, Shulman and his colleagues are developing the strategies of portfolios and assessment centers.[41]

Portfolios can capture "the contexts and personal histories of real teaching" better than any other evaluation strategy, TAP researchers contend. Portfolios contain both the "artifacts" of teaching—student papers, lesson plans, teacher-made tests, notes from parents, and the like—and teachers' written reflections on their work. In addition, technology makes it possible to record teaching on videotape. Videocassettes of teachers at work can help bring the other contents of portfolios to life. Just as photographers and other artists compile their best work for others to evaluate, teachers can put their best foot forward with portfolios.[42]

Regional assessment centers located in universities and school districts allow teachers to show what they can do under simulated classroom conditions. Teachers can deliver lectures, plan lessons, or explain to veteran teachers in their own field how they would use instructional aids to enhance a particular unit.

Technology opens many new possibilities, including computer-based simulations and videotaped teaching exercises.[43]

Can portfolios and assessment centers avoid the pitfalls of other evaluation techniques? Shulman and his colleagues are optimistic—perhaps overly so, given the subjectivity built into the strategies he is pioneering. Yet field tests indicate panels of trained examiners are not finding it difficult to reach a consensus when they evaluate portfolios and assessment center exercises. "Professional judgment" is the heart of the matter, TAP researchers insist, and teachers themselves must take charge of teacher evaluation.[44]

Portfolios and assessment centers are part of the national certification program the National Board for Professional Teaching Standards (NBPTS) is now putting into operation—a program that could be the first step toward a national career ladder. As we will see later in this chapter as well as in chapters 3 and 4, the NBPTS wants to create a teaching profession with clearly defined levels of competence and expertise and with different pay scales for each level. Here is merit pay, albeit in a new, more sophisticated form.

Many teachers, quite properly skeptical, are reserving judgment. Will a panel of peers evaluating a teacher through a portfolio or in an assessment center represent an improvement over a principal evaluating a teacher in the classroom? Will a union of insufficiencies—a marriage of several flawed evaluation strategies—somehow produce an acceptable plan?

We are looking closely at teacher evaluation as the basis of merit pay because evaluation is so often overlooked. Some of the merit pay plans we will examine in the next section are admittedly attractive, offering the hope of pulling teaching as an occupation out of a financial rut. Remember, though, that the plans are no better than the evaluation systems on which they rest.

## MERIT PAY, LATEST VERSIONS

### Two Recent Experiments

The pattern is clear. Merit pay plans come and go. Experiments that seem promising end in disappointment and failure. But advocates of merit pay keep trying. At best, we can liken these advocates to the Wright brothers, who finally built an airplane that could fly after other people had tried and failed for years. At worst, we can compare the advocates to alchemists who insisted that, under exactly the right conditions, lead really could turn into gold.

An especially promising experiment is under way in Granville County, North Carolina. In 1986, the district developed a merit pay plan that requires teachers to set four individual goals at the beginning of each school year. At least one goal must involve improving student performance on standardized tests. This plan is popular with the district's teachers, since about 90 percent are able to reach all four of their goals and receive the maximum 4 percent merit increase. Each school has lead teachers (a job classification we will discuss in the last section of this chapter) who earn an additional $1,200 for the extra duties they assume. Granville County's superintendent is proud of his district's rising test scores, which he cites as evidence that merit pay is improving teaching and learning.[45]

If this plan lasts, we may need to confer an Orville and Wilbur Wright award. Don't be so hasty, critics say. Let this airplane log some flying time, and it, too, will crash. Critics like to point to the failure of the most publicized merit pay experiment of the 1980s, Houston's Second Mile Plan.

Initiated in 1979, the Second Mile Plan received a great deal of media attention as a modern pioneer of merit pay, for it predated *A Nation at Risk* (1983). Houston's teachers could qualify for "bonus stipends" in several different ways, which ranged from teaching in a field with a staff shortage (secondary math or science, for example) to teaching in a school with better-than-predicted standardized test scores. On the positive side, more than two-thirds of Houston's teachers took home annual bonuses of as much as several thousand dollars. On the negative side, teachers said the plan sent the divisive message that the work of some teachers is more valuable than the work of others. Teacher organizations have argued for years that a high school physics teacher is worth no more and no less than a kindergarten teacher. Teachers also complained about pressure to teach the tests. Faced with teacher opposition, increasing costs, and a downturn in the Texas oil economy, the school board called off the eight-year experiment in 1987.[46]

## Merit Pay Plans that Last

By its very nature, merit pay violates the principle that only seniority and education should determine teacher salaries. Teachers organizations fought hard to establish that principle during the first half of this century. To make teachers more willing to compromise the principle as the century ends, researchers have several suggestions:

1. Define merit pay as "extra pay for extra work" rather than as a reward for outstanding performance.
2. See to it that "everyone wins" by awarding merit pay to almost every teacher.
3. "Make merit pay inconspicuous" by making participation voluntary.
4. Involve teachers in designing the plan.

A fifth suggestion might be: Start with a school district where "nearly everything seems to work well"—a system with strong community support, hard-working students, and happy well-paid teachers. All the experiments that have lasted more than a few years have been in such districts. These suggestions support the NEA and AFT's contention that merit pay would make better sense if teachers had decent salaries and working conditions to begin with.[47]

## State and Local Career Ladders

Whether the nation will heed this advice remains to be seen, but since the mid-1980s reformers have been building career ladders to help *restructure* teaching as an occupation. Teachers have long complained that teaching is not a *scaled* or *staged* occupation, that responsibilities and earnings increase relatively little over the course of their careers. Workers in many other occupations feel a satisfying sense of progress as they move through the ranks. Salaries rise and titles change as people get better at their work and take on new duties.

Teachers, though, face the same old routine year after year. Some teachers who want more responsibility and more money become administrators, but not every teacher is suited for administration. Besides, this limited path of career mobility leads many of the best and most ambitious teachers out of the classroom and into the front office, depriving students of contact with excellent instructors. Shouldn't it be possible for talented teachers to stay in the classroom and increase their responsibilities and earnings as their careers progress?

Answering this question affirmatively, state and local reformers have turned their attention to career ladders. Tennessee led the way in the mid-1980s, followed quickly by several other southeastern states. The movement spread to the Midwest and West, and by the late 1980s more than one-third of the states in the nation had career ladders in place or under construction. Eleven statewide ladders eventually went up, but then four states—all in the Southeast—pulled them down, complaining about high costs.[48]

The trend of the 1990s is toward local career ladders. In more than 20 states, hundreds of individual districts are building ladders modeled on the Carnegie Forum's national ladder. In chapter 4 we will examine the local career ladder in Rochester, home of the nation's most closely watched experiment in restructuring.[49]

Most career ladders consist of four or five rungs. Typically, teachers enter the occupation on an *apprentice* rung, where they are evaluated frequently and receive special guidance during their first year. Many career ladders are designed to bring new teachers into closer contact with experienced teachers. Veterans can serve as mentors to novices. Without such planned assistance, new teachers usually have to sink or swim on their own. They complain that teacher education programs do not prepare them well for their first year. They want on-the-job training. Apprenticeships may give teachers a way to pass the lore of their occupation from one generation of practitioners to the next.

After spending three to five years at the apprentice level, teachers who qualify for tenure step up to the *staff* rung of the ladder. Having passed a series of evaluations as apprentices, staff teachers are fully certified with the job security tenure provides. As chapter 5 explains, tenured teachers are entitled to continuing employment as long as their evaluations remain satisfactory. On most career ladders, teachers can remain at the staff level indefinitely if they wish. Moving up is voluntary. Staff teachers, like other teachers, draw their wages on a traditional salary schedule, but those who choose to climb the career ladder can qualify for incentive (that is, merit) raises.

The higher rungs may have such titles as (in ascending order) *career level I, career level II,* and *career level III,* with the latter sometimes also designated *lead teacher.* Teachers must serve a certain period of time at each level—typically five years—before they are eligible to apply for the next, and they must receive favorable evaluations in order to qualify.

Teachers who reach the top two rungs may sign 10- to 12-month contracts and take on such new responsibilities as working with apprentices, evaluating other teachers, and developing curricula. In some cases, they may teach the equivalent of four periods per day and spend the remaining time on their additional duties.

The quasi-administrative nature of these tasks leads critics to charge that career ladders are actually "job ladders" luring people out of teaching and into administration. The architects of career ladders reply that top-rung teachers are just that—teachers—for most of the day. A major goal of the ladders is to keep outstanding teachers in the classroom while allowing them to use their talents and experience in other ways.[50]

Advocates also call attention to what may be the most attractive feature of career ladders: the extra pay that comes with the extra work. Annual pay incentives can range from a few hundred dollars at career level I to several thousand dollars at career level III.[51]

How well are career ladders working? The most extensive evidence comes from Tennessee. According to former Governor Lamar Alexander, who helped design the nation's first statewide ladder as part of the education reforms he promoted, the Tennessee ladder is a tremendous success. When Alexander served as Secretary of Education in the Bush administration, he touted the ladder as an example of merit pay at its best.

Many Tennessee teachers disagree and claim the career ladder has been shaky from the start. The Tennessee Education Association (TEA), the state affiliate of the NEA, complains that Alexander and the state legislature built the ladder hastily, with only token involvement from classroom teachers. The evaluation system, based on behavioral evaluation and such other factors as a student questionnaire, a principal questionnaire, and a written test, got off to a particularly bad start with teachers. Eighty-five percent of teachers said the evaluation system could not work fairly and effectively, particularly in distinguishing excellent teachers from good teachers. Many teachers felt frustrated that the top two rungs of the ladder proved difficult to reach.[52]

Tennessee school officials tried to improve the evaluation system, and they defend the system's selectivity. To be sure, selectivity is something teachers are not used to—it has been sorely lacking in the occupation. Tennessee's average teacher salary of $28,248 ranks the state 37th in the nation, and some teachers say just the opportunity to compete for an income of $40,000 or more is a major step forward. Many teachers also welcome the chance to help one another. This attitude is most encouraging, for, as we will see in chapter 4, teachers themselves must take more responsibility if their occupation is ever to become a profession.[53]

But troubling questions remain. So far, statewide career ladders have appeared primarily in states whose teacher salaries rank below the national average. Will the ladders raise salaries substantially and make teaching a more attractive occupation? Or will the ladders give decent salaries to a few teachers without significantly raising average salaries—an updated version of sound and cheap?

The answers are mixed. On the one hand, the career ladder has not improved Tennessee's ranking among other states on teacher salaries—Tennessee remains stuck between 35th and 40th place. On the other hand, a few of the local career ladders in other states have raised salaries to truly impressive levels. The Rochester career ladder, for instance, quickly boosted average salaries above $45,000 and top salaries to $69,000.

The effects of career ladders on teacher morale and collegiality are also open to question. Some teachers frankly do not want to make their schools more like factories, corporations, or even law firms. They chose teaching as an occupation precisely because teachers are equals among equals, not climbers on their way past stallers. They like the fact that teachers do *not* joust with one another for slots on a bureaucratic hierarchy. How will these teachers react to a new game with new rules? With salaries and promotions at stake, will career ladders strengthen or weaken the spirit of cooperation?[54]

## A NATIONAL CAREER LADDER

Even though state and local ladders are getting mixed reviews, reformers are hard at work laying the groundwork for what could well become the ultimate career ladder: a national ladder designed for a national teaching profession. Two reports issued in 1986 drew up the blueprints: *A Nation Prepared: Teachers for the 21st Century* by the Carnegie Forum on Education and the Economy and *Tomorrow's Teachers: A Report of the Holmes Group* by a consortium of education deans and chief academic administrators from major research universities.[55]

Although the proposals in the reports differ in some respects, both advance the idea that teaching should be a *differentiated* occupation whose members have clearly defined levels of expertise, responsibility, and compensation. These reports call for fundamental reforms. If teaching heeds the call, the days of "equals among equals" are numbered. The occupation will frankly recognize that some teachers know more, can do more, and therefore should earn more than others.

We will examine the Carnegie and Holmes reports in several chapters of this book, but our major concern in this chapter is with the occupational ladder they envision. We will focus attention on the Carnegie ladder, which is already taking shape.

Carnegie's *A Nation Prepared* describes a four-level teaching force. The *licensed teachers* on the lowest rung have state licenses and are preparing for national certification. *Certified teachers,* the majority of the force, have passed evaluations developed by the National Board for Professional Teaching Standards (NBPTS), which the Carnegie Corporation helped establish in 1987. *Advanced teachers* have passed even more rigorous evaluations. *Lead teachers,* elected by teachers from among the advanced teachers, serve as the "instructional leaders" of their schools. Expertise, responsibility, and compensation increase as teachers move up the ladder. The lead teachers on the top rung, for instance, may serve as mentors for beginning teachers and intervenor/helpers for experienced teachers in trouble.[56]

If such fundamental reform of teaching sounds remote to you, consider how far the process has already gone. In districts where teachers, administrators, and school board members are restructuring teaching through collective bargaining, local versions of the Carnegie career ladder are already in place. AFT locals in big-city school systems are leading the way, in Rochester as well as in Dade County, Toledo, Cincinnati, and other districts. Urged on by President Shanker, the AFT has decided to roll the dice and gamble on a national career ladder—a radical break with the history of teaching.

The break may be too radical for the NEA, which sees merit pay written all over the Carnegie proposals. When the Carnegie Forum asked for an endorsement, the NEA offered support but "with reservations"—in contrast to the AFT's "full support." As former NEA president Mary Futrell explained, the idea of putting some teachers in charge of others "suggests that some teachers are more equal than others." To Futrell and her successor, Keith Geiger, creating a hierarchy of teachers looks suspiciously like "flawed and failed merit-pay and job-ladder plans." The NEA is proceeding cautiously with career ladders as well as other aspects of restructuring.[57]

Nevertheless, a national career ladder seems to be moving into place. The most powerful force behind the ladder is the NBPTS, which has the formidable financial and political support of the Carnegie Corporation. The NBPTS, a majority of whose members are classroom teachers, was chartered in 1987 to "establish high and rigorous standards for what teachers should know and be able to do, to certify teachers who meet those standards, and to advance related education reforms for the purpose of improving student learning in America."[58]

The board will soon begin issuing national teaching certificates that could help teachers move up the rungs of a national career ladder. Certification will be voluntary, much like national board certification for physicians, but the Carnegie Forum believes national teaching certificates will become so prestigious that teachers will seek them and states will recognize them. The complete national certification program will be in place by 1997–1998, and Carnegie and Holmes hope a national career ladder will not be far behind.

What might teachers earn on such a ladder? If we adjust the salaries recommended in the Carnegie Forum's *A Nation Prepared* (1986) for cost-of-living increases since the report was published, we can estimate the following ranges, which reflect local and state variations: licensed teachers, $18,500 to $31,000; certified teachers, $23,500 to $48,000; advanced teachers, $32,000 to $57,000; and lead teachers, $52,000 to $89,000. Compare these figures to the current salaries in Tables 2.1 and 2.3 and the salary schedules in Tables 2.5, 2.6, and 2.7. Prospective teachers will probably not stand up and cheer about their immediate prospects under the Carnegie proposal, but for those who make teaching a career, the long-term rewards are potentially much greater.[59]

Now here's the tough question: What methods of evaluation will accompany a national career ladder? The NBPTS is field testing portfolios, assessment center exercises, and paper-and-pencil tests.[60] In addition, the Carnegie Forum and Holmes Group endorse teacher accountability. The Carnegie report recommends basing teacher salaries in part on student test scores, even though it admits "no method that we know of for measuring student performance and connecting it to teachers' rewards is yet satisfactory."[61]

Will these new versions of merit pay prove to be the airplane that finally lifts off the ground, or will they be yet another failed attempt to turn lead into gold? Teachers are hedging their bets in the uncertain educational and economic climate of the 1990s.

## ACTIVITIES

1. Request salary schedules from the school systems in which you are most interested in teaching. Compare their schedules with the three representative schedules in this chapter. Inquire about state and local career ladders and other forms of merit pay.
2. Talk with a variety of currently employed teachers about merit pay, accountability, evaluation, and other issues discussed in this chapter. Interview retired teachers and compare their opinions.
3. Broaden your interviews to include political officials, particularly local and state school board members, state legislators, and others who have influence on teacher salaries.

## RECOMMENDED READINGS

American Federation of Teachers. *Survey and Analysis of Salary Trends* (Washington, D.C.: AFT, updated annually).
This report, along with the NEA's *Rankings of the States* (see note 20), is an excellent fact book on the economic status of America's teachers.

Murnane, Richard J., Judith D. Singer, John B. Willett, James J. Kemple, and Randall J. Olsen. *Who Will Teach? Policies that Matter* (Cambridge: Harvard University Press, 1991).
Arguing that higher salaries will attract and hold better teachers, the authors take a critical look at merit pay and teacher evaluation.

National Board for Professional Teaching Standards. *Toward High and Rigorous Standards for the Teaching Profession: A Summary,* 2d ed. (Detroit: NBPTS, 1991).
Along with the annual reports of the NBPTS (see note 60), this publication describes the board's ongoing efforts to restructure teaching as an occupation.

Shulman, Lee. "A Union of Insufficiencies: Strategies for Teacher Assessment in a Period of Educational Reform," *Educational Leadership* 46 (November 1988): 36–41.
Here is an important article by the nation's leading researcher/advocate of teacher portfolios and assessment centers.

## NOTES

1. Both quotes are from John Godar, *Teachers Talk* (Macomb, IL: Glenridge Publishing, 1990), pp. 74, 177.
2. American Federation of Teachers, *Survey and Analysis of Salary Trends, 1992* (Washington, D.C.: AFT, 1992), pp. 23, vi.
3. For state-by-state information on variations in the cost of living, see American Federation of Teachers, *Survey and Analysis of Salary Trends,* pp. 8, 16.
4. National Education Association, *Status of the American Public School Teacher, 1990–1991* (Washington, D.C.: NEA, 1992), pp. 74–75; U.S. Department of Commerce, Bureau of the Census, *Statistical Abstract of the United States, 1992* (Washington, D.C.: U.S. Government Printing Office, 1992), p. 447. The average American household income reported is for 1990.

5. National Education Association, *Status of the American Public School Teacher,* pp. 73–74.
6. Ibid., pp. 75–76.
7. American Federation of Teachers, *Survey and Analysis of Salary Trends,* pp. 23–25.
8. U.S. Department of Labor, Bureau of Labor Statistics, *Occupational Outlook Handbook, 1992–1993 Edition* (Washington, D.C.: U.S. Department of Labor, 1992), p. 121.
9. Ibid., p. 161; "The Pay Picture," *NEA Today* (April 1992), p. 13.
10. Judy Mann and Basia Hellwig, "The Truth about the Salary Gap(s)," *Working Woman* (January 1988): 61–62; U.S. Department of Labor, *Occupational Outlook Handbook,* pp. 17, 33.
11. Mann and Hellwig, "The Truth about the Salary Gap(s)," pp. 61–62; U.S. Department of Labor, *Occupational Outlook Handbook,* p. 66.
12. U.S. Department of Labor, *Occupational Outlook Handbook,* p. 83.
13. Ibid., p. 95.
14. Mann and Hellwig, "The Truth about the Salary Gap(s)," pp. 61–62.
15. U.S. Department of Labor, *Occupational Outlook Handbook,* p. 104; American Federation of Teachers, *Survey and Analysis of Salary Trends,* p. 35.
16. U.S. Department of Labor, *Occupational Outlook Handbook,* p. 147.
17. Don Cameron, "An Idea that Merits Consideration," *Phi Delta Kappan* 67 (October 1985): 110–112.
18. Blake Rodman, "Teachers Spurn an Unsolicited Starting-Pay Proposal," *Education Week* (February 19, 1986), p. 14. See also Randall W. Eberts and Joe A. Stone, *Unions and Public Schools: The Effect of Collective Bargaining on American Education* (Lexington, MA: Heath, 1984); and Anthony M. Creswell and Michael J. Murphy with Charles T. Kerchner, *Teachers, Unions, and Collective Bargaining in Public Education* (Berkeley, CA: McCutchan, 1980), chap. 11.
19. Roger Fisher and William Ury, *Getting to Yes: Negotiating Agreement without Giving In* (Boston: Houghton Mifflin, 1981).
20. National Education Association, *Rankings of the States, 1992* (Washington, D.C.: NEA, 1992), p. 19.
21. Ibid., pp. 19, 21, 59.
22. Albert Shanker, "The Making of a Profession," *American Educator* 9 (Fall 1985): 10–17, 46, 48.
23. Alec Gallup, "The Gallup Poll of Teachers' Attitudes toward the Public Schools," *Phi Delta Kappan* 66 (October 1984): 103.
24. Stanley M. Elam, Lowell C. Rose, and Alec M. Gallup, "The 23rd Annual Gallup Poll of the Public's Attitudes toward the Public Schools," *Phi Delta Kappan* 73 (September 1991): 50–51.
25. For analysis of merit pay in historical context, see Richard J. Murnane and David K. Cohen, "Merit Pay and the Evaluation Problem: Understanding Why Most Merit Pay Plans Fail and A Few Survive," *Harvard Educational Review* 56 (February 1986): 1–17; Susan M. Johnson, "Merit Pay for Teachers: A Poor Prescription for Reform," *Harvard Educational Review* 54 (May 1984): 175–185; and Raymond E. Callahan, *Education and the Cult of Efficiency: A Study of the Social Forces that Have Shaped the Administration of the Public Schools* (Chicago: University of Chicago Press, 1962), chap. 5.
26. The discussion in this section is based in part on case studies of the Atlanta Public Schools. See Joseph W. Newman, "A History of the Atlanta Public School Teachers'

Association, Local 89 of the American Federation of Teachers, 1919–1956'' (Ph.D. diss., Georgia State University, 1978), chap. 1; and Wayne J. Urban, "Progressive Education in the Urban South: The Reform of the Atlanta Schools, 1914–1918," in Michael H. Ebner and Eugene M. Tobin, eds., *The Age of Urban Reform: New Perspectives on the Progressive Era* (Port Washington, NY: Kennikat Press, 1977), chap. 9.

27. Arthur C. Boyce, "Methods of Measuring Teachers' Efficiency," *Fourteenth Yearbook of the National Society for the Study of Education, Part II* (Bloomington, IL: Public School Publishing, 1915); Lloyd Young, *The Administration of Merit-Type Teachers' Salary Schedules* (New York: Teachers College, Columbia University, 1933).

28. Arvil Sylvester Barr, "Measurement and Prediction of Teaching Efficiency: Summary of Investigations," *Journal of Experimental Education* 16 (June 1948): 203–283.

29. A highly influential book by the father of the movement is Leon M. Lessinger's *Every Kid a Winner: Accountability in Education* (New York: Simon and Schuster, 1970). For an opposing point of view, read Don T. Martin, George E. Overholt, and Wayne J. Urban, *Accountability in American Education: A Critique* (Princeton, NJ: Princeton Book Company, 1976).

30. Joel Spring, *Conflict of Interests: The Politics of American Education,* 2d ed. (White Plains, NY: Longman, 1993), pp. 20–21, 178.

31. The discussion in this section is based on Donald M. Medley, Homer Coker, and Robert S. Soar, *Measurement-Based Evaluation of Teacher Performance: An Empirical Approach* (White Plains, NY: Longman, 1984), chap. 3.

32. See, for example, Blake Rodman, "Rating Teachers on Students' Test Scores Sparks Furor, Legal Action in St. Louis," *Education Week* (September 17, 1986), pp. 1, 18.

33. The behavioral evaluation model developed by Donald Medley, Homer Coker, and Robert Soar is widely used, as is the Madeline Hunter/Clinical Supervision model. See Noreen B. Garman and Helen M. Hazi, "Teachers Ask: Is There Life after Madeline Hunter?" *Phi Delta Kappan* 69 (May 1988): 669–672.

34. Joseph O. Milner, "Suppositional Style and Teacher Evaluation," *Phi Delta Kappan* 72 (February 1991): 466.

35. Medley, Coker, and Soar, *Measurement-Based Evaluation,* pp. 41–45; B. Othanel Smith, Donovan Peterson, and Theodore Micceri, "Evaluation and Professional Improvement Aspects of the Florida Performance Measurement System," *Educational Leadership* 44 (April 1987): 16–19.

36. Milner, "Suppositional Style," p. 466.

37. Garman and Hazi, "Teachers Ask," pp. 670–672.

38. Milner, "Suppositional Style," pp. 464–467. Milner's research provoked a debate on North Carolina's TPAI in *Phi Delta Kappan* 72 (June 1991).

39. Jerome Bruner, *Actual Minds, Possible Worlds* (Cambridge: Harvard University Press, 1986), p. 126.

40. Kenneth Wolf, "The Schoolteacher's Portfolio: Issues in Design, Implementation, and Evaluation," *Phi Delta Kappan* 73 (October 1991): 130–131.

41. Lee Shulman, "A Union of Insufficiencies: Strategies for Teacher Assessment in a Period of Educational Reform," *Educational Leadership* 46 (November 1988): 36–41.

42. Wolf, "The Schoolteacher's Portfolio," pp. 132–134.

43. Bruce King, *Thinking about Linking Portfolios with Assessment Center Exercises: Examples from the Teacher Assessment Project* (Stanford, CA: TAP, Stanford University, 1990).

44. Wolf, "The Schoolteacher's Portfolio," pp. 135–136.

45. Daniel Gursky, "Against All Odds," *Education Week* (February 19, 1992), pp. 1, 16–17.
46. *The Second Mile Plan* (Houston: Houston Independent School District, n.d.); Elaine Say and Leslie Miller, "The Second Mile Plan: Incentive Pay for Houston Teachers," *Phi Delta Kappan* 64 (December 1982): 270–271.
47. Richard J. Murnane, Judith D. Singer, John B. Willett, James J. Kemple, and Randall J. Olsen, *Who Will Teach? Policies that Matter* (Cambridge: Harvard University Press, 1991), pp. 118–119; Murnane and Cohen, "Merit Pay and the Evaluation Problem," pp. 12–15.
48. Southern Regional Education Board, *The 1991 Survey of Incentive Programs and Career Ladders* (Atlanta: SREB, 1991).
49. Ibid.
50. Samul B. Bacharach, "Career Development, Not Career Ladders," *Education Week* (March 12, 1986), p. 28; Russell L. French, " 'Misconceptions' in Critique of Career Ladders," *Education Week* (May 14, 1986), p. 42.
51. Richard J. Coley and Margaret E. Goertz, *Educational Standards in the 50 States: 1990* (Princeton, NJ: Educational Testing Service, 1990), pp. 148–149.
52. Lynn Olson, "Pioneering State Teacher-Incentive Plans in Florida, Tennessee Still Under Attack," *Education Week* (January 15, 1986), pp. 1, 24–25; Olson, "Performance-Based Pay Systems Are Being Reexamined," *Education Week* (April 15, 1987), pp. 1, 16–17.
53. Carol B. Furtwengler, "Lessons from Tennessee's Career Ladder Program," *Educational Leadership* 44 (April 1987): 66–69.
54. Lynn Olson, "Performance Pay: New Round for an Old Debate," *Education Week* (March 12, 1986), pp. 1, 18–20; Susan J. Rosenholtz, "Education Reform Strategies: Will They Increase Teacher Commitment?" *American Journal of Education* 95 (August 1987): 534–562.
55. Carnegie Forum on Education and the Economy, *A Nation Prepared: Teachers for the 21st Century. A Report of the Task Force on Teaching as a Profession* (New York: Carnegie Forum, 1986); Holmes Group, *Tomorrow's Teachers: A Report of the Holmes Group* (East Lansing, MI: Holmes Group, 1986).
56. Carnegie Forum, *A Nation Prepared,* pp. 55–69, 87–95.
57. Ibid., p. 117.
58. National Board for Professional Teaching Standards, *Toward High and Rigorous Standards for the Teaching Profession: A Summary,* 2d ed. (Detroit: NBPTS, 1991), p. 3.
59. Carnegie Forum, *A Nation Prepared,* pp. 95–103.
60. National Board for Professional Teaching Standards, *1991 Annual Report* (Detroit: NBPTS, 1992), p. 10.
61. Carnegie Forum, *A Nation Prepared,* p. 92.

# CHAPTER 3

# Learning to Teach and Proving Your Competence

*Education courses require you to analyze and apply what you've learned. . . . I've been teaching the kids this semester. . . . I think I'll be O.K. I think I'll be good. . . . I think I've received a very good education.*
—Prospective Maryland teacher[1]

*Education is the only professional field where after people graduate they say they could have been better off without the training.*
—Former New York teacher[2]

The education of America's teachers has always been controversial, as a brief look at its history readily shows. In the early years of the nation, before teachers undertook special training, some citizens argued that teachers obviously needed help. Teachers lacked both knowledge and skill, a Massachusetts school reformer complained in 1826: They "know nothing, absolutely nothing, of the complicated and difficult duties assigned to them." "Literary and scientific" training, he later suggested, could help people learn what and how to teach.[3]

Not so, other citizens countered. Any intelligent person who had gone to school had already learned "the art of instructing others," and "if intelligence be wanting, no system of instruction can supply its place." Bright people can teach naturally, according to this argument, and dull people who try to teach are just asking for trouble—and dismissal.[4]

We still hear arguments on both sides of this debate. In fact, the opposing positions weave in and out of this chapter as themes. The advocates of formal teacher education have generally had the upper hand in the debate, but the issue of how teachers should prepare is lively once again.

The first public teacher training institution, a quasi-secondary school called a *normal school,* opened in 1839 in Lexington, Massachusetts, and very gradually the idea of teacher education caught on. In chapter 6, we will see that teacher education was one of the goals of the common school reformers who succeeded in building statewide public school systems throughout the nation. Yet in 1900, the typical elementary teacher was a woman who felt lucky if she had finished high school, much less received any formal training for her work. The typical secondary teacher was a man who had some college credit, a smattering of which may have been in *pedagogy,* the art and science of teaching, which was just developing as a university subject.[5]

What combination of knowledge and skill should form the content of teacher education? In what kind of institution should it take place? Does teacher education have anything to offer bright people? Can it turn average people into competent teachers? The search for answers to such questions continued into the twentieth century as universities assumed more responsibility, expanding their programs for high school teachers and developing programs for elementary teachers. Normal schools made a bid for status by transforming themselves first into teachers colleges, then into colleges, and finally into full-fledged universities. State boards of education began requiring teachers to obtain state certificates corresponding to higher levels of education.

But university degrees and state credentials have not put to rest the arguments over teacher education. On the contrary, the arguments have intensified during the late 1980s and 1990s.

Many students who enroll in a college or department of education expecting, reasonably enough, to learn how to teach do not realize they have stepped into the middle of a controversy. They soon find out, though, when they read a *Time* or *Newsweek* cover story that is critical of teachers and scornful of teacher educators or when they talk with business, engineering, or arts and sciences majors who ask, "What? You're taking education courses? Why would an intelligent person who has other options go into teaching?" As a prospective teacher, you undoubtedly have your own answers to such questions, but this chapter will give you a better understanding of *why* teacher education programs and their graduates generate so much controversy.

Just as chapters 1 and 2 offer hope as well as criticism, this chapter suggests the arguments over teacher education and competency may have a positive outcome. As I have said before, there are signs the occupation may be changing for the better.

Whether for better or for worse, the reforms of the 1980s and 1990s have opened a variety of new routes into teaching. The traditional route—through undergraduate teacher education programs—is now only one of several paths. In this chapter, we will look first at undergraduate programs, which still prepare the majority of new teachers. Then we will examine nontraditional routes, ranging from "professional" graduate programs advocated by the Carnegie Forum on Education and the Economy and the Holmes Group to shortcuts that drastically reduce specialized training. Depending on whose opinion we accept, opening these multiple routes may prove to be either the best or the worst reform ever in teacher education.

The trend toward higher standards in teacher education programs also deserves our attention. Raising standards, the watchword in teacher education during the 1980s and 1990s, generally means requiring teachers to take more standardized tests. A response to the public's latest discovery of the teacher competency issue, admission and certification tests have become controversial. Will more testing produce better teachers? Or are the tests keeping capable and deserving people, minorities in particular, out of the occupation?

We will conclude the chapter with a positive vision of teacher education as it might be. We will also see the negative consequences of allowing teacher education to remain as it is.

## MULTIPLE ROUTES INTO TEACHING

Preparation programs for new teachers are the focus of our attention in this chapter. You may recall from chapter 1 that school districts fill about 25 percent of their job openings with first-time teachers. How do these new recruits prepare for their work?

Seventy percent of new teachers, still the vast majority, follow the *traditional undergraduate route.* Most of these teachers major in education; others major in another field, usually an arts and sciences discipline, and take the education courses required for state certification.[6]

A growing number of new teachers, though, are following *nontraditional routes.* Twenty percent enter after completing a *master's-level program.* Depending on the particular program, the graduate path provides preparation that can range from a compressed version of an undergraduate program to a full-blown clinical program based on the Carnegie-Holmes model. The remaining 10 percent of new teachers come into the occupation via an *alternate program.* This path, too, can be quite varied, leading in some cases directly into the classroom—a sink-or-swim experience—and in other cases into a brief, but intensive training period followed by teaching under the supervision of a mentor.[7]

Now we will map these multiple routes. First, we turn to the path millions of teachers have followed, a route whose course has changed surprisingly little over the years.

## The Traditional Route: Undergraduate Teacher Education

Despite all the talk about education reform, there remains a remarkable sameness to undergraduate teacher education in the United States. Visiting campuses and talking with professors of education around the country, I notice variations in such things as course titles, sequences, and credit hours; I see different professors using different approaches; and I hear administrators boasting that their teacher education programs put more emphasis than their rivals' on, say, clinical and field experiences. But beneath these differences lies a framework that varies little from program to program and campus to campus.

At virtually all the 1,300 colleges and universities offering undergraduate programs for teachers, the curriculum falls into three broad areas:

1. *Liberal education* in the arts and sciences.
2. The *teaching field* (or fields) for which teachers will be responsible in the classroom—the "what" of teaching.
3. *Professional education* in methods and foundations—the "how" and "why" of teaching.

Although the names and specific content of these areas have changed over the years, teacher education programs have consisted of the same three areas since the days of normal schools.

For a century and a half, Americans have argued over how much emphasis each area should receive, with the debate usually centered on the trade-off between the third and the first two areas. In 1847, the principal of the State Normal School of Albany, New York, one of the nation's first teacher training institutions, spoke of the trade-off in terms that have changed little: "To be a teacher, one must first of all be a scholar. So much stress is now placed on method, and on the theory of teaching, that there is great danger of forgetting the supreme importance of scholarship and culture." Keep the concept of trade-off in mind as we survey each area in turn.[8]

***Liberal Education.***   This area consists of courses in the arts and sciences, the core of any college education. These courses are liberal in the sense that they are designed to liberate the mind from provincial thought, opening it to a variety of viewpoints. The arts and sciences transmit a common culture: knowledge educated people deem valuable, organized into such disciplines as history, English, foreign languages, mathematics, biology, and chemistry. These disciplines are more than bodies of knowledge; they represent different ways of knowing. Think for a moment about how differently historians and biologists organize and use knowledge or how differently philosophers and mathematicians solve problems.

Theodore Hesburgh, former president of the University of Notre Dame, suggests that liberal education enables people "to think clearly, logically, deeply, and widely"; to express themselves with the same facility; "to evaluate, to have a growing sense of moral purpose and priority"; and "to cope daily with the ambiguities of the human situation."[9] Although the case for liberal education is not primarily vocational, I could argue that of all citizens, teachers have the greatest need *in their work* for the skills that Hesburgh describes. As the Holmes Group states in *Tomorrow's Teachers* (1986), "Teachers must lead a life of the mind. They must be reflective and thoughtful: persons who seek to understand so they may clarify for others, persons who can go to the heart of the matter."[10]

But Hesburgh, the Holmes Group, and other professors and organizations in both education and the arts and sciences recognize that liberal education is imperfect. It, too, cries out for reform. Fragmentation, excessive specialization, poor teaching—prospective teachers encounter these problems far too often in liberal education courses. Professors of the arts and sciences are not always the academic exemplars some of them claim to be. A rivalry has raged for years between education and the arts and sciences. Many teacher educators, battle-weary and defensive, are reluctant to share any more of the teacher education program. Today, depending on the particular program and institution, liberal education usually accounts for one-third to one-half of the content of undergraduate teacher education. Is that enough? What is the trade-off with the other two areas?[11]

***The Teaching Field.***    This area involves preparation in the subject or subjects prospective teachers will convey to their students. One-fourth to one-third of the courses in teacher education programs are in the teaching field, and that range encompasses even more variation than the fractions suggest.

Consider first the case of prospective secondary teachers, some of whom (about 60 percent) major in secondary education while the rest (about 40 percent) major in the arts and sciences. All secondary teachers take their field courses in the arts and sciences, with English teachers studying in the English department, math teachers in the math department, and so forth. Secondary teachers who major in the arts and sciences take about one-third of their total programs in their teaching field. Those who major in secondary education, though, take about one-fourth of their total programs in their field, trading off three or four semester courses in the field in order to take three or four more courses in education.[12]

From an arts and sciences point of view, secondary education majors learn too little about the "what" of teaching, their academic subjects. The secondary education majors, of course, learn more about the "how" and "why" of teaching.

Aggravating this argument is the requirement in many states that secondary science and social studies teachers hold certification in at least two teaching fields. Designed to ease staffing problems by producing "switch-hitters," as one of my colleagues in secondary education recently explained, this requirement sacrifices mastery of a single subject for coverage of two or more subjects. The National Science Teachers Association and, to a lesser degree, the National Council for the Social Studies have expressed concern over the situation. Can a secondary science major learn enough from five or six semester courses in each subject to teach biology *and* chemistry? What about the secondary social studies major struggling to cover history, sociology, *and* economics in three or four courses each?[13]

The teaching fields for elementary, special, and physical education majors deserve separate consideration. These students receive about two-thirds of the bachelor's degrees in education, with elementary majors alone accounting for more than one-third. Where within the college or university should they take their teaching fields? We could argue that prospective elementry teachers, who must be responsible for many subjects, should take a sampler of courses in the arts and sciences. Special education teachers might go to the psychology department, while physical education teachers could concentrate on physiology in the biology department. In some programs, to be sure, these teachers do go to the arts and sciences for at least part of their teaching fields. Far more often, however, they take their teaching fields in the college of education, where they enroll in such courses as Sports Physiology, Behavior Modification of Emotionally Conflicted Children, and Math for Elementary Teachers.[14]

Many teacher educators argue that this practice is both logical and academically sound. They believe teaching field courses designed for teachers and focused on the classroom are more useful than courses designed for arts and sciences majors. The critics, when they are in a polite mood, argue that such courses take future teachers out of the academic mainstream, cutting them off from professors and students who are working in the disciplines. Less politely, the critics describe such courses as *Mickey Mouse.*

Name calling hurts, of course, and it diverts attention from the real questions: How valuable to a second-grade teacher is a math course in algebra or number theory? How many professors of biology know or care much about sports physiology? Do arts and sciences professors understand the academic world in which future elementary, special education, and physical education teachers will work?

*Professional Education.*   This is the most controversial area in teacher education programs. Here *Goofy* joins *Mickey Mouse* in the critics' stock of cartoon-character insults. In a more serious vein, *A Nation at Risk* (1983) set forth a common complaint: "The teacher-preparation curriculum is weighted heavily with courses in 'educational methods' at the expense of courses in subjects to be taught."[15]

Notice again the idea of a trade-off; also notice the use of "methods" as a generic description of virtually everything colleges and departments of education try to do. In fact, the professional education courses that make up one-fourth to one-third of teacher education programs are considerably more varied and complex.

Even the shorthand distinction I make above—"how" courses in methods versus "why" courses in foundations—does not do justice to the array of education courses found in college and university catalogs. Courses in methods of teaching are the most numerous, to be sure, and they are designed to be practical and helpful. In foundations courses, students use such disciplines as history, philosophy, sociology, and political science to study the relationship between school and society. The distinction between methods and foundations courses is clear enough, but other education courses deal with both hows and whys. Courses in evaluation and measurement, among the most technical in teacher education programs, can also raise questions of rationale and purpose, as can courses in educational psychology. Curriculum courses bring together knowledge of how, why, and what. Student teaching, the culmination of teacher education programs, *ideally* puts to the test a prospective teacher's entire repertoire of knowledge and skill.

*Ideally* is a word that symbolizes the problem with teacher education, according to critics. Teacher education programs abound in wishful thinking, they charge. Education professors, well meaning but out of touch with elementary and secondary schools, teach courses that run together in a blur. Students waltz in and glide through. Field experiences and student teaching offer a taste of the real world, but after graduation new teachers must literally teach themselves to teach in order to survive. Even though education professors rarely talk about discipline, out in the schools it becomes the first—and often the only—priority. Education courses that seemed fun at best and boring at worst turn out to be useless. Voicing feelings of frustration verging on bitterness, experienced teachers give their education courses low marks. Many teachers say the only worthwhile part of their professional education was student teaching.[16]

If the preceding paragraph seems harsh, I intend it to. Just as I tried to be honest about teacher satisfaction in chapter 1 and teacher salaries in chapter 2, I owe you an objective look at teacher education in this chapter. As the author of a teacher education textbook, though, I obviously believe professional education is valuable, and we professors of education do have our defenders.

Susan Ohanian, a veteran third-grade teacher whose writing about teaching has won her a reputation for pulling no punches, contends that

> teachers must stop asking education professors for the whole house. I know plenty of teachers who are disappointed, indignant, and eventually destroyed by the fact that nobody has handed them all four corners. But the best we can expect from any program of courses or training is the jagged edge of one corner. Then it is up to us to read the research and collaborate with the children to find the other three corners.[17]

There are no "stir-and-serve recipes for teaching," Ohanian insists. "We do not need the behaviorist-competency thugs to chart our course." Teachers deserve education courses that are intellectually challenging—and too many are "stupid," she acknowledges—but "much of the training must be self-initiated." Professors of education should open teachers' minds and give them a sense of purpose and direction. Ohanian concludes that the only way to learn how to teach is to teach.[18]

## Nontraditional Routes

Longtime observers of American education say they have seen it all before: The 1980s were a replay of the 1950s. In both decades, the public became convinced that public education had gone soft and insisted that the schools get back to basics. The finger of blame for the nation's educational problems pointed first at incompetent teachers and then at the teacher educators who had obviously mistrained them. Faced with a teacher shortage, Americans resolved to reform teacher education.

During the 1960s, though, the nation turned its attention to other matters, teacher educators won favor by pitching in to help solve the teacher shortage, and the critics went away for a while. The 1990s, according to veteran observers, will be like the 1960s. When the smoke clears, teacher education will be doing business as usual.

But the current wave of reforms *may* make more lasting changes in teacher education, if only because some of today's reformers are more politically astute than their predecessors. The new reformers are doing their homework in universities and legislatures, developing programs and pushing through bills that may change the way teachers prepare for their work. In fact, the new reformers have already been successful enough to make their earlier counterparts envious. Since 1983, at least 31 states have opened nontraditional routes into teaching, bringing the total number of such states to 39. About 30 percent of first-time teachers are now entering the occupation via nontraditional routes.[19]

Although the teacher education reform packages of the 1980s and 1990s vary in their details, three themes stand out:

1. Cut back professional education. Professional education has some value, the reformers seem to be saying, but not enough to take up one-fourth to one-third of an undergraduate program.
2. Strengthen the teaching field. America needs teachers who know their subjects.
3. Raise standards. This theme has a variety of meanings, but most often it is a call for brighter teachers with higher test scores. Remember the words of the nineteenth-century critic: "If intelligence be lacking, no system of instruction can supply its place."

As put into practice by today's reformers, the first two themes are crowding professional education out of undergraduate programs and reshaping it in a variety of new formats, which we will examine in this section of the chapter. The third theme reflects the controversy over teacher competency and teacher testing, which we will analyze in the next section.

***Carnegie and Holmes.***    In the mid-1980s, the Carnegie Forum on Education and the Economy and the Holmes Group captured center stage in the reform of teacher education. A well-matched pair of reports released in 1986—*A Nation Prepared* by the Carnegie Forum and *Tomorrow's Teachers* by the Holmes Group—presented their elaborate visions of a teaching profession whose members receive specialized training at the graduate level. Carnegie and Holmes called for the elimination of undergraduate degree programs in education. People with degrees in the arts and sciences and no formal teaching preparation would be able to enter the occupation, but all fully certified teachers would hold master's degrees in teaching. At the top of the new profession would be veteran teachers with doctorates in teaching, some of whom would hold adjunct appointments as university faculty members.[20]

Much, perhaps most, professional education would take place at "clinical sites." Here Holmes and Carnegie drew analogies to the teaching hospitals used to train medical doctors. Indeed, Carnegie spoke specifically of "interns" and "residents." Both reports envisioned clinical programs conducted jointly by teacher educators in the universities and experienced teachers in the schools. The goal is to improve instruction by helping tomorrow's teachers put into practice the best available knowledge about teaching, rather than mimic the survival strategies of today's teachers.[21]

These proposals for reform continue to generate controversy, but Carnegie and Holmes put things positively, preferring to say teacher education would be lengthened to five years rather than cut back to one year. Thus, they hope, teacher education can become an even more important part of the work universities do.

As we saw in the last chapter, the Carnegie Forum is a driving force behind the National Board for Professional Teaching Standards (NBPTS), the majority of whose members are classroom teachers. The board is hard at work developing tests and other assessment procedures to be used in awarding national teaching certificates. Because the Carnegie Corporation's prestige and powers of persuasion are formidable, the content of the tests may shape the content of teacher education programs—not necessarily a pleasant prospect, according to criticism we will examine later in this chapter.

As *A Nation Prepared* and *Tomorrow's Teachers* moved into the arena of state politics, the reports helped persuade about a dozen state legislatures to require future teachers to major in an arts and sciences discipline. During the late 1980s, one state after another seemed ready to join the trend. In the 1990s, though, the movement has slowed, and now it appears that most of the states with a serious interest in eliminating bachelor's degrees in education have already done so.[22]

The Holmes Group, a consortium of teacher education deans and chief academic officers at approximately 100 major research universities, continues to press its reform agenda within colleges of education. The strategy is to reform teacher education from the top down, by concentrating on the universities at the top of the academic pecking order.

Holmes proposes a number of costly and ambitious reforms designed to transform teaching into a full profession (see chapter 4), but the goal of eliminating bachelor's degree programs in education is controversial enough to stand out from the rest. About 30 universities invited to become charter members of the group declined, and several others have since withdrawn. Although some Holmes institutions have indeed shifted their professional education programs to the graduate level, leaving only an introductory course or two for undergraduates who plan to teach, other members are hedging their bets and maintaining parallel programs: a traditional four-year route as well as a nontraditional five-year route.[23]

Eliminating undergraduate education programs, which rank among the top "cash cows" on many campuses, is a move even large research universities will not make lightly. In smaller state universities and four-year public and private colleges, the change could touch off a riot. Why, it would threaten faculty jobs. It would deprive undergraduates of a popular major. It would . . .

Many teacher educators, even in Holmes Group institutions, are outspoken opponents of these reforms.[24] Professors of elementary, special, and physical education complain that they would be forced to abbreviate or simply eliminate much of the professional education curriculum. The Holmes Group recommends for elementary teachers a five-year preparation program including "area concentrations" in language and literature, mathematics, science, social science, and the arts. The undergraduate major would be in one of these areas; the other four, each "roughly equivalent in time commitment to a minor," would take up most of the remaining program.[25] Counting up the time left for instruction in methods, foundations, curriculum, evaluation, educational psychology, and other traditional areas, some professors believe the job simply cannot be done.

Without question, the Carnegie-Holmes reforms break with tradition. If they catch on, teacher education will have to change. Doing business as usual will not be possible, and, according to Carnegie and Holmes, that is precisely the objective. Yet teacher education is highly resistant to change. Fundamental reforms that not only upset its internal structure but also require external support—that is, public money and political commitment—may never have a chance.[26]

***Nontraditional Master's Degree Programs.*** Revamping existing master's degree programs offers an easier way to reform teacher education. In the political climate of the late 1980s and 1990s, with elected officials criticizing the way teachers are prepared, teacher educators have felt pressure to take preemptive action before politicians impose ideas of their own. Many colleges and departments of education are designing nontraditional master's programs for the large pool of people with bachelor's degrees outside education who want to change careers and give teaching a try.

Nontraditional master's programs drop the requirement that students must complete an undergraduate program in a particular teaching field—for example, elementary education or secondary mathematics—before beginning graduate study in that field. At one university, posters around campus advertise a nontraditional master's program designed to "prepare almost anyone with almost any college degree to teach in almost any field." That's quite a promise, even if the fine print does admit "certain restrictions."

By their very design, nontraditional master's programs are a compromise between what teacher educators think they should do and what political pressure compels them to do. But compared to the much shorter routes into teaching we will examine next, graduate programs requiring the equivalent of a full year of study (often stretched out over evenings and weekends to accommodate employed students) at least allow teacher educators to condense their courses, supervise field experiences and student teaching, and hope for the best. Fortunately, nontraditional master's programs seem to attract students who are experienced in the world of work and committed to helping young people. The dedication and maturity of these prospective teachers may be the programs' greatest assets.

In some respects, the nontraditional master's programs of the 1980s and 1990s are an updated version of the master of arts in teaching (MAT) programs developed to attract the arts and sciences graduates of the 1950s and 1960s. In both eras, a new path into teaching opened when teacher shortages threatened. Longtime observers are predicting that nontraditional master's programs, like the MATs before them, will fade fast when these shortages turn into surpluses. In this case, the veterans may be wrong. Already almost 20 percent of first-time teachers are entering the occupation via nontraditional master's programs, far more than the MATs ever attracted and far more than through the clinically based five-year Holmes Group programs.[27]

***The Texas Squeeze Play.*** While reformers throughout the nation are busy reconfiguring teacher education at the master's level, reformers in Texas and a few other states are simply squeezing it at the bachelor's level. In 1986, the Texas legislature not only abolished bachelor's degree programs in education but also prohibited prospective teachers from taking more than 18 semester hours of undergraduate professional education. This reform, fully effective since 1991, marked the first time a state legislature had set maximum rather than minimum requirements for teacher education. Now Virginia and New Jersey have placed similar restrictions.[28]

The Texas plan raises questions that as yet have no firm answers. Is it possible to learn how to teach from a bare-bones curriculum that can offer no more than six hours of "core" education courses, six hours of methods, and six hours of student teaching? Curiously, the Texas legislature allowed the state board of education to exempt teachers of early childhood education, reading, special education, bilingual education, and English as a Second Language from the 18-hour limit. Are professional education courses more valuable to these teachers than to secondary education and physical education teachers?[29]

Now a question with a clearer answer: Will the restrictions force teacher education programs in Texas to give up their accreditation from the National Council for Accreditation of Teacher Education (NCATE)? Already at least ten Texas institutions have dropped out of NCATE, the organization whose efforts to set national standards we will examine later in this chapter. The large, well-established program at Texas A&M, however, managed to win reaccreditation in 1992.[30]

Not satisfied with the state legislature's regulations, the Texas Higher Education Coordinating Board has extended the 18-semester-hour maximum to *graduate* education courses as well. Even those few institutions permitted to offer full graduate programs, such as the Holmes Group's Texas members, must also provide an undergraduate fast track to allow certification in no more than 18 hours. The dust of teacher education reform is still settling in Texas.[31]

*The New Jersey Shortcut.*   Since 1985, New Jersey has pioneered another kind of alternate program. The New Jersey shortcut puts college-educated people who want to teach into elementary and secondary classrooms—and puts them there fast. Clearly prompted by the threat of teacher shortages, the New Jersey plan carries on the political tradition we studied in chapter 1. Historically, state legislatures and boards of education have been more than willing to bend or alter teacher education and certification standards to put warm bodies in front of America's classrooms.

In all fairness, though, the officials in charge of the New Jersey shortcut are trying to put into those classrooms people who can teach as well as traditionally prepared teachers. And the strategy may be succeeding.

Under the New Jersey plan, a person with a bachelor's degree in an academic subject can become a provisional teacher by passing a test in that subject. An early goal of the plan was to encourage math majors to become math teachers and science majors to become science teachers, and many provisional teachers have done just that. The largest group, though, consists of people with noneducation bachelor's degrees who want to teach elementary school. After they pass a more general test covering several academic fields, into the schools the would-be teachers go.[32]

All New Jersey's provisional teachers take a compressed version of professional education course work during their first year, and they are supposed to receive 20 days of intensive summer training before they enter the classroom. They also work with experienced teachers who serve as mentors and are supposed to spend their first month under close supervision before assuming full responsibility. If the provisional teachers like their jobs, receive satisfactory evaluations, and make satisfactory scores on the National Teacher Examinations (NTE), they become fully certified teachers.

Amid dire predictions of failure from teacher educators, the New Jersey plan got off to a good start, and now about one-fourth of the state's new teachers are entering the occupation via the shortcut. A much larger percentage of provisional teachers than traditional-route teachers are racial or ethnic minorities. Predictably, though, critics and advocates see the plan differently.[33]

To understand the critics' point of view, notice how I used the term *supposed to* two paragraphs above. Critics point to program evaluations showing that provisional teachers are receiving less training and support than they are supposed to. Some candidates who take a real shortcut and completely miss the 20-day summer session have been allowed to move ahead and teach anyway. Although mentors are supposed to supervise provisional teachers 100 percent of the time during their first four weeks, an evaluation of the program found supervision taking place only 15 percent of the time and almost one-fourth of the provisionals receiving no supervision at all.[34]

Supporters of the shortcut tell another story. Provisional teachers are receiving evaluations as positive as those of traditionally prepared teachers, plus provisional teachers have a lower first-year attrition rate. The plan itself is receiving good marks from its "graduates." Provisional teachers rate working with their mentors as more beneficial than taking courses from teacher educators and school administrators who, according to the provisionals, have "little knowledge of the day-to-day demands of a classroom, and little to offer in the way of practical lessons or advice." Adding insult to injury, the alternate-route teachers are making higher scores on the NTE than graduates of traditional programs.[35]

Praised by former President George Bush and the nation's governors at their 1989 summit conference on education, the New Jersey plan has served as a model for alternate routes in at least ten other states: Colorado, Connecticut, Kentucky, Maryland, Minnesota, New Hampshire, Tennessee, Texas, Washington, and West Virginia. At least eight more states—Arkansas, Arizona, California, Georgia, Idaho, Mississippi, Missouri, and Ohio—have opened routes that are similar but restricted to shortages or to secondary teaching. Although such programs cut preparation too short to suit most teacher educators, they look incredibly long compared to the plans we will examine next.[36]

***Other Alternate Programs: Emergency Certification in Disguise.***    More than fifteen states have dusted off their old emergency teaching certificates, giving them a fresh coat of paint and a new look. Don't be misled by the "alternate program" sign that now hangs over this formerly unmarked door into the occupation. Emergency certification allows people to teach with *no* advance preparation if they agree to take a handful of education courses—in some cases, as few as three—during their first years on the job. Unsupervised and unassisted, these people must teach themselves to teach.[37]

It is telling that most emergency credentials go to teachers of poor, minority, and handicapped students, those whose parents often lack the political clout and sophistication to protest. In the words of Arthur Wise, president of NCATE, and Linda Darling-Hammond of Teachers College, Columbia University, such students must endure a "steady stream of substitute teachers alternating with the revolving-door parade of inexperienced, underprepared, and unsupported recruits, many of whom cannot survive even a year in the classroom."[38]

*A Tale of Two Occupations.*   Several times each year, the media carry the story of someone caught practicing medicine without a license. Usually the ersatz physician has a degree in biology or chemistry, a reassuring bedside manner, but no formal training in medicine. Doesn't the fact that such persons are often able to practice successfully for years, completely undetected, cast doubt on the necessity of going to medical school? Shouldn't we allow biologists and chemists to take a few courses in medicine, work with mentors, and see how well they can do as physicians?

Of course not. Most Americans believe medicine is too complex and important to treat in such a careless way. Medicine is a profession, after all, and we quite rightly insist that professions maintain high standards. Teaching, however, gets different treatment, as we will find in the concluding section of this chapter and in chapter 4.

## RAISING STANDARDS IN TEACHER EDUCATION

### Nostalgia for a Golden Age of Teaching

When Americans rediscovered teacher incompetency in the late 1970s, the media joined academic journals in tracing the problem back to teacher education. Prospective teachers were among the poorest students in colleges and universities, Americans heard repeatedly. At a time when many citizens were upset with declining scores on college entrance examinations, they learned the test scores of future teachers had fallen even faster than the scores of other students. Ranked against other undergraduates by their Scholastic Aptitude Test (SAT) and American College Testing (ACT) program scores, teacher education students consistently came in near the bottom, ahead only of students majoring in such fields as agriculture and home economics. Professors of education bore much of the blame, the media charged, for they had lowered their standards during the 1970s in response to declining enrollment in teacher education programs.[39]

*A Nation at Risk* captured the mood of the early 1980s when it stated that "not enough of the academically able students are being attracted to teaching" and "too many teachers are being drawn from the bottom quarter of graduating high-school and college students." How could teacher educators have let the nation down?[40]

Many news stories and journal articles left the impression that there was once a golden age of teaching: a time when teachers, if not exactly well paid, were uniformly bright and well educated. Educational historians tell a different story.

The mid- to late 1800s were certainly not golden years. School officials could not afford to be selective in hiring teachers—the problem was finding enough teachers to staff the rapidly growing common schools. Recall our discussion of turn-of-the-century teachers and their modest educational credentials. During the 1920s and 1930s, as researchers began administering standardized tests of academic ability, their studies showed that prospective teachers, many of whom were enrolled in normal schools and teachers colleges, ranked low when compared with the full range of college students. In some studies, teachers even ranked below high school seniors. At four-year colleges and universities, "eddies" and "aggies" had to put up with jokes about their shallow interests and weak intellect.[41]

Throughout this century as well as the last, teacher educators have complained that more prestigious, better-paying occupations were luring bright people away from teaching. Teacher educators documented their complaints in academic journals and books, waiting for the next public discovery of the teacher competency issue. Close on its heels, they knew, would be another round of criticism. The late 1940s and 1950s brought an especially strong media attack, the harshest since "muckraking" journalists uncovered poor teaching in turn-of-the-century schools. The 1950s critics lashed out at teachers and teacher educators, writing such scathing books as *And Madly Teach* (1949) and *Quackery in the Public Schools* (1953). Newspapers, news magazines, radio, and television joined the attack. And, since the late 1970s, Americans have taken up the teacher competency issue again.[42]

History is more than cycles and repetition, though. The social changes of the last three decades have affected teaching as an occupation in ways we are just beginning to understand. In particular, the women's movement and civil rights movement have been powerful influences.

The history of America's teachers is largely women's history, the story of women who have worked hard for little compensation. Since the 1960s, with the reduction of discrimination against women in higher education and in many occupations, teacher education programs have suffered a "brain drain" of bright, career-oriented students. It makes many Americans uncomfortable—even resentful—to realize they can no longer buy teachers of the same quality for the same price, nor even for a higher price. Teaching is a better-paid occupation than ever before, but the bright women who once formed a captive employment pool for teaching, nursing, and social work have other options now.[43]

To a degree, the same is true of minorities, especially African Americans. Many of the brightest African Americans, both women and men, once became teachers. Discrimination placed such severe limits on their chances of education and employment in other fields that teaching reaped a bounty of talented people. At the turn of the twentieth century, black teachers in many Southern cities had more years of schooling and held higher degrees than their white counterparts. Well into the 1960s, school systems did not have to worry about attracting talented African-American college students, for after graduation they had few choices.[44]

The brightest African-American college students, like the brightest women, are now going into the full professions. In contrast to women, however, the percentage of African-American high school students going on to college fell from the late 1970s through the mid-1980s. Although the percentage has now returned to earlier levels, the last few years have been spent merely recouping losses. African-American college students are turning away from teaching, to be sure; they are now *less* likely than whites to major in education. Unlike women, though, African Americans are not moving into higher-status fields in sufficient numbers to justify the consoling explanation that teaching's loss is law and medicine's gain.[45]

No, there never was a golden age of teaching, not even when teaching attracted a larger share of the brightest women and minorities. Even then, the overall intellectual quality of the teaching force was not very impressive. Even then, teacher competency was a serious concern. It is unfair and inaccurate, however, to paint teachers with a single brush. Teaching has always attracted a wide range of people, some of whom have been among the nation's most intelligent. I hasten to add that the public has always gotten better teachers than it has paid for. But the average American teacher, compared with all college students, has ranked low on standardized tests of academic ability as long as there have been standardized tests.

## Teacher Competency Today

If test scores meant nothing, as some argue, we might not need to be concerned. But there *is* a teacher competency problem, and it manifests itself in many other ways. Parents know something is wrong when teachers send home notes with grammatical and spelling errors in every sentence. Students worry when teachers routinely make mistakes in simple arithmetic on the chalk board. These concerns are legitimate. In teaching, of all occupations, there can be no excuse for weak literacy skills, for these skills are the tools of the trade.

Literacy is only one aspect of teacher competency. We cannot afford to take literacy for granted, but teachers must be more than literate. The three areas in teacher education programs suggest other areas in which teachers must be competent: general knowledge, knowledge of the teaching field, and knowledge of professional education. The ultimate test of teacher competency, of course, is performance in the classroom. Can the teachers teach? As we saw in the last chapter, though, evaluating teaching skills is difficult and controversial. The other aspects of competency, if no less controversial, lend themselves to an easier form of evaluation: pencil-and-paper testing.

Until the late 1970s, state boards of education did in a sense take it for granted that college graduates who had completed teacher education programs were competent. State boards issued teaching certificates to virtually everyone who finished a state-approved program, with no questions asked.

But, then, as the public rediscovered the teacher competency issue, state boards and legislatures began asking questions. Soon they mandated standardized tests as a check on the quality of teacher education. Today 39 states require some form of testing: 3 states for admission to teacher education programs only, 18 states for teacher certification only, and 18 states for both. Now we will take a closer look at the various types of teacher tests.[46]

## LITERACY TESTS

Many tests for students seeking admission to teacher education measure nothing more than simple literacy. Perhaps the "nothing more" is inappropriate, for it is essential that all teachers have the ability to use "our two principal symbol systems, words and numbers," as the former director of testing for the Dallas public schools so aptly states.[47] Perhaps it is time to stop apologizing for the emphasis teacher education programs are putting on literacy tests. Stressing literacy is putting first things first. The adjective *simple* does seem appropriate, though, since the admission tests are slanted toward such lower-level literacy skills as word recognition, punctuation, and basic computation. Moreover, the *cutoff* scores prospective teachers must make to pass the tests are usually set very low—in some cases, embarrassingly low.[48]

### Why Such Low Cutoff Scores?

In the process of setting the cutoffs, testing companies *norm* the tests by administering them to various groups—for example, to large samples of eighth-graders, tenth-graders, twelfth-graders, and college freshmen. The average score of each group is that group's *normal score,* or *norm.* Teacher education officials or state board of education members can then decide which norm to use as the cutoff score for admission to teacher education.[49]

One thing the public has generally overlooked in its latest discovery of teacher incompetency is that cutoff scores for admission to teacher education programs are usually set at the equivalent of tenth- to twelfth-grade norms; that is, the average tenth- or twelfth-grader could "pass" the tests.

For obvious reasons, teacher educators and state board members do not go out of their way to publicize the cutoffs, but, when pressed, they justify them in several ways. First, they want to maintain enrollment in teacher education programs. Raising the cutoffs, they believe, could cause enrollment to fall, worsen the teacher shortage, and put teacher educators out of work. Second, they cannot agree on the level of literacy necessary for teaching. Third, they want to be fair to prospective minority teachers, who do not score as well on the tests as prospective white teachers.[50]

All these justifications are controversial. To show they have some basis in experience, though, we need only consider what has happened in school systems administering their own literacy tests to applicants for teaching positions. After setting cutoffs at the tenth-grade norm, the Dallas Independent School District screened out more than half its applicants in the late 1970s and early 1980s—people who held bachelor's degrees and teaching certificates. With cutoffs set as low as the sixth-grade norm in Pinellas County, Florida, 15 to 30 percent of the applicants failed. In both systems, minorities failed at much higher rates than whites, an issue to which we will return later in this chapter. Other school systems using literacy tests have had similar results. The good news is that applicants have been doing better on the tests, in part because teacher education programs have been putting more emphasis on literacy.[51]

## Why Not Just Raise the Cutoffs?

Teacher educators are proceeding with caution. "America cannot afford any more teachers who fail a twelfth-grade competency test," the Holmes Group says.[52] Easier said than done. With the low cutoffs teacher education programs currently use, the rate of failure on admission tests throughout the nation averages 28 percent. If every program moved its cutoff to the equivalent of a college freshman norm, about half of all college freshmen would immediately become ineligible. (Since the norm is the average score of the group being tested, by definition about half the group falls below the norm.) Even more seriously, as many as 80 to 90 percent of all black college freshmen would be ineligible. Teacher educators could boast they had raised standards, but would they have raised the right standards?[53]

On the one hand, empirical research on the relationship between teachers' literacy test scores and their students' achievement test scores is inconclusive. Some studies show a modest correlation; others do not. Thus some teacher educators argue that emphasizing the literacy standard may keep potentially good teachers out of the occupation. These teacher educators make the same argument about SAT and ACT scores. Research does not show a definite link between the SAT and ACT of teachers and the achievement test scores of their students. Why, then, should teacher education programs turn away students with below-average scores on these tests? Doing so is arbitrary and discriminatory, some professors argue, and doing so can land you in court.[54]

On the other hand, we found in the last chapter that the entire area of research on measuring teacher influence on student test scores is fraught with problems. Because so many other factors inside and outside of schools outweigh the influence of teachers on student achievement, it is difficult to measure the effect of *any* teacher characteristic or behavior on student test scores. Frankly, this kind of research may never give teacher educators much guidance in setting standards.

Professors in other areas of higher education are often amazed that teacher educators spend so much time agonizing over standards and grasping for empirical studies to justify every change. Medical schools and law schools do not base their high admission standards on studies showing physicians and lawyers with higher test scores perform better operations and win more cases. Professors of medicine and law do not even conduct such studies. When setting standards, they simply state the obvious: Physicians and lawyers must be highly literate because their jobs demand it.

Surely professors of education can make the same case for teachers. When they have done so in court, they have won, for courts emphasize "job-relatedness": the demonstration of a *reasonable* relationship between what the test measures and what the job requires. It is only reasonable that people who constantly use literacy skills in their work, people whose jobs involve raising the literacy of others, be highly literate themselves.[55]

## TEACHER CERTIFICATION TESTS

This chapter's strong emphasis on literacy reflects the attention it is receiving in teacher testing, but teacher competency obviously involves more. For years, the most widely used certification tests have been the National Teacher

Examinations (NTE) developed by the Educational Testing Service (ETS) of Princeton, New Jersey. In 1990, more than 30 states used the NTE as part of their teacher education and certification requirements. ETS, the largest testing company in the world, also produces the SAT, the Graduate Record Examinations (GRE), and numerous other standardized tests. In 1992, ETS began phasing in a successor to the NTE, a new teacher assessment package we will examine later. National Evaluation Systems (NES) of Amherst, Massachusetts, and other testing companies are also in the teacher-testing business.[56]

The controversy over literacy tests is mild compared to the arguments over teacher certification tests. These examinations typically begin with communication skills and proceed to general knowledge, the teaching field, and professional education. Disgruntled teachers and prospective teachers, often with the backing of teacher unions, have challenged each part of these tests. Cultural bias, poor construction, irrelevance to the actual work teachers do—these are some of the charges the NEA, in particular, has pressed and often won in court. The arguments revolve around a deceptively simple question: What do teachers need to know?[57]

## General Knowledge

Prospective teachers sometimes complain that test items in the area of general knowledge are obscure, trivial, or irrelevant. I can tell when my students have taken a teacher certification test, for some of them invariably return with questions like these: "Why do I need to recognize the musical notation for the opening notes of the *Fifth Symphony*? Who cares who discovered radium? Where are the Alleghenies, anyway?" Students whose social and educational backgrounds have not prepared them for such questions may charge that the tests are culturally biased, and minority students are not the only ones who raise this issue. As we will see in chapter 8, the issue is one of social class as much as race and ethnicity.[58]

From one point of view, the above questions betray an appalling ignorance of—and indifference to—matters that should be common knowledge, at least to people with college degrees. Those who take this point of view throw up their hands in despair at the thought of teachers whose knowledge is so thin and spotty. There *is* cultural bias in the tests, these people argue, but the bias is toward a cultural heritage they want the schools to transmit. It is unfortunate and unjust that the schools do not expose every student to literate culture, but every prospective teacher has an obligation to acquire it.

From another point of view, there is no longer a consensus on the knowledge educated people should have in common, if indeed such a consensus ever existed. The best-selling books *Cultural Literacy: What Every American Needs to Know* (1987) by E. D. Hirsch, Jr., and *The Closing of the American Mind* (1987) by Allan Bloom have sparked a vigorous debate, one we will discuss in more detail in chapters 7 and 10. Some educated Americans do not believe it is possible to make a list of essential knowledge, which is exactly what Hirsch attempts. If Hirsch's list is nothing more than arbitrary, they suggest, then so is any test of general knowledge.[59]

## The Teaching Field

Tests in the teaching field are less controversial, but they, too, involve debates over what teachers need to know. We have already seen the disagreements over the teaching fields for elementary, special, and physical education teachers. Consider the difficulty involved in constructing a field test for elementary teachers in, say, mathematics. If the testing company asks classroom teachers, professors of education, and professors of mathematics for advice on the test, these people are likely to make different suggestions—especially in math, the subject most elementary teachers like least. The advisers must decide which areas of mathematics the test will cover, how broad and how deep the coverage will be, and so forth. Then a different group of advisers must repeat the process for every other subject in the elementary curriculum.[60]

Still to come is the highly technical work of actually constructing the test. Item writers compose the questions. Theirs is a critical job because in multiple-choice testing, the options listed are the only acceptable answers. An arithmetic problem has only one correct answer, to be sure, but in most academic fields, specialists often disagree over "right" and "wrong" answers. The more you know about literature, for example, the more likely it is that several answers—or no answers—to a question about a children's story appear to be correct. Thus all standardized tests reflect the "biases" of a variety of people, academic advisers as well as technicians at the testing company. Finally, the company field-tests the questions on a sample of elementary teachers, conducts statistical analyses of the results, and makes revisions in the test. Teacher education officials and state board members, of course, have the ultimate power to determine who passes and who fails because they establish the cutoff scores. Keep in mind that, next to literacy tests, teaching field tests are the most straightforward.[61]

## Professional Education

The least straightforward tests, as you must realize by now, are those of professional education. Teacher certification tests should reflect the *knowledge base* for teaching—what teachers need to know in order to do their work. Actually, the content of teacher education programs and teacher certification tests shows there are multiple knowledge bases for teaching, which we have called liberal education, the teaching field, and professional education. Rivalries and competition among the knowledge bases are common, and prospective teachers often feel they have been caught in an academic tug of war. As if that were not enough, teacher educators continue to disagree over what should constitute the professional knowledge base for teaching—the specialized knowledge that belongs to the occupation alone. Once again the question comes around: What do teachers need to know?[62]

NCATE has made strengthening the knowledge base one of its top priorities. Teacher education programs applying to renew their accreditation must convince NCATE they have given serious thought to the knowledge base, especially the professional education component. But NCATE allows a great deal of variation from one institution to another, and NCATE pays more attention to the *process* an institution goes through in designing its knowledge base than to the knowledge itself. Teacher educators have long emphasized process over product.[63]

As loose as this approach may seem, it does acknowledge that teacher educators are engaged in ongoing debates on the knowledge base. Seeing their professors shake hands and agree to disagree, prospective teachers correctly conclude that there is no one best way to teach. (Nor is there one best way to teach teachers.) But prospective teachers sometimes wring their hands in confusion when they have to take standardized certification tests.

Here is the problem they face. The professional education questions on certification tests often strike candidates as: (a) obvious; (b) confusing; (c) theoretical; (d) common sense; (e) all of these. The *best* answer, to use the parlance of the testing industry, is "e." Please understand that I am not insulting test makers and teacher educators. I am certainly not insulting prospective teachers. I am only suggesting that the lack of consensus about professional education makes testing teachers in that area most difficult.

To dramatize this problem, Linda Darling-Hammond published an analysis of the professional knowledge section of the old NTE. Examining a sample test provided by ETS, Darling-Hammond found that 15 percent of the questions required only "careful reading or knowledge of simple word definitions"; another 25 percent called for "agreement with the test's teaching philosophy," which she describes as "liberal" and "highly individualized"; and another 15 percent required "agreement with the test's definition of socially or bureaucratically acceptable behavior," which at least one item on the test itself characterized as "nonthreatening."[64]

Overall, according to Darling-Hammond, about 40 percent of the questions had no "right" answer. One question on techniques of "effective teaching," for example, gave prospective teachers a choice of several answers supported by different bodies of research. Test takers could mark an answer favoring mastery learning or an answer endorsing whole-group instruction. Both of these approaches have support in the research, and both have their advocates among teachers and teacher educators. But ETS counted these answers "wrong." Only those who opted for the answer favoring individualized instruction and pacing got the item right.[65]

## The Successor to the National Teacher Examinations

If the new-and-improved testing package form ETS lives up to its advance billing, it may be the vanguard of a "new generation of teacher assessments." Publicity from ETS promises more sensitivity to cultural and racial differences, less reliance on what test takers ruefully call the "multiple guess" format, and a better picture of what teacher candidates can actually *do*. The pencil-and-paper NTE, introduced in 1940, changed little over its half century of life. The NTE's computer-based successor promises to be state of the art and adaptable.[66]

A teacher candidate will take the new assessments in three stages. Stage I, administered during the sophomore college year (later for students in nontraditional programs), measures the basic literacy skills of reading, writing, and mathematics. Stage II, given when the candidate nears completion of a teacher education program, is a test of the teaching field and professional education. Stage III, administered during the teacher's first year in the classroom, is a performance-based assessment of teaching skills.

Stage I is a "multiple length test depending on how well you answer the questions," ETS officials explain. Seated at a computer, every candidate must answer a representative set of questions on reading, writing, and math; the computer stops asking questions of those who score high enough to meet state requirements. The computer puts test takers through a variety of paces in Stage I. There are some multiple-choice questions but prospective teachers must "construct their own responses" to other items. English teachers take heart. All candidates write essays.[67]

Technology makes it possible to custom-tailor Stage II to the teaching field of each candidate. A prospective social studies teacher, for instance, may be asked to write essays integrating history, geography, economics, and political science. An elementary teacher may have to show proficiency in a variety of academic subjects. A music teacher may have to answer questions on theory and submit a performance tape as well. Stage II can also be tailored to the requirements of the state where the candidate is applying for teacher certification. ETS allows state officials to select content from a "menu" of modules for each teaching field.

Stage II also covers professional education, and ETS is trying hard to avoid the pitfalls of the old NTE. One strategy for doing so is minimizing multiple-choice questions in favor of constructed-response items that ask the candidate how to handle hypothetical classroom situations. If, for instance, the candidate has to write a lesson plan or come up with a disciplinary procedure, a range of different answers can count as "right."

The Stage III assessment of teaching skill, still in the process of development in the early 1990s, will involve classroom evaluations conducted by state and local school officials. So many controversies cloud the history of performance evaluation. Hoping to break through the clouds, ETS is field testing interviews, work samples, videotapes, and other assessment strategies. As Lee Shulman suggests, such evidence can become part of an evaluation portfolio (see chapter 2).

Many readers of this book will be part of the first wave of prospective teachers to take the new assessments. Soon you may be able to judge for yourself whether, in the words of an NEA official, the NTE's successor is an "important rite of passage" or a "useless political barrier."[68]

## The National Board for Professional Teaching Standards

A few years into your teaching career, you may be able to make the same judgment about the assessments the NBPTS is developing. While the successor to the NTE is designed for initial state certification, the NBPTS wants to award national certificates to "experienced teachers who meet advanced standards of knowledge and practice and who wish professional and public acknowledgment of their superior professional skills."[69]

The NBPTS plans to issue certificates in four overlapping areas: early childhood, middle childhood, early adolescence, and adolescence and young adulthood. Within each area, teachers will be able to apply for either a generalist certificate or a certificate in a particular academic subject. Committees dominated by classroom teachers are now defining standards for each area, specifying "what teachers should know and be able to do"—a ticklish matter, as we have seen.[70]

Teacher-dominated committees are also confronting the problem of how to apply the standards to identify superior teachers. Convinced, like ETS, that multiple-choice testing can do only part of the job, NBPTS is considering such other strategies as "on-site observation, simulations of classroom practice, videotapes of a teacher's actual practice, oral defense of teaching portfolios, [and] examinations of subject-matter knowledge." Field testing of the new assessments began in the 1993–1994 school year, and the complete certification program should be in place by 1997–1998.[71]

It is most encouraging that *teachers themselves*—two words I will use often in the next chapter—are taking the lead in developing the first national system of teacher certification. Medicine, law, and other full professions have long recognized the value of national board certification, a process of peer recognition that extends above and beyond state licensing.

Optimistically, teaching may now be where medicine was in the 1870s—just beginning to develop a professional knowledge base that *actually works.* In medicine, it took several decades for the new scientific knowledge base to prove its worth. Only then, in the early 1900s, were medical educators and the American Medical Association able to drive out quacks and improve medical practice. Only then could they use examinations based on scientific medicine to raise standards.[72]

Teaching, as we have seen, is still an occupation in search of a specialized knowledge base. Giving teachers a major role in finding it—as NBPTS and, to a lesser degree, ETS have—is a great step forward. But before any group can develop fair examinations, teachers and teacher educators must reach a consensus on how to evaluate answers on tests and performance in the classroom. In our haste to move ahead, we cannot overlook this prior step. If we do, a least-common-denominator pseudoscience of education—a teach-by-the-numbers approach—will freeze into place, and the occupation will splinter into teachers who go along with it and teachers who see through it and reject it.

## TEACHER TESTING AND MINORITY TEACHERS

### A Precarious Situation

Fairness to minority teachers is one of the most difficult issues in teacher testing. The issue is part of a larger question: How can America's schools attract qualified minority teachers? The Carnegie Forum and Holmes Group recognize the urgent need to find answers. Academic journals feature articles with titles as alarming as "The Desperate Need for Black Teachers" and as hopeful as "Minority Teachers Can Pass the Tests."[73]

Even if there is room for hope, there is broad agreement that the current situation is precarious. At a time when the percentage of elementary and secondary minority students is increasing (see chapter 8), some studies show the percentage of minority teachers is decreasing. Consider African Americans as a case in point. The percentage of African-American students in public schools has risen to more than 16 percent, yet the percentage of African-American teachers fell from over 8 percent in 1971 to less than 7 percent in 1986. Extrapolating this trend, some observers predict that only 5 percent of America's teachers will be African American by the year 2000.[74]

What can be done? Almost everyone agrees that making teaching a more attractive occupation will help. As every chapter in part I of this book points out, there is certainly hope for the occupation. Attracting more minority teachers while raising standards, however, presents special problems. Even though the percentage of African-American students going on to college has apparently turned around after declining during the late 1970s and early 1980s, racial disparities remain. Fifty percent of black high school students enroll in college immediately after graduation, compared to almost 60 percent of white students. Blacks who do enroll tend to have lower SAT and ACT scores than whites. The black-white gap on the SAT, while closing, is still almost 200 points. Among the highest-scoring African-American students, fewer than 1 percent say they want to be teachers.[75]

Thus it is not surprising that teacher testing hits prospective teachers who are black harder than those who are white. The passing rate on Louisiana's teacher certification test in the mid-1980s was 78 percent for white candidates but only 15 percent for black candidates. In Georgia, the figures were 87 percent for whites and 34 percent for blacks. Other states have produced narrower gaps; unfortunately, they seem to have done so by setting lower cutoffs on the tests rather than by improving the education of minority teachers. In Texas, more than 99 percent of currently employed teachers, including 95.4 percent of African Americans and 98.9 percent of Hispanic Americans, passed a controversial literacy test the Texas State Teachers Association had tried unsuccessfully to block in court. The cutoff, though, was apparently the equivalent of an eighth- or tenth-grade norm. After Alabama agreed to lower the cutoff on its certification test to produce the same success rate for black and white students, 98 percent of all the candidates passed the test. At that point, the state decided the test was not worth the trouble and expense.[76]

In states with large minority populations, teacher testing has brought forth bitter accusations. Teacher testing is a racist ploy, some educators contend—the latest chapter in a long record of discrimination. No, others reply, it is a necessary step in improving the occupation—the real ploy is using the race issue to block higher standards.

## A Way Out?

Teacher education must find a way out of this dilemma, even if doing so proves to be difficult and expensive, as it certainly will. Listen to the counsel of Patricia A. Graham, former dean of the Graduate School of Education at Harvard:

The problem cannot be solved simply by raising the cutoff scores on tests, by ignoring the tests, by calling them racially biased, or by declaring them inappropriate for future teachers. The tests may contribute to the problem, but they are not central. The central problem is that blacks in the U.S. are not getting as good an education as whites are—and the education that whites are getting is not good enough.[77]

Thus Graham's major recommendation is improving elementary and secondary education.

She also suggests recruiting more minority college students and helping them succeed once they enroll. Graham points to the record of Grambling State University, a historically black school in Louisiana that is "fighting the scores instead of the tests." The performance of Grambling's students on Louisiana's teacher tests has improved substantially. Grambling has chosen not to challenge the tests, nor is it "teaching the tests," as so many institutions do for both black and white students. Instead, Grambling has tried to improve every area of its teacher education program.[78]

Graham also argues that the nation needs to invest more money and imagination in attracting bright minority college students to teaching. Noting the influx into teaching of people who are dissatisfied with their present jobs, Graham also calls for the recruitment of more minorities at mid-career or even later. She specifically mentions government workers and military retirees.[79]

These are just the kind of people who are now taking nontraditional routes into teaching. From my point of view as a teacher educator, one of the strongest arguments in favor of the new programs is that they may be able to attract more minorities into the occupation.

## Cautious Optimism

I will close this discussion with encouraging news: The NEA's ongoing studies suggest the decline in the percentage of African-American teachers may have ended. According to the NEA, 8 percent of public school teachers were black in 1991, an increase of slightly more than 1 percent over 1986. Moreover, NEA studies show a higher percentage of African-Americans among teachers under 30 than among teachers 30 to 39, which suggests that recent efforts to recruit minority teachers may be paying off. We must wait for other evidence to confirm these findings, but they may indicate that the nation is responding constructively to the urgent need for more minority teachers.[80]

## THE POSITIVE VISION OF JOHN GOODLAD

Although books about teacher education are rarely best-sellers, a happy exception to the rule is *Teachers for Our Nation's Schools* (1990) by John I. Goodlad, professor of education at the University of Washington and former president of the American Association of Colleges for Teacher Education. With this book and its companion volumes, *The Moral Dimensions of Teaching* (1990) and *Places Where Teachers Are Taught* (1990), Goodlad is raising new hopes for fundamental reform in teacher education.[81]

Goodlad examines many of the problems we have discussed in this chapter. Based on 5 years of research in 29 representative public and private institutions, Goodlad concludes that teacher education is a "Second-hand Rose" on most college and university campuses. Indeed, it suffers from "chronic prestige deprivation." Insecure teacher educators, divided among themselves, lack a clear sense of mission. Their standoffish colleagues in the arts and sciences offer abundant criticism but scant help. Politicians and other reformers impose a steady stream of regulations that fail to improve the enterprise. Students in teacher education programs, recruited with little care and reflecting little diversity, graduate without ever grasping their responsibilities to schools and society.

By now, this litany should sound familiar. Where is the positive vision?

The popularity of *Teachers for Our Nation's Schools* comes from Goodlad's willingness to argue, with no apologies, that teacher education should prepare teachers to transform schools and improve society. Goodlad offers his vision of what *should be* in contrast to what is. Teaching carries with it *moral imperatives,* Goodlad says. Teachers must enculturate young people into democracy; teachers must provide equitable access to knowledge; teachers must know how to "reach" and "connect with" students from a variety of backgrounds; and teachers must be stewards who accept responsibility for renewing the schools.

Goodlad's vision of teaching informs the 19 "postulates" he offers to guide the reform of teacher education. Readers seeking detailed blueprints will not find them in this book, but Goodlad's postulates do provide useful guidelines. Some are fairly specific. For example, Goodlad rejects "emergency" routes into teaching as I did earlier in this chapter. Other postulates are much broader. The one I will emphasize to close this chapter calls for preparing teachers to understand educational alternatives so they can "effect needed changes in school organization, pupil grouping, curriculum, and more."[82]

Goodlad's strongest indictment of teacher education programs is that they prepare teachers to fit into schools as they are. His strongest recommendation is to prepare teachers who can transform schools into what they should be.

Showing teachers how to teach by the cookbook will not do, he insists. Teacher educators must resist the pressure to turn out teachers who can follow instructional pacing guides, teach standardized tests, keep their heads down, and somehow survive. That kind of teaching—all too common in schools throughout the nation—is simply *wrong,* Goodlad states. It is wrong academically and wrong morally.

I must confess I find Goodlad's vision compelling. His ideas are refreshing because they are so different from the thinking that dominates education today. In chapters 7 and 10, we will see how his ideas draw on the theory of education known as *progressivism.* Advocates of this theory are challenging the *essentialism* that has reigned in the schools since the back-to-basics movement of the late 1970s and 1980s.

Like Goodlad, I feel optimistic about some of the changes I see occurring in the 1990s. But I, too, worry about the continued "technocratization" of teaching and teacher education.

With new certification assessments from the ETS and NBPTS coming on line, a new generation of high-stakes teacher tests is arriving. Although teachers and teacher educators are helping to develop these assessments, we must not allow them to dictate the knowledge base for teaching. We cannot afford to make preparation for *any* test the purpose of teacher education.

Goodlad urges us to set our sights higher. He urges prospective teachers to shake free of the status quo, to make intellectual waves. He wants you to shatter the prevailing belief that only a few students (mostly white and middle class) can learn while the rest are lost causes. Goodlad wants to convince you that "schools can and must change" and that much of the responsibility will soon rest in your hands. As a teacher educator, I hope you are ready to take up the challenge.[83]

## ACTIVITIES

1. Invite several professors of education and professors of arts and sciences into your class for a panel discussion of reform in teacher education, especially the opening of nontraditional routes into the occupation.
2. Talk with a public school administrator and an administrator in your college or university's teacher education program about the effects of raising standards on the quality of the teaching force. Be sure to discuss admission and certification tests and their effects on minority teachers.
3. Ask currently employed teachers for their views on the issues in this chapter, especially the strengths and weaknesses of teacher education programs.

## RECOMMENDED READINGS

Carnegie Forum on Education and the Economy. *A Nation Prepared: Teachers for the 21st Century* (New York: Carnegie Forum, 1986).
   Along with *Tomorrow's Teachers* by the Holmes Group (see note 10), this report charted the course of reforms that are still underway today.
Conant, James Bryant. *The Education of American Teachers* (New York: McGraw-Hill, 1963).
   Here is a classic study of teacher education by one of its most insightful and constructive critics.
Goodlad, John I. *Teachers for Our Nation's Schools* (San Francisco: Jossey-Bass, 1990).
   Supplemented by its two companion volumes (see note 81), this book is *the* teacher education study of the early 1990s.
Warren, Donald R., ed. *American Teachers: Histories of a Profession at Work* (New York: Macmillan, 1989).
   This anthology includes especially strong chapters on teacher education by Jurgen Herbst and William R. Johnson.

# NOTES

1. Lynn Olson, "A Month in the Life of a Prospective Teacher: 'I Feel Called to Do It,' " *Education Week* (December 12, 1990), pp. 17, 19.
2. The former New York teacher is Albert Shanker, now president of the American Federation of Teachers. Quoted in "Why Teachers Fail," *Newsweek* (September 24, 1984), p. 64.
3. James G. Carter, *Essays on Popular Education . . .* (1826) and *Outline of an Institution for the Education of Teachers* (1866), in David B. Tyack, ed., *Turning Points in American Educational History* (Waltham, MA: Blaisdell, 1967), pp. 153, 428.
4. Report of the Committee on Education of the Massachusetts House of Representatives (1840), in Rush Welter, ed., *American Writings on Popular Education: The Nineteenth Century* (Indianapolis: Bobbs-Merrill, 1971), p. 94.
5. See Donald R. Warren, "History and Teacher Education: Learning from Experience," *Educational Researcher* 14 (December 1985): 5–12. A recent book edited by Warren may become the definitive historical study: *American Teachers: Histories of a Profession at Work* (New York: Macmillan, 1989). This book will take its place beside Willard S. Elsbree's classic, *The American Teacher: Evolution of a Profession in a Democracy* (New York: American Book Company, 1939). For the history of normal schools, see Jurgen Herbst's, *And Sadly Teach: Teacher Education and Professionalization in American Culture* (Madison: University of Wisconsin Press, 1989), and Richard J. Altenbaugh and Kathleen Underwood's "The Evolution of Normal Schools," in John I. Goodlad, Roger Soder, and Kenneth A. Sirotnik, eds., *Places Where Teachers Are Taught* (San Francisco: Jossey-Bass, 1990).
6. I base these estimates on the following: U.S. Department of Education, National Center for Education Statistics, *The Condition of Education, 1992* (Washington, D.C.: U.S. Government Printing Office, 1992), pp. 148–149; Emily Feistritzer and David Chester, *Alternative Teacher Certification: A State-by-State Analysis* (Washington, D.C.: National Center for Education Information, 1991), pp. 9–10; Arthur E. Wise and Linda Darling-Hammond, "Alternative Certification Is an Oxymoron," *Education Week* (September 4, 1991), pp. 56, 46; and Ann Bradley, "Even as Gaps in Data Are Filled, Teacher-Supply Debate Lingers," *Education Week* (September 19, 1990), pp. 1, 14–15.
7. Ibid.
8. David Page, *Theory and Practice of Teaching: Or, the Motives and Methods of Good School-Keeping* (1849), in Tyack, *Turning Points in American Educational History*, p. 412.
9. Theodore M. Hesburgh, "The Future of Liberal Education," *Change* 13 (April 1981): 38–39.
10. Holmes Group, *Tomorrow's Teachers: A Report of the Holmes Group* (East Lansing, MI: Holmes Group, 1986), p. 47.
11. See *The Humanities in American Life: Report of the Commission on the Humanities* (Berkeley: University of California Press, 1980). I base my estimates of the amount of course work allocated to each area of teacher education on an examination of college and university bulletins.
12. U.S. Department of Education, Center for Education Statistics, *The Condition of Education, 1987 Edition* (Washington, D.C.: U.S. Government Printing Office, 1987), p. 48.
13. Robert Rothman, " 'Startling' Data Upset Certification Program for Science Teachers," *Education Week* (September 14, 1986), pp. 1, 15.

14. Diane Ravitch, "Scapegoating the Teachers," in *The Schools We Deserve: Reflections on the Educational Crises of Our Times* (New York: Basic Books, 1985), p. 95.
15. National Commission on Excellence in Education, *A Nation at Risk: The Imperative for Educational Reform* (Washington, D.C.: U.S. Department of Education, 1983), p. 22.
16. For contemporary criticism of teacher education, see C. Emily Feistritzer's, *The Making of a Teacher: A Report on Teacher Education and Certification* (Washington, D.C.: National Center for Education Information, 1984) and Reginald G. Damerell's *Education's Smoking Gun: How Teachers Colleges Have Destroyed Education in America* (New York: Freundlich Books, 1985). A well-balanced "inside" critique by two professors of education is Geraldine Joncich Clifford and James W. Guthrie's *Ed School: A Brief for Professional Education* (Chicago: University of Chicago Press, 1988). Two classic studies from the 1960s are James Bryant Conant's *The Education of American Teachers* (New York: McGraw-Hill, 1963) and James Koerner's *The Miseducation of American Teachers* (Boston: Houghton Mifflin, 1963). See also the earlier studies cited in note 42.
17. Susan Ohanian, "On Stir-and-Serve Recipes for Teaching," *Phi Delta Kappan* 66 (June 1985): 701.
18. Ibid., pp. 697, 699–700.
19. Feistritzer and Chester, *Alternative Teacher Certification,* p. 13.
20. Carnegie Forum on Education and the Economy, *A Nation Prepared: Teachers for the 21st Century* (New York: Carnegie Forum, 1986); Holmes Group, *Tomorrow's Teachers.*
21. Ann Bradley, "While All Agree on Value of Field Experience, Many Say Clinical Training Should Be Redesigned," *Education Week* (March 13, 1991), pp. 17–19, 22–24.
22. Lynn Olson, "Colleges of Education under Increasing Attack as Weak Link in the Drive to Improve Nation's Schools," *Education Week* (December 12, 1990), pp. 13, 25.
23. "Panel to Evaluate Holmes Group's Efforts," *Education Week* (April 11, 1990), p. 7; Lynn Olson, "Holmes Group Reflects on How to Sustain Its Momentum," *Education Week* (December 9, 1987), p. 6.
24. "Teachers," *Education Week* (October 28, 1987), p. 5.
25. Holmes Group, *Tomorrow's Teachers,* p. 95.
26. Lynn Olson, "Colleges of Education," p. 21; Ann Bradley, "Teacher Educators Told to 'Do More,' but with Less Help, New Survey Finds," *Education Week* (March 11, 1992), p. 11.
27. Wise and Darling-Hammond, "Alternative Certification," p. 46.
28. Lynn Olson, "Colleges of Education," pp. 14–15; Olson, "Texas Teacher Educators in Turmoil over Reform Law's 'Encroachment,'" *Education Week* (December 9, 1987), pp. 1, 19.
29. Ronald A. Lindahl and Jorge Descamps, "Texas Reforms Endanger Teacher Effectiveness," *Education Week* (November 11, 1987), pp. 28, 22.
30. Karen Diegmueller and Daniel Gursky, "Texas A&M Teacher Program Wins NCATE Endorsement," *Education Week* (May 20, 1992), p. 8.
31. "Texas Education Schools May Lose Accreditation," *Education Week* (May 24, 1989), p. 5.
32. Blake Rodman, "'Alternate Route' Said a Success," *Education Week* (February 24, 1988), p. 7.
33. Richard J. Murnane, Judith D. Singer, John B. Willett, James J. Kemple, and Randall J. Olsen, *Who Will Teach? Policies that Matter* (Cambridge: Harvard University Press, 1991), pp. 95–99.
34. Wise and Darling-Hammond, "Alternative Certification," p. 56.

35. Murnane et al., *Who Will Teach?,* p. 97; Rodman, " 'Alternate Route.' "
36. Feistritzer and Chester, *Alternative Teacher Certification,* pp. 17–18.
37. Ibid., p. 22; Wise and Darling-Hammond, "Alternative Certification," p. 56.
38. Wise and Darling-Hammond, "Alternative Certification," p. 56.
39. Two of the most widely discussed articles in education journals were W. Timothy Weaver's "In Search of Quality: The Need for Talent in Teaching," *Phi Delta Kappan* 61 (September 1979): 29–32, 46, and Victor S. Vance and Phillip C. Schlechty's "The Distribution of Academic Ability in the Teaching Force: Policy Implications," *Phi Delta Kappan* 64 (September 1982): 22–27. For criticism in the popular press, see "Teachers Are in Trouble," *Newsweek* (April 27, 1981), pp. 78–79, 81, 83–84.
40. National Commission on Excellence in Education, *A Nation at Risk,* p. 22.
41. These points are highlighted in several chapters of Donald R. Warren's *American Teachers: Histories of a Profession at Work* (New York: Macmillan, 1989).
42. Mortimer Smith, *And Madly Teach* (Chicago: Regnery, 1949); Albert Lynd, *Quackery in the Public Schools* (Boston: Little, Brown, 1953).
43. Weaver, "In Search of Quality"; Vance and Schlechty, "The Distribution of Academic Ability"; Michael Sedlak and Steven Schlossman, *Who Will Teach? Historical Perspectives on the Changing Appeal of Teaching as a Profession* (Santa Monica, CA: Rand Corp., November 1986).
44. Joseph W. Newman, "Reconstructing the World of Southern Teachers," *History of Education Quarterly* 24 (Winter 1984): 585–595.
45. U.S. Department of Education, National Center for Education Statistics, *The Condition of Education, 1992,* p. 28; U.S. Department of Education, National Center for Education Statistics, *The Condition of Education, 1991,* vol. 2 (Washington, D.C.: U.S. Government Printing Office, 1991), pp. 38–39; Patricia Albjerg Graham, "Black Teachers: A Drastically Scarce Resource," *Phi Delta Kappan* 68 (April 1987): 598–605.
46. Richard J. Coley and Margaret E. Goertz, *Educational Standards in the 50 States: 1990* (Princeton, NJ: Educational Testing Service, 1990), pp. 10–15.
47. Richard Mitchell, "Testing the Teachers: The Dallas Experiment," *Atlantic Monthly* (December 1978), pp. 66–70.
48. U.S. Department of Education, Office of Educational Research and Improvement, *What's Happening in Teacher Testing: An Analysis of State Teacher Testing Practices* (Washington, D.C.: U.S. Government Printing Office, 1987), pp. 5, 7, 36–37.
49. William A. Mehrens and Irving J. Lehmann, *Measurement and Evaluation in Education and Psychology,* 3d ed. (New York: Holt, Rinehart & Winston, 1984), chap. 13.
50. U.S. Department of Education, *What's Happening in Teacher Testing,* p. 5.
51. William J. Webster, "The Validation of a Teacher Selection System," paper presented at the annual meeting of the American Educational Research Association, Boston, April 1980; Thomas S. Tocco and Jane K. Elligett, "On the Cutting Edge: The Pinellas County Teacher Applicant Screening Program," *The Board* (Winter 1980): 5.
52. Holmes Group, *Tomorrow's Teachers,* p. 4.
53. See Carnegie Forum, *A Nation Prepared,* pp. 79–87.
54. Philip C. Schlechty and Victor S. Vance, "Institutional Responses to the Quality/Quantity Issue in Teacher Testing," *Phi Delta Kappan* 65 (October 1983): 101; Vance and Schlechty, "The Distribution of Academic Ability in the Teaching Force," *Phi Delta Kappan* 65 (October 1983): 25, 27.
55. Patricia M. Lines, "Testing the Teacher: Are There Legal Pitfalls?" *Phi Delta Kappan* 66 (May 1985): 618–622; W. James Popham and W. N. Kirby, "Recertification Tests for Teachers: A Defensible Safeguard for Society," *Phi Delta Kappan* 69 (September

1987): 45–49; U.S. Department of Education, *What's Happening in Teacher Testing*, pp. 15–17; and Blake Rodman, "Testing Practicing Teachers: The Battle Nobody Really Won?," *Education Week* (March 16, 1988), pp. 1, 13.

56. For a critical look at the ETS, read Allan Nairn and associates' *The Reign of ETS: The Corporation that Makes Up Minds* (Washington, D.C.: Ralph Nader Report on the Educational Testing Service, 1980). The board of trustees of ETS defends the organization in *1984 Public Accountability Report* (Princeton, NJ: ETS, 1984).

57. George F. Madaus and Diana Pullin, "Teacher Certification Tests: Do They Really Measure What We Need to Know?" *Phi Delta Kappan* 69 (September 1987): 31–38.

58. See Martha L. Bell and Catherine V. Morsink, "Quality and Equity in the Preparation of Black Teachers," *Journal of Teacher Education* 37 (March–April 1986): 17–18.

59. E. D. Hirsch, Jr., *Cultural Literacy: What Every American Needs to Know* (Boston: Houghton Mifflin, 1987); Allan Bloom, *The Closing of the American Mind* (New York: Simon & Schuster, 1987).

60. U.S. Department of Education, *What's Happening in Teacher Testing*, pp. 135–138.

61. David Owen critiques multiple-choice testing in *None of the Above* (Boston: Houghton Mifflin, 1985).

62. To appreciate the struggle, read Lee S. Shulman's "Knowledge and Teaching: Foundations of the New Reform," *Harvard Educational Review* 57 (February 1987): 1–22; and Hugh T. Sockett's "Has Shulman Got the Strategy Right?," *Harvard Educational Review* 57 (May 1987): 208–219.

63. See Karen Diegmueller, "Revamped NCATE Post Highs, Lows in Tides of Teacher-Education Reform," *Education Week* (February 26, 1992), pp. 1, 12–13, 15.

64. Linda Darling-Hammond, "Teaching Knowledge: How Do We Test It?" *American Educator* 10 (Fall 1986): 18–21, 46.

65. Ibid.

66. Educational Testing Service, *Working Papers toward a New Generation of Teacher Assessments* (Princeton, NJ: ETS, 1990).

67. See Karen Diegmueller, "E.T.S. Previews Revamped Examination for Teachers," *Education Week* (September 12, 1990), pp. 1, 13.

68. Ibid., p. 13.

69. National Board for Professional Teaching Standards, *1991 Annual Report* (Detroit: NBPTS, 1992), p. 8.

70. Ibid.

71. Ibid., p. 10.

72. For an insightful essay comparing the development of professionalism in medicine and teaching, see William R. Johnson's "Empowering Practitioners: Holmes, Carnegie, and the Lessons of the Past," *History of Education Quarterly* 27 (Summer 1987): 221–240.

73. John Hope Franklin, "The Desperate Need for Black Teachers," *Change* 19 (May–June 1987): 44–45; Barbara J. Holmes, "Do Not Buy the Conventional Wisdom: Minority Teachers Can Pass the Tests," *Journal of Negro Education* 55 (Summer 1986): 335–346.

74. U.S. Department of Education, National Center for Education Statistics, *The Condition of Education, 1991*, vol. 1 (Washington, D.C.: U.S. Government Printing Office, 1991), p. 68; National Education Association, *Status of the American Public School Teacher, 1990–1991* (Washington, D.C.: NEA, 1992), p. 78; Graham, "Black teachers," pp. 599, 605.

75. U.S. Department of Education, *The Condition of Education, 1992*, p. 28; Graham, "Black Teachers," pp. 605, 602.

76. Graham, "Black Teachers," p. 600; "Update," *Education Week* (September 10, 1986), p. 23; "Board Dumps Teacher Test," *Mobile Register* (July 13, 1988), p. 2B.
77. Graham, "Black Teachers," p. 601.
78. Ibid., pp. 603–604; Blake Rodman, "At Grambling: 'Fighting the Scores instead of the Tests,'" *Education Week* (November 20, 1985), p. 13.
79. Graham, "Black teachers," pp. 603–604.
80. National Education Association, *Status of the American Public School Teacher,* pp. 78, 176.
81. John I. Goodlad, *Teachers for Our Nation's Schools* (San Francisco: Jossey-Bass, 1990); Goodlad, Roger Soder, and Kenneth A. Sirotnik, eds., *The Moral Dimensions of Teaching* (San Francisco: Jossey-Bass, 1990); Goodlad, Soder, and Sirotnik, eds., *Places Where Teachers Are Taught* (San Francisco: Jossey-Bass, 1990).
82. Goodlad, *Teachers for Our Nation's Schools,* p. 61.
83. Ibid., p. 294.

# CHAPTER 4

# Joining a Teacher Organization and Empowering a Profession

*Joining [is] the professional thing to do. . . . We have three important responsibilities. Foremost, as always, is to carry out our role in educating our young people. . . . The second responsibility is to keep education in the limelight to point out ways to improve our schools. . . . Our third responsibility is to be involved politically as never before. We have friends of education to elect.*

—Alabama teacher[1]

*Recently I was involved with the statewide teachers' strike. . . . Our governor was made fun of and his plans were given sarcastic names. These kinds of tactics anger me to no end. . . . I am embarrassed to be associated with a teachers' group that uses such tactics.*

—Washington State teacher[2]

In the first three chapters, I have tried to paint a realistic picture of teaching as an occupation. The picture is not exactly rosy. America's teachers have their share of problems. The idealism and commitment new teachers bring to their work can vanish in the face of low salaries, poor working conditions, public doubts about teacher competency, and lingering questions about teacher education.

As I keep pointing out, though, a realistic assessment of the occupation does not have to be a hopeless assessment. Taking an honest look at their mutual problems encourages many teachers to seek solutions by working together in teacher organizations.

One of the first decisions you will make as a public school teacher is whether to join one of the two major organizations: the National Education Association (NEA) and the American Federation of Teachers (AFT). This chapter opens with a look at their similarities and differences and continues with a discussion of their strategies. Both the NEA and the AFT use *collective bargaining* and *political action* in their efforts to upgrade teaching as an occupation, and therein lies one of the great controversies of public education.

If you talk with people about the NEA and AFT, you will find few teachers (or other informed citizens, for that matter) have neutral opinions, because these organizations have a clear vision of what they want, and they pursue their vision aggressively. The AFT and NEA have helped shatter the "Miss Brooks" and "Mr. Chips" images of teachers as beloved servants. They would like to replace this image with one of teachers as competent professionals. No popular characters from books or the electronic media have completely captured that image, for teachers are still in the process of creating it.

Bringing the professional teacher to life will require a complete restructuring of the occupation, which is exactly what the NEA and AFT are trying to do. They do not use the word *professional* lightly. They want to win for teachers the rights and responsibilities society now reserves for physicians, lawyers, and members of a few other occupations. To some people, making teaching a profession represents the best hope for improving the public schools; to others, it is educational heresy. In the conclusion of this chapter we will explore why the goal of professionalism is so controversial and why it has eluded teachers for so long.


## NEA AND AFT

Throughout most of this century, the NEA and AFT have been in competition to organize America's teachers. Until the 1960s, the two groups were quite different. The NEA was a large, mild-mannered "professional association" that was better at collecting information, issuing reports, and talking about teachers' problems than at taking action to solve them. The AFT was a small, scrappy "union" that was trying hard but making little progress toward improving teachers' salaries, benefits, and working conditions.

Things changed during the 1960s and 1970s as the longstanding rivalry between the two intensified. The AFT's militant tactics began making sense to more teachers, its membership figures soared, and the NEA's "tea-sipping" ways seemed behind the times. Since then, the organizations have become much more alike—that is, the NEA has become militant, too—but several key differences remain, differences significant enough to keep the two from merging.[3]

Before we look at how the organizations differ, though, it is important to note how much they have in common. Today the AFT and NEA are both unions whose major goals are increasing the economic security of public school teachers and improving their working conditions. Both groups pursue these goals by looking after teachers' interests in the political area and, in most states, by representing teachers in collective bargaining sessions with school boards. Both are also professional associations that take stands on a variety of issues affecting students, teachers, and public education generally, issues ranging from the curriculum to teacher education to the federal budget. Convinced that a stronger teacher voice in *all* educational decisions can only improve the schools, both groups believe in teacher power. Above all, the AFT and NEA say they are trying to make public school teaching a true profession.

## Four Key Differences

But the similarities mentioned above obscure important differences in size, geographical strength, official positions on major issues, and labor relations. We will look at each of these in turn.

First, there is the matter of *size*. The NEA has about 2,100,000 members, the AFT about 750,000. The NEA, the largest union/employee organization/ professional association of any kind in the entire world, argues that its size gives it more clout. The AFT, pointing to its dramatic recent growth—it is more than 12 times as large today as in 1960—claims to represent the wave of the future. Both organizations recruit members from outside the ranks of teachers, encouraging paraprofessionals, support personnel, college professors, and others in the education field to join, but more than 70 percent of the members in both are classroom teachers. Overall, the NEA has organized about 60 percent of America's public school teachers, the AFT about 20 percent.[4]

Whether you join the AFT or NEA (or neither) may depend on where you teach, for the second difference between the two is their *geographical strength*. The AFT is essentially a big-city union, while the NEA dominates in suburban, small-town, and rural areas. The AFT, as a member of the American Federation of Labor–Congress of Industrial Organizations (AFL-CIO), the umbrella labor organization in the United States, has always been most successful where the labor movement is strongest and best established—in such major cities as New York, Chicago, Pittsburgh, Cleveland, Detroit, and St. Louis. Even though the AFT now has about 2,500 local affiliates, or "locals" (a good union word), and 22 state federations, there are so few members in some school systems—indeed, in some entire states—the organization has virtually no power there.

The NEA, by contrast, has associations in every state and more than 10,000 local affiliates, most of which now call themselves locals. The NEA boasts of its grassroots strength throughout the United States, proud of having brought together more than half the nation's highly diverse teaching force in one organization. Doing so has been no easy task. While the AFT has always required teachers to become local, state (if possible), and national members, the NEA has required "unified" membership only since the 1970s. Some of the NEA's state and local associations are well over a century old, and many teachers maintain stronger loyalties to their state and local associations than to the national. Some NEA members try to distance themselves from the national association, complaining that the NEA's politics are "too liberal" or its policies "too militant." The unified NEA is powerful, to be sure, but the diversity of which it is so proud can be a source of weakness as well as strength.[5]

The third difference between the organizations lies in their *official positions on major issues*. Although both make policy democratically—delegates elected in the locals come together in national summer conventions to confer, debate, and vote—since the mid-1970s, the NEA has been more willing than the AFT to take stands on broad social and political issues that, while not strictly educational, have an impact on the schools. These "human and civil rights issues" range from family planning to gun control to nuclear war. Most of the NEA's standards are considered liberal, which is ironic since the NEA has historically had the reputation of a moderate-to-conservative association while the AFT has been the liberal-to-radical union.[6]

Before the 1960s, for example, the NEA dragged its feet on race relations. It did not merge with the all-black American Teachers Association (ATA) until 1966, and some of the NEA's state and local affiliates in the South remained segregated until the late 1970s. The AFT, on the other hand, went on record in support of desegregation well before the landmark *Brown* decision (1954) and required its locals to desegregate in 1956. Standing history on its head, today's NEA is one of the nation's strongest advocates of minority rights—including affirmative action—while the AFT carefully positions itself in the middle of the road.[7]

On educational issues, the two organizations agree far more often than they disagree, but during the 1980s and 1990s, several important differences emerged. As the tide of conservatism that swept the nation reached the schools, the NEA dug in its heels and stuck to its longstanding opposition to merit pay and competency tests for currently employed teachers, while the AFT has been willing to compromise. As we saw in the last chapter, the AFT is more supportive of the Carnegie Forum and Holmes Group recommendations on how to restructure the occupation. Regarding trends in the public school curriculum, the NEA is sharply critical of the heavy emphasis on standardized testing, arguing that it denies a quality education to many, especially to poor and minority students. The AFT accepts more emphasis on testing as a necessary part of the drive toward "excellence in education," although it does admit testing can be overdone. Overall, the NEA takes a skeptical—some would say obstructionist—view of many recent educational reforms, while the AFT takes a hopeful—some would say opportunistic—view.

*Relations with the larger labor movement,* an issue we have already discussed briefly, are important enough to deserve separate consideration as a fourth difference between the NEA and AFT. Since its founding in 1957 as the National Teachers' Association, the NEA has been quite status conscious, billing itself as "professional" in an attempt to distinguish teachers from mere "workers." Thus, until recently, the NEA steered clear of organized labor.

The AFT, by contrast, has been affiliated with the American Federation of Labor since just after the AFT's founding in 1916. The AFT has always insisted that teachers are workers who aspire to be professionals. According to the AFT, joining a union and expressing solidarity with other workers does not make teachers less professional. Teachers and other workers can find strength in numbers in their mutual quest for better salaries, benefits, and working conditions, and the labor movement can support teachers as they try to gain the control over their occupation that physicians and lawyers have over theirs.

Until the 1960s, few teachers paid much attention to the AFT's calls to unionize. The NEA deliberately and effectively exploited antilabor sentiment, telling teachers they would be stooping to the level of blue-collar workers if they joined the AFT, "that labor union." Even after the NEA itself began using the tactics of organized labor, the association was reluctant to sew the union label into its jacket. Frankly, many NEA members are still uncomfortable with the label, especially those who live where organized labor is unpopular.[8]

But today's NEA *is* a union, recognized as such by the U.S. Department of Labor. The NEA is also a member of the Coalition of American Public Employees (CAPE), an organization whose major goal is winning collective bargaining rights for all public employees. Thus the NEA has, in a sense, joined the labor movement, but it refuses to join the AFL-CIO, arguing that doing so would compromise its independence. The AFT, for its part, refuses to leave the AFL-CIO, and this difference has frustrated efforts to merge the NEA and AFT.[9]

Still, the prospects of a merger look brighter in the 1990s than they have in decades. AFT president Albert Shanker and NEA president Keith Geiger have met and announced their willingness to consider the move. Like many of their members, the two leaders agree that teachers should belong to one organization and speak with one voice. The late 1980s saw the merger of the NEA and AFT locals in San Francisco, and in the early 1990s, the state affiliates of the two organizations in Wisconsin and Minnesota voted to explore the possibilities of merging. After years of often-bitter rivalry, these moves may be the harbingers of a new era in teacher unionism.[10]

## Labor, Management, and Gender

The list of differences between the NEA and the AFT was once much longer. One difference that has lost much of its significance is the NEA's willingness to admit school administrators as members.

Throughout most of the NEA's history, its administrative members, although only a small fraction of the association's total, aligned themselves with the even-smaller group of college professors and effectively ran the show. The NEA's internal structure virtually duplicated the larger structure of public education: A few administrators, mostly males, held sway over a large number of teachers, mostly females. The men who ran the NEA were the same men who ran the public schools. Most teachers joined the association not because they wanted to but because their superintendents and principals said to. Until power began to shift away from administrators in the 1960s, the NEA was not truly a *teacher* organization.[11]

Since then, classroom teachers have taken control of the NEA. As the organization has grown militant on *bread-and-butter issues*—another good union term encompassing salaries, benefits, and working conditions—many administrators have grown uneasy and left. Most of those who remain play minor roles.

This changing of the guard has been a source of much amusement to the AFT, which classroom teachers have always controlled. Some of the key leaders of the early AFT were women with a strong commitment to feminist causes, from voting rights to social and economic equality. Their struggle to make the voice of teachers heard in education was part of the larger struggle to make the voice of women heard in society. Although men eventually displaced women in the federation's leadership, the AFT—like other unions—has always drawn a line between workers and managers, arguing that their outlook, interests, and work are fundamentally different. According to the AFT, teachers cannot be expected to stand up for their rights in an organization controlled by their bosses.[12]

Only recently has the NEA come around to this adversarial, labor-versus-management point of view, and some members still find it hard to accept. In many rural and small-town districts, administrators still encourage teachers to join "our professional association, the NEA." In these districts, administrators and teachers enjoy a comfortable (if paternalistic) relationship, and teacher militancy is something that takes place only in the newspapers. The point to remember is that although gone are the days when administrators dominated the NEA and required teachers to join, rural and small-town systems are still a world apart from Chicago and New York.

## What Membership Means

Joining the NEA or AFT means different things in different systems. In some, it is a statement of militant professionalism; in others, an expression of concern with bread-and-butter issues; in others, a means of self-protection; in still others, just the thing to do. As a new teacher, you should find out what the organizations stand for in your state and your school system. If both groups are viable and actively competing for members, find out what one can do for you that the other cannot. You will probably discover both are proud, and rightly so, of what they have won for teachers through local, state, and national political activity. Ask what they have done about salaries, class sizes, preparation periods, noninstructional duties, and other matters that will affect your daily life as a teacher.

As you listen to their recruitment pitches, you will find that both organizations offer their members a wide range of services. The NEA publishes *NEA Today, Today's Education, NEA Research Bulletin,* and numerous other periodicals, while the AFT's publications include *American Teacher* and *American Educator.* Although the NEA is more involved in research and publication at the national level, members of both groups receive a variety of materials from their state and local organizations. State and local newsletters often contain information of immediate concern to teachers: job market news, recent court decisions, the status of education bills in the state legislature, activities in the local schools, and so forth.

Both the AFT and NEA offer their members life and supplemental health insurance and, more important, liability insurance that provides protection in lawsuits arising from job-related activities. Often one of the first things a teacher hears from NEA and AFT representatives is, "You'll wish you were a member if a student has an accident in your classroom and you get sued." As we will see in chapter 5, that message is fair warning, but it sometimes puts off teachers who think such things happen only to other people.

Both organizations will tell you that their local, state, and national dues, which usually total between $300 and $400 per year, are a sound investment. Ask for specific ways in which the investment has paid dividends. Something AFT and NEA representatives will certainly discuss with you in most school systems is collective bargaining, for both organizations would like to be your bargaining agent in negotiations with school boards.

## COLLECTIVE BARGAINING

Seated along one side of a long, narrow table are representatives of the teachers in a school system. Facing them across the table are representatives of the board of education. At issue is the master contract for the system's teachers, a thick document of more than 100 pages, and today the discussion is focused on new teachers' starting salary. Reminding the board of teacher shortages and stressing the importance of attracting capable people to the occupation, the teacher representatives ask for a raise of $1,000. The board representatives reply they are well aware of the supply-and-demand situation, but they are also aware of the tight budget.

A thousand dollars? Extravagant. Out of the question. Two hundred would be more like it. The negotiations wear on into the evening and into the days and nights that follow. No one is completely satisfied with the compromise raise of $450, but both sides feel pressured to work through the rest of the contract, which spells out teacher salaries, benefits, working conditions, and grievance procedures in great detail.

Most American public school teachers bargain with their school boards in sessions similar to this one. Twenty-eight states have laws outlining a collective bargaining process borrowed directly from labor-management relations. Teacher representatives and board representatives try to reach agreement on the terms of a contract, and if they are unable to agree, there are provisions for resolving the impasse. Thirteen states specify a milder form of bargaining that requires school boards to "meet and confer" with teachers. Here board members must listen to teachers in a formal session, but the boards retain the decision-making power. Six states have no laws on collective bargaining in the public schools, but some local boards in these states negotiate with teachers on a limited basis. Only three states, Mississippi, North Carolina, and Texas, prohibit collective bargaining for teachers.[13]

### AFT Points the Way

The AFT pioneered collective bargaining in public education. Its success with the practice not only helped the federation grow but also pushed the rival NEA toward unionism.

In the late 1950s, the AFT mounted an organizing campaign in the New York City schools in an effort to get the union moving again. At the time, New York's 50,000 teachers were splintered into a bewildering array of organizations according to their subjects and grade levels. The AFT's strategy, engineered by former high school teacher Albert Shanker and other experienced union leaders, was to hit hard on bread-and-butter issues common to all teachers, bring them together in a single unit, and win the right to bargain collectively with the board of education.[14]

After a bitter struggle punctuated by a one-day strike in November 1960, the board agreed to a collective bargaining election. In 1961, New York's teachers endorsed bargaining by a 3-to-1 margin and voted to be represented by AFT Local 2, the United Federation of Teachers. Local 2 won the right to bargain for the city's entire teaching force.

The AFT's victory went into the record books as a turning point in the history of teacher organizations. Teacher militancy spread quickly, first to other big cities and then beyond. During the 1960s and 1970s, the AFT grew four times as fast as the NEA. Albert Shanker went on to become president of the AFT, an office he still holds. The NEA had no choice but to take notice. After first trying to dismiss the AFT's militancy as "unprofessional," the NEA gradually followed suit.[15]

Today both organizations believe collective bargaining, combined with political action, offers the best hope for improving salaries, benefits, and working conditions. Both groups also regard the combination of bargaining and politics as the best strategy for professionalizing public school teaching.

## How Bargaining Works

The mechanics of collective bargaining are not difficult to understand. First, the teachers in a school system choose a union to represent them. Usually, the teachers vote by secret ballot; in other cases, they fill out authorization cards, or the locals competing for representation submit membership lists. The union that wins the support of the majority of teachers becomes the exclusive bargaining agent for all teachers in the system. (Some states allow the school board to negotiate with more than one local representing teachers, but this procedure is rare because it is time consuming and divisive.) The exclusive bargaining agent has the obligation to represent every teacher fairly—a tall order, since some teachers may be members of a rival union and others of no union. Most states have regulations to ensure that the bargaining union takes the interests of both members and nonmembers into account.[16]

In over half the states, *agency shop* or *fair share* contracts may require teachers who are not members of the bargaining union to pay the local a fee, generally the same amount as union dues. This fee reimburses the local for its work as the teachers' bargaining agent. But that means compulsory unionism, some teachers charge, arguing that these regulations force them in effect to join the union whether or not they want to, running roughshod over their freedom of choice. Prounionists reply that since the local is obligated to negotiate on behalf of all teachers, and since nonmembers and members alike reap the benefits won through bargaining, all teachers should share the costs. Although the U.S. Supreme Court has ruled agency shop regulations constitutional, the National Right to Work Committee, through its branch the Concerned Educators against Forced Unionism, is waging an ongoing battle against them.[17]

Once teachers have selected their bargaining agent, the union and the school board choose negotiating teams. In small school districts, a team of teachers (often the union officers) sits down at the table and talks directly with members of the board. In some districts, administrators are part of the board's team; in others, administrators have their own unions. As unions and boards become more sophisticated with collective bargaining, they usually seek the advice of lawyers who specialize in labor-management relations. The larger the school district, the more likely both sides are to call in even more outside help, with unions looking to their state and national offices and boards looking to their state and national associations. Both sides may also employ professional negotiators.

The bargaining process, more often than not, is long and slow. Occasional flashes of insight and humor lighten up the tedious deliberations. Usually, the process results in a new contract that all board members and all teachers have the right to examine and ratify.

If the two sides reach an impasse, most states have laws that outline steps for breaking the deadlock. The first step is typically mediation, in which a neutral third party makes suggestions in an attempt to promote a compromise. The mediator, whose recommendations are usually not made public, cannot mandate a solution. If mediation fails, fact finding is a second step. After both sides argue their cases before a fact-finding panel, the panel usually goes public with a set of recommendations that pressure the board and union to agree; however, the fact finders cannot dictate an agreement. Under binding arbitration, a third step in some states, the two sides agree to give a third party, chosen by mutual consent, the power to investigate their dispute and impose a solution.[18]

## What Bargaining Covers

The scope of collective bargaining varies considerably from district to district and state to state, but salaries, benefits, and working conditions are the bottom line. Some union leaders are content to negotiate bread-and-butter issues, for they know many *rank-and-file* teachers (yet another union term) want their bargaining agent to deliver the economic goods, period. Other leaders with broader goals envision the day when collective bargaining will give teachers a voice in virtually every policy decision in the public schools—from the content of the curriculum to teacher evaluation plans.[19]

As we will see later in this chapter, these leaders' vision is becoming a reality in some school systems. The eyes of teacher unionists throughout the nation are on the contracts recently negotiated in Rochester, Toledo, Miami–Dade County, Cincinnati, Albuquerque, Boston, Pittsburgh, and other urban districts. These contracts empower teachers with some of the rights and responsibilities Carnegie and Holmes recommend.[20]

Now there is talk of collective bargaining entering a new phase as teachers press toward "professional unionism." In the near future, all the cards may be on the table as teachers, administrators, and board members share power voluntarily, emphasizing cooperation rather than confrontation.[21]

To teachers in school districts that do not bargain at all, this vision seems remote indeed. Rochester, New York, and Raleigh, North Carolina, are two different worlds. Tough political battles lie ahead for teacher unionists who want to expand the scope of negotiations and extend bargaining rights to more teachers. The AFT and NEA support federal legislation that would allow every public school teacher in the nation to bargain. Opponents counter that such a law would violate states' rights and hand over control of public education to teacher unions. On balance, though, collective bargaining seems destined to stay, expand, and eventually involve teacher unions and school boards throughout the nation in the process of give and take.

## TEACHER STRIKES

Unions, bargaining, and strikes go together in the public's mind. When students return to school every fall, the news media run stories about teacher strikes, usually playing up those staged by AFT locals in big-city systems. "Do Chicago teachers strike every year?" one of my students asked me recently (and quite seriously). As many people see the situation, unions strike when they cannot get their way at the bargaining table, causing employers and often the public to suffer.

This analysis overlooks the fact that teachers who do not have collective bargaining rights also go on strike. A rash of teacher strikes broke out during the years of rapid inflation following World War II, well before the rise of collective bargaining in public education, and some strikes still occur in school systems that do not bargain. In fact, teachers in such systems say requiring board members to sit down, listen, and negotiate might well prevent strikes. To be sure, the AFT made its breakthrough in the 1960s by bargaining; threatening to strike; and, in some cases, carrying out its threats—but bargaining is not the *cause* of strikes.[22]

Instead, teacher frustration with low salaries and poor working conditions, aggravated by a sense of powerlessness, made teachers turn to collective bargaining in the first place and to strikes as a last resort. The state of the economy plays a leading role. Teacher strikes peaked during the double-digit inflation of the late 1970s and early 1980s, when increases in the cost of living far outstripped increases in teacher salaries. In 1979–1980 alone, AFT affiliates staged 34 strikes and NEA affiliates struck 208 times. During the mid- to late 1980s, with lower inflation and better raises, teacher strikes decreased to fewer than 100 per year, with most called by the NEA. The conservative national mood of the Reagan years, which spawned a get-tough-with-unions attitude, also made teachers less willing to strike.[23]

Now the economic turbulence of the 1990s is ushering in another era of labor unrest in the teaching force. As state and local governments reduce public education spending, many teachers see their salaries and working conditions absorbing a disproportionate share of the cutbacks. Strikes are increasing once again, although the yearly totals remain at less than half those of the late 1970s and early 1980s.[24]

Given the more than 15,000 local school districts in the United Sates, even the 242 strikes of 1979–1980 could hardly be called a runaway problem. Teachers, like other public employees, are aware of how much is at stake when they strike.

Strikes, risky under any circumstances, are literally desperate measures. Although the trend in state law is toward giving teachers a limited right to strike, in about half the states teacher strikes are still against the law, and the U.S. Supreme

Court has ruled school boards can fire teachers who engage in illegal strikes. Judges can levy fines against unions and individual teachers who strike illegally; in rare instances, striking teachers can find themselves in jail. Strikes can also alienate parents and the general public. Beyond these problems, teachers face an ethical question when they strike: Can they justify denying students the opportunity to learn?[25]

Rest assured that teachers who decide to strike do think seriously about these issues. Striking teachers gamble that the school board will not fire them in large numbers because of the difficulty in finding replacements. In some cases, teachers are willing to take the risk because they have community support. Conditions are so bad in some school districts that parents and other citizens side with teachers against the board. Other unions sometimes lend their support, especially if an AFT local is on strike.

Ethically, some teachers believe the short-term losses for students are outweighed by long-term gains for the whole school system. As the AFT and NEA like to point out, better salaries and benefits attract better teachers, and improving teachers' working conditions also improves students' learning conditions. If school boards force teachers to strike to reach those goals, the unions reason, then so be it.[26]

## POLITICAL ACTION

Less dangerous, if nearly as controversial, political action is a strategy teachers use to attain the same goals. As we will see in chapters 6 and 9, U.S. public schools have always been involved in politics. Tax revenues support the schools, public officials govern the schools, and teachers compete for a share of power and influence.

When administrators controlled the NEA, the association engaged in "dignified" political activity, lobbying Congress for federal aid to education and other measures. The NEA's state affiliates worked quietly with legislatures and school boards to secure tenure laws, retirement benefits, and health and sick leave provisions.[27]

The AFT also lobbied Congress, and some of its locals were deeply involved in city and state politics. Leaders of the more powerful AFT locals—such as Chicago, New York, and Atlanta—mastered the political arts only to encounter opposition from both the public and their own members. Many citizens argued, and some teachers agreed, that it was undignified and unprofessional for teacher organizations to engage in politics if that meant such things as supporting candidates for office and taking stands on political issues.

But since the 1970s, the NEA and AFT have done exactly that. Undignified behavior? Not unless the entire way we govern ourselves in the United States is undignified, teacher unionists answer. Politics is the name of the game, and during the 1970s, teachers realized the members of almost every organized occupational group were playing the game. Some groups—physicians, lawyers, farmers, manufacturers—had been playing it seriously and successfully for years.

Unprofessional behavior? Quite the contrary, say the unionists, for teachers are using politics to win more control over their occupation, and control is the very essence of professionalism.[28]

Today, it is difficult to find a professional association or union more active in U.S. politics than the NEA or the AFT. At all three levels of government—federal, state, and local—teacher organizations operate with clout and sophistication. In 1976, the NEA broke long years of official silence on presidential elections by endorsing the Democratic ticket of Jimmy Carter and Walter Mondale. Since then, candidates for the Democratic presidential nomination have eagerly courted both the NEA and the AFT. The two organizations now maintain a high profile in races for the U.S. Senate and House of Representatives. Candidates for state office, from governors to legislators, come under the unions' political scrutiny. So do aspiring local politicians, from mayors to school board members.[29]

## PACs

Both the NEA and AFT have political action committees (PACs) to raise money through teachers' voluntary contributions. Together, the teacher PACs collect more than $5 million to be spent on federal campaigns during a given two-year presidential election cycle, with the NEA-PAC typically outraising the AFT's Committee on Political Education (COPE) by about 3 to 1. The NEA may have the larger war chest, but both organizations are able to make direct contributions of as much as $10,000, the maximum federal law allows, to endorsed Senate or House candidates—$5,000 in a primary and $5,000 in a general election. Indirect contributions to candidates—providing volunteers and equipment for a telephone bank, for instance, or funding a "Friends of" campaign—can run to $100,000 or more.[30]

This level of political activity is high enough to get the candidates' attention, to say the least, and the NEA and AFT believe endorsements and contributions make elected officials more likely to act in the interest of teachers. Considering the competition teachers face in their quest for power and influence, both organizations have matured politically in an amazingly short time. The NEA's contributions usually rank it among the top four federal PACs in the nation, trailing only such groups as the National Association of Realtors, the International Brotherhood of Teamsters, and the American Medical Association. The AFT generally ranks among the top 30 federal PACs.[31]

State and local affiliates of the NEA and AFT also raise substantial sums through PACs, enabling the unions to have clout in state, city, and county governments. In agricultural states, for instance, organized teachers often do battle with the farm bureau and forestry association over school taxes, while in industrial states, teacher unions may square off against manufacturers and bankers associations.

## Who Gets Endorsed

It should come as no surprise that most of the candidates teacher organizations endorse are moderate to liberal and Democratic, for such politicians tend to be prounion and willing to "invest in public education," which is a nice way of saying they are willing to spend more money on the schools. The NEA and AFT have stuck with Democratic presidential tickets despite their unimpressive showing against Republicans in the 1980, 1984, and 1988 elections. True to the pattern set during the 1980s, George Bush and Dan Quayle made a point of *not* seeking the support of teacher unions during the 1992 campaign, while Bill Clinton and Al Gore pursued and won the endorsements. This time, the Democrats also won the election.[32]

Teacher organizations have posted a more consistent record in congressional elections, where candidates who are Democratic and less conservative have a better chance of winning. More than 75 percent of the congressional candidates endorsed by the NEA during the 1980s and 1990s, for instance, have been elected. The NEA boasts that it has an average of 6,000 members in every congressional district—a formidable political force.[33]

Does this mean every teacher unionist is a moderate-to-liberal Democrat who votes accordingly? No. Teachers have diverse political views and party affiliations, and polls taken during the 1980s and 1990s suggest almost as many teachers vote for Republican presidential candidates as for their Democratic opponents. But bread-and-butter issues are usually the decisive factors in political endorsements, just as they are in collective bargaining. Faced with one candidate committed to holding down taxes and social spending and another candidate more willing to raise taxes and increase spending, the NEA and AFT have little difficulty choosing the latter.[34]

## Grassroots Politics and Teacher Power

Today, both organizations are digging in at the grassroots level, paying more attention than ever to local school board, state school board, state legislative, and gubernatorial races. AFT and NEA locals invite candidates to screening sessions in which teachers ask point-blank questions: How will you vote on teacher salary increases? On raising retirement benefits? Where do you stand on agency shop regulations? On raising state taxes? Based on the candidates' answers, teachers vote whether or not to make an endorsement in the various races and decide how much to contribute to each endorsed candidate.

After attending one such session, I was impressed by how forceful were the teachers and how polite were the candidates—in this case would-be state legislatures. After the candidates left, a frank discussion took place, the teachers voted, and the treasurer of the local association sat down to write out checks of several hundred dollars each. Weren't teachers simply buying politicians? I asked several members. They replied that the candidates were "making the rounds. Last night they went to the chamber of commerce; tomorrow night they'll be at the bar association; next week they'll visit the labor council and farm bureau. Why should teachers sit on the sidelines when everyone else is playing the game?"

Teacher organizations see political action and collective bargaining as complementary strategies—both are roads to power. Teachers exercise power indirectly by endorsing political candidates and lobbying in Congress and state legislatures. Teachers wield power directly when they bargain with school boards. Both strategies are controversial because they give power to a group that historically has had little.

Discussions of teacher power inevitably lead to questions about professionalism: What are the characteristics of a profession? To what degree does teaching have those characteristics? Can political action and collective bargaining make teaching more professional? The next section explores these questions.

## A TEACHING PROFESSION?

Because *profession* has such a nice ring, people use the word in a variety of ways. The question "What is your profession?" may simply mean "What kind of work do you do?" Some people use *professional* in an attempt to add status and prestige to an occupation. Thus we hear of professional entertainers and professional secretaries. To other people, a professional is anyone who excels in a particular occupation—a highly professional mechanic or salesperson, for instance.

If we apply more stringent criteria, though, only a few occupations qualify as professions. Medicine, law, and theology—the oldest and most familiar—were originally called the learned professions. Dentistry, architecture, and engineering are among the other occupations that have established themselves as professions.[35]

Developments in medicine and law over the last 150 years have set the modern standards for professionalism, but only in this century have doctors and lawyers become fully professional, organizing and controlling their occupations in ways that distinguish them from other types of work. Based on comparative studies of many occupations, sociologists have developed a set of characteristics to define the professions. They have paid particular attention to medicine, often referring to it as the "prototype" profession because medicine exhibits the characteristics to a greater degree than any other occupation.[36]

We can distill the discussion of professionalism in the sociological literature to a set of three major characteristics:

1. A profession performs a unique, essential social service.
2. A profession has a defined, respected knowledge base.
3. A profession has autonomy.

You have probably noticed that throughout this book I avoid referring to teaching as a profession. I call it an occupation. My choice of words does not reflect a lack of respect for teaching—I respect it immensely—but rather the fact that teaching does not possess the characteristics of professionalism to the extent medicine, law, and several other occupations do. Teaching does, however, exhibit the characteristics to a greater degree than most lines of work, prompting people to call teaching—along with nursing and social work—a *semiprofession* or, more optimistically, an *emerging profession*.

Terminology is important. I am careful with my choice of words because I want them to remind you that teachers must make fundamental changes in their occupation if they want to make it more professional.

Our discussion of professionalism pulls together many of the main issues from the preceding chapters, touching on supply and demand, salaries, teacher competency, and teacher education. The key to professionalism, though, is the role teachers themselves must play. Physicians and lawyers moved their occupations along the road to professionalism by taking collective action through the American Medical Association (AMA) and the American Bar Association (ABA). Many teachers believe they can professionalize their occupation by working together through the NEA, the AFT, or a merged organization.

## A Unique, Essential Social Service

The first characteristic of a profession suggests that society regards some work as so vital—healing the sick is the best example—it gives the members of one occupation exclusive rights to perform the work. Society allows the profession to "corner the market," in other words, to ensure that the service is available at a high level of quality. Society must regard the service as essential, and it must be convinced that only the members of the profession can render the service to acceptable standards. Otherwise, society will not grant a monopoly for performing the service.[37]

Certainly Americans believe teaching young people is an essential task, and society has given one occupational group, public school teachers, a monopoly of sorts in public education. As we saw in chapter 3, standards for teacher education and certification vary considerably around the nation, but a person cannot teach in any state's public schools without first obtaining a certificate from the state. Even though the certificate may be issued on an emergency or a provisional basis, it is required nonetheless.

Teaching in private schools is another matter. Most states do not require private school teachers, who make up about 10 percent of the nation's teaching force, to meet state education and certification standards. This situation opens a loophole without parallel in medicine, law, and most other professions. As we will see in chapter 11, there are some good arguments against state regulation of private schools and their teachers. On the other hand, our society would not tolerate two classes of physicians—one licensed by the state, the other unlicensed, but both doing the same work—because we regard medicine as so important we cannot entrust it to unlicensed practitioners.

But teaching? Many people believe almost anyone can do it. Parents teach their children, after all, and most people have taught on the job, in church, or in a similar situation. Can teaching be so complex that only one occupational group, people with state certification based on an approved teacher education program, can perform the service? Many Americans answer no. Teacher education doesn't have the best reputation in the world, and state officials are quite willing to bend or break certification requirements when teacher shortages hit. Such factors make it difficult to argue that one group should have exclusive rights to teach in the public schools, much less that their rights should extend to private schools.

Although public school teachers and private school teachers will probably never become a unified professional group, promising developments related to the first characteristic of professionalism are under way. In the last chapter, I expressed cautious optimism about teacher education and certification for public school teachers. Higher standards are sending the message that not just anyone can teach. The recommendations of the Carnegie Forum and Holmes Group for completely restructuring the occupation hold great promise and deserve a fair trial.

But by allowing people with no formal teacher training to enter the occupation on its lowest rungs, aren't Carnegie and Holmes sending a mixed message? If bright people with just arts and sciences degrees can teach, the states may ignore the rest of the Carnegie-Holmes recommendations—especially the costly ones—and simply open quick-entry alternate paths (described in chapter 3) into teaching. Why go to the extra trouble and expense?

Citizens do receive mixed messages. Not just anyone can teach, to be sure, yet, on the other hand, the job requires little or no specialized training. Perhaps anyone who is intelligent and liberally educated can teach. And back we go to the nineteenth-century debates over teacher education.

## A Defined, Respected Knowledge Base

America's continuing uncertainty about these issues relates also to the second characteristic of a profession: a defined, respected knowledge base. Professionals have expertise not shared by the general public. People recognize that a body of knowledge called "the law" exists, for instance, and they recognize attorneys as experts in the law. Professionals acquire their knowledge in specialized training programs, usually in graduate-level university programs. Bar examinations for lawyers, like similar examinations in other professions, assure the public that professionals are in command of their knowledge before they enter practice.[38]

Teaching does not fare well on this characteristic. The controversy over teacher education haunts the occupation here, too. Both inside and outside of universities, there is little agreement on the knowledge teachers must master. One of the most damaging aspects of the controversy, as we have seen, is that teachers themselves belittle their training in education. Once they begin teaching, they tend to ignore their training and improvise. Teachers say they learn far more on the job than from their undergraduate and graduate education courses.

In this area of professionalism, just as in the first one, so much is riding on the outcome of the Carnegie and Holmes experiments. If they are successful, they may allow teaching to put some of its ghosts to rest. Every teacher will be able to claim expertise in a recognized academic discipline. Every teacher who moves up the career ladder will receive graduate-level training with a strong clinical emphasis.

But is the body of knowledge about teaching strong enough to support such a program? What, exactly, is the role of the National Board for Professional Teaching Standards (NBPTS) in defining the professional knowledge base? What is the role of the long-awaited successor to the National Teacher Examinations, the new teacher-testing package the Educational Testing Service began phasing in during 1992?

Medicine, as I pointed out in the last chapter, developed a knowledge base that actually worked *before* devising tests to measure it. In teaching, we are putting the cart before the horse if we expect a national board and a national testing company to devise tests before we have agreed on what works and what doesn't. The consensus on knowledge must come first, then it can be followed by the tests. It is encouraging, though, that teachers themselves have the strongest voice on the NBPTS.

Other voices are also speaking out in the nationwide discussion of the knowledge base. Lee Shulman's Teacher Assessment Project at Stanford University, another experiment supported by the Carnegie Foundation, is trying to push teachers and teacher educators toward a consensus on the knowledge base (see chapter 2). Another push is coming from the National Council for Accreditation of Teacher Education (NCATE), which is requiring faculty members in the teacher education programs it accredits to look critically at their curriculum—to debate what teachers need to know (see chapter 3).

## Autonomy

The words *teachers themselves,* which I am using throughout this discussion, hold the key to professionalism in teaching. Autonomy, the third characteristic of a profession, is the right the members of an occupation have to make their own decisions and use their own judgment. The members themselves are in charge. Professionals have two kinds of autonomy: individual and group.

As *individuals,* professionals have the right to perform their work as they see fit, based on knowledge acquired through specialized training. Physicians, for example, enjoy a wide range of autonomy in their daily work. Society trusts them to make one decision after another as they diagnose their patients' illnesses and prescribe appropriate treatments. Physicians may turn to their colleagues for help and advice, but they do not have to check with a boss or supervisor before they act.[39]

As a *group,* physicians control their occupation through a network of state and national boards that set standards for medical education, licensing, and practice. Group autonomy is a relatively recent development in medicine. Although the AMA was founded in 1846, it took the organization three-quarters of a century to win physicians the right to regulate themselves. In the late 1800s, medical education was notoriously poor. Licensing was a sham. "Quacks" were an embarrassment to competent physicians and a danger to people seeking medical care.[40]

Then a series of developments turned the occupation around. Over several decades, scientific medicine gradually won acceptance among physicians. Because scientific medicine worked, prospective physicians became willing to attend university medical schools to learn how to practice. This revolution in knowledge and training was already under way when the Carnegie Foundation for the Advancement of Teaching published *Medical Education in the United States and Canada* in 1910. Popularly known as the Flexner Report, this study was a call to continue upgrading the occupation. The Flexner Report capped—not caused— the trend toward scientific medicine.[41]

The report's greatest value was as a political document, for the AMA was able to use it to convince Congress and the state legislatures that physicians should control their occupation. Give physicians the right to regulate themselves, the AMA promised, and they will give the nation better medical care. The AMA fought and won its political battles, and medicine became a self-regulating profession with the AMA as its major professional association. Along the way, the AMA also became one of the nation's most effective "unions," highly successful at safeguarding its members' interests.

The lesson for teachers is that while there are good reasons to be optimistic about the prospects for professionalism, teachers have a long way to go in their quest for autonomy. Consider this old saying among teachers: "I may have to follow school board policies and take orders from the principal, but when I close the classroom door, I'm in charge." To a degree, this statement is true—or rather was true. Until the late 1970s, teachers did have a fair amount of individual autonomy in the workplace, at least informally. Teachers were able to use methods they thought appropriate, administer tests they had designed, and grade students using their best judgment. Being able to work with relatively little direct supervision, escaping bureaucracy by closing the door, was one of the most attractive features of the occupation.

The back-to-basics movement and minimum competency testing changed the situation drastically, ushering in an era of standardized teaching, testing, and grading. Teachers now feel pressure from their bosses, school board members and school administrators, to teach by the cookbook. As we will find in chapter 10, the cookbook—often called an instructional pacing guide—tells them what to teach, how to teach it, when to teach it, and which tests to use to measure how much students have learned about it. As one teacher recently joked with me, "The packing guide tells me everything but when to go to the restroom, and that will probably be covered in next year's edition."

The sad truth is that teachers have lost rather than gained individual autonomy. Backed into a corner, those in some school systems are fighting back with collective bargaining, trying to carve out areas in which they can use their judgment. Local unions now find themselves having to negotiate for a stronger teacher voice in student promotion and other decisions that once rested entirely with teachers themselves.

Teachers have never had much group autonomy, which is another way of saying they have never won the right to control their occupation. One reason is that most teachers are public employees, paid with public money, while most physicians and lawyers are in private practice, paid by their clients on a fee-for-service basis. (Predictably, as the public pays a larger share of the nation's medical bills, physicians rail against creeping government restrictions on their autonomy.) The public tries to regulate what it pays for, to be sure, but something more fundamental is involved in public education: a long tradition of state and local governance, grounded in the belief that citizens should control "their" schools (see chapter 9). Given this tradition, we must face the fact that teachers will never have the group autonomy of physicians or lawyers.

# PRESSING TOWARD PROFESSIONALISM

## State Professional Standards Boards:
## A Case Study of NEA Strategy

As teacher organizations are quick to point out, though, the public regulates every profession to some degree. The task that lies ahead in teaching, as the NEA and AFT see it, is finding a way to balance public power and teacher power. In setting standards for teacher education and certification, these organizations want teachers to have more, but obviously not absolute, autonomy. And, in typical fashion, the NEA and AFT are pursuing the goal differently.

The NEA is using its clout in state politics to push for *state professional standards boards,* commissions with the authority to set standards for educating and certifying teachers. These boards include classroom teachers as voting members. Although state boards of education already consult with teachers on such matters—most states, in fact, have teacher advisory councils—the NEA looks forward to the day when teachers themselves can actually vote on the standards rather than merely give advice.

The NEA's ultimate goal is a professional standards board in every state, with teachers holding a majority of votes on each. Beginning in the late 1960s, California, Oregon, Minnesota, and a few other states established professional standards boards, but for years no state was willing to give teachers a controlling voice.[42]

The breakthrough the NEA was working for came in 1987, when the Nevada legislature created a nine-person board, with teachers holding four of the seats, a school counselor or psychologist holding the fifth, and the remaining seats occupied by two administrators, a dean of education, and a state board of education member. Since teacher organizations represent school counselors and psychologists, the NEA proudly hailed the Nevada board as the nation's first "teacher-dominated" professional standards board.[43]

The NEA, encouraged by this victory, has stepped up its campaign in other states. In 1989, the Iowa legislature established a professional standards board, with teachers holding the largest bloc (although not quite a majority) of seats. That same year, the Minnesota legislature redesigned its professional standards board to put teachers in the majority. Georgia created an autonomous teacher-dominated board in 1991. Indiana followed in 1992. Now the NEA's state affiliates, sometimes in concert with the AFT, are pressing for professional standards boards in other states.[44]

Teachers also hold a majority of the seats on the National Board for Professional Teaching Standards. Although this board does not have the power to set standards directly, it hopes the certificates it issues will become prestigious enough to make the states want to follow its lead. The AFT lost little time throwing its support behind the national board, on which the AFT has a better chance of holding its own with the NEA than on the state boards the NEA is almost certain to dominate. The NEA hesitated, expressing reservation after reservation before finally warming up to the NBPTS.[45]

The different approaches of the two unions are not necessarily in conflict, though, for most professions have national *and* state standards boards. In fact, the work of the NBPTS and state standards boards can be complementary.

The NBPTS makes a distinction between *licensing* and *certification,* a distinction long recognized in most professions but not yet in teaching. Physicians, for example, receive licenses to practice medicine from individual state boards, and those who wish to can seek certification in medical specialties from national boards. Using this model, state and national boards may be able to work together in education. The NBPTS would like state standards boards to be responsible for licensing teachers—for setting standards to govern how teachers enter and advance in the occupation based on education and experience. The NBPTS hopes to be responsible for certifying teachers—for setting standards to recognize teachers whose performance is outstanding.[46]

The prospects of teacher empowerment are exciting, but opposition is already mounting, coming primarily from school board members and school administrators. In Nevada, the bill creating the teacher-dominated professional standards board passed the legislature with only one dissenting vote, despite the efforts of the state board of education, state department of education, and local school boards to defeat it. The executive secretary of the Nevada Association of School Boards stated bluntly, "These are not doctors, lawyers, accountants, and engineers. These are public employees, working in the public sector, and much public benefit is lost with them having total control." Unable to block the establishment of the professional standards board, opponents did persuade the Nevada legislature to give the state board of education veto power in certain areas. Opposition is running high in other states as well.[47]

Opponents charge that teacher autonomy breaks the administrative chain of command within school systems and reduces the power of the state and local boards that represent the public. The charge is accurate. Instead of trying to deny it, teacher organizations will have to counter that changing the balance of power in public education is desirable. They must argue, as physicians did, that teachers can improve the quality of their services if they have more autonomy.[48]

In order to convince the public, teachers must begin to set standards of performance for their occupation. Unlike the NEA's existing Code of Ethics for the Education Profession and the AFT's Bill of Rights, two documents that sit on the shelf collecting dust, the performance standards must be specific, and teachers themselves must enforce the standards. The Carnegie Forum says more accountability—some form of merit pay based on student achievement—must go hand in hand with more autonomy. Since teacher organizations have consistently opposed holding teachers accountable for student test scores—with good reason, as we have seen—accountability will be a bitter pill to swallow. But the AFT seems willing to try.[49]

Broadening the definition of accountability to include factors other than student test scores may make the pill more palatable. The new accountability may involve peer evaluation, for example. Teachers evaluating teachers, another Carnegie recommendation, would be a major step toward professionalism, but peer evaluation is also controversial. Some teachers are as reluctant to take on the responsibility as some administrators and board members are to share it.[50]

## Restructuring in Rochester: A Case Study of AFT Strategy

Notice how every change we consider leads to several others. We are talking about a complete realignment of teaching as an occupation and more—a complete overhaul of America's schools. The situation is certainly not hopeless, though. Since the late 1980s, some local teacher organizations have been negotiating experimental versions of the Carnegie recommendations with their school boards, tying together salaries, evaluation, and autonomy. *Restructuring* has become a watchword of school reform, and it holds the promise of empowering teachers.[51]

AFT locals jumped off to an early lead in the race to restructure, attracting media attention with the innovative contracts they negotiated in Rochester, Toledo, Miami, Pittsburgh, and other big-city school systems. The AFT gave its locals the green light, encouraging them to take calculated risks and shake free of some of the traditional contract restrictions in labor-management relations.[52]

The NEA, by contrast, moved slowly and cautiously. As the discussion below suggests, restructuring is fraught with uncertainty, so the NEA says it is only wise to look before leaping. Having looked and seen its rival moving ahead, the NEA is now boasting of its own leadership in restructuring, trying to direct the course of local and state experiments through its National Center for Innovation in Education.[53]

Perhaps the AFT and NEA should not merge. Perhaps their differences in style and approach offer teachers valuable alternatives. In the case of restructuring, different approaches seem desirable, for restructuring can involve virtually every aspect of schooling.

But a concept that means everything can also mean nothing, and in some school districts the watchword of restructuring is nothing more than a buzzword. Trying to appear trendy, some districts "restructure" by forming teacher committees with no real power, or by using parent involvement as a public relations ploy, or by making cosmetic changes in the curriculum. When educational reform turns out to be phony, teachers, parents, and students come away disappointed, cynical about educational buzzwords. If the record of school reform since the late 1980s proves anything, it proves there are endless ways to render restructuring meaningless.

In Rochester, however, restructuring has produced real changes, and now the school district is trying to sort them out and decide which are worthwhile. Rochester has been in the public eye since 1987, when a spirit of friendship and trust between the president of the AFT local, Adam Urbanski, and the superintendent of schools, Peter McWalters, produced a "revolutionary" teacher contract. The goal of restructuring in Rochester—easy to state but hard to reach— is to find solutions to the problems that beset virtually all big-city school systems, such problems as low student achievement and low teacher morale, high student dropout rates and high teacher burnout rates.[54]

In exchange for better salaries and more control over their work, Rochester's teachers promised to improve the education of their students, 70 percent of whom are poor and an equal percentage of whom are members of racial and ethnic minorities. The predominately white teaching force promised to be more *accountable,* using this word in its broad sense to reassure the public of teacher commitment to meeting student needs.[55]

With the contract signed and the promises made, restructuring in Rochester focused on school organization and governance, parent involvement, and teaching as an occupation. The district created middle schools, developed magnet programs (discussed in chapter 8), and eliminated high school attendance zones to give students and parents a degree of "educational choice" (see chapter 11). Every school in the system formed a school-based planning team with the principal as chair and teachers as the majority of members. High school planning teams also include students and parents. A home-based guidance program went into effect in middle and high schools to bring teachers, parents, and students into closer contact.[56]

The key component of restructuring is the ongoing effort to reshape teaching as an occupation. The 1987 contract installed a Carnegie-inspired four-step career ladder that soon raised the average teacher salary from $33,000 to $46,000, with top salaries ranging up to $69,000. Differentiated staffing now gives teachers greater responsibilities as they move up the ladder. The lead teachers at the top divide their time among such activities as demonstration teaching, staff development, and involvement in the Peer Assistance and Review Program. This program provides mentors for beginning teachers and intervenor-helpers for experienced teachers who receive unsatisfactory evaluations. Because all these reforms involve teacher evaluation, a Career in Teaching panel has been struggling to devise a fair performance-appraisal system.[57]

A rush of national attention caught the school district by surprise, and, ready or not, Rochester became the most-watched laboratory of teacher professionalism. The Rochester experiment is putting the Carnegie recommendations to the test. And what are the results?

"Real change is real hard." This candid assessment from union president Urbanski goes to the heart of the matter. Teachers and administrators are gradually adjusting to their new roles, but the long years they spent jealously guarding their old turfs make it difficult to share territory. Teachers have discovered how time consuming school-based planning can be, and some teachers would rather give the responsibility back to administrators. Parents and students seem unsure of their roles on planning teams, although the assertive behavior of a few parents reminds educators of why they have historically kept "community activists" at arm's length.[58]

Different levels of teacher responsibility and remuneration are gaining acceptance, but only after misunderstanding and resentment. The role of lead teachers has proven difficult for some teachers to grasp and accept. The peer intervention program allows lead teachers to make career decisions about troubled colleagues—decisions only administrators had the authority to make before restructuring. Some principals, too, find the autonomy of lead teachers hard to take. The administrators' union made an unsuccessful attempt to block the intervention program.[59]

Winning acceptance for restructuring is turning out to be just as difficult within the community as within the school system. By the time the original contract came up for renegotiation in 1990–1991, teachers could sense a gulf forming between themselves and the community, a gulf that only widened as the economy went into recession. As many taxpayers saw restructuring, "We paid teachers big bucks in '87, and we're not getting our money's worth, so why should we pay them again?" Most teachers had a very different view. They were doing their best, but the community was expecting too much, too soon. Within the walls of the schools, restructuring was slowly making changes, yet the citizens of Rochester—70 percent of whom are white and fewer than 20 percent of whom have children in the public schools—wanted visible, dramatic changes.[60]

Accountability became the main point of contention. In the minds of many citizens, accountability took on the politically charged meaning we discussed in chapter 2: pay for performance, pay for results. This brand of accountability is far more specific than what teachers had in mind when they signed the 1987 contract. Responding to mounting demands for measurable results, the administration and union presented the kind of evidence taxpayers have come to expect: scientific-looking statistical indicators of rising test scores, falling dropout rates, rising college enrollment rates, and so forth. Meanwhile, Urbanski and McWalters tried to draw up a contract acceptable to both rank-and-file teachers and school board members.[61]

Two proposed contracts went down to defeat in rapid succession. In September 1990, Rochester's teachers overwhelmingly rejected a contract that offered raises of as much as 34 percent over three years but tied the raises to performance ratings based on portfolios. Each portfolio was to contain lesson plans, student work, parent comments, an administrator evaluation, a peer evaluation, and similar evidence. "Professional practice review committees" composed of two teachers and an administrator were to evaluate the portfolios against a "code of professional practices," and their evaluations were to determine raises. Here was an accountability plan that reflected the spirit of the Carnegie Forum's *A Nation Prepared.*[62]

Teachers felt the plan went too far, too fast, however, and they received support from none other than Lee Shulman, the advocate of portfolios we first met in chapter 2. Shulman, who served as a consultant during the contract negotiations, said teachers had "every right to be suspicious, because [portfolios had] never been tried out in the field." Shulman said he understood why teachers were reluctant to "take a brand-new approach and throw it into the highest-stake environment."[63]

The many citizens of Rochester who did not understand put pressure on the school board to reject the second proposed contract in January 1991. This proposal entailed a much simpler evaluation plan that called for classifying teachers as either satisfactory or unsatisfactory. Satisfactory teachers were to receive raises averaging 27 percent over three years; unsatisfactory teachers were to be referred to the intervention program and receive lower raises. Believing this contract would have amounted to an easy raise for virtually all of Rochester's 2,500 teachers, the school board unanimously rejected it.[64]

With the help of a state mediator, in April 1991 teachers and board members finally ratified a contract that gave raises of 14 percent over two years to satisfactory teachers, referred unsatisfactory teachers to intervention, and charged a task force with developing a new evaluation plan. The nation's most publicized experiment in school restructuring had survived a major crisis, but, as Adam Urbanski says, "Real change takes real time."[65]

Several lessons seem clear. Teachers will not accept even the best-intended reforms, even those with the high gloss of professionalism, if they sense a threat to their salaries and job security. Much more research, development, and planning will be necessary to convince teachers to buy into portfolios and other innovations. Taxpayers, behaving just as defensively as teachers in tough economic times, will be reluctant to foot the bill for restructuring. By 1992, the Rochester schools were staring at a $10-million budget deficit, and disagreements over how to reduce the deficit were further straining the spirit of cooperation among board, administration, and union. Even if everyone agrees that the goal of school reform is to improve the education of young people, differing perceptions of accountability will make it hard to reach agreement on whether restructuring is helping or hurting. And no, a teaching profession will not spring to life overnight.[66]

## Professionalism, Feminism, and Unionism

Two strong undercurrents of opposition continue to hold professionalism down. One is antifeminism. Our discussion in the preceding chapters highlights the perception of teaching as women's work. To the extent some people still view women as second class and subordinate, teachers—along with nurses and social workers—will run into resistance in their bid for professional status. Today, this opposition is rarely expressed openly, even though it occasionally slips out in such remarks as "After all, most teachers are only working for a second income" or "Women are naturals at teaching kids in the classroom, but they could care less about running a school district."

The other undercurrent, antiunionism, comes to the surface more often. Critics charge that teacher organizations are using professionalism selfishly, to make life better for their members. Teachers are coming out the winners, some citizens claim, with students, parents, and the general public the losers. Consider again the example of professional standards boards. There is little doubt that the unions will use their influence on the boards to set teacher education and certification standards high enough to reduce the supply of new teachers, a move that could drive up teacher salaries. Moreover, the organizations give every indication that they will oppose relaxing the standards in response to teacher shortages. They will insist that if school boards want qualified teachers, the only ways to attract them are better salaries, benefits, and working conditions. Self-serving, critics say.

The NEA and AFT counter that what is good for teachers is good for public education. The unions argue that while all professional associations try to take care of their own members, ultimately they have the interests of their clients at heart. Certainly physicians were thinking about themselves when they restricted access to their occupation. By making medicine a highly selective occupation, physicians ensured those who got in a comfortable living.

But they were also thinking about the public. When shortages of physicians develop today, state medical boards do not allow people with partial or no medical education to fill in, even on an emergency basis. Instead, the profession maintains its standards, fees for medical care rise, medicine becomes even more attractive to young people, and a greater supply of licensed, fully trained physicians eventually meets the need. The AMA argues that what the public loses in short-term convenience it gains in long-term quality. Don't Americans deserve the same quality in public education, the AFT and NEA ask?[67]

Yes, but. . . . Trying to answer that question sends us back to others we have already considered. Can we justify giving one occupational group exclusive rights to teach in the public schools? Is the knowledge base for teaching strong enough to support an emerging profession? Is the public ready to trust teachers and their organizations with more autonomy?

The questions are old, but some of the answers are new. Since the early 1980s, people have been taking the questions seriously, for teacher organizations, respected study commissions, and some public officials are serious about making teaching a profession. Part of your job will be helping to find new answers if you take your place among America's teachers in the 1990s.

## ACTIVITIES

1. Invite representatives of the NEA and AFT to speak to your class about their organizations' similarities and differences. Press them on what the differences really mean at the local level.
2. Talk with people who have a variety of opinions about teacher organizations. Begin with classroom teachers, then expand your interviews to include school administrators, school board members, parents, labor and business leaders, politicians, officials of the Democratic and Republican parties, and reporters.
3. Attend a collective bargaining session and a teacher organization's screening session for political candidates.
4. Discuss the concept of professionalism with representatives of the medical association and bar association in your community. Ask them to trace any parallels they see between the professionalization of their occupations and teaching.

## RECOMMENDED READINGS

The best source of current information on the NEA is the latest edition of the *NEA Handbook* (Washington, D.C.: NEA). For current information on the AFT, see recent issues of the newsletter *American Teacher*.

Kerchner, Charles Taylor, and Douglas E. Mitchell. *The Changing Idea of a Teachers' Union* (London: Falmer, 1988).
The authors optimistically forecast the emergence of "professional unionism."

Lane, John J., and Edgar G. Epps, eds. *Restructuring the Schools: Problems and Prospects* (Berkeley, CA: McCutchan, 1992).
With an opening chapter by Albert Shanker and other chapters by scholars as well as practitioners, this book examines the pros and cons of restructuring.

Murphy, Marjorie. *Blackboard Unions: The AFT and the NEA, 1900–1980* (Ithaca, NY: Cornell University Press, 1990).
A history of teacher unionism as a movement, this study provides an especially good account of the AFT's early years and the NEA's recent transformation into a union.

Urban, Wayne J. *Why Teachers Organized* (Detroit: Wayne State University Press, 1982).
Urban paints a realistic, sympathetic portrait of teachers striving for economic improvement and job security.

## NOTES

1. Anita Raby, "President's Message," *Alabama School Journal* (Special Membership Edition, 1990), p. 2; Raby, "From the President," *Alabama School Journal* (August 24, 1990), p. 5.
2. Gwyn J. Booth, "Hold the Sarcasm," *NEA Today* (February 1992), p. 38.
3. For a critical historical study of the two organizations, see Marjorie Murphy's *Blackboard Unions: The AFT and the NEA, 1900–1980* (Ithaca, NY: Cornell University Press, 1990). William Edward Eaton's *The American Federation of Teachers, 1916–1961* (Carbondale: Southern Illinois University Press, 1975) remains the classic account of the AFT. Wayne J. Urban is currently working on a history of the NEA.
4. The National Education Association's *1991–92 NEA Handbook* (Washington, D.C.: NEA, 1991) and the American Federation of Teachers, *The 1990–92 Report of the Officers of the American Federation of Teachers* (Washington, D.C.: AFT, 1992) provided much of the information for my discussion of the differences between the two organizations.
5. For the history of the state and local associations that provided the foundation for the NEA's rise to power, see Willard S. Elsbree's *The American Teacher: Evolution of a Profession in a Democracy* (New York: American Book Company, 1939).
6. The NEA's stands have provoked bitter attacks. See Sally D. Reed's *NEA: Propaganda Front of the Radical Left* (Washington, D.C.: National Council for Better Education, 1984); Dan C. Alexander, Jr.'s *Who's Running Our Schools? The Case Against the NEA Teacher Union* (Washington, D.C.: Save Our Schools Research and Education Foundation, 1986); and Phyllis Schlafly's *Child Abuse in the Classroom* (Westchester, IL: Crossway, 1985).
7. Michael John Schultz, Jr., *The National Education Association and the Black Teacher: The Integration of a Professional Organization* (Coral Gables: University of Miami Press, 1970); Eaton, *The American Federation of Teachers,* pp. 159–160.
8. Murphy, *Black Board Unions,* ch. 11.
9. Ibid., p. 255.
10. Ann Bradley and Karen Diegmueller, "Shanker Remarks Renew Possibility of Merger of Two Teachers' Unions," *Education Week* (August 1, 1990), pp. 1, 21; Bradley, "Teachers' Unions in San Francisco Decide to Merge," *Education Week* (October 18, 1989), pp. 1, 9; Bradley, "N.E.A. Affiliate in Wisconsin Backs Union-Merger Accord," *Education Week* (May 8, 1991), p. 8; "Column One," *Education Week* (February 26, 1992), p. 6.

11. Wayne J. Urban, *Why Teachers Organized* (Detroit: Wayne State University Press, 1982), chap. 5.
12. Murphy, *Blackboard Unions,* chap. 4.
13. Louis Fischer, David Schimmel, and Cynthia Kelly, *Teachers and the Law,* 3d ed. (White Plains, NY: Longman, 1991), pp. 41, 48–49.
14. Eaton, *The American Federation of Teachers,* pp. 161–166; Stephen Cole, *The Unionization of Teachers: A Case Study of the UFT* (New York: Praeger, 1969).
15. Anthony M. Creswell and Michael J. Murphy, with Charles T. Kerchner, *Teachers, Unions, and Collective Bargaining in Public Education* (Berkeley, CA: McCutchan, 1980), chaps. 3–4.
16. Helpful sources of information on the mechanics of bargaining include Cresswell and Murphy's *Teachers, Unions, and Collective Bargaining*; Fischer, Shimmel, and Kelly's *Teachers and the Law,* chap. 3; and William G. Webster, Sr., *Effective Collective Bargaining in Public Education* (Ames: Iowa State University Press, 1985).
17. Fischer, Shimmel, and Kelley, *Teachers and the Law,* pp. 44–45. See the brochure *Compulsory Unionism in Education* (Springfield, VA: Concerned Educators against Forced Unionism, 1984).
18. On impasse procedures, see Cresswell and Murphy's *Teachers, Unions, and Collective Bargaining,* pp. 365–375 and Webster's *Effective Collective Bargaining,* chap. 14.
19. Lorraine M. McDonnell and Anthony Pascal, *Teacher Unions and Educational Reform* (Santa Monica, CA: RAND Corp., 1988); Randall W. Eberts and Joe A. Stone, *Unions and Public Schools: The Effect of Collective Bargaining on American Education* (Lexington, MA: Heath, 1984), pp. 20–30; Cresswell and Murphy, *Teachers, Unions, and Collective Bargaining,* chap. 8; Webster, *Effective Collective Bargaining,* chap. 12.
20. Marilyn Rauth, "Exploring Heresy in Collective Bargaining and School Restructuring," *Phi Delta Kappan* 71 (June 1990): 781–784, 788–790.
21. Charles Taylor Kerchner and Douglas E. Mitchell, *The Changing Idea of a Teachers' Union* (London: Falmer Press, 1988); Stuart C. Smith, Diana Ball, and Demetri Liontos, *Working Together: The Collaborative Style of Bargaining* (Eugene, OR: ERIC Clearinghouse on Educational Management, 1990).
22. Cresswell and Murphy, *Teachers, Unions, and Collective Bargaining,* p. 81.
23. "Teacher Strikes," *Education Week* (September 24, 1984), p. 4.
24. Karen Diegmueller, "Teachers' Strikes Up 36% Amid Signs of Growing Tension," *Education Week* (September 18, 1991), p. 5; Diegmueller, "Strikes Abating, But Labor Unrest Appears on the Rise," *Education Week* (November 20, 1991), p. 8.
25. Fischer, Shimmel, and Kelly, *Teachers and the Law,* pp. 50–52.
26. Cresswell and Murphy's *Teachers, Unions, and Collective Bargaining* analyzes strikes on pages 341–364.
27. Urban's *Why Teachers Organized,* chapters 2–6, discusses the early political involvement of the NEA, AFT, and local teacher organizations in Chicago, New York, and Atlanta. For a case study of one city, see Joseph W. Newman's, "A History of the Atlanta Public School Teachers Association, Local 89 of the American Federation of Teachers, 1919–1956" (Ph.D. diss, Georgia State University, 1978).
28. For the recent political history of the NEA and AFT, see Martin R. Berube's *Teacher Politics: The Influence of Unions* (Westport, CT: Greenwood Press, 1988).
29. Mark Pitsch, "Three Democratic Hopefuls Bid for N.E.A.'s Endorsement," *Education Week* (January 8, 1992), p. 10.
30. Mark Pitsch, "Teachers' Unions' PAC's Gave $5.2 Million in '89–'90 Elections," *Education Week* (November 28, 1990), p. 18.

31. Peter West, "Campaign Reforms Could Cut Unions' Clout, Some Say," *Education Week* (May 23, 1990), pp. 13, 16; Julie A. Miller, "1987–1988 Federal Election Contributions: The N.E.A. Ranks 4th; the A.F.T., 28th," *Education Week* (November 29, 1989), p. 21.

32. "The NEA Representative Assembly," *NEA NOW* (July 20, 1992), pp. 1–2.

33. NEA Government Relations/National Council of State Education Associations, *1990 Election Results* (Washington, D.C.: NEA, November 1990).

34. Peter Schmidt, "Teachers' Unions Jockey to Sway Races in Pivotal Election Year," *Education Week* (October 10, 1990), pp. 1, 17.

35. See Amitai Etzioni's *The Semiprofessions and Their Organizations: Teachers, Nurses, and Social Workers* (New York: Free Press, 1969). Another often-cited study of teaching is Myron Lieberman's *Education as a Profession* (Englewood Cliffs, NJ: Prentice-Hall, 1956).

36. Ernest Greenwood, "Attributes of a Profession" and Dietrich Rueschemeyer, "Doctors and Lawyers: A Comment on the Theory of the Professions," in Ronald M. Pavalko, ed., *Sociological Perspectives on the Occupations* (Itasca, IL: F. E. Peacock, 1972), chaps. 1 and 3; Eliot Freidsen, ed., *The Professions and Their Prospects* (Beverly Hills: Sage, 1973).

37. Greenwood, "Attributes of a Profession," pp. 8–9.

38. Ibid., pp. 4–6.

39. Greenwood, "Attributes of a Profession," pp. 6–12.

40. Kenneth M. Ludmerer, *Learning to Heal: The Development of American Medical Education* (New York: Basic Books, 1988); Morris Fishbein, *A History of the American Medical Association, 1847–1947* (Philadelphia: Saunders, 1947).

41. Abraham Flexner, *Medical Education in the United States and Canada* (New York: Carnegie Foundation for the Advancement of Teaching, 1910). For an excellent discussion of these issues, see William R. Johnson's "Empowering Practitioners: Holmes, Carnegie, and the Lessons of History," *History of Education Quarterly* 27 (Summer 1987): 221–240.

42. Blake Rodman, "N.E.A. Pursues Its Plan to Establish State Boards Controlled by Teachers," *Education Week* (April 29, 1987), pp. 1, 20.

43. Blake Rodman, "Nevada Creates 'Teacher Dominated' Licensing Board," *Education Week* (August 4, 1987), p. 7.

44. Ann Bradley, "Backers of Teacher-Dominated Boards for Licensing Win in Minnesota, Iowa," *Education Week* (September 13, 1989), pp. 8, 12; Bradley, "Georgia Legislature Approves Bill Creating Independent Standards Board for Teachers," *Education Week* (March 13, 1991), p. 32; Mark Pitsch, "Indiana Bill to Create Teacher-Majority Bill Advances," *Education Week* (February 19, 1992), p. 22.

45. Rodman, "N.E.A. Pursues Its Plan"; Ann Bradley, "N.E.A. Assails Board's Policy on Prerequisites for Certification," *Education Week* (January 17, 1990), pp. 1, 11.

46. National Board for Professional Teaching Standards, *Toward High and Rigorous Standards for the Teaching Profession: A Summary,* 2d ed. (Detroit: NBPTS, 1991).

47. Rodman, "Nevada Creates 'Teacher-Dominated' Licensing Board"; Bradley, "Backers of Teacher-Dominated Boards"; "News in Brief," *Education Week* (February 5, 1992), p. 20.

48. Lynn Olson, "Certification Panel Gets Cool Reception from Some Administrators," *Education Week* (May 27, 1987), pp. 1, 16–17.

49. Lynn Olson, "Carnegie Forum's Plan for Revamping Schools Is Seen as Tough Task," *Education Week* (May 27, 1987), pp. 1, 16–17.

50. Ibid.

51. John J. Lane and Edgar G. Epps, eds., *Restructuring the Schools: Problems and Prospects* (Berkeley, CA: McCutchan, 1992).
52. Rauth, "Exploring Heresy."
53. Gary D. Watts and Robert M. McClure, "Expanding the Contract to Revolutionize School Renewal," *Phi Delta Kappan* 71 (June 1990): 765–774; Ann Bradley, "N.E.A. Creates Center to Promote School-Renewal Efforts," *Education Week* (February 26, 1990), p. 5.
54. Blake Rodman, "Friendship and Trust: Unusual Keys to Radical Pact," *Education Week* (September 30, 1987), pp. 1, 20–21.
55. Ann Bradley, "Rochester Contract Woes Ignite Debate over 'Accountability,'" *Education Week* (February 6, 1991), pp. 1, 14.
56. Ann Bradley, "After Two Tough Years in Rochester, School Reformers Look to the Future," *Education Week* (October 18, 1989), pp. 1, 10–12.
57. Ibid.
58. Adam Urbanski, "'Real Change Is Real Hard': Lessons Learned in Rochester," *Education Week* (October 23, 1991), p. 29; Bradley, "After Two Tough Years"; Bradley, "Rochester Contract Woes."
59. Bradley, "After Two Tough Years."
60. Bradley, "Rochester Contract Woes."
61. Ibid.; Urbanski, "Real Change."
62. Ann Bradley, "In Rochester, Skepticism, Confusion Greet News of 'Revolutionary' Pact," *Education Week* (September 26, 1990), pp. 1, 13; Bradley, "Rochester Contract Woes."
63. Bradley, "Rochester Contract Woes."
64. Ibid.
65. Ann Bradley, "On Third Try, School Board and Teachers Agree on Two-Year Contract in Rochester," *Education Week* (May 1, 1991), p. 4; Urbanski, "Real Change."
66. Ann Bradley, "Rochester to Lay Off 160 to Close Budget Deficit," *Education Week* (March 11, 1992), p. 11.
67. Arthur E. Wise, "A Case for Trusting Teachers to Regulate Their Profession," *Education Week* (October 8, 1986), p. 24; Wise, "States Must Create Teaching Standards Boards," *Education Week* (January 11, 1989), p. 48.

# CHAPTER 5

# Exercising Your Rights and Fulfilling Your Responsibilities

*I don't think I'll ever need to see an attorney. I work hard. I'm good. That's all the legal protection I'll need.*

— Prospective Florida teacher

*I never thought it would happen to me. The kids liked me, and so did most of the parents. Why didn't the principal?*

— Former Ohio teacher[1]

Teachers need to know where they stand with the law. Teachers who know their legal rights and responsibilities can put some of their doubts and fears to rest. No, the law is not so complex it is impossible to understand. No, there is not a lawyer lurking around every corner, just waiting to file suit against you. Much of the legal paranoia teachers share with other Americans is simply a fear of the unknown. By the time you reach the end of this chapter, I hope you will feel a sense of relief from knowing more about your rights and responsibilities in three areas: *employment, liability,* and *expression.*

On the other hand, becoming more familiar with school law should also give you a greater sense of caution. When we discuss employment, for instance, you will see that teacher tenure is not the ironclad guarantee to a lifetime job it is reputed to be. In the area of liability, one of the issues we will examine is the teacher and AIDS, and you may be surprised to learn what your responsibilities are concerning students who have the disease. When we discuss expression, you will find that although academic freedom protects teachers, that protection has limits.

Throughout this chapter, you will see that the law is a two-edged sword: It gives teachers rights to exercise; it also gives them responsibilities to fulfill.

This chapter, which concludes part I, is not the only chapter that involves school law. Collective bargaining, teacher testing, merit pay—these are only three of the issues in the preceding chapters that illustrate the influence of law on teaching as an occupation. In part II of this book, the spotlight is on students more often than teachers, and the law helps illuminate such issues as school desegregation, bilingual education, and gender equity. The focus of chapter 9 is the political arena in which the law originates. The debates we will examine in part III also involve legal questions. Who should control the curriculum? Should the government regulate private schools? Every chapter in *America's Teachers* bears the influence of school law.

## EMPLOYMENT

### Contracts

When you obtain your first teaching job, you will sign a *contract* with a local school board. A contract is a legally binding agreement, a statement of the rights and responsibilities of both parties, the teacher and the board. A contract typically specifies such things as salary, grade level or subject area, and length of school day and school year. A contract also obligates the teacher and the board to follow state school laws, state board of education policies, and local board regulations. In school districts with collective bargaining, the contract binds both parties to the master contract the teacher organization and the board have negotiated. Most teachers sign annual contracts, although some work under continuing contracts that remain in effect until one party gives notice of intent to change the agreement.[2]

Read your contract carefully. You may want to discuss it with an official of the local teacher organization, since lawyers retained by the organization have almost certainly scrutinized the document, as have the school board's attorneys.

### Tenure

In most states, teachers have the protection of *tenure,* which is a status of protected employment granted to teachers after satisfactory service during a probationary period. While teachers are on probation (usually for three years), it is easy for school boards to dismiss them. After teachers receive tenure, dismissal is difficult.

Tenure laws are controversial. Do they protect good teaching? Or shield incompetence? It is impossible to understand the pros and cons of tenure without knowing its history.

Public school teachers campaigned for the passage of tenure laws in the early 1900s, stressing their need for protection from "petty political and social attacks." To say teachers were vulnerable is to understate the situation. State school laws allowed local boards to fire teachers at will by simply not renewing their contracts. Teachers lost their jobs because of administrative whim, political patronage, social prejudice, and religious intolerance. In most states, dismissed teachers received neither a statement of the charges against them nor an opportunity to defend themselves at a hearing. They were simply out of work and out of luck.[3]

Teacher organizations took the case for tenure to the public and the state legislatures. Flagrant miscarriages of justice often tipped the balance of opinion in the teachers' favor: teachers who were dismissed for having the "wrong" religion or belonging to the "wrong" political party; those who were fired for discussing a controversial issue from several points of view rather than just the "right" one; those who lost their jobs because they smoked or drank in public (or even in private). Citing examples like these to dramatize the case for tenure, teachers argued that they deserved the same kind of protection from arbitrary dismissal that civil service laws gave to other government employees.

After the District of Columbia passed a teacher tenure law in 1906 and New Jersey followed suit three years later, the quest for job security gradually spread across the nation. Supported by the NEA, AFT, and independent state teacher organizations, teachers in city school systems led the tenure campaigns. By 1937, 17 states had passed some form of tenure legislation. Most of the early tenure laws applied just to urban teachers, but during the 1940s and 1950s, state legislatures extended tenure to rural teachers as well.

Think of tenure laws as a bargain struck between teachers and local school boards. Tenure allows the boards to dismiss teachers for almost any reason during the probationary period, but after that the boards must have a very good reason. As part of the bargain, tenure laws leave teachers vulnerable while they are on probation. They are literally on trial.

The future teachers in my classes often feel uneasy when they learn that school boards can dismiss an untenured teacher simply by not offering a new contract. In most states, the untenured teacher is entitled to no explanation and no hearing—and, of course, no further employment. I remind my students that this sense of insecurity is exactly what *all* teachers, 25-year veterans no less than beginners, felt without tenure. I hasten to add that even untenured teachers who can prove that their dismissal violates state or federal law—that they were fired because of their race or sex, for instance—can win back their jobs if they are willing to go to court.

## Dismissal

Obviously, tenure does not give absolute job security to any teacher. It does, however, put the burden on the school board to prove a tenured teacher unfit for further employment. In most states, the local board must prove a tenured teacher guilty of one of the "three *i*'s": incompetence, insubordination, or immorality. Some states add the *u* of unprofessional conduct or even broader grounds, such as "good and just cause."

*Incompetence* is the inability to perform the job the contract calls for. To prove a teacher incompetent, school officials must show a pattern of behavior, a clear record of failure. In dismissal cases that reach the court system, charges of incompetence most often center on a teacher's inability to maintain classroom discipline. As we saw in chapter 3, incompetence can also be the inability to speak or write grammatically, or it can be a lack of subject-matter knowledge. Incompetence can stem from a physical or mental condition—impaired hearing, for instance, or mental illness—that renders the teacher incapable of effective work. The mere existence of a handicap is not proof of incompetence, however. The board must produce evidence that the teacher cannot perform adequately. In most dismissal cases, teachers face charges of not one but several kinds of incompetence—a "collapse of performance."[4]

*Insubordination* is the willful violation of reasonable rules or the deliberate defiance of school officials. A reasonable rule, according to the courts, is one that officials have the authority to issue, that is clear enough to be understood, and that does not violate a teacher's constitutional rights. In cases involving alleged defiance of school officials, the courts often look for a pattern of behavior rather than a single incident. When a tenured teacher consistently refuses to comply with reasonable requests from a principal or supervisor, for example, the courts are likely to rule in favor of dismissal.[5]

Although definitions of *immorality* vary from community to community and change from time to time, the courts have narrowed the range of immoral conduct that can deprive tenured teachers of their jobs. In general, the conduct must interfere with a teacher's effectiveness before it can become grounds for dismissal. In *Morrison v. State Board of Education* (1969), a landmark case involving homosexuality, the California Supreme Court ruled that "an individual can be removed from the teaching profession only upon a showing that his retention in the profession poses a significant danger of harm to either students, school employees, or others who might be affected by his actions as a teacher." The courts usually distinguish between public and private conduct, and they usually protect what adults do in private. But when a teacher's private conduct becomes a matter of public controversy that spills over into the classroom and impairs his or her effectiveness, the courts generally support dismissal. Moreover, immoral conduct involving teachers and their students—a sexual relationship, for instance, or the use of alcohol or other drugs—is a sure ticket out of the occupation. We will return to the issues of lifestyle and other forms of personal expression in the last section of this chapter.[6]

The term *unprofessional conduct* is disturbingly vague, yet the courts have sometimes upheld the dismissal of tenured teachers on these and other broad grounds. The courts have reasoned that since society entrusts teachers with the important responsibility of working with young people, which calls into play numerous personal qualities ranging from "cleanliness" to "wisdom and propriety," school boards must have considerable discretion to determine who is fit for the task. In some cases, the courts have interpreted unprofessional to mean immoral; in other cases, unprofessional has been construed as unethical. The latter interpretation presents special problems, since teaching's two most prominent statements of ethics, the NEA's Code of Ethics and the AFT's Bill of Rights, have no legal standing. Even so, the courts have upheld the dismissal of teachers who use their classrooms for activities other than teaching, such as urging students to support a particular political candidate. The courts have also allowed the dismissal of "uncooperative" teachers. *Unprofessional conduct* and similar phrases are the catchalls of tenure law.[7]

In addition to the three *i*'s and the *u*, tenured teachers can lose their jobs as a result of *reduction in force,* or "riffing." When enrollment in a school district falls sharply, when a district decides to reorganize its curriculum for economic reasons, or when a financial crisis makes severe budget cuts necessary, school boards can dismiss tenured as well as untenured teachers. Seniority usually dictates whose jobs go first. Although riffing has been relatively rare, it posed a threat to teachers during the tax and budget-cutting era of the late 1970s and early 1980s, and it made a comeback in the hard economic times of the early 1990s.[8]

## Due Process

Tenured teachers have the right to *due process* the Fourteenth Amendment guarantees to all citizens. Tenure gives teachers ownership of their jobs, for the courts have ruled that tenured teachers have a "property interest" in their positions. Because of the Fourteenth Amendment, no state can "deprive any person of life, liberty, or property, without due process of law." In *Goldberg v. Kelly* (1970) and other cases, the U.S. Supreme Court has ruled that due process rights include a statement of charges, sufficient time to prepare a defense, a hearing before a fair tribunal (usually the local school board), representation by legal counsel, the opportunity to present evidence and cross-examine witnesses, a transcript of the hearing, and appeal of adverse rulings.[9]

Trying to dismiss a tenured teacher is expensive and time consuming. School boards can anticipate legal costs running into the tens of thousands of dollars. The NEA and AFT usually pay the expenses of their tenured members whose jobs come under fire, although there are important exceptions. The organizations will not stand behind a confessed child molester, for example, or an admitted drug dealer. Without question, though, teacher organizations make it more difficult for school boards to dismiss tenured teachers, leading some citizens to charge that tenure laws and union attorneys conspire to protect poor teaching. The NEA and AFT have a different point of view. They argue that teachers, like all citizens, are innocent until proven guilty.[10]

Even though local school boards win most of the dismissal cases that go to court, very few cases even reach the hearing stage before a local board. Unwilling to spend time and money on dismissal proceedings, some administrators and board members simply tolerate tenured teachers they know to be unfit for the classroom. Parents become incensed, and rightly so, when principals claim their hands are tied because of tenure laws. Some principals transfer unfit teachers from school to school—a game called "pass the turkey" in the literature on tenure.[11]

Other principals take more constructive approaches. One is remediation: trying to help teachers improve. Assistance from other teachers often proves helpful, which makes the peer evaluation and peer intervention programs we considered in chapters 2 and 4 seem very promising. If remediation fails, the principal can try confrontation. After observing an inadequate teacher and compiling a "thick folder" of evidence, the principal can confront the teacher with stacks of evaluation forms, dated observations, complaints from parents, and so forth. The object is to convince the teacher that resignation is a better option than a dismissal hearing and possible court battle. If confrontation fails, the principal can take the folder of evidence to a superior and argue for a dismissal hearing.[12]

The point is that administrators have options. They can do *something*. The laws outline grounds for dismissal, and it is the responsibility of administrators, admittedly an unpleasant and demanding one, to see that unfit teachers do not remain in the classroom.

## LIABILITY

A student falls in the classroom and breaks an arm. Several students come to school bearing signs of child abuse. Parents confide in a teacher that their child has tested positive for the HIV virus that causes AIDS. Despite a teacher's best efforts, some students learn very little. What are the rights and responsibilities of teachers in each of these situations? Can teachers be sued and held liable for failing to fulfill their responsibilities? In the excellent guidebook *Teachers and the Law* (1991), Louis Fischer, David Schimmel, and Cynthia Kelly provide answers.

### Injuries to Students

According to Fischer, Schimmel, and Kelly, a student who is hurt while under a teacher's care must prove four things in order to hold the teacher liable for the injury:

1.  The teacher owed a duty of care to the student.
2.  The teacher was negligent.
3.  The teacher's negligence was the cause of the student's injury.
4.  The student was actually damaged by the teacher's negligence.[13]

In most injury cases that go to court, there is little question that the teacher had a duty to care for the student, and there is little question that the student sustained monetary damages. The dispute usually centers on the second and third requirements. Was the teacher negligent, and if so, did the negligence cause the injury?

The courts place great emphasis on the concept of *reasonable care*, "the degree of care a teacher of ordinary prudence" would exercise.[14] Take the example of a student who falls and breaks an arm in a teacher's classroom. Court proceedings would probably revolve around several key questions. Was the teacher in the room at the time of the injury? Unless the teacher had an excellent reason not to be, his or her absence in itself could increase the chances of the teacher's being found liable. Could the teacher have foreseen the accident? Could the teacher have taken steps to prevent the accident? If the accident happened unpredictably—if the student simply lost balance and fell—the teacher would probably have little to worry about in court. But if the student slipped on water, for instance, or tripped over a wire, there would be further questions about whether the teacher had made a reasonable effort to remove the hazards or keep the students away. Did the student fall while running? If so, did the teacher make a reasonable effort to stop the running? Questions like these help the court decide whether the teacher was negligent and whether the negligence resulted in the injury.

Teachers should know they can be held liable for injuries occuring outside as well as inside the classroom. Teachers who provide transportation for students to field trips, athletic events, or debate tournaments are taking a risk, and the permission slips, waivers, and covenants not to sue that parents sign usually do not protect teachers from negligence suits. Regardless of what the piece of paper says, the courts generally allow an injured student to sue.[15]

Teachers can reduce their risk with liability insurance. They should find out how much coverage (if any) they have through their school district's policy. Does the policy cover teachers in the classroom? Does it protect them while they are supervising extracurricular activities? Does it cover transporting students in a private automobile? A major benefit of membership in the AFT or NEA is being able to buy low-cost liability insurance designed especially for teachers. While it is possible to be overinsured, it is wise for a teacher to have personal liability insurance to supplement whatever protection the district's policy provides.

## Reporting Child Abuse and Neglect

The laws of every state require teachers to report suspected cases of child abuse and neglect. Every state grants teachers who make such reports immunity from civil and criminal suits. State laws vary in their requirements, but most call for an oral report to an administrator followed by a written statement. Let me stress that the law will protect teachers who act in good faith. Teachers should not hesitate to file a report if they believe a student is a victim of abuse or neglect. In most states teachers can be fined or imprisoned if they do *not* make the report, and in some states they can be sued for negligence.[16]

The National Child Abuse Prevention and Treatment Act of 1974 defines child abuse and neglect as

> physical or mental injury, sexual abuse or exploitation, negligent treatment, or maltreatment of a child under the age of eighteen or the age specified under the child protection law of the state in question, by a person who is responsible for the child's welfare, under circumstances which indicate that the child's health or welfare is harmed or threatened thereby.[17]

According to recent estimates, at least 2,000,000 children suffer abuse and neglect every year. Looking just at sexual abuse, 1 of every 4 girls and 1 of every

10 boys will fall victim before their eighteenth birthday. Ninety percent of these cases go unreported. These statistics suggest why it is important for teachers to pay close attention to the mental and physical condition of their students.[18]

Statistics can only hint at the human dimensions of the problem, but they can put teachers on notice that they are *likely* to have abused and neglected children in their classes. Do not be blind to the problem.

## The Teacher and AIDS

How schools should respond to Acquired Immune Deficiency Syndrome (AIDS) is one of the most pressing issues in American education today. Almost every state mandates some form of AIDS education, and many teachers—certainly not just high school biology teachers—have a role in providing students information about the disease.[19]

Because of the highly charged controversies surrounding AIDS, some states and local school boards issue detailed teaching guides that tell teachers what to say, what not to say, and how to answer student questions. Should a teacher mention the word *condom* to a class of fifth-graders, or should the teacher suggest only sexual abstinence? In how much detail should a teacher describe the sexual acts that can transmit the disease? AIDS guidelines vary from state to state and district to district, and they raise academic freedom issues we will consider in the last section of this chapter. Teachers should be familiar with the state and local AIDS policies applicable to them.[20]

Of greater emotional as well as legal concern for teachers is the issue of how to deal with students who have contracted the Human Immunodeficiency Virus (HIV) that causes AIDS. What should a teacher do after learning a student has tested positive? Many teachers are concerned that they could be sued for negligence for not reporting a student with the virus or, on the other hand, sued for invasion of privacy or infliction of emotional distress for making a report.

Medical facts about AIDS shape judicial opinion. All teachers should know that AIDS has three stages. In the *carrier* stage, people test HIV-positive but show no symptoms; in the *AIDS-related complex* (ARC) stage, symptoms of an impaired immune system appear; and in the *full-blown* stage, the immune system breaks down and opportunistic infections develop. AIDS is progressive, incurable, and fatal, even though many people live for years in the final stage. The disease advances through the three stages faster in some people than in others, and carriers may not realize they have the HIV virus for several years—until the first symptoms of ARC appear.[21]

Teachers should also know that people contract the AIDS virus in a limited number of ways, primarily through sexual contact, sharing hypodermic needles, transfusions of contaminated blood, and perinatal contact between mother and child. One of the few positive things about AIDS is that it is hard to get; people do not catch the virus through casual contact. It is most encouraging for teachers that there are no known cases in which a child has caught the virus from a classmate or playmate.[22]

Based on this medical evidence, the courts are generally ruling that students who have AIDS can come to school. Judges are applying to AIDS victims (those in any stage of the disease) Section 504 of the Rehabilitation Act of 1973:

No otherwise handicapped individual in the United States . . . shall, solely by reason of his handicap, be excluded from participation in, be denied the benefits of, or be subjected to discrimination under any program or activity receiving Federal financial assistance.[23]

The courts sometimes allow school systems to isolate or exclude, on a case-by-case basis, AIDS victims whose condition or behavior—biting or drooling, for example—*might* pose a "significant risk" to others.[24]

The word *might* is appropriate because, again, AIDS is difficult to catch. Even people in close physical contact with AIDS victims—caregivers who bathe them and dress their skin lesions—have not contracted the HIV virus. As for biting and drooling, the virus is detectable in the saliva of only 1 of 18 or 20 people who have AIDS. It bears repeating that there are no known cases in which a child has transmitted the virus to a classmate or playmate.[25]

Medical evidence does not always put fears to rest, however. AIDS strikes terror in the hearts of many students, parents, and teachers. The media carry stories of irate crowds literally driving students with the disease out of the school—in some cases running their families out of town. Thus the courts have had to weigh the student's right to privacy against the public's right to know.[26]

The verdict is clear. The student's right to privacy, which is protected by the Family Educational Rights and Privacy Act (1974) and the Education of All Handicapped Children Act (1975), prevails. These federal laws allow the release of medical information on a student to qualified persons—to a teacher, principal, or school nurse, for example—only to protect health and safety. In the absence of a threat to health and safety, information on a student's medical condition is strictly confidential.[27]

In light of the legal obligations to educate and protect all students, many school districts form special teams to make case-by-case decisions about students in any stage of AIDS. Such teams often consist of a student's doctor, a doctor representing the school board, a public health officer, the school nurse, and the student's teacher(s). After reviewing information on the student's medical condition and behavior, the team makes a recommendation to the superintendent on whether the student should remain in school and whether anyone else needs to know he or she has AIDS.[28]

What school systems try to avoid is the public uproar that can occur if a student's condition becomes widely known. A teacher who breaches a parent's confidence and leaks information about a student with AIDS can start a chain of events that can force the student out of school—the law and the courts notwithstanding. In addition to inviting a lawsuit, the teacher's action can discourage other parents and students from coming forward with information about the illness.[29]

Many school systems have developed policies on how teachers should report AIDS cases. Find out whether your system has a policy and, if so, what it provides. In the absence of a clear policy, a confidential report to the principal is probably the teacher's safest course of action.

AIDS policies in school systems, like court decisions on the disease, are relatively new and still evolving. With the number of cases reported in school systems continuing to increase, though, teachers may soon become all too familiar with how to deal with the disease. The Recommended Readings at the end of this chapter include one of the best sets of AIDS guidelines for teachers.[30]

## Educational Malpractice

Malpractice suits against physicians are common. The soaring cost of malpractice insurance is prompting some physicians to raise their fees, change their specialties, or even leave the profession. Teachers face the same kind of lawsuits, although far less frequently. Some parents have argued that just as teachers can be held liable for physical injuries to students under their care, they should also be liable for mental injuries—for educational malpractice. Although no educational malpractice suits have yet succeeded, two precedent-setting cases raise issues teachers need to consider—issues we have examined in a different light in other chapters of this book.

The most famous case, *Peter W. v. San Francisco Unified School District* (1976), involved a young man who sued the San Francisco public schools because he had graduated from high school with only a fifth-grade reading level. Peter produced evidence in court that his IQ scores were at least average and that teachers and administrators had informed his mother on numerous occasions he was making adequate progress in school. Peter claimed the school system had acted negligently by giving him inadequate teachers, assigning him to inappropriate reading groups, and socially promoting him from one grade to the next. The system's negligence had damaged him, he charged, by reducing his chances of finding a job.[31]

When weighing Peter's claim of negligence, the judge considered the lack of an agreed-on knowledge base in education, an issue we analyzed in chapters 3 and 4. By what standard could he find the school system negligent, the judge wondered, when "the science of pedagogy itself is fraught with different and conflicting theories of how or what should be taught?"[32]

The judge ran into a further problem when he looked for a link between teacher behavior and student achievement. He concluded that student achievement is "influenced by a host of factors which affect the pupil subjectively, from outside the teaching process"—such factors as the home, the media, and an assortment of "physical, neurological, emotional, cultural, [and] environmental" forces. How could anyone isolate the influence of teachers—indeed, of schools—and hold them responsible for a student's reading ability? This, of course, is one of the questions we asked about teacher evaluation in chapter 2.[33]

The judge rejected Peter's claim, adding that a ruling in the student's favor would encourage countless other lawsuits of the same kind and place an impossible burden on the schools and society. Peter W.'s lawsuit was an attempt to force accountability with a vengeance, and the judge turned it back.

Another case, *Hoffman v. Board of Education of the City of New York* (1979), appeared to have a better chance of succeeding. Danny Hoffman entered kindergarten with a severe speech defect. Scoring 74 on an intelligence test emphasizing verbal skills, Danny was placed in a class for mentally retarded students. Even though the school psychologist who administered the test recommended retesting within two years, stating that the child "obviously understands more than he is able to communicate," the school system never retested Danny. He graduated from high school after spending 11 years in classes for the retarded.[34]

At 18, Danny took an intelligence test required by the Social Security Administration. Because he scored in the normal range, he lost both his Social Security benefits and his eligibility for rehabilitation training. At that point, Danny sued the New York public schools for negligence. He charged the school system with a serious error, a mistake that had damaged him intellectually and psychologically. A lower court ruled in Danny's favor, awarding him $750,000 (later reduced to $500,000) in damages. The lower court stated that unlike the *Peter W.* case, *Hoffman* was a case of clearcut malpractice.[35]

The New York Court of Appeals reversed the decision. By a 4-to-3 margin, the justices ruled that the courts cannot second-guess schools on academic matters. A court of law is not the appropriate place to question the "professional judgment of educators," the majority wrote. Instead, students and parents who are unhappy with educational decisions can use the educational appeals process provided by state school laws.[36]

*Peter W.* and *Hoffman* established precedents other courts have followed in the educational malpractice suits of the 1980s and 1990s. But will the precedents remain in place? The mounting pressure for accountability and the increasing willingness of courts to question the judgment of physicians, lawyers, and other professionals make it possible that educational malpractice suits may yet succeed.

# EXPRESSION

## Academic Freedom

Academic freedom for teachers is based on the First Amendment, which guarantees teachers, along with all other citizens, the right to free speech. Teachers argue that since their jobs involve working with knowledge and testing ideas, they need special protection as they experiment, question, and criticize. Democracy demands free teaching, they insist.

But the courts have not always recognized the concept of academic freedom. Although the First Amendment went into effect in 1791 as part of the Bill of Rights, only in the twentieth century have elementary and secondary school teachers won a degree of protection for their academic work in the classroom. Even college professors, who work with older students and are responsible for generating new knowledge, have faced an uphill struggle for academic freedom. During this century, teachers at all levels of education have won major victories, but the courts have made it clear that academic freedom is far from absolute.

Despite the protection of tenure laws, teachers still come under fire for assigning controversial readings and discussing controversial issues. Consider the case of Alabama teacher Marilyn Parducci, who had her eleventh-grade English class read Kurt Vonnegut, Jr.'s, comic satire "Welcome to the Monkey House." After several students and parents complained, the teacher's superiors told her to stop using the story, which they branded "literary garbage." The teacher refused. Defending the literary value of the work, she continued to discuss it in the classroom, whereupon the school system fired her for insubordination.[37]

The lawsuit she initiated to get her job back led to a precedent-setting court decision, *Parducci v. Rutland* (1970). The federal district judge who heard the case observed that academic freedom, while "fundamental to a democratic society," does have limits. Trying to define some of the limits, the judge considered two major questions. Had the school system shown that the assignment was inappropriate for the age group or grade level? Had the system shown that the assignment interfered with discipline or disrupted the educational process? On both counts, the judge weighed the evidence and answered no. Thus he ruled in favor of the teacher, stating that her dismissal had been "an unwarranted invasion of her First Amendment right to academic freedom."[38]

Such controversies rarely cost teachers their jobs, though they often cost books their place in the classroom or in the library. Citizen complaints about books are increasing, and few teachers or librarians seem to be as willing as Marilyn Parducci to stand their ground and defend their decisions. One or two parental complaints may be enough to make a teacher change an assignment or a librarian remove a book from the shelf. Even worse, from the standpoint of academic freedom, is the subtle form of censorship known as *prior restraint*, which occurs when teachers or librarians never assign or never order certain books for fear of causing controversy, even though they believe the books have educational value.[39]

School boards have the right to ban textbooks and library books, the courts have held. But board members must base their decisions on legitimate educational reasons, not on their disagreement with social, political, or religious ideas.[40]

A school board can ban John Steinbeck's *Of Mice and Men* and Judy Blume's *Deenie* if the board can make a reasonable case that the sexually explicit language in the book is educationally inappropriate for a particular age group or grade level. Even if teachers disagree with the justification the board members present, the board can still ban the book as long as it couches its arguments in legitimate educational concerns.[41]

When evaluating such arguments, judges distinguish between what they regard as unlawful and what they regard as unwise. In a recent Florida case, a panel of judges who admitted they sided with teachers on the educational merits of two literary classics, Chaucer's "The Miller's Tale" and Aristophanes' *Lysistrata*, still allowed a local school board to ban them, for the board presented a justification related to legitimate educational concerns. The members argued that the classics were too "explicit" and "vulgar" for high school students, and the judges accepted the justification as questionable but constitutional. The point—not an easy one for advocates of teacher power to accept—is that the ultimate authority to make educational decisions about the curriculum rests with school board members, not with teachers.[42]

On the other hand, a board cannot ban books about teenage pregnancy, the Vietnam War, the Islamic faith, or any other topic just because the board objects to the social, political, or religious ideas in the books. Teachers who believe in the educational merits of books that generate controversy will have to find evidence that board members are trying to keep ideas away from students.[43]

With the American Library Association's *Intellectual Freedom Manual* (see Recommended Readings at the end of this chapter) as a reference, teachers can stand their ground. Many school districts have developed procedures to resolve disputes over contested books. If a dispute goes to court, the school board must show a legitimate educational reason for its decision to ban a book. Denying students access to controversial ideas is not a legitimate educational reason.[44]

In all cases regarding controversial issues in the classroom, the courts emphasize relevance to the curriculum. In general, the courts have found teachers who deal with controversial topics that are a logical part of the subject at hand—a lecture on racism in an American history class, for instance, or a discussion of human sexuality in a biology class—to be operating within the limits of academic freedom. Yet the limits stretch only so far. A teacher who continually injects politics into a math class is probably out of bounds, and anything a teacher does that substantially disrupts the class may not be protected by academic freedom.[45]

The courts generally protect teachers who use controversial teaching methods, *if* they can produce reasonable evidence that other members of the occupation consider the techniques valid. Remember, though, that state and local school boards clearly have the right to determine the content of the curriculum and prescribe particular teaching techniques. The cookbook curriculum I discuss as a threat to autonomy in several chapters of this book may be unwise, or so many teachers think, but it is also legal. Regarding the example of AIDS instruction we discussed earlier, school systems have the right to control what teachers say about the disease. Teachers should check their instructional guides before they utter the words *safe sex.*[46]

The courts have ruled that academic freedom is fundamental to a democratic society, then, but they have also placed limits on the concept. When deciding where to draw the lines, the courts consider such factors as the age and grade level of students, effects on discipline and the educational process, relevance to the curriculum, the judgment of other educators, and state and local curriculum requirements.

## Right of Public Dissent

With the rise of teacher unionism and the push for teacher power, teachers are more likely than ever to express their disagreement with administrators and school board members. Are teachers protected when they go public with their criticism?

In *Pickering v. Board of Education* (1968), the U.S. Supreme Court considered a suit brought by Marvin Pickering, a tenured Illinois high school teacher who lost his job because of a critical, sarcastic letter he wrote to the editor of a local newspaper. In it, Pickering took his superintendent and school board to task on the sensitive issue of school finance. He faulted his superiors for the way they raised and spent money, accusing them of shortchanging academics to enrich athletics. He also criticized the ''totalitarianism'' that stifled teacher dissent in the schools. The school board fired Pickering, claiming he had damaged the reputations of his superiors and impeded the efficient operation of the school's system. Pickering filed suit to regain his job, arguing that the First Amendment protected his right to speak out.[47]

Although a state court upheld the dismissal, the U.S. Supreme Court ordered Pickering reinstated. Several points in the decision deserve our attention. Most important, the Supreme Court upheld the teacher's right to make public statements on matters of public concern. Obviously, said the justices, school finance is a public concern. They argued that

> free and open debate is vital to informed decision making by the electorate. Teachers are, as a class, the members of a community most likely to have informed and definite opinions as to how funds allocated to the operation of the schools should be spent. Accordingly, it is essential that they be able to speak out freely on such questions without fear of retaliatory dismissal.[48]

Even though Pickering had made several erroneous statements in his letter, the court found no evidence that he had done so intentionally. Nor did the court find evidence that his letter had harmed anyone's reputation or interfered with the operation of the school system.

The court did place limits on the teacher's right of public dissent, implying that had his criticism disrupted his working relationship with an immediate superior—a principal or assistant principal, for example—the dismissal might have been justified. The court also observed that the need for confidentiality—the need to safeguard the privacy of a student's records, for instance—could override a teacher's right to speak out on a matter of public concern.[49]

The most important limitation on public dissent came in another Supreme Court decision, *Connick v. Meyers* (1983). The court held that ''when a public employee speaks not as a citizen upon matters of public concern, but instead as an employee upon matters only of personal interest,'' the courts cannot interfere with personnel decisions. According to this decision, not everything that goes on inside a school is a matter of public concern.[50]

In a later Florida case, a federal judge ruled that a teacher who had criticized teacher assignment policies—including the long-controversial practice of assigning coaches to social studies classes—had not raised a legitimate public concern. Instead, the teacher was simply disgruntled over ''internal school policies.'' School finance is a public concern; job assignments, according to the judge, are not. The judge observed that ''in the wake of *Connick,* the federal courts have substantially broadened the employer's rights to control employee speech activities that *relate to his employment.*"[51]

Teachers can publicly criticize their school systems, then, but only if their dissent involves a matter of public concern. Teachers can speak out within their systems on any educational issue, but even then they must be wary of causing disruptions and upsetting working relationships.

## Other Forms of Expression

Now our focus expands to encompass broader forms of expression, such matters as personal appearance, political activities, and private life. As I pointed out in the discussion of tenure and dismissal, the courts have established the general principle that a teacher's behavior must impair effectiveness in the classroom before the behavior can become grounds for dismissal.

Decisions are constantly changing, though, and a prime example of how they change with the times is the matter of personal appearance. When long hair, beards, and mustaches were popular during the late 1960s and 1970s, the courts often came to the defense of male teachers who wore these styles. Arguing that grooming is a symbolic expression and therefore protected by the First Amendment, the courts tended to put the burden on the school system to prove the hair disrupted the classroom. In more recent cases, the burden of proof has shifted to the teacher. Unless the teacher can prove a school system's grooming regulations irrational or unreasonable, judges are increasingly allowing the regulations to stand. Teachers of the 1990s, male or female, who sport shaved heads or spiked hair may be forced to choose between their hairstyles and their jobs.[52]

Nor are the courts giving teachers much leeway in dress. Rejecting arguments that clothing is symbolic expression, judges have validated regulations requiring male teachers to wear coats and ties and female teachers to wear skirts longer than minis. Even so, the decisions suggest that the courts might protect articles of religious clothing—a Jewish teacher's yarmulke, for instance—or clothing that marks racial or ethnic pride—such as a black teacher's dashiki.[53]

The courts have also sent mixed signals on political activities. Reversing earlier decisions, the U.S. Supreme Court has made it clear that teachers cannot be dismissed because of their membership in radical organizations. Teachers can belong to the Communist Party or Ku Klux Klan, for example, and still retain their jobs. If teachers show they intend to further the illegal aims of an organization, however, they can be fired. Regarding participation in political activities, the courts have held that teachers, like all citizens, can vote, contribute to political candidates, express opinions on political issues, and display bumper stickers. But as public employees, how far can teachers go? Can teachers, like federal employees, be prohibited from managing political campaigns and playing other key roles? The NEA and AFT encourage their members to become involved in partisan politics. Even though no court has yet curtailed such activity, a test case could go to trial in the 1990s.[54]

Meanwhile, the courts have rendered conflicting decisions on whether teachers have to resign if they are elected to public office and, indeed, whether they can run for office without resigning. This issue has become quite contro-versial in some states. Is it a conflict of interest for teachers to serve in a state legislature, where they cast votes on education bills that directly affect their jobs? The answer may be yes in one state and no in the state next door. Look for more litigation on political activity as teachers continue to push for power.[55]

Finally, there are the lifestyle issues we discussed earlier in this chapter. The landmark decision in this area of expression is *Morrison,* which protected the rights of a homosexual teacher. Again, the critical issue is the degree to which teachers' private lives affect their work. Marc Morrison kept his job, but the courts have upheld the dismissal of other gay and lesbian teachers when students, parents, and colleagues have protested their continued employment. Decisions affecting unmarried teachers who become pregnant or simply live with someone of the opposite sex are also mixed. The courts consider the circumstances of each case, sometimes affirming and sometimes rejecting the teacher's right to remain in the occupation.[56]

## ACTIVITIES

1. Talk with several principals about the legal issues surrounding teacher tenure, especially the dismissal of unfit teachers. Interview several officers of a teacher organization and compare the responses.
2. Start an information file on AIDS. Education journals are running more and more stories on the disease, often emphasizing legal issues. Write to state and local boards of education for policies that will apply to you as a teacher.
3. Where do you stand on the expression issues in this chapter? Stage a classroom debate on academic freedom, public criticism of school system policies, or a teacher's right to have an unconventional lifestyle.

## RECOMMENDED READINGS

American Library Association, Office of Intellectual Freedom. *Intellectual Freedom Manual,* 3d ed. (Chicago: ALA, 1989).
   This guide offers valuable suggestions to educators who wish to safeguard their academic freedom.
Fischer, Louis, David Schimmel, and Cynthia Kelly. *Teachers and the Law,* 3d. ed. (White Plains, NY: Longman, 1991).
   The authors give straightforward, plain-English answers to teachers' questions about the law.
National Association of State Boards of Education. *Someone at School Has AIDS* (Alexandria, VA: NASBE, 1989).
   Recommended by the Centers for Disease Control, this booklet is an excellent resource for teachers, administrators, and school board members.
Zirkel, Perry A. "De Jure," a monthly column in *Phi Delta Kappan.*
   Zirkel covers a wide range of issues in school law, including the teacher-focused concerns discussed in this chapter.

# NOTES

1. Both quotes are from interviews conducted by my students in clinical and laboratory experiences in educational foundations, Winter quarter 1992.
2. Louis Fischer, David Schimmel, and Cynthia Kelly, *Teachers and the Law,* 3d ed. (White Plains, NY: Longman, 1991), chap. 1.
3. For the history of teacher tenure, see the National Education Association's *The Problem of Teacher Tenure,* Research Bulletin, vol. II, no. 5 (Washington, D. C.: NEA, 1924); Cecil Winfield Scott's *Indefinite Teacher Tenure: A Critical Study of the Historical, Legal, Operative, and Comparative Aspects* (New York: Bureau of Publications, Teachers College, Columbia University, 1934); and the Commission on Educational Reconstruction, American Federation of Teachers' *Organizing the Teaching Profession* (Glencoe, IL: Free Press, 1955), chap. 4.
4. Edwin M. Bridges, *The Incompetent Teacher: Managerial Responses,* rev. ed. (Bristol, PA: Falmer, 1992); Fischer, Schimmel, and Kelly, *Teachers and the Law,* pp. 28–29.
5. Fischer, Schimmel, and Kelly, *Teachers and the Law,* pp. 27–28.
6. *Morrison v. State Board of Education,* 461 P.2d 375 (Cal. 1969); Fischer, Schimmel, and Kelly, *Teachers and the Law,* pp. 29–30.
7. Fischer, Schimmel, and Kelly, *Teachers and the Law,* pp. 30–31.
8. Ibid., pp. 31–34.
9. *Goldberg v. Kelly,* 397 U.S. 254 (1970).
10. Bridges, *The Management of Teacher Incompetence* (Stanford, CA: Institute for Research on Educational Finance and Governance, Stanford University, August 1983), pp. 19–20.
11. Ibid., pp. 23–25, 13–14.
12. Bridges, *The Management of Teacher Incompetence,* pp. 14–21.
13. Fischer, Schimmel, and Kelly, *Teachers and the Law,* pp. 72–73.
14. Ibid., p. 58.
15. Ibid., pp. 63–64.
16. Bruce Beezer, "Reporting Child Abuse and Neglect: Your Responsibility and Your Protections," *Phi Delta Kappan* 66 (February 1985): 434–436.
17. National Child Abuse Prevention and Treatment Act of 1974 (P. L. 93-247), quoted in Fischer, Schimmel, and Kelly, *Teachers and the Law,* p. 77.
18. Marnell Holtgraves, "Help the Victims of Sexual Abuse Help Themselves," *Elementary School Guidance and Counseling* 21 (December 1986): 155–159.
19. National Commission on Acquired Immune Deficiency Syndrome, *America Living with AIDS* (Washington, D.C.: NCAIDS, 1991).
20. See Debra Viadero's "C.D.C. Urges AIDS Instruction in Every Grade," *Education Week* (February 3, 1988), p. 4.
21. Cathy Allen Broadwell and John L. Strope, Jr., "Students with AIDS," *West's Education Law Reporter* 49 (January 5, 1989): 1105–1114.
22. Debra Viadero and Peter Drotman, "Expert's Answers to Frequently Asked Questions about AIDS," *Education Week* (September 30, 1987), p. 6.
23. Rehabilitation Act of 1973, Section 504, quoted in Broadwell and Strope, "Students with AIDS," p. 1106.
24. Broadwell and Strope, "Students with AIDS," pp. 1106–1110; Perry A. Zirkel, "AIDS: Students in Glass Houses?" *Phi Delta Kappan* 70 (April 1989): 646–648.
25. Viadero and Drotman, "Expert's Answers," p. 6.
26. David L. Kirp and Steven Epstein, "AIDS in America's Schoolhouses: Learning the Hard Lessons," *Phi Delta Kappan* 70 (April 1989): 585–593.

27. Debra Viadero, "AIDS in Schools: Compassion vs. 'the Public's Right to Know,' " *Education Week* (January 20, 1988), pp. 1, 26; Broadwell and Strope, "Students with AIDS."
28. Viadero, "AIDS in Schools," p. 26.
29. Ibid.
30. Ellen Flax, "AIDS Virus Becoming More Common among At-Risk Youths, Studies Find," *Education Week* (November 13, 1991), p. 10.
31. *Peter W. v. San Francisco Unified School District,* 131 Cal. Rptr. 854 (Cal. App. 1976).
32. Ibid.
33. Ibid.
34. *Hoffman v. Board of Education of the City of New York,* 64 A.D. 2d 369, 410 N.Y.S. 2d 99 (1978).
35. Ibid.
36. *Hoffman v. Board of Education of the City of New York* 49 N.Y.2d 317, 424 N.Y.S.2d 376 (1979).
37. *Parducci v. Rutland,* 316 F. Supp. 352 (N.D. Ala. 1970).
38. Ibid.
39. "Schools Fend Off More Attempts at Censorship," *USA Today* (August 30, 1990), p. 1; Henry Reichman, *Censorship and Selection: Issues and Answers for Schools* (Chicago: American Library Association, 1988).
40. Eugene C. Bjorklun, "School Book Censorship and the First Amendment," *Educational Forum* 55 (Fall 1990): 37–48.
41. Fischer, Schimmel, and Kelly, *Teachers and the Law,* p. 133.
42. *Virgil v. School Board of Columbia County, Florida,* 862 F.2d 1517 (11th Cir. 1989).
43. Bjorklun, "School Book Censorship"; Fischer, Schimmel, and Kelly, *Teachers and the Law,* pp. 133–134.
44. Ibid.
45. Fischer, Schimmel, and Kelly, *Teachers and the Law,* pp. 132–138.
46. Ibid., pp. 138–140; David Rubin with Steven Greenhouse, *The Rights of Teachers: The Basic ACLU Guide to a Teacher's Constitutional Rights,* rev. ed. (New York: Bantam Books, 1984), pp. 130–131.
47. *Pickering v. Board of Education,* 225 N.E.2d 1 (1967), 391 U.S. 563 (1968).
48. *Pickering v. Board of Education,* 391 U.S. 563 (1968).
49. Ibid.
50. *Connick v. Myers,* 461 U.S. 138 (1983).
51. *Ferrara v. Mills,* 596 F.Supp. 1069 (S.D. Fla. 1984), 761 F.2d 1508 (11th Cir. 1986). Emphasis in the original.
52. Fischer, Schimmel, and Kelly, *Teachers and the Law,* pp. 354–357.
53. Ibid., pp. 357–358, 367–368.
54. Rubin, *Rights of Teachers,* pp. 74–82; Fischer, Schimmel, and Kelly, *Teachers and the Law,* pp. 175–183.
55. Ibid.
56. Fischer, Schimmel, and Kelly, *Teachers and the Law,* pp. 235–247; Rubin, *Rights of Teachers,* pp. 147–158.

# PART II

# Schools and Society

# CHAPTER 6

# History of American Education

## DEBATES AND PATTERNS

This chapter uses debates and patterns to introduce the history of American education. The debates we will hear took place before the Civil War and at the turn of the twentieth century, yet they have a surprisingly contemporary ring. The patterns we will see have appeared over the course of this century, and they are still shaping the schools. All historians try to avoid reading the present into the past—they call that the sin of "presentism"—but most historians believe studying the past can help us live better in the present.

I have tried to capture the excitement of educational history by focusing on debates that occurred during two eras of educational reform. In both periods the future of the schools—and, indeed, the future of the nation—hung in the balance as citizens debated fundamental questions about education: Whose children should go to school? What kinds of schools should they attend? What should they study? Who should control the schools?

Debates over these issues were especially heated in the mid-nineteenth century and at the turn of the twentieth century. Looking back, it is easy to see why. Both eras were periods when the United States itself was changing rapidly, times when many people were convinced they could improve the nation if only they could channel change in a constructive way. In both eras, reformers who wanted to change the schools took their place alongside reformers with plans to remake other social institutions. And in both eras, citizens spoke out freely for and against the proposals for reform.

After listening to the debates, we will turn our attention to twentieth-century patterns of education. We will examine four patterns: the competition for control of the schools, the local/state/federal balance of power, the quest for equal educational opportunities, and trends in the curriculum. Some historians argue that these patterns show more stability than change, claiming the basic structure and purposes of American education have changed little during this century. Other historians disagree, contending the growing strength of teacher organizations and the development of the cookbook curriculum (to cite two examples we discussed earlier) are fundamental changes—major breaks with the past.

## HISTORICAL INTERPRETATION

To understand why historians disagree, you need to realize history is not a literal record of the past. History is an *interpretation* of the past. History reflects the spirit of the times in which it is written; how historians view their own era influences how they view the past. Historians select from the past those ideas and events that seem significant to them and then interpret what they have selected through the lens of their own experience. Although they do not deliberately distort the past, historians readily acknowledge that they "cannot jump out of [their] intellectual skin."[1]

You should be aware of several major varieties of historical interpretation. In the early 1900s, *celebrationist* historians dominated the history of American education. We call them celebrationists because they wrote glowing, inspirational accounts that were full of praise for both the nation and its schools. The United States was a country of great virtue, in their interpretation, and much of its virtue flowed from its wonderful schools. Concerned with preserving and extending public education, celebrationist historians saw the rise of public schools as a triumph of good over evil.[2]

By the 1920s and 1930s, *liberal* historians were criticizing the idealized picture the celebrationists had painted. In the liberal interpretation, the nation and its schools were basically good, but both had problems that cried out for attention. The liberals pointed out some of the biases in schools and society— biases against poor people and African Americans, for instance. Liberal historians of these decades stressed conflict, the clash of competing ideas and interests. The emphasis on conflict became especially pronounced during the Great Depression. As times changed, though, so did the liberal interpretation. During the 1940s and 1950s, liberal historians downplayed conflict and competition and emphasized consensus and cooperation. Liberal historians of these decades seemed confident the United States could solve its problems, and they called on public educators to play key roles in building a better nation.[3]

*Revisionist* historians displaced liberals as the dominant interpretive force during the late 1960s and 1970s. Revisionist history portrayed the nation and its schools as flawed—fundamentally flawed, according to the harsher revisionists. In the revisionist interpretation, public schools were deliberately designed to protect the status of elite groups and keep the children of other groups in their place. Revisionist history written during these years had a pessimistic tone, for most revisionists believed it was impossible to improve the schools without making fundamental changes in society, changes that people with wealth and power have successfully resisted.[4]

During the 1980s and 1990s, two major trends have shaped historical interpretation. As always, the spirit of the times is leaving its stamp on historical scholarship. Reflecting the more conservative national mood of the Reagan-Bush era, *neoconservative* historians—it would be unfair to call them celebrationists, but they do seem nostalgic for a golden age of American education—are offering their interpretation of such issues as changes in the curriculum, the effects of desegregation, and the place of traditional values in the schools. Revisionist and liberal historians, of course, are challenging the neoconservative point of view.[5]

The second trend of the 1980s and 1990s involves *multiple-perspective* historians who are trying to portray the complexity of the past with more subtlety and sensitivity. This movement in history parallels a similar development in other academic fields, the trend toward *postmodern criticism,* which we will examine in more detail in chapter 7. Postmodernists argue that where people stand in the social structure shapes their perception of ideas and events. The factors of social class, race, ethnicity, and gender exert a powerful influence on how people construct meaning from their experience. Thus when historians look into the past, they can see many layers of meaning built up around any idea or event. The historians' job is to show how the different layers correspond to different social perceptions. Although multiple-perspective historians usually make it clear where they stand—they may be liberals, revisionists, or neoconservatives—they want their readers to see a past full of contradictions and ambiguities through the eyes of different people and different social groups.[6]

As you read this chapter, remember you are reading interpretations of the past. I have included debates to expose you to different points of view, but you should be aware that as I wrote the chapter, I constantly had to decide which debates to include and which to omit, how to present opposing positions on the issues, and so forth. In other words, this chapter is interpretive from beginning to end. Let me challenge you to judge the past for yourself as you read. Be critical and think of different interpretations. I hope the chapter helps you catch the spirit of historical debate, the clash of opinion *in* the past as well as *about* the past.

## COMMON SCHOOL REFORM
## IN HISTORICAL CONTEXT

During the three decades before the Civil War, public education as we know it began to take shape. Americans built statewide public school systems—*common school* systems, they were originally called. Controlled to some degree by the state governments, common schools were different from the various kinds of locally controlled schools with which Americans were familiar. Common schools, according to the reformers who advocated them, would be common to all children; they would teach a common political creed; and they would instill a common morality based on nonsectarian religion.

Until the 1960s, most educational historians gave common school reform a favorable review. Celebrationists were hard pressed to criticize it at all. Liberals have generally viewed the common schools crusades as noble, if imperfectly conducted. Revisionists, however, have charged that school reformers ran roughshod over the values and interests of certain groups—poor people, religious minorities, political dissenters—in the drive to bring schooling under state control. Neoconservative historians have come to the defense of the reformers, arguing that revisionists have exaggerated the drawbacks and downplayed the benefits of common schools. And now multiple-perspective historians are trying to reveal the many and sometimes conflicting motives people had for favoring or opposing common school reform.

These contrasting historical interpretations recall the debates over schooling that occurred before the Civil War. In order to understand the debates, we need to be familiar with the locally controlled schools that common school reformers wanted to replace.

## District Schools, Academies, and Other Schools

Had we been able to tour the new nation in the late 1700s and early 1800s, we would have seen a great deal of variation in education. In New England, where traditions of schooling were strongest, *district schools* had dotted the countryside well before the American Revolution. Massachusetts had led the way in 1642 with legislation requiring parents and guardians to make sure their children could read, and that legislation was followed by a 1647 act requiring every town of 50 or more families to appoint a reading and writing teacher.[7]

The religious and political influence of the Puritans on these developments was unmistakable. They believed universal literacy would prevent the development of a pauper class, enable citizens to understand the law, and—most important—save souls. The 1647 school act was known as the "Old Deluder Satan Law," for it was intended to help people resist the wiles of the devil himself.

The "New England model" of district schools grew out of this heritage. New England towns and townships were, on the average, 6 miles square. By the mid-1700s, most of them contained several population centers or villages. As population growth continued, the towns gradually delegated control over the schools to the individual villages, which began to function as school districts. This decentralized model of schooling took local control of education to the extreme. The citizens of each village set their own school taxes and, through a committee of selectmen, hired the teacher (usually a man), established the length of the school year, and determined the course of study.[8]

The one-room district school took in boys and girls ranging from about 5 to 15. Their attendance, limited by weather, distance, and farm work, was irregular. Literacy, morality, and religion were the heart of the curriculum, with memorization and recitation the dominant pedagogy. The teacher rarely stayed in one school for more than a session or two. For the children of the wealthiest New Englanders, tutors offered an alternative to the district school. The sons of the elite could then enroll in a *Latin grammar school,* a private school with a classical orientation.

District schools moved west after the Revolution with the passage of the Northwest Ordinances of 1785 and 1787. These laws, which governed the settlement of the territory west of the Allegheny Mountains, laid out land in townships 6 miles square, with each township divided into 36 sections, each 1 mile square. The sixteenth section, which fell close to the center of the township, was set aside for education—it often became the site of a district school. Other acts of Congress applied the sixteenth-section principle to the settlement of territory outside the Old Northwest. In this way the decentralized New England model came to many of the states admitted to the new nation. District schools were scattered throughout the Midwest by 1850 and across the Great Plains and Far West during and after the Civil War.

District schools were never as popular in the South, though, even in the newer southern states that entered the union with sixteenth-section lands earmarked for education. In the antebellum South, a different model of education prevailed. The children of the wealthy had their tutors and private schools; "middling" whites attended academies (which we will discuss next), denominational schools, or the few district schools; poor whites received little or no formal education; and in most states, African slaves were prohibited by law from learning to read and write.[9]

In the Middle Atlantic states—New York, New Jersey, Pennsylvania, and Delaware—yet another model of schooling developed. Here differences in ethnicity, language, and religion drew people into a variety of denominational schools, among them Dutch Reformed, Quaker, Jewish, and Roman Catholic. District schools and academies were more numerous in the Middle Atlantic region than in the South, but the pull of private religious education was strong.

*Academies* offered schooling to students who were at least middling in social status—or had aspirations to be. Billing themselves as more practical than the Latin grammar schools, academies took in students whose ages usually ranged from about 14 to 25. The education academies provided was supposed to be both "ornamental" and "useful," as Benjamin Franklin explained in his 1749 proposal for an academy in Philadelphia. Franklin outlined plans for a school that would place more emphasis on English grammar, composition, and public speaking than on Latin and Greek. History, mathematics, and science—subjects to which Latin grammar schools paid little attention—would be prominent in the curriculum. Carpentry, printing, farming, and other practical skills would also have a place. Such a course of study, Franklin argued, would prepare students to get ahead in life.[10]

But the academies that became increasingly popular throughout the nation in the first half of the nineteenth century rarely had so practical a slant. Ironically, Franklin's proposal led to the establishment of a school that evolved into the University of Pennsylvania, a classically oriented institution. Parents wanted their children to get ahead, to be sure, but most parents believed an education in the classics was the key to social mobility. Thus the academies stressed practicality in moderation, careful not to steer too far away from the subjects that were the mark of middle- and upper-class culture.[11]

From our twentieth-century vantage point, academies were a curious blend of "public" and "private." Typically, academies held public charters and received public funds, though they also charged tuition and were governed by private boards of trustees. Academies also blurred the line we draw between high schools and colleges. Most academies were more like the former; a few were more like the latter. Indeed, academies were sometimes called "people's colleges." Academies were usually coeducational, although some, like Emma Willard's Troy Female Seminary and Mary Lyon's Mount Holyoke Seminary, were exclusively for females. Such institutions made their reputations by offering women educational opportunities that were unavailable elsewhere. The popularity of academies grew rapidly between the Revolution and the Civil War.[12]

In the early years of the nation, then, Americans attended a variety of locally controlled schools. Such figures as Benjamin Franklin, Noah Webster, Benjamin Rush, George Washington, Thomas Jefferson, and James Madison spoke out in support of the "general diffusion of knowledge" among the populace. The republican spirit of the new nation included the belief that schooling had a crucial role to play in promoting nationalism, patriotism, and a balance between freedom and order. Most Americans were in agreement that schooling was a good thing and that the nation needed more of it.[13]

But this broad consensus concealed fundamental disagreements over the purposes and control of schooling. Jefferson and Rush, for instance, differed over whether schools should impose order and virtue on students (Rush's position) or simply cultivate the inborn reason and moral sense that students bring to school (Jefferson's position). Clearly, Jefferson and Rush also disagreed over the nature of human beings. Interestingly enough, in the late 1700s, Jefferson and Rush both proposed statewide school systems to put their educational ideas into practice—and their proposals fell on deaf ears. For more than half a century after the Revolution, Americans saw little need to involve the state governments in schooling.[14]

## The Impact of Modernization

The nation was changing. By the 1830s, three major trends were under way, exerting their strongest influence on New England and the Middle Atlantic states. Urbanization, industrialization, and immigration—historians call them the forces of *modernization*—were altering the way Americans felt about their nation and its schools.[15]

These three trends were closely related. A worldwide movement of people from the farm to the city had begun, prompted by changes in agriculture and accelerated by the lure of factory jobs. Many of those who swelled the population of cities like Boston, New York, and Philadelphia had been born in the rural areas of this nation, but many others were newly arrived from abroad. Immigration from Ireland and Germany was heavy in the three decades before the Civil War, bringing to the United States large numbers of people whose language was not English and whose religion was not Protestant. These immigrants seemed especially "foreign" to Americans of British descent.

The entire process of modernization seemed threatening to many, for the traditional community controls that worked well in small towns and rural areas seemed to break down in industrial cities. Agrarian communities were usually homogeneous, composed of people with similar backgrounds and beliefs. Out in the country, family, church, and neighbors kept people in line—everyone knew everyone else's business. In the heterogeneous cities, by contrast, people could and did go their own way. The social and economic distance between rich and poor seemed to widen. The popular press constantly reminded the public of the consequences of urban poverty, playing up sensationalized accounts of crime and degradation: men turning to strong drink, women turning to prostitution, and children working in factories or roaming the streets at all hours. To some citizens, it seemed the cities were already out of control and the entire nation would soon be in danger. Something had to be done.

Out of this ferment came an upsurge of reform, a remarkable variety of movements that had in common the urge to perfect and control the modernizing society. Urbanization, industrialization, and immigration held out the promise of great rewards, not the least of them economic development—thus the drive to perfect society—but they exacted a frightening toll that was painfully obvious on city streets—thus the quest for control. Temperance crusaders, prison reformers, advocates of women's rights, pacifists, abolitionists—these and many others worked to win popular support for their causes, sometimes competing and sometimes cooperating. Often an individual reformer worked for several causes simultaneously or moved from one to another over the course of a lifetime.[16]

School reformers mounted an educational crusade, often quoting scripture to prove the changes they sought were the most fundamental: "Train up a child in the way he should go: and when he is old, he will not depart from it" (Proverbs 22:6). Pay the schoolmaster today, they exhorted, or pay the jailer tomorrow. Thus the common school movements of the antebellum era were one piece in an elaborate mosaic of reform.

Before the pace of modernization quickened in the 1830s, some Americans were already finding fault with the district schools. Even in Massachusetts, which prided itself as the nation's educational leader, decentralization had yielded a patchwork of schools that varied tremendously from one district to the next. The lack of uniformity was evident in many ways, including the quality of teachers. It troubled Massachusetts educator and legislator James G. Carter that his state had established no qualifications for teaching. The selectmen of each district, usually advised by local clergy, hired whomever they pleased. The result, as we saw in the introduction to chapter 3, was often the employment of teachers "who [knew] nothing, absolutely nothing, of the complicated and difficult duties assigned to them"—or so Carter claimed. With an eye toward raising standards and eventually enforcing them statewide, in 1826 he proposed a network of state colleges to train teachers.[17]

But Carter had more on his mind, as the following warning on the perils of decentralization indicates:

> If the policy of the legislature, in regard to free schools, for the last twenty years be not changed, the institution, which has been the glory of New England will, in twenty years more, be extinct. If the State continue to relieve themselves of the trouble of providing for the

instruction of the whole people, and to shift the responsibility upon the towns, and the towns upon the districts, and the districts upon individuals, each will take care of himself and his own family as he is able, and as he appreciates the blessing of a good education. The rich will, as a class, have much better instruction than they now have, while the poor will have much worse or none at all. The academies and private schools will be carried to much greater perfection than they have been, while the public free schools will become stationary or retrograde.[18]

Carter's basic argument was that the state could no longer afford to entrust something as vital as schooling to the whims of local people. He envisioned schools less stratified by social class, accessible—at least at the lower levels—to rich and poor alike. Girls as well as boys would attend. Reaching this goal, he insisted, would require some degree of state control.

In time, the Massachusetts legislature responded favorably to Carter's arguments. The first public *normal school* (teacher training institution) in the state as well as the nation opened in Lexington in 1839. But Carter had already won his greatest victory in 1837 with the creation of a state board of education, also the first in the nation, and the appointment of Horace Mann as its secretary. Mann, who would soon be called the father of public education in the United States, set out on a 12-year crusade to establish common schools throughout Massachusetts.

Gradually other states followed suit. In 1838, Connecticut established a state board of education with Henry Barnard as its secretary, and during the 1840s and 1850s, common school movements appeared in most of the states outside the South. Even in that region there were common school crusaders, although before the Civil War the movement was not very successful outside a few cities.[19]

Common school reformers had ambitious goals. They wanted to provide at least three years of tax-supported schooling for every white child in the nation. In the cities, they usually set their sights higher, proposing grammar schools and high schools for students who wished to go beyond the primary level. Reformers wanted to upgrade teaching by setting standards for training and hiring teachers, who increasingly were young women (see chapters 1 and 3). Centralizing some of the control of schooling at the state level was the key to reaching the other goals, reformers were convinced, for they found how hard it was to rely on the power of persuasion alone.[20]

Even though Carter, Mann, Barnard, and other reformers were tireless promoters, collecting statistics, publishing reports and journals, and traveling from community to community to drum up interest in common schools, initially they obtained mixed results. But they were persistent, and they knew how to play the game of state politics. Some of them were lawyers, former holders of other political offices, or veterans of other reform crusades. Horace Mann was all of these: an attorney and former legislator who numbered temperance, prison and asylum reform, and abolition among his many causes.[21]

Battles over centralization would continue throughout the nineteenth century, even longer in the South, but state legislatures gradually gave state boards of education the ultimate political weapon: the power of the purse. With the passage of statewide school taxes, state boards could withhold funds from local districts to force compliance with state standards.[22]

Still, the reformers found some things very resistant to change—teacher behavior, for instance. It was one matter for reformers to convince state legislators to set standards for training and hiring teachers; it was quite another to persuade teachers to change how they taught.

Barbara Finkelstein's study *Governing the Young* (1989) reveals that despite the reformers' best efforts to upgrade the teaching force, teacher behavior changed very little. Teachers saw themselves as intellectual overseers and drillmasters, and they were set in their ways. Largely rejecting the child-centered pedagogies of the day, paying little heed to the reformers' goals of developing critical intelligence and self-discipline in students, teachers were content to enforce rote work and instill the dominant values of their local communities. Carter, Mann, Barnard, and other common school crusaders became the first in a long series of reformers to discover how difficult it is to make changes in the day-in, day-out routine of teaching and learning.[23]

## DEBATES OVER COMMON SCHOOL REFORM

The common school campaigns peaked in intensity during the 1840s and 1850s. Feelings ran high in legislative chambers, courthouses, town halls, and lyceums across the nation as citizens debated educational issues. When the reformers stood up to argue that district schools were not reaching many children, a typical reply was that local people could simply increase their financial support and improve the schools, making them more attractive to all students. To the argument that many teachers were unqualified, the reply came that better wages would attract better teachers—if the people really wanted them. As we saw in chapter 3, the opponents often added that training in pedagogy was useless. The existing district schools had no inherent weaknesses, the opponents of common schooling suggested. It was the responsibility of local citizens to strengthen the schools as they saw fit. State-regulated common schools and normal schools were totally unnecessary.[24]

As the debates unfolded, it became clear that the reformers were using the word *common* not in the sense of "ordinary" or "only for the poor," but in three more inclusive ways. Common schools would be common to all children; they would teach a common political creed; and they would instill a common morality based on nonsectarian religion.[25]

Interestingly, outside the South most of the opponents conceded the desirability of the first kind of commonality, although we know that few advocates on either side envisioned racially integrated schools. Still, conceding the importance of schooling for all children weakened the opponents' case when the discussion turned to "laggard" districts in which people seemed to care little about providing schools of any sort. In those instances, Horace Mann and other reformers argued, the best interest of both the children and the nation compelled the state to step in.

The political, moral, and religious dimensions of commonality drew sharp attacks, even though the reformers tried to walk a tightrope in hopes of avoiding controversy. Orestes Brownson, editor of *The Boston Quarterly Review,* did his best to shake the tightrope in his critique of Horace Mann's *Second Annual Report of the [Massachusetts] Board of Education* in 1839. Brownson wrote:

> Education, then, must be religious and . . . political. Neither religion nor politics can be excluded. Indeed, all education that is worth anything is either religious or political and fits us for discharging our duties either as simple human beings or as members of society.[26]

Building on this premise, Brownson posed the dilemma America's public schools have always faced. If they exclude politics and religion, some people will regard the education they provide as worthless. If politics and religion are included, some people will take offense.

## Politics

Orestes Brownson was a Democrat. Before the Civil War, his party supported schooling for all citizens but often opposed common schools. State governments should leave local schools in the hands of local people, said the Democrats. Common school reformers were more likely to be Whigs. Their party advocated an active role for the states as well as the federal government in securing internal improvements for the nation. In Massachusetts and other states, the common school crusade was dividing people along traditional party lines.

Turning his attention to the common political creed that Horace Mann, a prominent Whig, wanted to teach in the schools, Brownson dryly observed:

> Establish, then, your Whig board of education; place on it a single Democrat, to save appearances; enable this board to establish normal schools and through them to educate all the children of the common-wealth, authorize them to publish common-school libraries, to select all the books used in school, and thus to determine all the doctrines which our children shall imbibe, and what will be the result? We have then given to some half a dozen Whigs the responsible office of forming the political faith and conscience of the whole community.[27]

Mann and the common schoolers would admit nothing of the sort. They rejected the idea that teachers had to avoid discussing politics and government entirely or else offend students by taking sides on partisan issues. As Mann put it,

> Surely, between these extremes, there must be a medium not difficult to be found. . . . Those articles in the creed of republicanism, which are accepted by all, believed in by all, and which form the common basis of our political faith, shall be taught to all. But when the teacher, in the course of his lessons or lectures on the fundamental law, arrives at a

controverted text, he is either to read it without comment or remark; or, at most, he is only to say that the passage is the subject of disputation, and that the schoolroom is neither the tribunal to ajudicate, nor the forum to discuss it.[28]

The common schoolers were able to walk the tightrope in the arguments over the political aspects of commonality. Most Americans seemed content with the "middle course" Mann suggested—a course involving *controlled* political discussion. To be sure, since Mann's day a variety of groups from across the political spectrum have objected that their views were not getting a fair hearing in the public schools, but the protests have never convinced large numbers of Americans to abandon the schools.

## Morality and Religion

The common schoolers fell off the tightrope in their quest for a common morality based on nonsectarian religion. For most nineteenth-century Americans, religion and morality were firmly linked. Few people even entertained the thought that the common schools could inculcate morality without also inculcating religion. In the context of the times, morality divorced from religion was no morality at all. But in an increasingly heterogeneous nation, where Catholics, Jews, people of other non-Protestant faiths, and people of no religious faith were becoming more numerous every year, how could the schools provide a common moral and religious education?

Mann naïvely believed the answer lay in removing specific religious doctrine from the schools while retaining a common, nonsectarian creed as the basis for moral education. The nonsectarian creed he had in mind, however, was not a distillation of principles from religions around the world. Even though Mann was a Unitarian, he centered his faith on Christ, and he was well aware that most Americans thought of themselves as Christians. Thus *nonsectarian* came to mean "nondenominational Christian" in the language of Horace Mann and most other leaders of the common school movement.[29]

Once again, Mann believed he had found a middle course, a compromise. How could anyone object to moral lessons based on nondenominational Christianity? Mann expressed it this way:

> In this age of the world, it seems to me that no student of history, or observer of mankind, can be hostile to the precepts and the doctrines of the Christian religion, or opposed to any institutions which expound and exemplify them.[30]

Orestes Brownson found the compromise unacceptable. He spoke for many opponents of common schooling when he said:

> The board assure[s] us Christianity shall be insisted on so far, and only so far, as it is common to all sects. This, if it mean anything, means

nothing at all. All who attempt to proceed on the principle here laid down will find their Christianity ending in nothingness. Much may be taught in general, but nothing in particular. No sect will be satisfied; all sects will be dissatisfied. For it is not enough that my children are not educated in a belief contrary to my own; I would have them educated to believe what I hold to be important truth.[31]

Brownson was a Roman Catholic. Like other members of his faith, he rejected moral instruction based on general Christian principles as watered-down and meaningless—some Catholics branded it "godless"—calling instead for moral instruction grounded explicitly in the doctrines of Catholicism. Would such instruction be possible in common schools regulated by the state? No, but it would be in district schools that left decisions on moral and religious education in the hands of local citizens. Many Catholics and a small number of Protestants took this position along with Brownson.

In effect, the content of moral and religious education would be subject to majority rule in each district. In Catholic districts, Catholicism would prevail in the schools; in Methodist districts, Methodism would dominate; and so on. Those who were unhappy with the schools in their district could open parochial schools and receive public funds to support them, a widely accepted practice before the rise of common schools.

Brownson's vision of publicly funded sectarian schools clashed with Mann's vision of moral and religious commonality. Sectarian schools were divisive, Mann argued. He was relieved that most Protestants seemed content to teach their children specific religious principles at home and in church. Protestants generally accepted common schools that based moral instruction on what was called nonsectarian religion. Catholics, though, continued to protest, not only in Massachusetts but also wherever they were a significant religious minority. Mann became alarmed as other disputes over commonality broke out, making the possibility of compromise seem increasingly remote.[32]

We have already seen how common schoolers construed "nonsectarian religion" as "nondenominational Christianity." Catholics took the argument a step further, charging that "nondenominational Christianity," as put into practice in the common schools, was really "nondenominational Protestantism." Daily reading of the King James version of the Bible, "without note or comment," was standard practice in common schools. It was fast being written into law as state legislatures and state boards of education began to regulate the schools. Catholics objected that they used another translation of the Bible, the Douay version, and that it was dangerous to read the scriptures without commentary—students might interpret them incorrectly without guidance. The common schools were filled with Protestantism, they further complained. Many textbooks were replete with slurs against Catholics in general and Irish immigrants in particular. Protestant teachers and students often ridiculed Catholic students. How could Catholic parents send their children to such schools?

The most-publicized battle over these issues occurred in New York City during the 1830s and 1840s. Trustees of the Public School Society were determined to increase Catholic enrollment, for they were convinced that Catholic children, especially those of recent immigrants, needed common schooling to fit into society; otherwise, they might grow up as unsocialized outsiders. The trustees offered to edit some of the offensive passages from the textbooks, but they would not budge on reading the King James Bible without explication. After Catholics rejected the offer and petitioned for public funds to support their parochial schools, a statewide political controversy erupted. In 1842, the legislature intervened to make New York City part of the state's common school system, at the same time banning the use of public funds to support sectarian religious instruction.[33]

Although similar battles would be fought in other places, the confrontation between Protestants and Catholics in New York City set two precedents. In state after state, legislatures withdrew financial support from sectarian education, and in city after city, Catholics withdrew into their own schools.

## THE TRIUMPH OF COMMON SCHOOLS

By the outbreak of the Civil War, common school reformers could sense they had turned a corner. The failure to enlist Catholics in the school crusades had been a setback, to be sure, but there had been many victories. The idea of commonality had spread west and south as state legislatures committed themselves to the goals of tax-supported primary schooling for all white children, higher standards for training and hiring teachers, and a degree of centralized control vested in state boards of education. Even in the South, common schools were a reality in some cities, and southern legislatures were trying to translate the commitment they had made on paper into actual schools for the rural South. Thus the framework to support statewide school systems was either in place or under construction throughout most of the nation.

For 50 years after the Civil War, educators kept busy building, reinforcing, and expanding the systems. Two trends illustrate their progress.

The passage of compulsory school attendance laws, which appeared first in Massachusetts in 1852, quickened after the war. By 1900, the laws were on the books in 30 states; by 1910, in 40 states; and by 1918, in every state. Enforcement of the laws, haphazard at best before the turn of the century, became serious as state governments tightened their reins of control.[34]

A parallel development was the rise of public high schools. By now it should come as no surprise that Massachusetts led the way—Boston English High School opened in 1821—with other New England states, the Middle Atlantic states, and then the rest of the nation gradually following.

Nineteenth-century public high schools present a paradox to educational historians. With regard to gender, the schools were surprisingly egalitarian. They gave girls a chance to compete on relatively equal footing with boys—and the girls competed well. Girls outnumbered and often outperformed boys in public high schools, a pattern that lasted into the early twentieth century. Regarding social class, the schools were highly exclusive. As late as 1890, only about 4 percent of all the young people in the eligible age group attended public high schools, while private high schools enrolled another 2 percent. Public secondary education had a limited appeal in the nineteenth century, primarily to middle-class Americans who lived in cities. The wealthy, the poor, and the rural, in fact, sometimes challenged the right of governments to levy taxes for public high schools, arguing that the few who wanted secondary education for their children should pay for it themselves.[35]

A landmark decision of the Michigan Supreme Court in the *Kalamazoo* case (1874) handed public educators yet another victory over their critics, legally establishing a place for high schools as one rung on an educational ladder extending from primary schools through colleges and universities. The *Kalamazoo* decision strengthened the framework of public school systems and readied them for unprecedented expansion in the early twentieth century. Public elementary schools soon bulged at the seams, and by 1920, almost one-third of the eligible age group was enrolled in secondary education, overwhelmingly in public high schools.[36]

## PROGRESSIVE SCHOOL REFORM
## IN HISTORICAL CONTEXT

Once the students got to school, though, what were educators to do with them? This question goes to the heart of school reform during the progressive era, as historians call the period from the election of President William McKinley in 1896 through the U.S. entry into World War I in 1917. During these years, public schools changed in several lasting ways. Arguing that the schools should meet the needs of an increasingly heterogeneous student body, educators diversified the curriculum and broadened the schools' responsibilities. Increasingly, students took different courses and different programs depending on their abilities and "probable destinies" in life. The schools assumed more responsibility for the students' health and home life, for instance, and for the work they would do after graduation.[37]

One of the major legacies of progressive school reform is the strong link it forged between going to school and getting a job. Nineteenth-century educators had felt pressure to make schools relevant to work, but in the early twentieth century, educators became job brokers. Now their goal was fitting students into vocational slots—very narrow slots, in some cases, and very early determined. Schools sorted and selected students as never before. Ability grouping and tracking, ostensibly based on academic talent and individual goals, divided students along social lines as well. Wealthy kids here, middle-class kids there, working-class kids over there. Boys here, girs there. Blacks here, whites there— with subdivisions, of course, for various white ethnic groups.[38]

Educators believed immigrant children and African-American children confronted the schools with special problems. How should the schools respond? The debates in the next section of this chapter, focused on the cultural theories of *assimilation, pluralism,* and *separation,* suggest some of the strategies educators considered.

Historians differ in their interpretations of progressive school reform. To celebrationists, some of whom were reformers themselves, the diversified curriculum and the new responsibilities the schools assumed were in the best interest of students as well as society. Liberal historians, regarding progressive reform as basically well-intended, have nevertheless argued that certain reforms—vocational tracks and low-ability classes, for example—often harmed the very students they were designed to help. Revisionists have said they know why. The thrust of progressive reform was *not* to help students, especially those on the lower rungs of the social ladder, but to serve the interests of corporate capitalism. Neoconservatives have defended corporate capitalism, of course, but they, too, have been critical of public educators for fragmenting the curriculum and taking on too many social and economic responsibilities. Now multiple-perspective historians are urging us to look beyond caricatured portraits of reformers, supporters, and opponents to see how ordinary people have made their influence felt in the schools.

Keep these different interpretations in mind as you read about progressive school reform. Our major concern here is with how the reforms affected immigrant and African-American children. At the end of this chapter and in chapter 7, we will take a closer look at the curricular changes that began during the progressive era. Chapter 8 explores another legacy of progressive reform: the stratification of schools by social class.

## Modernization Accelerates

Even though the reform movements that occurred during the progressive era were quite diverse, the popular belief that the nation could take charge of its affairs and move forward gave the era a degree of unity. The need for reform seemed great because the forces of modernization—urbanization, industrialization, and immigration—were once again in high gear, confronting the nation with problems and opportunities similar to those the pre–Civil War reformers had faced.

But now the stakes seemed even higher. In 1860, only 20 percent of Americans had lived in cities. By 1920, the figure had climbed to 51 percent, with more than 5 million people crowded into New York City and more than 2 million into Chicago. Industrialization continued to fuel the growth of urban America, but Horace Mann and his contemporaries, certainly no strangers to change, could hardly have anticipated the pace and scale of industrial development after the Civil War: the rapid growth of big business, the extreme concentration of wealth in the hands of the most successful capitalists, and the flight of workers into labor unions.[39]

Many of the workers who took jobs in steel mills, meat-packing plants, garment factories, and other industrial settings were immigrants. The "new" immigration that occurred after 1870 made the "old" immigration seem mild by comparison. In the largest mass movement of people in history, approximately 28 million men, women, and children arrived in the United States from 1870 through 1920, so that by the twenties more than one-third of all the people in the nation were foreign-born or children of the foreign-born.

Beyond their sheer numbers, more than half the newcomers were from Central, Eastern, and Southern Europe, bringing with them a host of differences in language, religion, food, work habits, and other cultural traits. To people who had already put down their roots in this country, these new immigrants seemed even more alien than the old Irish and German immigrants.

Just as in the decades before the Civil War, calls for change went out as Americans decided something had to be done. The resulting reforms show that *progressive* could mean different things in different contexts. Some reforms were designed to improve the lot of ordinary people: housing regulations to clean up the squalor of tenements, food and drug acts to ensure standards of purity, and labor legislation to establish a reasonable work day and to get children out of the labor force. Other "progressive" reforms betrayed a lack of faith in ordinary people. Immigrants were greeted with laws designed to minimize their influence on the nation, and African Americans lost rather than gained rights during the period. Today, three-quarters of a century later, some of these reforms appear quite liberal, others profoundly conservative, still others a curious mixture.[40]

## Liberal and Conservative School Reformers

School reform during the progressive era was just as complex. John Dewey stands out as the major educational theorist of the era. The theory he and his followers developed, in fact, became known as *progressivism.* Social worker Jane Addams and African-American sociologist W. E. B. DuBois were among the liberal reformers who were concerned, like Dewey, with social justice and social service. In this chapter we will call Addams and DuBois to the podium to present the case for liberal reform. In the next chapter, we will pay closer attention to Dewey. Conservative reformers, represented here by school administrator and historian Ellwood P. Cubberley and African-American leader Booker T. Washington, had a different set of priorities, an agenda centered on social order and business efficiency.

Conservatives outnumbered liberals and often held positions that gave them more direct influence on the schools. Moreover, most of the teachers, administrators, and school board members who were responsible for putting educational reforms into practice on the front lines took an eclectic yet fundamentally conservative approach, paying lip service to the ideas of a Dewey, perhaps, but acting more like a Cubberley in their day-to-day work.[41]

## Ordinary People: Students, Parents, Teachers, and Others

Since the 1980s, historians have paid more attention to the ways ordinary people—students, parents, teachers, and others—influenced school reform. Multiple-perspective history reveals that ordinary people did not just stand by passively and let things happen to them. They also stood up and made things happen their way.

Three multiple-perspective studies capture this phenomenon especially well. In *Power and the Promise of School Reform* (1986), William J. Reese describes the "grass-roots" efforts of women's groups, parent-teacher coalitions, labor unions, socialists, and others to reshape schools during the progressive era. Voicing a variety of local concerns, these groups often won compromises and concessions from more powerful business interests. *Outside In* (1989) presents Paula S. Fass's argument that European immigrants, African Americans, women, and Catholics—cultural "outsiders" at the turn of the century—transformed American education as they moved through the schools. The education system we know today is the result of a tug of war between liberalism and conservatism as the schools came to grips with diversity. And in *The Education of Blacks in the South, 1860–1935* (1988), James D. Anderson portrays African Americans as active agents in their own education, people working to take charge of their lives and advance themselves. Their burning desire to learn threatened whites, for blacks used schools to resist racial and class oppression.[42]

As you read the debates in next section, keep in mind the complexities and contradictions of school reform. The process of reform involved much more than prominent people speaking while ordinary people listened.

## DEBATES OVER PROGRESSIVE SCHOOL REFORM

Nowhere is the complexity of reform more clearly illustrated than in the debates over the schooling of immigrant and African-American children, debates strikingly similar to those we hear today. Two cultural theories dominated the debates.

According to the theory of *assimilation,* it was the duty of the schools to fit children into society by washing out cultural differences and ironing in values and behaviors that conformed to Anglo-American ways. Here was the idea of the "melting pot" as most Americans understood it—a crucible that would melt away the immigrants' cultural differences.

According to the theory of *separation,* by contrast, certain cultural groups were so different that their children were better off attending separate schools, preparing them to reside in separate neighborhoods, hold separate jobs, and lead separate lives as adults. Members of these groups were not candidates for the melting pot, for they were regarded as too different to assimilate—that is, as incurably inferior.

The schools, taking their cues from the rest of the nation, used these theories to develop two distinct educational agendas: schools to promote assimilation for immigrant children and schools to foster separation for African-American children. Also singled out for separation throughout the Southwest were Mexican Americans and Native Americans, with California adding Asian-American children to the list of those schooled separately.[43]

### Assimilation for Immigrant Children

Ellwood Cubberley stated the case for immigrant assimilation in the textbooks he wrote for teachers and administrators. Cubberley, who rose quickly through the ranks of teachers and administrators to become dean of education at Stanford University, was one of the most prominent education professors of his day and a leading celebrationist historian. His textbooks went into numerous editions, influencing several generations of American educators. Had you decided to become a teacher 60 or 70 years ago, your introduction to education might well have been a course taught with one of Cubberley's books.[44]

In the well-thumbed volume from which I took the following quotation, the administrator who originally owned the book underlined and annotated Cubberley's views on the new immigrants:

> These Southern and Eastern Europeans were of a very different type from the North and West Europeans who preceded them. Largely illiterate, docile, often lacking in initiative, and almost wholly without the Anglo-Saxon conceptions of righteousness, liberty, law, order, public decency, and government, their coming has served to dilute tremendously our national stock and to weaken and corrupt our political life. . . . They have created serious problems in housing and living, moral and sanitary conditions, and honest and decent government, while popular education has everywhere been made more difficult by their presence. The result has been that in many sections of our country foreign manners, customs, observances, and language have tended to supplant native ways and the English speech, while the so-called "melting pot" has had more than it could handle. The new peoples, and especially those from the South and East of Europe, have come so fast that we have been unable to absorb and assimilate them, and our national life, for the past quarter of a century, has been afflicted with a serious case of racial indigestion.[45]

Nevertheless, Cubberley looked to the future with characteristically progressive optimism. If immigrant children would only attend public schools rather than the "foreign-language parochial schools," Cubberley opined as he gestured toward the Catholic and Lutheran churches, they would begin to lay aside their Old World culture and pick up American ways. The diversified public school curriculum, he believed, offered vocational courses that would help immigrant children make a contribution to society. The process of Americanization might take two or three generations to complete, but Cubberley felt sure the public schools, "our greatest agency for unifying the diverse elements of our population," were up to the task.[46]

## The Middle Course of Pluralism

Few public educators disagreed with Cubberley. A strong consensus supported the policies of assimilation he advocated. Two liberal reformers who did dissent were Jane Addams and John Dewey, both of whom tried to chart a middle course between assimilation and separation. Certainly it would be undesirable if each immigrant group went its own way, turning inward and never learning what it means to be American. Such separation would fragment the nation, they acknowledged. But total assimilation would also be unwise, they insisted, for already it was driving a wedge between immigrant parents and their children, depriving the immigrants as well as other Americans of a valuable cultural heritage.

The middle course Addams and Dewey were seeking eventually became known as *pluralism*. According to this theory, every person is expected to learn the common culture—which in this nation consists of the English language, American history, and the American political system, among many other things—but other cultures are not only tolerated but encouraged. As Addams told the National Education Association in 1908:

> [T]he schools ought to do more to connect these children with the best things of the past, to make them realize something of the beauty and charm of the language, the history, and the traditions which their parents represent. . . . If the body of teachers in our great cities could take hold of the immigrant colonies, could bring out of them their handicrafts and occupations, their traditions, their folk songs and folk lore, the beautiful stories which every immigrant colony is ready to tell and translate; could get the children to bring these things into school as the material from which culture is made and the material upon which culture is based, they would discover by comparison that which they give them now is a poor meretricious and vulgar thing. Give these children a chance to utilize the historic and industrial material which they see about them and they will begin to have a sense of ease in America, a first consciousness of being at home. I believe if these people are welcomed upon the basis of the resources which they represent and the contributions which they bring, it may come to pass that these schools which deal with immigrants will find that they have a wealth of cultural and industrial material which will make the schools in other neighborhoods positively envious.[47]

Addams's commitment to pluralism was based on her experience as a social worker and leader of the settlement house movement. In 1889, she founded Hull House in Chicago to encourage contact between privileged women (like Addams herself) and poor people, believing both could profit from the exchange. Mutual respect was the cornerstone of her philosophy. Addams envisioned settlement houses as community centers offering educational, social, and recreational programs; she hoped they would serve as models for public schools and other public agencies.[48]

A few public educators who shared Addams's pluralistic outlook started pioneer programs in what we now call *multicultural education*. Leonard Covello, who immigrated with his parents from Southern Italy at the turn of the century, experienced culture shock as a student in the New York City public schools. Feeling strong pressure to turn his back on Italy if he wanted to succeed in America—a teacher even changed his name from the original Leonardo Coviello—the young man complied, only to have second thoughts about assimilation after he graduated from college and began a career in education.[49]

Covello devoted the rest of his life to promoting pluralism. As a teacher in the New York City system, Covello worked with Italian students and parents to build pride in their heritage. When he became a principal, Covello turned a high school enrolling 25 different ethnic groups into the kind of community center Addams envisioned. Ordinary people from ethnic neighborhoods—the largest groups were Italian, Puerto Rican, and African—helped shape the new school. Students performed plays in Italian and Spanish. Parents spoke out in advisory meetings conducted in several languages. The curriculum upheld racial and ethnic tolerance.[50]

Such schools were rare. To Addams's disappointment, most public educators found little they wanted to emulate at either Hull House or schools like Covello's, for most educators saw little they wanted to save in immigrant cultures. Instead, their emphasis was on preparing immigrants for the work force. Addams was alarmed that the vocational programs into which many immigrant children were tracked led to dull, repetitive jobs that, she predicted, would produce alienation and drug abuse.

In Addams's day, as today, the issue of language was especially sensitive. Why should public schools encourage the use of any language but English? critics wanted to know. Hadn't the schools always used English as the only medium of instruction?

Conveniently ignored in most of the debates was the history of bilingual public schools in such cities as Cincinnati, Clevelend, Indianapolis, St. Louis, New Orleans, and San Francisco, some of which were using languages other than English as a medium of instruction before the Civil War. Responding to parents who wished to preserve their ethnic culture, some public schools offered bilingual instruction, usually in German and English, as late as World War I, when antiforeign sentiment forced the programs to close. Although bilingual public schools were the exception, not the rule, they set an early precedent for a pluralistic approach to public education, an approach that became popular in the 1960s and thereafter.[51]

## Separation for African-American Children

If immigrants were tossed into the melting pot and expected to emerge, completely assimilated, within a few generations, African Americans received no such treatment. Some immigrants were enthusiastic supporters of assimilationist public schools; others, as Cubberley pointed out, rejected them for parochial schools. Africans, with few exceptions, did not have a choice. In parts of the nation, most notably the rural South, they were lucky if they could go to school at all. As the progressive era opened in 1896, the U.S. Supreme Court handed down its decision in the *Plessy v. Ferguson* case, which placed the stamp of judicial approval on the "separate but equal" doctrine. The decision gave a Louisiana railroad company the right to segregate African-American passengers in train cars that were clearly separate and supposedly equal, and it quickly became the legal basis for segregation in other walks of life, including public education.

The result was a steady deterioration in the quality of education for African Americans as a bad situation became worse. In the South, where more than

90 percent of African Americans lived, the gaps in financial and physical resources between white schools and black schools widened. At the end of Reconstruction in 1877, the South had spent $1.50 to $2.00 per white student for every dollar spent per black student, a ratio of almost 2 to 1; by the end of the progressive era, the ratio had increased to perhaps 4 to 1. These figures estimate regional averages; we know the gap was wider, appallingly wider, in many rural systems, and some historians put the overall ratio of white to black expenditures as high as *15* to 1. Whatever the exact figures, it is obvious that "separate but equal" really meant "separate and unequal."[52]

The worst situation was in the South, but elsewhere racial attitudes hardened as lines were drawn to separate blacks and whites, either by law (as in the South) or by custom (as in most of the nation). Race riots and lynchings left ugly scars across the face of the country. In an era often remembered for social progress and uplift, African Americans found their educational rights eroding along with their voting rights, property rights, and other civil rights.

Yet African Americans fought back, as we can tell by listening to the debates over their education during the progressive era. The most important debate was between Booker T. Washington and W. E. B. DuBois, two leaders whose social and educational views were as different as their backgrounds.[53]

Washington, born in Virginia just before the Civil War, literally worked his way *Up from Slavery,* as he explained in his aptly titled autobiography. The education he received at Hampton Institute, an industrial school for African Americans in Virginia, convinced him that hard work, practical training, and cooperation with whites were the keys to success for blacks. He put his ideas into practice as head of Tuskegee Institute in Alabama, building the school from the ground up as a national model for the education of African teachers, farmers, and other workers. Washington soon became the best-known and most influential African American of his day.[54]

DuBois, born in Massachusetts just after the Civil War, attended integrated public schools, graduated from all-black Fisk University in Nashville, studied abroad at the University of Berlin, and capped his education at Harvard University, where he became the first African in the nation to earn a Ph.D. As a professor at Atlanta University and later as a leader of the National Association for the Advancement of Colored People (NAACP), DuBois spoke out sharply against all forms of racial discrimination. He pushed for equal access to schools at every level, but his heart was in higher education, which he hoped would prepare "the talented tenth"—the most gifted 10 percent of young African Americans—to become the leaders of their race.[55]

DuBois was too radical and outspoken for the times; Washington was so popular he was often invited to address white audiences, a distinction few other blacks could claim. By the 1890s, Washington was already in demand on the lecture circuit, but his 1895 speech at the Cotton States and International Exposition in Atlanta cemented his reputation as "the spokesman for his race."

On this occasion, the audience consisted of whites and blacks, seated in separate sections. Washington's thesis was that the two races would have to cooperate in order to move the South forward economically. He carefully distinguished between economic and social progress, though. With words chosen to admonish blacks and reassure whites, Washington said:

> The wisest of my race understand that the agitation of questions of social equality is the extremest folly, and that progress in the enjoyment of all the privileges that will come to us must be the result of severe and constant struggle, rather than of artificial forcing. . . . The opportunity to earn a dollar in a factory just now is worth infinitely more than the opportunity to spend a dollar in an opera house.[56]

Delivering the line that would prove to be the most quoted in the speech, Washington held his hand high: "In all things that are purely social we can be as separate as the fingers, yet one as the hand in all things essential to mutual progress." Thus Washington struck the conservative chords of social order and business efficiency.[57]

Despite his reference to factory work, the industrial education Washington advocated for African Americans did not emphasize preparation for city jobs in plants and machine shops. Instead, the accent was on rural life, for Washington believed blacks could make their greatest contribution in farming and farm-related crafts. Moreover, he used the word *industrial* much as we use *industrious* today, stressing such values as efficiency, punctuality, thrift, obedience, and cleanliness more than specific job skills. Above all, he urged African Americans to adopt the proper attitudes toward work and their place in the economic order. As he cautioned in the Atlanta speech:

> Our greatest danger is, that in the great leap from slavery to freedom, we may overlook the fact that the masses of us are to live by the production of our hands, and fail to keep in mind that we shall prosper in proportion as we learn to dignify and glorify common labor and put brains and skill into the common occupations in life, shall prosper in proportion as we learn to draw the line between the superficial and the substantial, the ornamental gewgaws of life and the useful. No race can prosper till it learns that there is as much dignity in tilling a field as in writing a poem. It is at the bottom of life we must begin, and not at the top.[58]

Industrial education worked its way into African-American schools at every level. In some elementary schools, it threatened to crowd academic studies into a corner, and as the small number of black students who were able to continue their formal education discovered, it was firmly entrenched in high schools and colleges as well.[59]

It angered DuBois that the ideas Washington articulated were so widely accepted. Few blacks and fewer whites paid attention as DuBois and other activists outlined dissenting points of view. Ellwood P. Cubberley's teacher education textbooks, for instance, contained words of praise for Washington and industrial education with no mention of the alternatives. As Cubberley explained matter of factly to future teachers and administrators, the black's "peculiar mental makeup and character have made his vocational and industrial education almost a necessity." These words struck college-educated African Americans like a slap in the face.[60]

In the early 1900s, DuBois established himself as Washington's most vocal critic. As a professor at Atlanta University, DuBois knew firsthand how difficult it was to raise money for African-American colleges and universities with a strong academic orientation. Northern philanthropists were sending money South, to be sure, but Washington's endorsement of industrial education carried so much weight that Tuskegee, Hampton, and similar schools were receiving the lion's share. Atlanta, Fisk, and other institutions with more traditional academic programs found it difficult to compete. Adding insult to injury, white philanthropists sometimes required them to develop industrial programs as a condition for receiving financial support.

DuBois believed "progress in human affairs is more often a pull than a push, a surging forward of the exceptional man, and the lifting of his duller brethren slowly and painfully to his vantageground." How could the black race produce the professionals and leaders it needed when the deck seemed to be stacked against academic programs?[61]

In his book *The Souls of Black Folk* (1903), DuBois grappled with that question and went considerably further, offering a pointed critique of Booker T. Washington's overall approach to black-white relations. Calling Washington's 1895 speech the "Atlanta Compromise" and referring to him with more than a hint of sarcasm as "the most distinguished Southerner since Jefferson Davis," DuBois charged that Washington had asked African Americans to trade their political power, civil rights, and higher education for "industrial education, the accumulation of wealth, and the conciliation of the South." They had made the bargain, DuBois noted, and three things had occurred:

1. The disfranchisement of the Negro.
2. The legal creation of a distinct status of civil inferiority for the Negro.
3. The steady withdrawal of aid from institutions for the higher training of the Negro.

These movements are not, to be sure, direct results of Mr. Washington's teaching; but his propaganda has, without a shadow of a doubt, helped their speedier accomplishment. . . . And thus Mr. Washington faces the triple paradox of his career:

1. He is striving nobly to make Negro artisans business men and property owners; but it is utterly impossible, under modern competitive methods, for workingmen and property-owners to defend their rights and exist without the right of suffrage.
2. He insists on thrift and self-respect, but at the same time counsels a silent submission to civic inferiority such as is bound to sap the manhood of any race in the long run.
3. He advocates common-schooling and industrial training, and depreciates institutions of higher learning; but neither the Negro

common schools, nor Tuskegee itself, could remain open a day were it not for teachers trained in Negro colleges, or trained by their graduates.[62]

Although DuBois's ideas may sound more acceptable than Washington's to our modern ears, we must remember to judge both men by the standards of their times rather than ours. By all accounts, both were sincere and well-intended, and both saw education as resistance to oppression. Washington was not trying to sell African Americans short—he was trying to make the best of a miserable situation. In fact, historical evidence has come to light indicating that Washington worked behind the scenes to support civil rights litigation he could not afford to endorse in public. By the same token, DuBois was not the elitist his blunt statement on "the exceptional man" and "his duller brethren" might suggest. Most of the African-American college students he taught came from poverty backgrounds. DuBois saw what they could achieve when given the opportunity, and he refused to compromise their future. His work with the NAACP helped pave the way for the modern civil rights movement.[63]

## PROGRESSIVE SCHOOL REFORM IN PERSPECTIVE

When progressive reformers, liberal and conservative, stepped back to survey what they had accomplished, conservatives could see more reasons to be pleased. Assimilation and separation were well-established in educational theory and practice. Pluralism was so undeveloped and unrefined it had yet to be named.

To be sure, all school reformers could point with pride to shared victories. Public schools were virtually everywhere, with centralized, statewide systems in place even in the South. The passage and enforcement of compulsory attendance laws was filling the schools with unprecedented numbers of students. The 1920 census found that over 90 percent of children aged 7 to 13 were in school, and more students were continuing their formal education through high school. Reflecting the growing consensus that the schools had to assume new social and economic responsibilities to meet the needs of a diverse student body, the diversified curriculum was rapidly winning acceptance. Another victory virtually all educational reformers could celebrate was the trend toward more specialized training for teachers. Colleges and universities were adding departments of pedagogy during the progressive era, state teachers colleges were emerging, and state normal schools and high school normal programs were in their heyday. In an era that fell in love with statistics, the facts and figures on the schools looked good.

Liberal reformers could take heart that a new theory of education, *progressivism,* was receiving a great deal of rhetorical support, especially among professors of education and school administrators. Since progressivism was so closely associated with John Dewey, the leading liberal reformer, liberals had high hopes that progressivism would eventually usher in a new era of social service and social justice in the schools.

Imagine their disappointment when, in the years after World War I, the nation took a conservative turn and "returned to normalcy"—business as usual. The spirit of liberal reform was a dead letter as far as the schools were concerned, but professors of education continued to preach, and administrators increasingly encouraged teachers to practice "progressive" methods of classroom instruction. By the 1920s, the methodology had been dubbed *progressive education.*[64]

Liberals were also disappointed that the academic discipline of psychology, to which many "progressive" educators were turning in their quest to make teaching and learning more scientific, was becoming another justification for the new status quo. As intelligence testing became widespread in the schools during the 1920s, educators gathered evidence that seemed to support what they were already doing: placing immigrant children, African-American children, and poor children generally in low-ability classes and vocational programs.[65]

Thus it was the form but not the substance of progressivism that influenced the schools after the war, the rhetoric but not the spirit. At the end of this chapter and throughout the next one, we will examine the controversy over how much the schools changed as a result of progressive influence, whether or not they improved, and who deserves the credit—or the blame.

## TWENTIETH-CENTURY PATTERNS OF EDUCATION

We can now look back on more than nine-tenths of the twentieth century and identify major trends in the schools. Because many of the chapters in this book provide historical perspectives on the issues they examine, the purpose of this section is to outline broad patterns to help structure the analysis presented elsewhere. Four patterns stand out as especially important: competition among school board members, administrators, and teachers for control of the schools; the changing balance of educational power among the local, state, and federal levels of government; the quest for equal educational opportunities; and trends in the curriculum.

### Competition for Control of the Schools

This first pattern has roots in the progressive era. "Get the schools out of politics" was the rallying cry of conservative reformers who charged local school boards with inefficiency and corruption.

The problem, they said, was that school boards in major cities had too many members with too many different points of view to do business efficiently. The boards were packed with "petty local politicos" elected from the various wards (political subdivisions) of the city. According to the reformers, such board members lacked a vision of what was good for the system as a whole—they were interested only in the schools in their own wards, and, to make matters worse, some of them were on the take, soliciting bribes, kickbacks, and payoffs. The reformers' solution: smaller school boards with members elected or appointed at-large, with each member representing the city as a whole rather than an individual ward.[66]

The trend toward smaller boards with at-large members swept the nation during the progressive era, spreading from major cities into other school systems. One result was the appearance on local boards of more people the reformers liked to call "the better sort"—successful businesspeople and professionals, most upper middle and upper class—and a sharp drop in the number of members with lower socioeconomic status.

A closely related trend was the rise to power of "professional" school administrators. As enrollments increased and the management of school systems became ever more complex, local board members gladly turned over more responsibility to superintendents and their growing administrative staffs. "Let the experts manage the schools" was another popular slogan during the progressive era, signaling a shift of power away from board members and toward upper-level administrators. As the twentieth century wore on, local superintendents consolidated their power, claiming that only experienced educators with advanced degrees from university departments of educational administration had the expertise necessary to run the schools. A self-conscious class of "professional" educators was emerging.[67]

Teachers felt lost in the shuffle. In some respects, they had felt more comfortable before progressive reform. Many teachers had known the board member who represented their ward—a shopkeeper from the neighborhood, perhaps. The smaller, at-large board seemed remote, aloof—a group of elites. The worst development from the teachers' point of view was the attempt to apply the "sound and cheap" principles of scientific management to the schools. Merit pay and promotions based on evaluations by administrators and supervisors posed the greatest threat, as we saw in chapter 2.

In 1920, 86 percent of America's teachers were women. Just when the numerical dominance of women in the occupation was greater than at any time before or since, women were losing power in the school system hierarchy. Most elementary school principals had been women in the late nineteenth century. During the twentieth century, women watched these administrative positions go increasingly to "school men," as male educators like to be called to set themselves apart. High school principalships had always belonged to men. Educational historian David Tyack describes the situation bluntly:

> Hierarchical organization of the schools and the male chauvinism of the larger society fit as hand to glove. The system required subordination; women were generally subordinate to men; the employment of women as teachers thus augmented the authority of the largely male administrative leadership.[68]

In the early decades of this century, teachers organized to protect their interests and improve their economic security. Their early organizations were local groups responding to local problems. Teacher organizations gave women the opportunity to lead, but these groups, too, were often dominated by school men. With the NEA in the hands of college professors and administrators, some local teacher organizations affiliated with the AFT, a small, struggling union.[69]

From the 1920s through the 1950s, teachers had to strain to make their voice heard in school system policy, even when they spoke through an AFT local. Since the 1960s, though, the situation has changed. The AFT led the way by showing how collective bargaining can amplify the teachers' voice. After scoring organizing victories in New York City and several other large systems, the AFT became a power to be reckoned with. In short order, the NEA also became a teacher union, a national giant with strength in every state and in most local school systems. For the first time, teachers had a collective voice in educational policy making at all three levels of government, and the voice of female teachers was stronger than ever.

As we saw in chapter 4, the new power of teacher organizations is highly controversial. Supporters say teachers are beginning at last to act like professionals rather than employees; detractors say just the opposite is true.

## The Local/State/Federal Balance

The increasingly complex politics of teacher organizations add their own weight to the educational balance of power among the local, state, and federal levels of government, the second pattern of twentieth-century education we will consider. Recall the debates over the merits of local versus state control of public education—the tension between the idea that citizens should be able to run their local schools as they see fit and the idea that a degree of centralized control is necessary to ensure minimum standards of education. Notwithstanding the statewide standards promoted by school reformers, local school boards still enjoyed a great deal of autonomy at the turn of the century, for the regulations state legislatures and state boards of education imposed left plenty of discretion at the local level.

As the century unfolded, the states gradually tightened their reins of control, often in response to controversies and shortcomings in local school systems. Several examples illustrate the trend. Complaints about the content of textbooks— often involving religion or politics, just as in Horace Mann's day—led to more power for state textbook committees. But local school officials usually were able to choose from several titles on the state-approved list or, in some states, simply to ignore the list. Arbitrary dismissals of teachers triggered the passage of state tenure laws, often after successful campaigns by teacher organizations. But local boards could still fire probationary teachers without stating a reason, and administrators could make life miserable for tenured teachers who violated local mores.

Financial problems also enhanced state control. During the Great Depression, thousands of local school systems declared insolvency and closed. Faced with already wide gaps in spending between rich systems and poor systems within virtually every state, legislatures stepped in to provide relief, mandating minimum levels of local support as a condition for receiving state aid. Lawsuits from citizens and advocacy groups led to a still greater state role in school finance beginning in the 1960s. As chapter 9 points out, the latest round of litigation is pushing many states closer than ever toward equalizing expenditures from one district to the next.

Financial problems were also behind the trend toward consolidation of local school systems. In 1900, there were approximately 150,000 independent school districts in the United States; today there are about 15,000. State legislatures justified consolidation on the grounds of economic and academic efficiency— more programs could be offered to more students at lower cost—but local people complained their control over the schools was slipping away.[70]

Such complaints are not new; most of them would seem familiar to Horace Mann. What would strike him as novel, though, is the federal government's growing involvement in public education during the twentieth century. Even a Whig like Mann, an advocate of active government, never envisioned public education as a major item on the federal list of "internal improvements." But in 1917, the federal government made its first annual appropriations to secondary schools through the Smith-Hughes Act, which was designed to promote vocational education. For the next few decades, the federal role was focused, with Congress trying hard not to step on state and local toes. A series of federal relief acts aided schools during the Depression, the 1944 G.I. Bill helped veterans further their education, and the 1958 National Defense Education Act (NDEA) entered the schools in the space race.

The real breakthrough came during the 1960s and 1970s, when the federal government began targeting most of its assistance toward students whose education had been a low priority in state and local school systems: poor, minority, disabled, and female students. Judicial activism in the federal courts complemented the high profile Congress maintained in public education, and Lyndon Johnson said he wanted to go down in history as an "education president."

We will take a closer look at federal involvement in other chapters, especially chapter 9, but here it is important to note the mixed reviews the new federal role received. Once again debates over centralized control, this time control at the federal level, broke out across the nation, and during the 1980s, Ronald Reagan capitalized on a strong backlash as he cut federal involvement in education.

Part of the backlash reflected the general distrust Americans have always had of central government, though part of it was based on the newer and more specific concern that the federal government was paying too much attention to certain groups of students—poor, minority, disabled, and female—and promoting their advancement at the expense of the rest. This development was an ironic reversal of the situation during the first half of the twentieth century, when members of the same groups criticized the federal government for its lack of interest in their plight.[71]

## The Quest for Equal Educational Opportunities

As we examine the third pattern of twentieth-century education, we will consider African Americans as a case in point. Since the 1920s, the NAACP and other organizations working on behalf of African Americans have brought legal pressure to bear on public schools and colleges, seeking better treatment for black students and teachers. The results were disappointing at first. Southern states continued to spend several times as much money on white as on black children, and in other regions, particularly in large industrial cities, schools became more rather than less segregated. In the late 1930s, however, the tide began to turn as African Americans won court decisions that eventually led to equal salaries for black and white teachers.[72]

Other litigation began the long process of desegregation. The major victory came with the U.S. Supreme Court's landmark decision in *Brown v. Board of Education of Topeka* (1954). The court unanimously overturned *Plessy v. Ferguson* (1896) for elementary and secondary schools, declaring that "in the field of public education the doctrine of 'separate but equal' has no place." The struggle to translate the court's words into action continues today.[73]

The modern civil rights movement that gathered strength in the post-*Brown* era not only helped improve educational opportunities for African Americans but also inspired other Americans to press for better education for their children. During the 1960s and 1970s, members of other racial and ethnic minority groups, women, the disabled, and the poor mounted their own campaigns.

The schools responded in a variety of ways, often by developing special programs with federal funds. Renewed interest in bilingual instruction and the growth of multicultural education led to arguments reminiscent of earlier debates over assimilation, separation, and pluralism. Despite the backlash against federal involvement in education during the 1980s, educators continued to show concern—at least rhetorical concern—for students who became known as the "at risk." In chapters 8 and 9, we will analyze the current status of the quest for equal educational opportunities.

## Trends in the Curriculum

The final twentieth-century pattern is a fascinating study of the relationship between educational theory and educational practice. Historians enjoy investigating the evolution of the *formal* curriculum, the one discussed in teacher education courses and written down in school board policies. Usually the historical analysis focuses on major studies and reports that have influenced the curriculum. To show how the curriculum has changed during this century, historians often begin by describing the nineteenth-century curriculum as subject centered, revolving around a set of academic subjects that were said to strengthen the mind in the same way that physical exercise strengthens the muscles. The report most often cited to illustrate this "mental discipline" approach came from the NEA: the *Report of the Committee of Ten on Secondary School Studies* (1893).[74]

The NEA's study committee, dominated by college presidents, argued that the best way to prepare students for life was to discipline their minds with the academic subjects that would also prepare them for college—this at a time when only 6 percent of the eligible age group went to high school and only 2 percent went on to college. Although the committee recommended several alternatives to the then-fashionable concentration on Latin and Greek, it affirmed the idea that schools should challenge *all* high school students with a subject-centered curriculum, and it suggested that elementary schools take a similar approach.

This point of view came under attack in the twentieth century, but two subject-centered theories of education, *essentialism* and *perennialism,* continued to influence the schools. I will argue in chapters 7 and 10 that essentialism—its most recent incarnations are back to basics, the new basics, and excellence in education—has had more influence on educational practice than any other theory.

But at times during this century there has been a strong pull away from a curriculum centered on subjects and a push toward a curriculum that attempts to balance academic content, social needs, and student interests. The report historians usually cite to illustrate this trend also came from the NEA, but this report appeared at the end of the progressive era, 25 years after the Committee of Ten: the *Cardinal Principles of Secondary Education* (1918). The study group that produced the report, the Commission on the Reorganization of Secondary Education, was dominated by high school principals and professors of education who urged the development of diversified, more flexible curriculum with different programs designed to prepare *all* students for *all* aspects of life.[75]

By 1918, almost one-third of the eligible age group was going to high school, and the NEA's commission envisioned a time when almost all students would. (By 1930, half the age group was in high school, and today the figure is near 95 percent.) To meet the needs of a hetergeneous student body, the NEA commission recommended that educators reorganize and supplement the traditional academic subjects in order to pay more attention to such areas as health, leisure, and vocation.[76]

The *Cardinal Principles* reflect *progressivism,* the modern theory of education developed primarily by John Dewey and his followers. As we will see in the next chapter, though, Dewey was often unhappy with what happened when progressivism was translated into practice in the schools.

Describing twentieth-century changes in the curriculum as an ongoing battle between mental discipline and the *Cardinal Principles* or as a contest between traditional and modern theories of education allows historians to simplify an immensely complicated process and explain it in understandable terms. Now historians are beginning to investigate what teachers actually *did* with the formal curriculum. We know progressivism was popular in teacher education programs by 1920, but how and when did the progressive methods teachers and administrators learned about in their education courses actually work their way into elementary and secondary classrooms? How much did teachers change the formal curriculum after they shut the classroom door? Our answers to such questions are tentative at best.[77]

Larry Cuban's book *How Teachers Taught* (1984) is forcing historians to rethink their standard explanations, for Cuban has discovered more constancy than change in twentieth-century classrooms. Using photographs, textbooks, tests, recollections of teachers and students, and other sources that historians have often neglected, Cuban argues that teacher-centered instruction—in which the teacher stands up front and spends most of the time talking to the whole class—has remained dominant throughout this century.[78]

Even though progressives have urged teachers to become more student centered by letting students exercise more responsibility and by teaching them individually or in groups, most teachers have not changed. Cuban estimated that since 1900, about two-thirds of America's teachers, including over 90 percent of high school teachers, have stuck firmly to teacher-centered instruction. About 25 percent of teachers have tried a few student-centered techniques, developing "hybrids" that blended with their routine. Only 5 to 10 percent have been true believers in student-centered instruction. Like their nineteenth-century counterparts we studied earlier, twentieth-century teachers have resisted pressure to alter their style.[79]

Why so little change? According to Cuban, the organizational structure of schools and the occupational culture of teaching work against change. The structure of schools requires teachers to maintain order, cover a body of material, and show evidence that students have learned. Quite simply, teacher-centered instruction helps teachers get the job done. Student-centered instruction, on the other hand, is risky. It reduces the authority of teachers. It disrupts the quiet routine. From the teachers' point of view, more freedom for students may or may not result in more learning. Most teachers prefer to settle for tried-and-true methods rather than invest their time and energy—scarce commodities—in an experiment.[80]

Have teaching methods really changed so little since the days of the NEA's Committee of Ten? Before accepting or rejecting Larry Cuban's arguments, you need to become familiar with philosophies and theories of education, for they offer a way of thinking about teaching and learning that complements the historical analysis in this chapter.

## ACTIVITIES

1. Now that you have read this chapter, think about your own interpretation of American educational history. Is your interpretation celebrationist, liberal, revisionist, neoconservative, or multiple perspective?

2. Debate some of the issues in this chapter with friends whose interpretations of history differ from yours.

3. Conduct an oral history project. Interview older citizens with diverse social and educational backgrounds about their school experiences.

4. Compile a history of an older elementary or secondary school to see the local effects of national educational trends. Oral history, microfilmed newspaper accounts, and school system records are some of the sources you may be able to use.

## RECOMMENDED READINGS

Anderson, James D. *The Education of Blacks in the South, 1860–1935* (Chapel Hill: University of North Carolina Press, 1988).
    Already a classic, this book shows how African Americans used education to resist political and economic subordination.
Cremin, Lawrence A. *The Transformation of the School: Progressivism in American Education, 1876–1957* (New York: Knopf, 1961).
    Cremin's study remains the best introduction to the progressive impulse in education.

Kaestle, Carl F. *Pillars of the Republic: Common Schools and American Society, 1780–1860* (New York: Hill & Wang, 1983).
The definitive work on common schools, this study has clear themes and rich detail.

Perkinson, Henry J. *The Imperfect Panacea: American Faith in Education, 1865–1990,* 3d ed. (New York: Random House, 1990).
Students looking for a short, readable survey of the history of American education can do no better than this book.

## NOTES

1. Robert Allen Skotheim, ed., *The Historian and the Climate of Opinion* (Reading, MA: Addison-Wesley, 1969), p. 2.
2. Ellwood P. Cubberley, one of the conservative reformers mentioned later in this chapter, was also a major celebrationist historian. His textbook *Public Education in the United States: A Study and Interpretation of American Educational History* (Cambridge, MA: Houghton Mifflin, 1919) remained a standard in teacher education courses as late as the 1950s.
3. See Merle Curti's *The Social Ideas of American Educators* (New York: Scribner, 1935) and Lawrence A. Cremin's *The Transformation of the School: Progressivism in American Education, 1876–1957* (New York: Knopf, 1961).
4. Examples of revisionist educational history include Michael B. Katz's *The Irony of Early School Reform: Educational Innovation in Mid-Nineteenth Century Massachusetts* (Boston: Beacon Press, 1968); Clarence J. Karier, Paul C. Violas, and Joel Spring's *Roots of Crisis: American Education in the Twentieth Century* (Chicago: Rand McNally, 1973); and Samuel Bowles and Herbert Gintis's *Schooling in Capitalist America: Educational Reform and the Contradictions of Economic Life* (New York: Basic Books, 1976).
5. Diane Ravitch is the most prominent of the new conservatives. She stirred up controversy among educational historians with the publication of *The Revisionists Revised: A Critique of the Radical Attack on the Schools* (New York: Basic Books, 1978) and *The Troubled Crusade: American Education, 1945–1980* (New York: Basic Books, 1983).
6. For examples of multiple-perspective history, see David Tyack and Elizabeth Hansot's *Managers of Virtue: Public School Leadership in America, 1820–1980* (New York: Basic Books, 1982); William J. Reese's *Power and the Promise of School Reform: Grass-Roots Movements during the Progressive Era* (Boston: Routledge & Kegan Paul, 1986); and Joel Spring's *The American School, 1642–1990: Varieties of Historical Interpretation of the Foundations and Development of American Education,* 2d ed. (White Plains, NY: Longman, 1990).
7. Two important studies of the colonial era are Bernard Bailyn's *Education in the Forming of American Society: Needs and Opportunities for Study* (Chapel Hill: University of North Carolina Press, 1960), which called attention to the importance of educational agencies other than schools, and Lawrence A. Cremin's *American Education: The Colonial Experience, 1607–1783* (New York: Harper & Row, 1970).
8. One of the best accounts of district schools is Robert L. Church and Michael W. Sedlak's *Education in the United States: An Interpretive History* (New York: Free Press, 1976), chap. 1.

9. Gerald L. Gutek traces the colonial roots of these regional variations in *Education in the United States: An Historical Perspective* (Englewood Cliffs, NJ: Prentice-Hall, 1986), chap. 1.
10. Albert Henry Smith, ed., *The Writings of Benjamin Franklin,* vol. 3 (New York: Macmillan, 1904–1907), pp. 395–421.
11. Church and Sedlak, *Education in the United States,* chap. 2.
12. Spring, *The American School,* pp. 17–22; H. Warren Button and Eugene F. Provenzo, Jr., *History of Education and Culture in America,* 2d ed. (Englewood Cliffs, NJ: Prentice-Hall, 1989), pp. 85–90.
13. Spring, *The American School,* chap. 3.
14. Ibid.
15. Two studies of modernization and its effects are Clinton Rossiter's *The American Quest, 1790–1860: An Emerging Nation in Search of Identity, Unity, and Modernity* (New York: Harcourt Brace Jovanovich, 1971) and Robert H. Wiebe's *The Segmented Society: An Introduction to the Meaning of America* (New York: Oxford University Press, 1975).
16. An old but still useful study emphasizing the "humanitarian" aspects of the various reform crusades is Alice Felt Tyler's *Freedom's Ferment: Phases of American Social History from the Colonial Period to the Outbreak of the Civil War* (Minneapolis: University of Minnesota Press, 1944).
17. James G. Carter, *Essays on Popular Education . . .* (1826), in David Tyack, ed., *Turning Points in American Educational History* (Waltham, MA: Blaisdell, 1967), p. 153.
18. Ibid, p. 155.
19. An excellent study of the movements is Carl F. Kaestle's *Pillars of the Republic: Common Schools and American Society, 1780–1860* (New York: Hill & Wang, 1983). For a study of the South, see Joseph W. Newman's "Antebellum School Reform in the Port Cities of the Deep South," in David N. Plank and Rick Ginsberg, eds., *Southern Cities, Southern Schools: Public Education in the Urban South* (Westport, CT: Greenwood Press, 1990), chap. 1.
20. Church and Sedlak, *Education in the United States,* chap. 3.
21. Ibid. See also Jonathan Messerli's *Horace Mann: A Biography* (New York: Knopf, 1972) and Edith Nye MacMullen's *In the Cause of True Education: Henry Barnard and the Nineteenth-Century School Reform* (New Haven, CT: Yale University Press, 1991).
22. Church and Sedlak, *Education in the United States,* chap. 3.
23. Barbara Finkelstein, *Governing the Young: Teacher Behavior in Popular Primary Schools in Nineteenth-Century United States* (New York: Falmer Press, 1989).
24. A typical defense of district schools came from the Committee on Education of the Massachusetts House of Representatives in 1840, reprinted in Rush Welter, ed., *American Writings on Popular Education: The Nineteenth Century* (Indianapolis: Bobbs-Merrill, 1971), pp. 85–96.
25. Spring discusses various aspects of commonality in *The American School,* chap. 5.
26. Orestes Brownson, *The Boston Quarterly Review* (October 1839), in Michael B. Katz, ed., *School Reform: Past and Present* (Boston: Little, Brown, 1971), p. 280.
27. Ibid., p. 281.
28. Horace Mann, *Twelfth Annual Report of the [Massachusetts] Board of Education* (1848), in Lawrence A. Cremin, ed., *The Republic and the School: Horace Mann on the Education of Free Men* (New York: Bureau of Publications, Teachers College, Columbia University, 1957), p. 97.

29. Joseph W. Newman, "Morality, Religion, and the Public Schools' Quest for Commonality," *Review Journal of Philosophy and Social Science* 4 (Winter 1980): 18–32.

30. Mann, *Twelfth Annual Report,* p. 102.

31. Brownson, *The Boston Quarterly Review* (1839), in Katz, *School Reform,* pp. 280–281.

32. R. Freeman Butts, *Public Education in the United States: From Revolution to Reform* (New York: Holt, Rinehart & Winston, 1978), pp. 114–120.

33. Two studies of the confrontation in New York are Carl F. Kaestle's *The Evolution of an Urban School System: New York City, 1750–1850* (Cambridge: Harvard University Press, 1973), pp. 145–158; and Diane Ravitch's *The Great School Wars: New York City, 1805–1973* (New York: Basic Books, 1974), pp. 3–79.

34. Butts, *Public Education,* p. 181.

35. David Tyack and Elizabeth Hansot, *Learning Together: A History of Coeducation in American Public Schools* (New Haven: Yale University Press, 1990); U.S. Department of Education, National Center for Educational Statistics, *Digest of Education Statistics, 1991* (Washington, D.C.: U.S. Government Printing Office, 1991), p. 64.

36. *Stuart et al. v. School District No. 1 of Kalamazoo* (1874). Edward A. Krug has written the classic histories of secondary education: *The Shaping of the American High School, 1880–1920* (New York: Harper & Row, 1964) and *The Shaping of the American High School, 1920–1941* (Madison: University of Wisconsin Press, 1972).

37. The pioneering study of these changes is Cremin's *The Transformation of the School.*

38. See Harvey Kantor and David B. Tyack, eds., *Work, Youth, and Schooling: Historical Perspectives on Vocationalism in American Education* (Stanford: Stanford University Press, 1982); David F. Labaree, *The Making of an American High School: The Credentials Market and the Central High School of Philadelphia, 1838–1939* (New Haven: Yale University Press, 1988); and John L. Rury, *Education and Women's Work: Female Schooling and the Division of Labor in Urban America, 1870–1930* (Albany: State University of New York Press, 1991).

39. Robert H. Wiebe's *The Search for Order, 1877–1920* (New York: Hill & Wang, 1967) provides an excellent historical context, emphasizing the impact of modernization.

40. John D. Buenker, *Urban Liberalism and Progressive Reform* (New York: Scribner, 1973); Gabriel Kolko, *The Triumph of Conservatism: A Re-Interpretation of American History, 1900–1916* (New York: Free Press of Glencoe, 1963).

41. Church and Sedlak, *Education in the United States,* chap. 9.

42. Reese, *Power and the Promise of School Reform*; Paula S. Fass, *Outside In: Minorities and the Transformation of American Education* (New York: Oxford University Press, 1989); James D. Anderson, *The Education of Blacks in the South, 1860–1935* (Chapel Hill: University of North Carolina Press, 1988).

43. Raymond A. Mohl, "Cultural Assimilation versus Cultural Pluralism," *Educational Forum* 45 (March 1981), pp. 323–332.

44. Joseph W. Newman, "Ellwood P. Cubberley: Architect of the New Educational Hierarchy," *Teaching Education* 4 (Spring 1992): 161–168.

45. Cubberley, *Public Education,* pp. 485–486.

46. Ibid., p. 489. For excellent studies of the tension between ethnic identity and Americanization, see Fass's *Outside In* and Maxine Schwartz Seller's *To Seek America: A History of Ethnic Life in the United States* (Englewood, NJ: Jerome S. Ozer, 1988).

47. Jane Addams, "The Public School and the Immigrant Child" (1908), in Daniel Calhoun, ed., *The Education of Americans: A Documentary History* (Boston: Houghton Mifflin, 1969), pp. 421–423.

48. Ellen Condliffe Lagemann, ed., *Jane Addams on Education* (New York: Teachers College Press, 1985).
49. Covello describes his experiences in the autobiographical *The Heart Is the Teacher* (New York: McGraw-Hill, 1958), rereleased in 1970 as *The Teacher in the Urban Community.*
50. David B. Tyack discusses Covello's school in *The One Best System: A History of American Urban Education* (Cambridge: Harvard University Press, 1974), pp. 239–240.
51. Tyack, *The One Best System,* pp. 106–109.
52. Anderson, *The Education of Blacks,* chap. 5; Louis R. Harlan, *Separate and Unequal: Public School Campaigns and Racism in the Southern Seaboard States, 1901–1915* (Chapel Hill: University of North Carolina Press, 1958), pp. 255–256. See also Horace Mann Bond's *The Education of the Negro in the American Social Order* (Englewood Cliffs, NJ: Prentice-Hall, 1934) and Henry Allen Bullock's *A History of Negro Education in the South: From 1619 to the Present* (Cambridge: Harvard University Press, 1967).
53. Anderson, *The Education of Blacks,* pp. 65, 77, 102–109.
54. Booker T. Washington, *Up from Slavery* (New York: Doubleday, 1901).
55. W. E. B. DuBois, *The Autobiography of W. E. B. DuBois: A Soliloquy on Viewing My Life from the Last Decade of Its First Century* (New York: International Publishers, 1968).
56. Booker T. Washington, "Address . . . [on] September 18, 1895," in Calhoun, *The Educating of Americans,* p. 351.
57. Ibid., p. 350.
58. Ibid.
59. Donald Spivey, *Schooling for the New Slavery: Black Industrial Education, 1868–1915* (Westport CT: Greenwood Press, 1978).
60. Cubberley, *Public Education,* p. 744.
61. W. E. B. DuBois, *The Souls of Black Folk* (Chicago: A. C. McClurg, 1903), chap. 6.
62. Ibid., chap. 3.
63. See Louis R. Harlan's *Booker T. Washington: The Making of a Black Leader, 1856–1901* (New York: Oxford University Press, 1972) and *Booker T. Washington: The Wizard of Tuskegee, 1901–1915* (New York: Oxford University Press, 1983).
64. Cremin, *The Transformation of the School.*
65. Erwin V. Johanningmeier, *Americans and Their Schools* (Chicago: Rand McNally, 1980), chap. 13.
66. Joseph M. Cronin, *The Control of Urban Schools: Perspectives on the Power of Educational Reformers* (New York: Free Press, 1973).
67. Raymond E. Callahan, *Education and the Cult of Efficiency: A Study of the Social Forces that Have Shaped the Administration of the Public Schools* (Chicago: University of Chicago Press, 1962); David Tyack and Elizabeth Hansot, *Managers of Virtue: Public School Leadership in America, 1820–1980* (New York: Basic Books, 1982); William Edward Eaton, ed., *Shaping the Superintendency: A Reexamination of Callahan and the Cult of Efficiency* (New York: Teachers College Press, 1990).
68. Tyack, *The One Best System,* p. 60.
69. Wayne J. Urban, *Why Teachers Organized* (Detroit: Wayne State University Press, 1982); Marjorie Murphy, *Blackboard Unions: The AFT and the NEA, 1900–1980* (Ithaca, NY: Cornell University Press, 1990).
70. Educational historians need to pay more attention to relations between the local and state levels. One study that does provide some historical perspective is Frederick M. Wirt and Michael W. Kirst's *Schools in Conflict: The Politics of Education* (Berkeley, CA: McCutchan, 1982).

71. Joel Spring, *The Sorting Machine Revisited: National Educational Policy since 1945,* rev. ed. (White Plains, NY: Longman, 1989); Henry J. Perkinson, *The Imperfect Panacea: American Faith in Education, 1865–1990,* 3d ed. (New York: Random House, 1991), chap. 5; Frank J. Munger and Richard F. Fenno, Jr., *National Politics and Federal Aid to Education* (Syracuse, NY: Syracuse University Press, 1962); Hugh Davis Graham, *The Uncertain Triumph: Federal Education Policy in the Kennedy and Johnson Years* (Chapel Hill: University of North Carolina Press, 1974).
72. Meyer Weinberg, *A Chance to Learn: The History of Race and Education in the United States* (London: Cambridge University Press, 1977).
73. Richard Kluger, *Simple Justice: The History of* Brown v. Board of Education *and Black America's Struggle for Equality* (New York: Knopf, 1976).
74. *Report of the Committee of Ten on Secondary School Studies* (Washington, D.C.: National Education Association, 1893).
75. Commission on the Reorganization of Secondary Education, *Cardinal Principles of Secondary Education* (Washington, D.C.: U.S. Government Printing Office, 1918).
76. U.S. Department of Education, *Digest of Education Statistics,* p. 64.
77. The best historical studies of the curriculum are Herbert M. Kliebard's *The Struggle for the American Curriculum, 1893–1958* (Boston: Routledge & Kegan Paul, 1986) and Edward A. Krug's two-volume set *The Shaping of the American High School, 1880–1920* and *The Shaping of the American High School, 1920–1941.*
78. Larry Cuban, *How Teachers Taught: Constancy and Change in American Classrooms, 1890–1980* (White Plains, NY: Longman, 1984).
79. Ibid., chap. 6.
80. Ibid.

# CHAPTER 7

# Philosophies and Theories of Education

## "WHY" QUESTIONS

Every chapter in this book asks "why" questions, questions of rationale and purpose, but this chapter digs deepest into human experience for answers. Here we will use the discipline of philosophy to study schools and society. Most introduction to education textbooks challenge prospective teachers to personalize educational philosophy by developing their own, a request that seems reasonable enough. As you read this chapter, try to relate each philosophy and each theory to your own experience. As we go about our careers and lives, we have all-too-little time to ask "why" questions, and thus we may never see the values and assumptions underlying what we do and what we believe. One value of philosophy, then, is that it requires us to pause and reflect on deeply personal matters.

But as much as philosophy has helped me understand myself and my teaching, it has given me even more guidance as I have tried to make sense of the changes I have seen in education during my lifetime. Studied in conjunction with history, philosophy has helped me analyze controversies that seem to reappear, albeit in slightly different guises, with surprising regularity. For instance, why do Americans keep sending their schools back to basics every few years? What is back? What is basic? And what are the alternatives? Although I cannot guarantee you will have all the answers after you read this chapter, you will have some of them. Just understanding the questions is a step forward.

The chapter opens with an overview of four schools of philosophy: *idealism, realism, pragmatism,* and *existentialism.* These are philosophies of life, encompassing education as well as other aspects of living. After a brief look at each philosophy, we will turn to a more extensive discussion of three educational theories: *perennialism, essentialism,* and *progressivism.* These theories apply the philosophies directly to education.

**175**

## FOUR PHILOSOPHIES

Each philosophy offers answers to three basic questions:

| | |
|---|---|
| What is real? | Each philosophy has a *metaphysics,* a particular explanation of the nature of reality. |
| How do we know? | The answers each philosophy provides to this question constitute its *epistemology,* or view of the nature of knowledge. |
| What is of value? | Each philosophy has an *axiology,* or value system. Such questions as "What is right?" and "What is good?" are in the realm of *ethics.* "What is beautiful?" is a matter of *aesthetics.* |

### Idealism

The roots of idealism lie in the thinking of the Greek philosopher Plato. Idealists believe reality is ultimately spiritual. The physical world we know through our senses is only a manifestation of the spiritual world. Idealists acknowledge a *macromind*—a universal force, a creator, a God—who is responsible for the whole of existence. We humans have souls and *microminds.* Our souls resided with the macromind in a transcendental realm before they united with our bodies, giving our microminds a spiritual character that can never be lost.

Idealists believe our major responsibility on earth is getting our microminds as closely in touch as possible with the macromind. We can do so by looking inward rather than outward. Since our souls once lived in the spiritual realm, our minds are capable of recalling absolute and unchanging truth. Truth is already in our minds. We should not look for it outside of ourselves. We cannot rely on our five senses in the search for truth, because our senses give us distorted information on the physical world, and the physical world is itself an imperfect manifestation of the spiritual world. We must seek the truth within our minds, relying on contemplation and introspection.

We cannot go it alone, though. We need help on our quest. Idealists believe we can recall the truth if we stimulate our minds with the best thoughts of the best human minds. Some human minds have grasped more truth than others, which is another way of saying some microminds reflect the macromind far better than others. Most humans operate at the level of opinion, often incorrect opinion, and only a few have been very successful in the quest for truth. But how can we identify these enlightened thinkers? How can we examine their thought?

We must concentrate on ideas that have stood the test of time, idealists answer. Throughout history, educated people have cherished certain works of literature and art, for example, works that have endured because they are superior representations of the truth. The minds of the writers and artists who produced them were more closely in touch with the truth than were the minds of their contemporaries. Because our time on earth is limited, we must use it wisely, concentrating on the best literature and art and the best of our human heritage. This heritage, organized in the form of academic disciplines, is the curriculum idealists want us to study in school.[1]

## Realism

Realism is another old philosophy, with roots in the thinking of Plato's student Aristotle. All realists emphasize the physical world. Some believe nothing else exists, although others say a spiritual realm exists as well. When trying to explain the origins of the physical world, most realists admit the likelihood of a divine being or creator, although here again realism provides room for several points of view. Some realists believe the physical world is a result of mere chance; others argue that a divine being set the world in motion and then sat back to watch; still others insist that the creator maintains active involvement with the world. Realists are also divided over whether humans have souls, but they agree that humans have minds capable of rational thought, a quality that distinguishes us from other creatures on earth.

Our major responsibility is getting to know the physical world. We can do so by using our senses and our rationality. In contrast to idealists, realists urge us to look outward rather than inward. Using our senses, we collect information on the physical world. Using our rational minds, we process the information by sorting, classifying, and abstracting it. And thus we acquire knowledge.

Like idealists, realists believe in absolute and unchanging truth, though to realists truth lies in the natural law that governs the universe—the law of gravity, for example, and the laws of reproduction and genetics. Humans know the truth to the degree they understand natural law. Not all realists are scientists, of course, but realists argue that all people who seek reliable knowledge about the world must conduct their quest in the same way, by relying on their senses and their rationality.

Experiencing the world is the best way to learn about it, realists say, but given our limited time, we cannot afford to learn randomly, taking life as it comes. We must structure learning based on the experiences of those who have preceded us. Over the years, educated people have sorted and classified what they have learned into academic disciplines, the organized bodies of knowledge we know by such names as history, mathematics, literature, and science. These subject-matter disciplines provide the framework for formal education.[2]

## Pragmatism

Compared with idealism and realism, pragmatism is a newcomer. Its roots lie in late nineteenth-century America, in the work of mathematician Charles Sanders Pierce, psychologist William James, and philosopher John Dewey. All three were deeply influenced by Charles Darwin's theory of evolution, with its emphasis on change and adaptation. Like realists, pragmatists urge us to concentrate on the physical world. Some pragmatist believe there is nothing else, others refuse to speculate, while still others believe in a spiritual realm but say it can be known only through faith, not reason. Pragmatists agree, though, that change is the most important characteristic of physical reality and that the human mind, endowed with rationality, can understand reality by coming to grips with change.

John Dewey, whose work as a school reformer we examined briefly in the last chapter, believed adapting to change is the major challenge we face in life. He urged us to take an experimental approach to life. Drawing on the work of Darwin, Dewey viewed human beings as organisms interacting with their environments. He called this interaction process *experience*—a key concept in pragmatic philosophy. Experience brings us face to face with a series of problems, and we learn as we try to solve the problems. Dewey urged the use of the scientific method in problem solving, both in schools and throughout society.

Wedded as they are to change and adaptation, pragmatists do not believe in absolute and unchanging truth. For pragmatists, truth is what works. Truth is relative, because what works for one person may not for another, just as what works at one time or in one place or in one society may not work in another. Pragmatists admit that the concept of relative truth, applied to morality, could lead to chaos. They insist, though, that morality is social rather than personal. Certainly a society cannot allow people to act just as they see fit, completely unrestrained. But a society inevitably changes its morality over time, and one society's morality may be another's immorality.

Like realists, pragmatists believe we learn best through experience, but pragmatists are more willing to put that belief into practice. While realists are concerned with passing organized bodies of knowledge from one generation to the next, pragmatists stress applying knowledge—using ideas as instruments in problem solving. Realists and idealists call for a curriculum centered on the academic disciplines; pragmatists prefer a curriculum centered on problems, a curriculum that draws the disciplines together to solve problems—an *inter-disciplinary* approach.[3]

## Existentialism

"Existence precedes essence," declared Jean-Paul Sartre, the French philosopher who popularized existentialism in the years after World War II. Unlike the other philosophies we have discussed, which seek to define the nature of human beings and then suggest how we should live, existentialism begins with the fact of existence. We have no choice about being born, but from that point on we face an infinite number of choices. Each of us must define his or her own essence. Each of us is an experiment of one. Each of us has the freedom—and the obligation—to choose how to live. No one else can make these decisions for us.

Although a few existentialists have tried to combine their philosophy with traditional religion, most are not interested in speculating about a creator and a spiritual realm. Rather, they urge us to get on with the task of defining our lives in the physical world, which is devoid of purpose and meaning according to most existentialists. They make much of the concept of *angst,* the feeling of pervasive dread that comes with the realization that each of us is alone in a meaningless world. Yet rather than being overwhelmed with desperation, we should go go forward with hope, for we can create the lives we want. We can choose to be self-determined. We can give meaning to our lives.

As we saw in the discussion of pragmatism, leaving people free to determine their own morality runs the risk of anarchy. This risk is present to an even greater degree in existentialism. But unlike pragmatists, who try to deal with the problem by making morality social rather than personal, existentialists are unwilling to trust society, for they view society as often—some of them would say usually—oppressive. Instead, they ask each of us to choose morals with the interests of all of us in mind. As Sartre said, "I am responsible for myself and for all."

With their concern for promoting choice and independence, existentialists prefer an education that offers students as many alternatives as possible. Certainly there should be no set curriculum; students must be free to explore as they see fit. Existentialists do believe some subjects are better suited than others to promoting self-expression. Literature, the arts, and other subjects that raise questions rather than present answers are high on the existentialists' list.

Unlike idealism, realism, and pragmatism, existentialism has not yet produced a theory of education comparable to those we will examine in the next section. Existentialism has influenced the schools, though, and we will conclude this section by looking at its effects.

Van Cleve Morris, one of the best-known advocates of existentialist education, points out how the rise of the late 1960s counterculture brought a kind of "street existentialism" into the schools. Humanistic psychology and values clarification became popular. Many students and some teachers vowed to "do their own thing." Caught up in the spirit of the times, school officials made graduation requirements more flexible so students could choose relevant, meaningful courses. Some educators questioned the value of grades—what right did one human being have to impose a value judgment on another? These trends were beneficial in part. If nothing else, they forced an examination of educational rituals. "You'll act this way because I think it's good for you" was no longer an acceptable justification.

But unfortunately, says Morris, this "parody of existentialism . . . left out the most important thing existentialism teachers: *personal responsibility.*" Genuine existentialists resent the charge that their philosophy has ushered a "no-fault morality" into the schools, a value system no more complex than "If it feels good, do it." Yet some critics are saying just that, roping together existentialism and pragmatism and branding them as modern philosophies with disastrous effects on school and society. Since the late 1970s, as we will see in the following sections, theories of education based on the traditional philosophies of idealism and realism have been basking in their popularity, while educational theory based on modern philosophy has been on the outside looking in.[4]

## THEORIES OF EDUCATION: AN OVERVIEW

Educational theories are applications of philosophy to education. The two older philosophies, idealism and realism, have combined to produce two theories of education, perennialism and essentialism. These traditional theories went almost unchallenged in their dominance of education until the last 100 years. The modern philosophy of pragmatism applied to education has produced progressivism, a theory that has competed with the traditional theories throughout the twentieth century. Looking back on the century, we will see an especially competitive tug of war between essentialism and progressivism.

Out in the schools, it is difficult to find any of the three theories in pure form. When theory goes into practice, some things change in translation. Most teachers are eclectic, blending this theory with that and alternating the mix from time to time. Thus we will examine educational theory alongside educational practice, pointing out discrepancies between what the theorists say and what actually goes on in the schools.

The questions with which educational theory deals are less sweeping than What is real? How do we know? and What is of value? Nevertheless, the concerns of educational theory are far reaching. Each theory tries to answer four basic questions:

What is the purpose of education?

What is the content of the school curriculum?

What is the place of students?

What is the role of teachers?

Now we will see how perennialism, essentialism, and progressivism answer the questions.

## PERENNIALISM

*Perennial* means "everlasting." This theory of education, derived from the philosophies of idealism and realism, emphasizes knowledge that has endured. From idealism perennialists get their interest in spiritual knowledge, in ideas that seem so transcendent they must reflect a higher intelligence. From realism comes the perennialists' willingness to study the physical world using their senses and rationality. Perennialism itself has stood the test of time. It is an old educational theory that shaped the development of European universities and dominated U.S. higher education until the late nineteenth century. Perennialism exerts a continuing influence through the work of Robert M. Hutchins, former president and chancellor of the University of Chicago, and Mortimer J. Adler, for many years the preeminent philosopher at Hutchins's university. Indeed, Adler and his Paideia Associates are leading a revival of interest in perennialism.

Hutchins presented a succinct rationale for perennialism in his book *The Higher Learning in America* (1936): "Education implies teaching. Teaching implies knowledge. Knowledge is truth. Truth is everywhere the same. Hence, education should be everywhere the same." The education perennialists advocate focuses on both intellect and character, on enlightenment as well as goodness. Perennialists believe a careful study of our cultural heritage reveals more agreement than disagreement on such questions as What is beautiful? and What is moral? Intent on passing time-honored concepts from one generation to the next, perennialists look for continuities in human existence.[5]

Perennialists stress the authority relationship in teaching and learning. If teachers are knowledgeable people of good character, as perennialists insist they must be, then they should not hesitate to take command in the classroom. Students are incompletely formed human beings; they should not come to school expecting to dictate the terms of their education, for they have less knowledge and maturity than the adults with whom they will be working. The very idea of a "student voice" in a "democratic classroom"! Students may question ideas, of course—perennialists require them to think critically—but they must never challenge their teachers' authority.

## The Great Books

Critics have joked that perennialists won't even read books written after 1900, much less use them in school. The joke exaggerates the point, but the charge is just accurate enough to irritate perennialists. In fact, they do like modern works, though they are more comfortable with those that have stood the test of time. During the 1930s, Robert Hutchins, Mortimer Adler, and other perennialists tried to revive classical tradition in higher education with a curriculum based on the "great books of Western civilization." They assembled a set of books ranging from Plato's *Republic* to the Bible to the U.S. Constitution to Einstein's *On the Electrodynamics of Moving Bodies,* works that in their judgment represent the best of Western civilization.[6]

A great book, they argued, is one that accomplishes just what it sets out to do—it does not need to be rewritten. A great book is always contemporary—it does not need to be reinterpreted. A great book can be read by almost anyone. A great book helps people develop standards of taste and judgment. Unfortunately, many of the debates over perennialism as an educational theory have been little more than arguments over the books on Hutchins and Adler's shelf. Why did they choose this book but not that one? Do Asian, African, and other non-Western cultures have adequate representation? What about modern fiction? Can very young students understand the books? These arguments, still flying back and forth between great-books fans and great-books critics, have settled nothing.

## *The Paideia Proposal*

Adler, chair of the board of editors of *Encyclopedia Britannica* and now professor of philosophy at the University of North Carolina at Chapel Hill, has revitalized perennialism with the publication of *The Paideia Proposal* (1982). Adler and his Paideia Associates are no longer arguing the merits of a particular set of books. Instead, they are promoting a particular kind of education for all students. Make no mistake about it, this is a far-reaching proposal. What the Paideia Group advocates is schooling that is the same for everybody, with no tracking and virtually no electives. For 12 years, all students pursue the same curriculum, which Adler organizes into "three distinct modes of teaching and learning."[7]

He calls the first mode *acquisition of knowledge.* Using didactic methods, teachers acquaint students with fundamental knowledge in three subject-matter areas: language, literature, and fine arts; mathematics and natural sciences; and history, geography, and social sciences.

The second mode of teaching and learning is *development of skill.* Here teachers act like "coaches" who help students learn to *do*; that is, they help students acquire the basic skills of reading, writing, speaking, listening, observing, measuring, estimating, and calculating. Students get their only elective in this area: choice of a second language.

*Enlargement of understanding,* the third mode, goes to the heart of perennialism by emphasizing ideas and values. Teachers conduct seminars in which they use not didactics and coaching but the Socratic method of questioning and discussing. Students study not textbooks but books and art forms that represent the best of human endeavor.

Very much alive in his nineties, Adler genuinely enjoys responding to criticisms of *The Paideia Proposal* and its two companion volumes, *Paideia Problems and Possibilities* (1983) and *The Paideia Program* (1984).[8] I once had the privilege of seeing him in action at an academic conference as, with obvious relish, he took on a roomful of friendly and not-so-friendly critics. "You are an elitist, just as perennialists have always been," one critic charged. "Your proposal sounds like the curriculum of an exclusive prep school 'back East.'"

"You are the elitist," Adler replied. "I am trying to make education in the United States truly democratic by giving all students the high-quality schooling that has been reserved for a privileged few."[9]

"You are trying to educate all children as if they were all alike, when actually they are all different," another critic stated. "There is infinite variety in human beings. One child may be a rose, so to speak, while another may be a tulip and still another a violet. Just as roses, tulips, and violets require different amounts of light, water, and heat to thrive, so, too, do children need different kinds of education."

"Your analogy is fundamentally flawed," Adler shot back, with more than a hint of irritation. "The plants you named are members of different species. All human beings are members of the same species. Children are inherently alike, and all deserve the same excellent education."

Somewhat more cautiously, another critic stood up and said, "But students do differ in their academic abilities. Let's face it—some are smarter than others. The curriculum you advocate may suit the academically gifted, but it is inappropriate for below-average or even average students."

Smiling now, Adler replied, "Certainly some people have a greater capacity for learning than others. Some of us are large containers who can hold a great deal; some of us are medium-sized; some of us are small containers with small capacities. The mistake educators make is pouring different liquids into the different sizes. The large containers often get wine, the excellent education offered in the best public and private schools. The medium-sized containers get water, an education of lesser quality. Perhaps the greatest tragedy is that the small containers usually get dirty water—make-work courses, vocational training, a curriculum that is admittedly third class. We in the Paideia Group want to pour the same wine into all containers, irrespective of size. We want to educate all students up to their capacity."

Adler seemed less confident fielding questions about teachers and teacher education. Given prevailing salaries and working conditions, can this nation attract the moral, intelligent people needed to make the Paideia Proposal work? Given the kind of education students receive in the vast majority of public and private schools today, is it reasonable to expect these students to become the kind of teachers Adler wants? Even if all prospective teachers receive a liberal arts education in college, as Adler demands, will they be able to bring perennialism to life in the classroom? Adler admits that finding favorable answers to these questions will not be easy, but he insists that we try: "An ideal—even a difficult one—excites everyone's imagination. To say it cannot be done is to beg the question. We've got to try it."[10]

Adler and his associates are putting their ideals to the test in the real world of the public schools. They have taken over selected schools in Atlanta, Chicago, and Oakland, where they are educating—a better word might be *reeducating*—teachers and challenging students with a perennialist curriculum. The Paideians asked for "tough" schools full of the students who otherwise might be getting dirty water. Their success in these schools, publicized in their newsletter *The Paideia Bulletin,* has prompted more than 100 other school districts to implement some version of the Paideia reforms.

It is hard not to admire Adler for trying, but it is also hard to imagine perennialism succeeding on a large scale in the United States. Although Adler defends himself well at academic meetings, easily deflecting charges of elitism, he may find it impossible to counter the socioeconomic biases that run so deep in the history of American education. Simply stated, public educators have consistently given up on certain children—poor and minority students in particular. Perennialists have tended to wall themselves off in private schools with carefully selected students, proudly cultivating the very image of elitism Adler is trying to dispel.

Adler harbors no illusions that reform will be easy. Although he feels more optimistic now, as his career draws to a close, than when he began teaching in the 1930s, he cautions there is "no quick fix." In fact, Adler admits the reforms in *The Paideia Proposal* may take "the better part of two generations to achieve." While some advocates of essentialism, the educational theory we will examine next, are promoting reform by the cookbook—step by step, to the letter, and right into the oven—Adler is holding out for reform that is more gradual, complex, and fundamental.[11]

Known for skewering his critics, Adler often rebukes educators and politicians for not "fully understand[ing] the shape of an adequate reform or all the obstacles to be overcome in achieving it." One of Adler's favorite essentialist targets is the equally sharp-tongued William J. Bennett, secretary of education during the second term of the Reagan administration. According to Adler, Bennett is selling the quick fix. Bennett is one of today's leading spokespersons for essentialism, and Adler holds him partially responsible for the educational excesses of our nation's most recent back-to-basics movement, especially the "uncritical, almost superstitious" faith in testing, testing, testing (see chapter 10). Bennett and other essentialists—including Chester E. Finn, Jr., Diane Ravitch, and E. D. Hirsch, Jr.—are more than happy to defend themselves, and you should weigh the arguments on all sides as you read the next section.[12]

## ESSENTIALISM

Of all the theories of education, essentialism has had the greatest influence on U.S. elementary and secondary schools. Its popularity may wax and wane, but essentialism never fades away entirely. It is like a durable undercoat of paint. Educational reformers may cover it temporarily with other theories, but when times and fashions change, essentialism reappears. Essentialists sometimes say their theory is what remains when we peel away the "fads and frills" of American education. To go back to basics is to go back to essentials, although it is becoming increasingly difficult to get a consensus on what is essential and what is not.

Essentialism, like its close relative perennialism, is grounded in the philosophies of idealism and realism. Idealism gives essentialism its emphasis on the human mind as a precious, some would say sacred, treasure that—if properly educated—can show the way to a full, rich life. Realism gives essentialism an emphasis on the physical world. Since people live in the world, they must acquire the knowledge and skills necessary not only to survive but also to live well.

Although the term *essentialism* was not coined until the 1930s, when traditional educators were organizing to do battle with progressive educators, the principles of essentialism dominated the district schools and common schools of nineteenth-century America. The twentieth century has witnessed a struggle between essentialists and progressives (whose ideas we will study next), with the former having more influence on daily practice in the schools and the latter having a stronger voice in colleges of education.

Essentialism and perennialism, grounded as they are in idealism and realism, have a great deal in common. Both theories of education dismiss the criticism "some students can't handle your curriculum" with a terse "certainly they can—all but the very small percentage of students who have severe mental deficiencies." Advocates of both theories are comfortable with the image of students as receptacles or containers into which teachers pour knowledge. Both theories are conservative in a cultural sense, for both emphasize passing a cultural inheritance from one generation to the next.

There are also important differences between essentialism and perennialism. The essentialist curriculum is less wedded to the classics. It is likely to contain more modern literature, for instance, and to feature more knowledge and skills of recent vintage—computer science and word processing. Notwithstanding Adler's attempts to avoid debates over the great books in promoting the Paideia Proposal, most perennialists do have a preference for older, tried-and-true works, and even though Adler says he has found a place for the manual arts in his curriculum, perennialist schools are not exactly rushing to add courses in cooking and auto repair. Essentialists, on the other hand, have long favored industrial arts courses in theory, although in practice they tend to look the other way when only the less academically talented students sign up.

Accordingly, essentialism has a stronger vocational emphasis. In theory, essentialists and perennialists both say there is more to life than getting and holding a job, but in practice essentialists are more likely to try to sell students on the value of academic subjects in the job market: "You'll need this math course if you want to work in a high-tech company." This strand of essentialism has grown especially strong since the early 1980s, when business leaders began promoting school reform as they key to making the United States more productive and competitive in the world economy. Adler and the perennialists realize almost everyone has to work, yet they believe too much emphasis on job preparation inevitably tracks "small container" students into vocational courses, robbing them of a first-rate education.

Perhaps the most significant practical difference between essentialism and perennialism is that essentialists have more faith in standardized testing. To a greater degree than the advocates of any other educational theory, in fact, essentialists see standardized testing as a yardstick of student progress, a quality-control check on teachers, and a guarantee of accountability for the taxpaying public. Perennialists, by contrast, join progressives in arguing that standardized testing has been so overdone it has corrupted the entire teaching-learning process.

During this century, essentialism has surged forward three times, in each case capitalizing on recurring public beliefs that the schools have become too soft and too involved in social engineering. In the late 1930s, William Bagley led the essentialist crusade. During the 1950s, the "academic critics"—a group of essentialist professors of the arts and sciences—launched their attacks. And from the late 1970s through the present, essentialist banners have been flying again. During its most recent revival, essentialism has inspired reforms ranging from minimum competency testing to the "Excellence in Education" campaign outlined in *A Nation at Risk* (1983) to former President George Bush's America 2000 strategy.

## William C. Bagley and the 1930s

William C. Bagley, a professor of education at Teachers College, Columbia University, emerged during the 1930s as the most prominent and articulate spokesperson for essentialism. Faced with the social upheaval of the Great Depression, Bagley looked to the schools to provide stability in the midst of change. Above all, he argued, the schools should equip students with the basic academic skills they need to survive in society and continue their education. He charged that many students were graduating from high school "essentially illiterate." Tracing such problems back to the elementary schools, Bagley called for a renewed emphasis on reading, writing, and arithmetic. If essentialism stands for nothing else, it stands for mastery of the 3Rs.[13]

But it stands for much more, Bagley said. The schools must conserve and transmit our cultural heritage. "An effective democracy demands a community of culture," he maintained. "Educationally this means that each generation must share a common core of ideas, meanings, understandings, and ideals, representing the most precious elements of the human heritage.''[14] Like many traditional educators, Bagley downplayed differences of opinion regarding the content of the curriculum. ''There can be little question as to the essentials,'' he asserted, urging a program of history, geography, health, science, the fine arts, and the industrial arts, supported by continuing instruction in the 3Rs.[15]

Schools must also stress morality, Bagley maintained. Such cornerstone values as honesty and respect for other people's property are as essential to the orderly operation of schools as they are to the very existence of society. So are obedience, discipline, and hard work. Much learning is simply not fun, Bagley argued, and students should not come to school expecting to have a good time. Essentialists talk so much about the importance of work that they sometimes appear to believe in work for its own sake. Essentialist teachers wear the mantle of authority in the classroom, insisting on order and making no apologies for instilling traditional values in students.

## The Academic Critics of the 1950s

The academic critics were articulate, colorful, and for the most part bitter in their attacks on American education. The titles of their books tell much of the story: Arthur E. Bestor's *Educational Wastelands: The Retreat from Learning in Our Public Schools* (1953) and *The Restoration of Learning* (1955) were the perfect complements to Mortimer Smith's *And Madly Teach* (1949) and *The Diminished Mind: A Study of Planned Mediocrity in Our Public Schools* (1954). James B. Conant offered less biting criticism in *Education and Liberty: The Role of Schools in a Modern Democracy* (1953) and *The American High School Today* (1959).[16]

Whether their tone was vicious or gentle, the academic critics agreed on key points. The public schools, by embracing a progressive theory of education that made them responsible for meeting every need of every student, had strayed from their central purpose: providing intellectual training in the basic skills and academic disciplines. This change had harmed all students, the critics maintained, but gifted students had suffered the most. The schools had abandoned their Jeffersonian mission of identifying bright students, whatever their backgrounds, and preparing them to lead the nation. The academic critics had no difficulty casting villains for their drama. John Dewey led the list, followed by professors of education who infected teachers with progressivism. Teacher education was the biggest joke on college campuses, yet state certification standards were written so only people trained in colleges and departments of education could become teachers.

Arthur Bestor and Mortimer Smith, as professors of history, leaned heavily on the liberal arts in their proposals for reform. In 1956, they helped organize the Council for Basic Education, which is still one of the most prominent voices of essentialism.

James Conant, trained in chemistry, appreciated the liberal arts but placed more emphasis on science and math. After the Soviet Union put Sputnik I into orbit in 1957, Conant's ideas became tremendously popular. Fed up with progressive pedagogy, Americans turned to the schools to help the nation win the space race. Congress passed the National Defense Education Act (NDEA) in 1958; math, science, and foreign language teachers suddenly found themselves in great demand; and students across the nation found out what it meant to build a science project. Essentialism was in the driver's seat.

Many Americans look back on the late 1950s and early 1960s with a kind of "Happy Days" nostalgia, recalling the era as a time of academic excellence. To be sure, the schools were excellent for some students in some schools. If you were lucky enough to live in a well-off suburban district and were fortunate enough to be in the college preparatory track, you probably did receive a rigorous, academically demanding education, particularly in the technologically oriented subjects that were in vogue.

Excellence was not uniformly distributed, though. Within those same suburban districts it was business as usual for students in the lower-ability groups, especially for those in the vocational tracks. Essentialism probably did bring more academic rigor to the students caught in the middle—those in the general track—although their program continued to be less demanding than the college prep curriculum. Moreover, academic excellence was out of reach of the nation's poorest school systems, even with the federal government's financial assistance.

It is also questionable that the new math, new science, and new social studies deserved the label of excellence. If we take the word of the students, teachers, and parents who struggled with them, they were academic disasters. Arts and sciences professors do not like to be reminded that they led the schools down the "new" paths, only to beat a hasty retreat when the innovations failed.

## Back to Basics through Behavioral Essentialism: The 1970s, 1980s, and 1990s

Since the mid-1970s, going back to basics has been all the rage. To people who have studied the history and philosophy of American education, much of the recent rhetoric of school reform has a familiar ring. There are echoes of William Bagley in the calls for good old-fashioned morality and discipline in the classroom. Charges that the schools became soft and affective in the mid-1960s as they tried to engineer a racially integrated society recall the academic critics of the 1950s. James Conant would surely approve the renewed emphasis on science and math, although this time we are racing not the Soviet Union but Japan, West Germany, and other friendly industrial powers. And once again it has become fashionable to poke fun at teacher education, much to the delight of the Council for Basic Education.

Public pressure on the schools to stress the 3Rs—"Teach our children reading, writing, and arithmetic if you teach them nothing else"—is also familiar. Although the pressure has varied in intensity over the years, it has always been a force to be reckoned with. More thoughtful essentialists have tried to remind the public that basic skills are just the beginning of formal education. But when theory meets practice, essentialism has consistently promoted such a fixation on basic skills that some students have received drill in the 3Rs and hardly anything else. It has always been easy for college professors to blame parents, teachers, and administrators for corrupting essentialism in this way, but the corruption has occurred nevertheless. It is widespread today.

What is different about the latest back-to-basics movement is that behavioral psychology is influencing the schools to a far greater degree than ever before, as educators learn to combine behaviorism and essentialism in powerful new ways. We will return to this issue in chapter 10, but here it is important to note how the new *behavioral essentialism* emphasizes observable, measurable results.

The marriage of behaviorism and essentialism has produced a generation of standardized tests designed to offer the public "scientific proof" that students are learning. In response to the public outcry for more basics and higher test scores, the curriculum for most students has narrowed. Educators have deemphasized music, art, health, and physical education—and, in some cases, even science and social studies—because they are not basic enough, or so it seems, particularly for elementary school students. Given the difficulty of measuring higher-level academic skills with multiple-choice/true-false tests, the curriculum has tilted, even in middle and secondary schools, toward lower-level skills. In math classes, students spend far more time practicing computation than solving application problems. In history, they memorize lists of battles and generals rather than analyze issues and trends.

As behavioral essentialism swept the schools in the late 1970s and early 1980s, scores on tests of lower-level skills rose. The public was impressed. But most teachers knew better.

Some prominent essentialists, to their credit, were as skeptical as the teachers. *A Nation At Risk,* the report that shaped the educational debates of the 1980s, was essentialist to the core. Prepared by the Reagan administration's National Commission on Excellence in Education, the report curtly rejected the obsession with minimum competency testing and lower-level skills. It proposed instead a curriculum built on Five New Basics, all of them to be taught with a higher-level emphasis. Four years of English, three years of mathematics, three years of science, three years of social studies, and one-half year of computer science should be the *minimum* requirements for *all* high school students, the commission urged. Foreign language was the sixth basic for college-bound students, and the report also gave a nod of approval to the fine and performing arts.[17]

With its references to "the essentials of a strong curriculum" and their role in preserving "the mind and spirit of our culture," *A Nation at Risk* tried to pull essentialism out of its behavioral rut. Unfortunately, the attempt was only partially successful, for the report had its share of inconsistencies and contradictions. On the one hand, it tried to be egalitarian by insisting on a higher-level curriculum for all students; on the other, it deliberately evoked nostalgia for the schools of the late 1950s and early 1960s, conveniently ignoring the grossly unequal educational opportunities that characterized the era. Along the same lines, the Cold War and Sputnik rhetoric was so strong in the report, which called on science and math to ride to the rescue of America once again, that teachers of other subjects wondered how they would fare under this Conant-like version of essentialism.

Even the attack on minimum competency testing and the lower-level mediocrity it promotes struck some teachers as halfhearted, for the report turned right around and recommended the development of a "nationwide (but not federal) system of state and local standardized tests," a proposal President Bush would push in the early 1990s. Teachers who were already under pressure to teach to numerous existing national, state, and local tests were not encouraged.[18]

Now, more than a decade after *A Nation at Risk,* the pileup of test upon test is creating serious doubts about behavioral essentialism. I realized sentiment was shifting when my local school district and my state, among the first in the nation to jump on the testing bandwagon in the late 1970s, began *repealing* standardized test requirements in the late 1980s. "Enough of a good thing, I guess," one local school board member told me, preparing to switch to the "critical thinking skills" bandwagon. The same switch is under way in many other states and school districts. Veteran teachers are telling their younger colleagues they have seen it all before.[19]

As the 1990s unfold, behavioral essentialism is indeed losing some of its luster. Judged by its own criteria—standardized test scores—the movement has not been a resounding success. Scores on tests of higher-level skills have declined throughout the reign of back to basics, and some of the rising lower-level scores of a decade ago have stagnated or fallen. Behavioral essentialism is in trouble. Thoughtful advocates of essentialism are trying hard to project a more appealing image of their theory as it might be, an image that contrasts sharply with essentialism as it is.[20]

## Contemporary Essentialists

Some of essentialism's best contemporary advocates are scholars who took leaves from their university careers to accept political appointments in the Reagan and Bush administrations. Moving back and forth between higher education and the federal government, William Bennett, Diane Ravitch, and Chester Finn are using the prominence they have attained in both worlds to advance the cause of traditional education.

Bennett, the most colorful and audible of the three, left academia to chair the National Endowment for the Humanities and then to serve as Ronald Reagan's second secretary of education. In *James Madison High School* (1987) and *James Madison Elementary School* (1988), Bennett sets forth his vision of essentialism as it might be. Rich in Western culture and steeped in the democratic ethic, the work ethic, and the Judeo-Christian ethic—Bennett regards these as the common elements of U.S. culture—the James Madison curriculum moves well beyond the 3*R*s. We will use this curriculum as a model of thoughtful essentialism in chapter 10.[21]

Students should *know* things when they get out of school, Bennett says. In *The De-Valuing of America* (1992), he looks back on his federal service and summarizes with disarming simplicity the lessons he learned: "Students should finish high school knowing not just the 'method' or 'process' of science or history; they should actually know some science and history. . . . They should know that for every action there is an equal and opposite reaction, and they should know who said 'I am the state' and who said 'I have a dream .' . . . They should know where the Amazon flows, and what the First Amendment means."[22]

Bennett knows how to use the English language to great effect. One of the most popular conservative speakers in the nation, often described as senatorial or presidential timber, he stays involved in education and politics as a fellow at the Hudson Institute and the Heritage Foundation.

Finn and Ravitch are helping Bennett carry on the essentialist campaign. Finn, a professor at Vanderbilt University, served as assistant secretary of education under Bennett, and Ravitch left Teachers College, Columbia University to become assistant secretary in Lamar Alexander's Department of Education during the Bush administration. Having founded the Educational Excellence Network, Finn and Ravitch brought to Washington their credentials as defenders of traditionalism. Both are advocates of the humanities, and Ravitch is a well-known neoconservative historian (see chapter 6) who has written several books and published numerous articles in the *Atlantic Monthly, New Republic, New York Times,* and other high-profile media.[23]

Ravitch and Finn captured national attention in 1987 with their book *What Do Our 17-Year-Olds Know?,* which announced that U.S. students are ignorant of the most basic factual knowledge. In the tradition of Bagley, Bestor, and Bennett, essentialists update and recycle this criticism during every back-to-basics movement. Ravitch and Finn focused their concern on history and literature. What do students know about the Civil War, for instance? The Great Depression? Shakespeare? Faulkner? Based on the results of a test administered by the National Assessment of Educational Progress (NAEP), their answer was "Not much."[24]

The timing of this announcement was perfect, for E. D. Hirsch, Jr., an English professor at the University of Virginia, had already made the best-seller lists in 1987 with *Cultural Literacy: What Every American Needs to Know.* Perennialist Allan Bloom released *The Closing of the American Mind,* a biting critique of higher education, that same year. Ravitch, Finn, Hirsch, and Bloom all stress the importance of passing a cultural heritage from one generation to the next, and their books have touched off a debate over the role of the schools in increasing cultural literacy. We will hear this debate in chapter 10.[25]

Chester Finn's *We Must Take Charge* (1991) is *the* essentialist call to arms of the 1990s. "This book is about ignorance, about discomfort, and about education," he begins. Using military imagery, Finn argues that the essentialist battle for the schools is America's best hope for averting catastrophe. The nation is still at risk, he warns, urging "civilians" outside the education establishment ("the blob," Bennett calls it) to get angry, alarmed, and armed. Concerned citizens must take charge to ensure all students sound instruction in a national core curriculum. The academic critics of the 1950s and the excellence reformers of the 1980s were aiming at the right target, Finn says, but their campaign fell short of the mark. Now it is time to finish the job.[26]

The heavy emphasis in *We Must Take Charge* on "outcomes-based" accountability, which Finn proposes to achieve through a national system of standardized tests, draws him into a defensive debate on the merits of behavioral essentialism. Finn seems far more convinced than Bennett, Ravitch, or Hirsch that standardized testing is *the* way to straighten the kinks out of American education. The love of the humanities that was so strong in Finn's earlier work—a quality that still shines through in the writing of Bennett, Ravitch, and Hirsch—is barely visible in this book. Nor does Finn write with Bennett's moral fervor. But for civilians who are looking for a campaign guide to test-driven school reform, *We Must Take Charge* is the ultimate field manual.

Lamar Alexander says reading Finn's book saved him six months as U.S. Secretary of Education. Sure enough, when Bush and Alexander unveiled their America 2000 strategy, a national system of standardized tests was the centerpiece of their plan. Along with the proposal to give parents and students tax-supported choice among private as well as public schools (see chapters 9 and 12), national achievement testing has become a lightning rod for political controversy.[27]

Many teachers who share the essentialist concern for conserving and transmitting a cultural heritage express serious reservations about test-based accountability: Haven't we had enough of that at the state and local levels? Haven't we already driven that car over the cliff? Of course we have, say advocates of progressivism, whose theory of education we will examine next.

## PROGRESSIVISM

While John Dewey was a professor at the University of Chicago during the 1890s, he went shopping for school furniture. Dewey had just started a laboratory school at the university with a group of parents who were unhappy with the traditional education their children were receiving. Now the problem was finding suitable desks and chairs, and none of the school supply stores in Chicago had what he was looking for.

Finally one dealer made a remark that struck Dewey as so insightful he included it in his book *The School and Society* (1899): "I am afraid we have not what you want. You want something at which the children may work; these are all for listening."[28]

For Dewey, that comment got to the essence of the traditional classroom, "with its rows of ugly desks placed in geometrical order, crowded together so that there shall be as little moving room as possible, desks almost all of the same size." Listening is the only educational activity that can take place in such a setting, Dewey claimed, "because simply studying lessons out of a book is only another kind of listening; it marks the dependency of one mind upon another. The attitude of listening means, comparatively speaking, passivity, absorption; . . . the child is to take in as much as possible in the least possible time."[29]

An old joke in colleges of education is that Dewey wanted the words "Here Lies the Man Who Convinced Americans to Unbolt School Desks from the Floor" chiseled on his tombstone. Funny or not, the joke does point out the symbolic importance of something as ordinary as school furniture. Dewey looked into traditional classrooms and saw passivity, rigidity, and uniformity locked into place. Teachers, the dispensers of knowledge, took their places at the front. Students, the receivers of knowledge, sat in their places at the rear.

Like many observers, Dewey saw similarities between classrooms and factories, but unlike many, Dewey did not approve of what the similarities suggest. Schools should not be places where adult "supervisors" give orders while child "employees" grudgingly sit and listen, their minds often a thousand miles away. Instead, schools should be places where adults serve as guides and advisers to students who are actively involved in their education, doing things that are interesting to them as well as important to society.

Dewey was both philosopher and educator, and the principles of pragmatism, the philosophy he helped develop, directly influenced his educational ideas. Given a world in which change is the central feature, education must help people adapt. Not for Dewey was the education preferred by idealists and realists, an education based on truths passed from one generation to the next, an education students absorb. Dewey called instead for an education based on what works for the present generation, an education students *experience* as they interact with the environment. Students are not receptacles or containers, Dewey argued, they are organisms. They need to be active. They learn best by doing.

The theory of education Dewey advocated came to be known as progressivism, for it developed during what historians call the progressive era in American history. As we saw in the last chapter, at the beginning of the twentieth century a spirit of reform was in the air. Because John Dewey was a liberal reformer, progressivism in education has always been linked to liberalism. The linkage is less direct than it may seem, however, because most of the people who translated educational theory into practice—teachers, administrators, school board members—were moderates and conservatives. It took time for Dewey's progressivism to work its way into teachers colleges and from there into the schools, and when *progressive education* did appear in classrooms, it was often difficult to recognize the original ideas. Beyond the social and political differences that separated theorists and practitioners, Dewey's writing was dense, ponderous, and easily misinterpreted. Few educators read his work carefully, and those who did disagreed over how to use his ideas in the classroom.[30]

Throughout his long life, which spanned the Civil War and the atomic age, Dewey kept claiming his ideas had been misquoted, misunderstood, and misapplied in the schools. We should be sympathetic, but only to a point. After all, as a pragmatist Dewey insisted that the ultimate test of a theory is the difference the theory makes in practice. Just as we saw that perennialists, despite Hutchins and Adler's egalitarian rhetoric, have reserved their brand of education for a few students in a few schools, and that educators have consistently corrupted essentialism, denying its full benefits to many students despite the good intentions of Bagley, Bestor, and Bennett, we must evaluate progressivism in the same way, judging not only theory but practice.

Dewey based his educational theory on his view of democracy. As he explained in his best-known book, *Democracy and Education* (1916), democracy is more than a form of government. It is a way of life. The essence of democracy is people working together cooperatively to find solutions to common problems. The schools in a democratic society bear a great responsibility, for they must help give people the problem-solving skills that they need to make democracy work. Dewey was very much the liberal progressive in his belief that ordinary people can contribute to society if the schools help them to do so. And he went even further: Unless America's schools equip all students to solve problems, democracy cannot survive.[31]

## Children, Society, and Their Problems

On which problems should the schools focus? According to Dewey, there are two sources from which problems can be selected: children and society. Students can suggest problems they are having, and society is full of problems crying out for solutions. Unfortunately, Dewey continued, the traditional curriculum does justice to neither. A collection of facts and skills pigeonholed into academic subjects, the curriculum may make sense to college-educated adults, but it is remote from children's experience and out of touch with pressing social problems.

Imagine how Dewey's ideas must have sounded at the turn of the century. They were nothing short of heresy to traditionalists. What? Ask the *children*? But they're too immature to make suggestions about their education. And why bring the problems of society into the classroom? Shouldn't schools keep a safe distance from society, striving to be above politics, beyond controversy, and apart from the unpleasant realities of life?

Dewey replied to traditionalists in several ways. Hadn't they noticed the bored looks on children's faces? To the degree the schools ignore problems that concern students, the schools are meaningless to students. Hadn't traditionalists noticed how difficult it was to move the nation forward, even in a progressive era? To the degree the schools ignore problems that beset society, the schools are useless to society. Moreover, in *The Child and the Curriculum* (1902) and later works, Dewey urged traditionalists to recognize that student problems and social problems are identical. The questions even the youngest children ask—Do others like me? Should I share my belongings? What makes automobiles run? Why are vegetables better for me than candy?—are scaled-down versions of questions society asks. Students do not come to school to get ready for life. They are already alive. Education is not preparation for life. It *is* life.[32]

Dewey wanted schools to be miniature societies, "embryonic communities" that simplify, purify, and integrate culture. In his laboratory school at the University of Chicago, students engaged in such "real-life activities" as gardening, weaving, woodworking, and metalworking. Since everyone has to eat, Dewey and his fellow teachers found it easy to build on the natural interest children have in food. As students worked in the school garden, they began to understand—many for the first time—where food comes from and how important it is to any society. With student interest presumably running high, resourceful teachers provided gentle guidance as students investigated how food production has changed over the years, why some nations have more food than others, how seeds germinate—the possibilities were endless. Science, geography, history, and other academic subjects were no longer the center of the curriculum. Instead, the curriculum was at once child-centered and society-centered, with subject matter brought into play as necessary to study particular problems or issues.

In 1904, Dewey moved from the University of Chicago to Columbia University in New York City, where his reputation grew steadily. Although he concentrated more on philosophy than education after the publication of *Democracy and Education* in 1916, Dewey soon became the nation's preeminent educational theorist. He developed a strong following among the faculty of Columbia's Teachers College, attracting a group of dedicated professors who spread his ideas—more precisely, their interpretation of his ideas—to numerous teachers and administrators. As Teachers College established itself as the top school of education in the country, Dewey and his followers were in an influential position indeed. During the 1920s, 1930s, and 1940s, they were the pacesetters in educational theory.

## Progressivism in the Classroom

How much educational practice changed is a hard question to answer, as Larry Cuban's book *How Teachers Taught* suggests (see chapter 6). As early as World War I, though, there were signs of growing interest in progressivism. In 1918, the Commission on the Reorganization of Secondary Education, a committee of the National Education Association, issued what would prove to be one of the most significant educational reports of this century. Titled *Cardinal Principles of Secondary Education,* the report called on secondary educators to broaden their aims, to do more than offer a relatively small group of students a traditional academic curriculum. The report encouraged schools to prepare *all* students for *all* aspects of life. The cardinal principles were an ambitious statement of the schools' responsibilities for seven broad areas of life: health, command of fundamental processes (basic academic skills), worthy home membership, vocation, civic education, worthy use of leisure, and ethical character.[33]

Despite warnings that the schools were asking for more than they could handle, progressivism gained ground. Another breakthrough came in that same year when William Heard Kilpatrick, a Teachers College professor who had studied under Dewey, published "The Project Method." This article was Kilpatrick's attempt to translate Dewey's ideas into a set of practical guidelines for teachers. *Foundations of Method* (1925), Kilpatrick's elaboration on the article, became *the* methods textbook in many teacher education programs.

Education should revolve around "wholehearted purposeful activity in a social situation," Kilpatrick declared. Using the problems and questions students brought to school as a point of departure, teachers could help students design projects that taught social lessons and conveyed academic content as well. If students were curious about buying and selling, they could set up a store in the classroom. Using play money, they could learn to make change. The thoughtful teacher could stock the shelves with items chosen to stimulate further learning. Buying a cotton shirt could get a student interested in where cotton is grown and how clothes are made. The student who spent money too quickly would have to face the realities of budgeting. If another student turned into a loan shark, the teacher could help the class decide how to handle the situation.[34]

Kilpatrick's project method seemed easy to understand and easy to use in the classroom—deceptively easy, as it turned out. Almost immediately distortions appeared, and the popular press had a field day with progressive education. By some accounts, a few teachers simply turned things over to the students. With "What do you want to do today, kids?" as their major question, these teachers provided little guidance. Other teachers were willing to be more directive but found it difficult to come up with a steady stream of projects that did justice to children, society, and subject matter. Teacher educators and curriculum specialists rushed in with preplanned projects that laid out almost everything in advance— stimulation, problems and questions, subject-matter content, probable outcomes, and new interests—but spontaneity and student motivation suffered.

Journalists of the 1920s sniped away at child-centered private schools that seemed to lack structure of any kind, at least to the casual observer. Why, the children sang, danced, and made pottery all day! They read books and did arithmetic only when they wanted to. And so the caricatures went. Journalists who were aware of the Progressive Education Association, organized in 1919 with an accent on child-centered private education, could lampoon the first two principles on the association's charter, "freedom to develop naturally" and "interest the motive of all work." "Scientific study of pupil development," another principle, somehow received less attention in the press.[35]

To many citizens and some teachers, progressivism became little more than a set of slogans: Learning by doing. Educating the whole child. Teaching students, not subjects.

Dewey, Kilpatrick, and other theorists spoke out against the distortions of progressivism in the schools and the distortions of the distortions in the press. The image of progressivism as totally permissive was especially irritating to Dewey. "The child does not know best," he reminded his supporters and detractors alike. Trusting students to make intelligent decisions with little or no adult guidance "is really stupid. For it attempts the impossible, which is always stupid; and it misconceives the conditions of independent thinking." Nor did Dewey agree with his Teachers College followers on all matters. Tired of seeing progressivism reduced to playing store, Dewey cautioned against projects so trivial they miseducated students. Kilpatrick's method was only one alternative, he pointed out.[36]

Whereas Kilpatrick seemed almost ready to discard the entire subject-matter curriculum and replace it with a series of projects, Dewey wanted to make academic subjects more responsive to the needs of students and society. If the curriculum began with the experiences of students, as the students gained maturity they could delve into subject matter in a rigorous way that might even please the traditionalists. Dewey's scientific method of problem solving was structured and systematic. He also believed there was a time and place for didactic instruction—for a teacher to stand at the chalkboard and show students how to work a math problem, for example—and a time and place for students to memorize and practice their multiplication tables. In other words, Dewey was no pedagogical libertine.[37]

It troubled Dewey that much of what passed as progressive education had only tenuous connections to social reform. Before World War I, progressivism in education had been part and parcel of the larger reform movements. After the war, progressive education went its own way, enjoying its greatest popularity in private schools. During the 1930s, as the nation faced the Great Depression and the rise of totalitarian governments abroad, Dewey was encouraged as progressive education became more society centered. This version of progressivism made more headway in public schools. It was impossible for educators to ignore unemployment, bread lines, and fascism, and progressive education offered a way to infuse social issues into the curriculum. The social studies, which progressive educators had developed during the 1920s as an interdisciplinary problem-centered subject, enjoyed an upswing in popularity. Students took field trips and studied problems in their own communities. Kilpatrick's project method seemed ideally suited to this kind of progressivism, since students and teachers could design their projects around studies of city and county governments, housing conditions, New Deal public works programs, and the like.

## Social Reconstructionism

A politically focused form of society-centered progressivism called *social reconstructionism* also developed during the 1930s. Inspired in part by Dewey's reaction against the permissiveness and lack of social concern in child-centered progressivism, social reconstructionists went to another extreme with their desire to use the schools to engineer a new society.

George S. Counts, a Teachers College professor, galvanized the annual meeting of the Progressive Education Association in 1932 with his speech "Dare Progressive Education Be Progressive?" Calling on teachers to become leaders of social change, Counts urged them to take stands on controversial social issues and to prepare students for the emerging society. Teachers should increase their power by joining teacher unions and casting their lot with the labor movement and other forward-looking groups. Counts's book *Dare the School Build a New Social Order?* (1932) became the charter document of reconstructionism.[38]

Counts, Kilpatrick, and several of their colleagues at Teachers College, most notably Harold Rugg and John Childs, joined other professors in education and the arts and sciences to publish *The Social Frontier,* a journal that served as the voice of reconstructionism. John Dewey, a regular contributor to the journal, was at the center of all this activity, even though he occasionally chided his followers for their naïve faith in the power of schools to change society.

Social reconstructionism, a fusion of progressive pedagogy and left-of-center politics, had little direct influence on the schools. Even though the nation became more liberal during the 1930s, most educators and school board members simply did not share the reconstructionists' vision of an emerging society that, if not exactly socialist, was clearly collectivist. Predictably, reconstructionism drew the fire of people who were educationally conservative, politically conservative, or both. A series of social studies textbooks produced by Harold Rugg fell victim to a censorship campaign in the late 1930s and 1940s, and conservative critics have cited the social reconstructionists' writings as evidence of a left-wing conspiracy to control the schools.[39]

## Life Adjustment

By the time the academic critics launched their attack in the 1950s, progressive education had undergone a name change. Now the dominant strain of progressivism was called *life adjustment* education. More than the name had changed. Dewey's ideas could hardly be recognized. On a rhetorical level, to be sure, life adjustment incorporated elements of both child-centered and society-centered pedagogy, but in theory and practice it departed from Dewey's progressivism at almost every turn.

The rationale for life adjustment was that schools were not preparing large numbers of students for the realities of modern life—particularly the world of work. There were well-developed programs for the 20 percent of students who were college bound and the 20 percent who were in the vocational track, but what were the schools doing for the majority, the 60 percent in the middle? Surely they did not need a rigorous academic program, the life adjusters asserted, and just as surely they did not belong in wood shop or metal shop.[40]

What they did need was training in good habits that would pay off on almost any job; help with their immediate personal problems as well as the ones they would face as adults; advice on how to spend their leisure time, which was predicted to be more plentiful in the years after World War II; and preparation for good citizenship. Students in the general track soon found themselves in such courses as Developing an Effective Personality, Marriage and the Family, and Metropolitan Living. Designed to focus and integrate the curriculum, courses revolving around class discussions and field trips became quite popular.

John Dewey turned 90 as life adjustment education hit its stride and the academic critics mounted their attack. He wrote little about education in his last years, but it is easy to imagine his disappointment with what was passing for progressivism in education. Perhaps he held his peace because he found himself agreeing with the critics on many points.

Certainly the basic assumption of life adjustment education, that only students who were headed for college needed a curriculum with substantial academic content, made Dewey recoil. He knew vocational educators were the theorists and strongest advocates of life adjustment, which surely made him suspicious. Dewey had parted company with vocational educators in the early 1900s when he realized they wanted to give job skills to a few students—the academic castoffs, most of them poor and minority students—while he wanted to give all students the chance to work with their hands and sample a variety of occupations. Now a vocational education mentality was limiting the education of another group of students, those in the large general track; essentialists were getting the credit for saving the schools; and Dewey was getting the blame.

## Blame It on Progressivism:
## Bashing the 1960s and 1970s

Dewey died in 1952, but today it is fashionable to blame progressivism for everything that went wrong in the schools from the mid-1960s through the mid-1970s. William Bennett, Diane Ravitch, Chester Finn, Jr., and E. D. Hirsch, Jr., have turned sixties-and-seventies bashing into an essentialist spectator sport. Whenever progressivism shows signs of stirring and reviving, essentialists point to progressivism as the culprit that messed up America's schools. Surely the nation would not want to go down *that* road again. As Finn puts it, beware the slippery slope!

When students demanded more relevant courses during the 1960s and 1970s, educators responded by making things easy and elective, encouraging students to pick and choose their way through a cafeteria-style curriculum that included science-fiction English courses, values clarification social studies courses, consumer math courses, and the like. Even the brightest students sometimes steered clear of foreign languages, advanced math and science, and other demanding courses while teachers, parents, and other adults stood by and watched. No matter that this do-your-own thing pedagogy resembled a distorted version of existentialism more than a distorted version of progressivism— essentialists chalk it up as another failed experiment in progressive education. Compensatory education, school integration, and affirmative action are, of course, the social engineering legacy of progressivism.

Essentialists who are fundamentalist Christians (see chapter 11) go even further. During the 1960s and 1970s, as the United States underwent a moral revolution that brought sex, drugs, and rock and roll into the schools, to some people it seemed the schools themselves were to blame. Didn't John Dewey say values are relative? Hasn't he had a lot of influence on education? Don't some teachers practice values clarification? Affirmative answers to such questions provide fundamentalist Christians all the evidence they need to implicate progressivism (and often existentialism, too) in a secular humanist conspiracy.

No one expresses the moral and academic indignation of essentialists better than William Bennett. Just look at what happened when liberals led America astray during the 1960s and 1970s, he says: "We neglected and denied much of the best in American education. We simply stopped doing the right things. We allowed an assault on intellectual and moral standards. . . . We experienced the *worst* education decline in our history." Bennett voices the desire to return to better days, to set things straight—the same desire he articulated as director of President Bush's antidrug program.[41]

In the educational politics of the 1980s and early 1990s, Bennett and other officials of the Reagan and Bush administrations tried to lay claim to essentialism as the conservative (and therefore Republican) theory of education, labeling progressivism as the liberal (and therefore Democratic) approach. All is fair in politics, of course, but we should be wary of such neat labels. They are not an exact fit for the two theories as they have been practiced in recent school reform. During this most recent back to basics movement, people with diverse political views and party affiliations jumped on the essentialist bandwagon as it rolled through local and state school systems. For a while, almost everyone seemed to be an essentialist.

In another sense, though, the careful use of labels *can* help us describe changing national moods. It now appears that the election of President Bill Clinton, a political moderate, represented a significant step away from the political conservatism of the 1980s. The nation that took this step may also be willing to try a less conservative theory of education, progressivism.

In the last two sections of this chapter, we will look at the varieties of contemporary progressivism from which Americans can choose. We will begin with its most radical version.

## Critical Theory and Postmodernism

The progressive impulse to reconstruct society through education is once again gaining strength. *Critical theory* is a pedagogy designed to "empower the powerless and transform existing social inequalities and injustices." Through the hard-to-penetrate writing of Henry A. Giroux, Stanley Aronowitz, Peter McLaren, and other radical scholars, critical theory is reaching a small audience inside colleges of education. The more accessible writing of Jonathan Kozol is taking critical theory to large popular audiences as well.[42]

Critical theory is a contemporary extension of social reconstructionism. Beginning with the premise that "men and women are essentially unfree and inhabit a world rife with contradictions and asymmetries of power and privilege," critical theorists resolve to help students and teachers escape oppression. Since the mid-1970s, they have tried to fuse progressive pedagogy and radical politics, acknowledging the influence of Dewey, Counts, and other society-centered progressives.[43]

But critical theorists say their twin goals of empowering individuals and transforming society are more explicitly political than the goals of Dewey and his colleagues, for critical theorists claim they have developed a better understanding of the link between knowledge and power. They argue that what is regarded as worthy of study in school—indeed, the very concept of "knowledge" itself—privileges some students and penalizes others.[44]

To understand their argument, we must see how critical theory in colleges of education fits into the movement in higher education toward *postmodern criticism.* University scholars in a variety of academic disciplines have grown more sensitive to the influence of class, race, ethnicity, and gender. Postmodernists argue that these cultural factors strongly affect how people construct meaning from their experience. Postmodernists believe women and men, for example, see things differently.

Traditional academic scholarship, however, glosses over such differences, holding up men as the standard and presenting masculine views as reality. History, as it comes across in school, is primarily an account written by men about men; literature is primarily a text of men's feelings and perceptions. Thus, postmodernists contend, what passes for knowledge in school *marginalizes* women.

In similar ways, knowledge as traditionally defined marginalizes poor people and members of racial and ethnic minorities.

Critical theorists in colleges of education, along with their postmodern counterparts in departments of history, English, and other academic disciplines, are trying to listen to the voices of marginalized groups. To help students hear these voices, critical theorists are urging educators to "interrogate the *canon*," the body of knowledge deemed worthy of serious study.

Critical theorists were not the first scholars to make this demand. Well before the mid-1970s, scholars were debating the contents of the canon, arguing over which works to put in and which to leave out. Critical theorists and other postmodernists, though, are now questioning "the priority of canonicity itself." Critical theorists want each school's students and teachers to negotiate the content of the curriculum, to select the knowledge that can help empower the particular people in that particular situation.[45]

"The curriculum can best inspire learning only when school knowledge builds upon the tacit knowledge derived from the cultural resources that students already possess," Aronowitz and Giroux argue in *Postmodern Education* (1991). It becomes the teachers' job to relate traditional academic subjects to projects that students and teachers have jointly chosen. Such projects might center on "rap music, sports, the Civil War, neighborhoods, youth in society, race relations, sexuality, or almost anything else."[46]

In the postmodern high school, students and teachers are free to negotiate virtually every aspect of education. "There are no requirements imposed from above," Aronowitz and Giroux point out. Here is a pedagogy designed to be as different as possible from the essentialism of Bennett and company. Critical theory is progressivism pushed to the limit.[47]

Not only are the critical theorists' ideas radical, their language is often difficult and sometimes impossible. When pressed on this complaint, critical theorists reply they are leaving "lite" writing and "popcorn imagery" to others, thank you. They feel they must create a new language so they can "deconstruct and challenge dominant relations of power and knowledge legitimated through traditional forms of discourse."[48] Such words make for tough reading, but Peter McLaren has written a plain-English introduction to critical theory in *Life in Schools* (1989). The popular books of Jonathan Kozol, which we will review in the last section of this chapter, are giving critical theory its broadest exposure.[49]

Critical theorists pride themselves on being outside the mainstream. Relishing their role as outsiders and outlaws, critical theorists are making other progressives look less radical as Americans search for alternatives in the aftermath of the conservative Reagan-Bush era.

## A Progressive Revival?

In the first edition of *America's Teachers* (1990), I concluded this discussion of progressivism on a pessimistic note. Progressivism was out of step with current educational theory and practice, I wrote. Now I feel differently. As behavioral essentialism loses favor, educators are searching for something to replace it. Progressivism is making a modest comeback.

"I'm talking about schools that have high standards—incredibly high standards, in fact—but standards that are met through mutual trust and mutual respect." Tom Peters, coauthor of the best-seller *In Search of Excellence* (1982), uses these words to introduce "Why Do These Kids Love School?" (1990), a PBS television program about innovative schools. After nodding to John Dewey and taking viewers on a tour of a private school that practices an almost pure strain of child-centered progressivism, the program surveys variations on the progressive theme in nine public schools.[50]

Viewers see a magnet school in Lowell, Massachusetts, that functions as a "microsociety" in which students run the political and economic system. (The September 21, 1992, issue of *Time* praised this school before an even larger audience.) An alternative school in Jackson, Mississippi, encourages students of different abilities to work as a group and assist one another—a strategy known as *cooperative learning* (see chapter 8). A school in Minneapolis helps students learn through all their senses, not just vision and hearing. By stressing high standards and associating such schools with "excellence," the producers of "Why Do These Children Love School?" hope to deflect sixties-and-seventies bashing and give progressivism a fresh start.[51]

In the changing social and political climate of the 1990s, progressivism may once again have a turn. Of all the scholarly studies of education released in the early part of the decade, the one that continues to attract the most public attention is Jonathan Kozol's *Savage Inequalities* (1991). Kozol first captured a national audience in 1967 with *Death at an Early Age* (1967), an account of his inner-city teaching career with poor African-American children. Now, with *Savage Inequalities,* he is once again moving the social reform agenda of progressivism to center stage. President Clinton has said "every educator in America should read Jonathan Kozol's *Savage Inequalities.*"[52]

Kozol, the winner of the National Education Association's Friend of Education Award in 1992, is trying to restart a conversation very few people wanted to have during the 1980s. He wants to talk about inequality and segregation. The reforms of the 1980s never reached schools like those Kozol visited in East St. Louis, Chicago, San Antonio, New York, Camden, and Washington, D. C. Making a mockery of the *Brown* decision, these schools remain separate and *un*equal. Urban schools for the minority poor are miserable by any standards, Kozol insists, but rather than dwelling on test scores, dropout rates, and other quantitative indicators, he shows us overcrowded classrooms, dangerous hallways, filthy conditions. These schools are "extraordinarily unhappy places," he says, far worse than any schools he saw during the 1960s.[53]

Kozol lets us hear the voices of those trapped inside—teachers, parents, and especially students. A fifth-grader in Washington, D.C., says if her school somehow got more money, she would want to "make it a beautiful clean building. Make it *pretty*. Way it is, I feel ashamed." These students realize suburban schools are vastly different, and they are resentful.[54]

Voices from the suburbs that ring the central cities also speak in *Savage Inequalities.* These voices, mostly those of middle-class whites, boast their public schools exemplify "what is possible when citizens want to achieve the best for their children." In a self-congratulatory mood, a community magazine published in Chicago's wealthy New Trier suburb applauds its schools by observing "a supportive attitude on the part of families . . . translates into a willingness to pay" for quality. Suburban Americans would not allow *their* children even to walk past the inner-city schools Kozol visited, much less try to learn there. Yet these same Americans believe higher graduation requirements, more standardized testing, and more homework can make the schools good enough for *other people's* children.[55]

Kozol believes in desegregation, as do most of the minority students he interviews, but the main reform he advocates is financial: spending at least as much on urban schools as on suburban schools. Kozol attacks America's school finance system, which by relying on local property taxes enables wealthier school districts to raise far more money. As we will see in chapter 9, lawsuits are under way throughout the nation to try to reduce the spending gap between rich and poor districts. But Kozol's disquieting conclusion is that better-off Americans will continue to resist equalization because "they are fighting for the right to guarantee their children the inheritance of an ascendant role in our society."

> There is a deep-seated reverence for fair play in the United States, and in many areas of life we see the consequences in a genuine distaste for loaded dice; but this is not the case in education, health care, or inheritance of wealth. In these elemental areas we want the game to be unfair and we have made it so; and it will likely so remain.[56]

Kozol's words hit home. Written to reach the widest possible audience, *Savage Inequalities* spells out a message that is much more accessible and only slightly milder than the work of Henry Giroux, Stanley Aronowitz, Peter McLaren, and other critical theorists. Kozol is taking critical theory to the masses.

Writing in a more moderate progressive vein, Ernest Boyer focuses attention on the nation's youngest children in *Ready to Learn* (1991). Boyer, president of the Carnegie Foundation for the Advancement of Teaching, looks at the families and communities in which preschool children live. He listens to kindergarten teachers who report that more than one-third of students enter school unprepared to learn. Boyer sees families and communities under stress, and in *Ready to Learn* he resolves to "move beyond the tired old 'family versus government' debate" that has hamstrung efforts to relieve the stress.[57]

Boyer calls for the creation of a new support network for families. He proposes a seven-step strategy encompassing "a healthy start, empowered parents, quality preschool, a responsive workplace, television as teacher, neighborhoods for learning, [and] connections across the generations." This proposal will hearten political liberals and educational progressives, but will it be able to rise above the family-versus-government debate?[58]

Studying Boyer's proposal alongside a very different plan exposes the political dimensions of educational theory. Boyer took the title of his book from the first of six education goals adopted by former President Bush and the nation's governors: "All children in America will start school ready to learn." Bush's America 2000 plan—politically conservative and educationally essentialist—held government involvement to a minimum by telling families and communities to take care of themselves. Boyer's proposal comes down on the side of government activism, affirming the progressive belief that government is obligated to help people help themselves.[59]

Under President Clinton, who had a hand in drafting the six education goals as governor of Arkansas, the debate continues. As we will see in chapter 9, Clinton takes an eclectic approach to the politics of education, mixing progressivism and essentialism, liberalism and conservatism. On the issue of government activism, though, Boyer has an ally in the White House for the first time in years.

Meanwhile, teachers are struggling to make their voices heard over the din of school reform. Ernest Boyer has the reputation of a good listener, and so does Theodore R. Sizer, chair of the education department of Brown University. Since the 1980s, while *A Nation at Risk* and other essentialist reports have been telling teachers how to do their jobs better, Sizer, Boyer, and John Goodlad (whom we met in chapter 3) have been listening to teachers explain why their jobs are so difficult.

To Sizer, Boyer, and Goodlad, the "Work Harder, Reach Higher, Do More" advice of essentialism seems simplistic and unrealistic given the conditions teachers and students face every day. Sizer's *Horace's Compromise* (1984), Boyer's *High School* (1983), and Goodlad's *A Place Called School* (1984) proposed fundamental changes in the occupation of teaching, the organization of schools, and the relationship between students and teachers. Based on thousands of hours of classroom observation, these studies predicted that the noses-to-the grindstone essentialist remedy would not work.[60]

Now Sizer has released *Horace's School* (1992), a work of "nonfiction fiction" that reintroduces Horace Smith, the frustrated high school teacher who was the subject of Sizer's 1984 book. Forced by his working conditions to compromise his ideals, Horace wondered in the early 1980s whether the reforms getting under way then would help him and his students. Sadly, Sizer reports that the promise of better education through school reform never came true.[61]

In the 1990s, Horace still has to compromise. He still has too many students to teach. He still has to cover too many topics in too little depth. He still has to fragment his work into 52-minute bites of sound and sight punctuated by bells and class changes. Horace's students are still compromising, too, bargaining informally with their teachers for "the least hassle," learning how to adjust their standards downward as they move through the system.

*Horace's School* presents reform proposals that contrast with the "more of the same" reforms of the 1980s. At Franklin High School, the model school Sizer envisions, students and staff are divided into more manageable, largely self-contained units called "houses." Each teacher is responsible for no more than 80 students. The curriculum is organized into three areas: math/science, history/philosophy, and the arts. Faculty members work together in multidisciplinary teams. All share responsibility for teaching oral and written expression, inquiry techniques, and study skills.

Franklin High's teachers have reached consensus on what high school graduates should be capable of doing, and they have designed student "exhibitions," a type of *performance assessment* (see chapter 10), to replace "seat time" as the basis for awarding diplomas. Unlike pencil-and-paper tests, which typically give students one shot at telling what they know, exhibitions take place over an extended time period to let students show what they can do. While some exhibitions involve formal expression in words and numbers—writing an essay or solving a set of problems, for example—others are to be as varied as drawing a map, composing a piece of music, or demonstrating the skills acquired in a community service job. Students keep their work in *portfolios* that are open to inspection by parents, teachers, and state officials.

Granting more autonomy to individual schools and individual teachers is the key to successful reform, Sizer maintains. Regarding external regulation, his motto is "The least imposition is the best imposition." At Franklin High, standardized testing is limited to periodic assessments of reading, writing, and basic math. Anything more is not only unnecessary but counterproductive, Sizer argues, criticizing proposals to create a national curriculum driven by national tests.

Yet Franklin High does not shirk accountability, he insists. Student portfolios, test results, site visits, and annual reports to the community provide all the information anyone could need to judge the school's effectiveness.

These ideas have a track record of success, Sizer points out. They are working right now in schools across the nation. Sizer chairs the Coalition of Essential Schools, a group of about 200 schools in 23 states that are field testing reform. The proposals in *Horace's School* are based on the experiences of the coalition. "Essential Schools" may be a traditional-sounding name, but the progressive theory of education these schools are putting into practice would hearten John Dewey.

Sizer, however, feels unsure about when—or whether—Horace Smith will be able to make a better set of compromises. "I fear," Sizer confesses, "that the preferred alternative to careful rethinking will be continued pushing, prodding, testing, and protesting our largely mindless, egregiously expensive, and notably unproductive current system. It is not a pretty prospect."[62]

"And yet, he concludes, "there are glimmers of hope."[63] I hope you are forming your own opinion on the prospects of fundamental reform. In the chapters that follow, we will continue our study of the social and political forces shaping the schools.

## ACTIVITIES

1. Visit the central office of a local school system and ask for a copy of the system's philosophy of education (sometimes called a statement of goals and purposes). Compare it with the philosophies and theories in this chapter. Try to obtain an earlier statement of goals from the same system and analyze the changes.

2. Interview currently employed teachers who represent a variety of philosophies and theories.

3. Talk with retired teachers about swings of the educational pendulum—how one educational theory may have displaced another during their careers.

4. Observe in a public or private school that seems to be dominated by a theory of education different from yours.

## RECOMMENDED READINGS

Adler, Mortimer J. *The Paideia Proposal: An Educational Manifesto* (New York: Macmillan, 1982).
This book, assisted by its two companion volumes (see note 8), breathed new life into perennialism.
Finn, Chester E., Jr. *We Must Take Charge: Our Schools and Our Future* (New York: Free Press, 1991).
From its forceful title to its forthright advocacy of standardized testing, Finn's study defends essentialism as it has evolved during the latest back-to-basics movement.
Ozmon, Howard, and Samuel Craver. *Philosophical Foundations of Education,* 4th ed. (Columbus, OH: Merrill, 1990).
Ozmon and Craver offer one of the best surveys of philosophies and theories of education.
Sizer, Theodore R. *Horace's School: Redesigning the American High School* (Boston: Houghton Mifflin, 1992).
John Dewey would surely enjoy seeing how Sizer has adapted progressivism and put it to work in this model school.

## NOTES

1. For further reading, see J. Donald Butler, *Idealism in Education* (New York: Harper & Row, 1966).
2. For further information, see William O. Martin's *Realism in Education* (New York: Harper & Row, 1968) and John Wild's *Introduction to Realist Philosophy* (New York: Harper & Row, 1948).
3. See Ernest E. Bayles' *Pragmatism in Education* (New York: Harper & Row, 1966) and John Childs' *American Pragmatism and Education* (New York: Holt, Rinehart & Winston, 1956).
4. Three studies from the 1960s, when existential education enjoyed rising popularity, are Van Cleve Morris's *Existentialism in Education: What It Means* (New York: Harper & Row, 1966); Maxine Greene's *Existential Encounters for Teachers* (New York: Random House, 1967); and George F. Kneller's *Existentialism and Education* (New York: John Day, 1964). To go directly to the source, read Jean-Paul Sartre's *Being and Nothingness,* translated by Hazel E. Barnes (New York: Philosophical Library, 1958). The Morris quotations are from his chapter "Establishing a Philosophical Point of View," in Donald E. Orlosky, ed., *Introduction to Education* (Columbus, OH: Merrill, 1982). Emphasis in the original.
5. Robert M. Hutchins, *The Higher Learning in America* (New Haven: Yale University Press, 1936), p. 66.
6. Robert M. Hutchins, *Great Books: The Foundation of a Liberal Education* (New York: Simon & Schuster, 1954). See also the excellent discussion in Christopher J. Lucas's *Foundations of Education: Schooling and the Social Order* (Englewood Cliffs, NJ: Prentice-Hall, 1984), chap. 3.

7. Mortimer J. Adler, *The Paideia Proposal: An Educational Manifesto* (New York: Macmillan, 1982).

8. See Mortimer J. Adler's *Paideia Problems and Possibilities* (New York: Macmillan, 1983) and *The Paideia Program: An Educational Syllabus* (New York: Macmillan, 1984).

9. Based on my notes and recollections, I have reconstructed these exchanges, which took place at the annual meeting of the American Educational Studies Association, Milwaukee, on November 4, 1983.

10. "Quality, Not Just Quantity," *Time* (September 6, 1982), p. 59.

11. Mortimer J. Adler, *Reforming Education: The Opening of the American Mind,* ed. Geraldine Van Doren (New York: Macmillan, 1988), p. 314.

12. Ibid., pp. 314, 312.

13. Two key documents of the early essentialist movement are William C. Bagley's *Education and Emergent Man* (New York: Ronald Press, 1934) and "An Essentialist's Platform for the Advancement of American Education," *Educational Administration and Supervision* 24 (April 1938): 241–256. Lucas analyzes essentialism in *Foundations of Education,* chap. 2.

14. Bagley, "An Essentialist's Platform," p. 253.

15. William C. Bagley, "The Case for Essentialism in Education," *Journal of the National Education Association* 30 (October 1941): 202.

16. Arthur E. Bestor, *Educational Wastelands: The Retreat from Learning in Our Public Schools* (Urbana: University of Illinois Press, 1953); Bestor, *The Restoration of Learning* (New York: Knopf, 1955); Mortimer Smith, *And Madly Teach* (Chicago: Regnery, 1949); Smith, *The Diminished Mind: A Study of Planned Mediocrity in Our Public Schools* (Chicago: Regnery, 1954); James B. Conant, *Education and Liberty: The Role of Schools in a Modern Democracy* (Cambridge: Harvard University Press, 1953); Conant, *The American High School Today* (New York: McGraw-Hill, 1959).

17. National Commission on Excellence in Education, *A Nation at Risk: the Imperative for Educational Reform* (Washington, D.C.: U.S. Government Printing Office, 1983).

18. Ibid.

19. Linda Darling-Hammond, "The Implications of Testing Policy for Quality and Equality," *Phi Delta Kappan* 73 (November 1991): 220–225.

20. Ibid.

21. William J. Bennett, *James Madison High School: A Curriculum for American Students* (Washington, D.C.: U.S. Department of Education, 1987); Bennett, *James Madison Elementary School: A Curriculum for American Students* (Washington, D.C.: U.S. Department of Education, 1988).

22. William J. Bennett, *The De-Valuing of America: The Fight for Our Culture and Our Children* (New York: Summit Books, 1992), p. 61.

23. Chester E. Finn, Jr., Diane Ravitch, and Robert T. Fancher, eds., *Against Mediocrity: The Humanities in America's High Schools* (New York: Holmes & Meier, 1984). For a collection of Diane Ravitch's writings on education, see *The Schools We Deserve: Reflections on the Educational Crises of Our Times* (New York: Basic Books, 1985).

24. Diane Ravitch and Chester E. Finn, Jr., *What Do Our 17-Year-Olds Know?: A Report on the First National Assessment of History and Literature* (New York: Harper & Row, 1987).

25. E. D. Hirsch, Jr., *Cultural Literacy: What Every American Needs to Know* (Boston: Houghton Mifflin, 1987); Allan Bloom, *The Closing of the American Mind* (New York: Simon & Schuster, 1987).

26. Chester E. Finn, Jr., *We Must Take Charge: Our Schools and Our Future* (New York: Free Press, 1991), p. xiv.

27. See the special section on national testing in the November 1991 *Phi Delta Kappan.*
28. John Dewey, *The School and Society* (Chicago: University of Chicago Press, 1899 [1927]), p. 32.
29. Ibid.
30. The classic study of the movement is Lawrence A. Cremin's *The Transformation of the School: Progressivism in American Education, 1876–1957* (New York: Knopf, 1961). Also useful are Henry J. Perkinson's *The Imperfect Panacea: American Faith in Education, 1865–1990,* 3d ed. (New York: Random House, 1991), chaps. 2 and 5; and Lucas's *Foundations of Education,* chap. 6.
31. John Dewey, *Democracy and Education: An Introduction to the Philosophy of Education* (New York: Macmillan, 1916). Also see Robert B. Westbrook's *John Dewey and American Democracy* (Ithaca, NY: Cornell University Press, 1991).
32. John Dewey, *The Child and the Curriculum* (Chicago: University of Chicago Press, 1902).
33. Commission on the Reorganization of Secondary Education, *Cardinal Principles of Secondary Education,* Bulletin No. 35 (Washington, D.C.: U.S. Government Printing Office, 1918).
34. William H. Kilpatrick, "The Project Method," *Teachers College Record* 19 (September 1918): 319–335; Kilpatrick, *Foundations of Method* (New York: Macmillan, 1925).
35. See Patricia A. Graham's *Progressive Education: From Arcade to Academe—A History of the Progressive Education Association, 1919–1955* (New York: Teachers College Press, 1967).
36. John Dewey, *Art and Experience* (New York: Capricorn Books, 1934), pp. 40, 32.
37. Dewey published many of his criticisms of progressive education in *Experience and Education* (New York: Macmillan, 1938).
38. George S. Counts, *Dare the School Build a New Social Order?* (New York: John Day, 1932).
39. C. A. Bowers, *The Progressive Educator and the Depression: The Radical Years* (New York: Random House, 1969). Theodore Brameld of Boston University became the major voice of social reconstructionism in the 1950s and 1960s. See his books *Toward a Reconstructed Philosophy of Education* (New York: Holt, Rinehart & Winston, 1956) and *Education for the Emerging Age* (New York: Harper & Row, 1965).
40. Lucas, *Foundations of Education,* pp. 183–185; Cremin, *Transformation of the School,* pp. 332–338.
41. William J. Bennett, *Our Country and Our Children: Improving America's Schools and Affirming the Common Culture* (New York: Touchstone, 1989), pp. 9–10.
42. Peter McLaren, *Life in Schools: An Introduction to Critical Pedagogy in the Foundations of Education* (White Plains, NY: Longman, 1989), p. 160.
43. Ibid., p. 166.
44. Stanley Aronowitz and Henry A. Giroux, *Education Under Siege: The Conservative, Liberal, and Radical Debate over Schooling* (South Hadley, MA: Bergin & Garvey, 1985).
45. Stanley Aronowitz and Henry A. Giroux, *Postmodern Education: Politics, Culture, and Social Criticism* (Minneapolis: University of Minnesota Press, 1991), p. 17.
46. Ibid., p. 15.
47. Ibid., p. 21.
48. Ibid., pp. 90–91.
49. See note 42. Another book targeted toward a wide audience is Joe L. Kincheloe and Shirley R. Steinberg's *Thirteen Questions: Reframing Education's Conversation* (New York: Peter Lang, 1992).

50. "Why Do These Kids Love School?" produced by Dorothy Fadiman and KTEH-TV (San Jose: Concentric Media, 1990). Mary Anne Raywid describes the video in "Why Do These Kids Love School?" *Phi Delta Kappan* 73 (April 1992): 631–633. Thomas J. Peters and Robert H. Waterman, *In Search of Excellence: Lessons from America's Best-Run Companies* (New York: Harper & Row, 1982).
51. Kevin Fedarko, "Can I Copy Your Homework—And Represent You in Court?" *Time* (September 21, 1992), pp. 52–53.
52. Jonathan Kozol, *Savage Inequalities: Children in America's Schools* (New York: Crown, 1991); Kozol, *Death at an Early Age: The Destruction of the Hearts and Minds of Negro Children in the Boston Public Schools* (Boston: Houghton Mifflin, 1967). The quotation is from "Meet Bill Clinton," *NEA Today* (October 1992), p. 11.
53. Kozol, *Savage Inequalities,* p. 5.
54. Ibid., p. 181.
55. Ibid., pp. 66–67.
56. Ibid., p. 223
57. Ernest L. Boyer, *Ready to Learn: A Mandate for the Nation* (Lawrenceville, NJ: Princeton University Press, 1991), p. 10.
58. Ibid., p. 135.
59. U.S. Department of Education, *America 2000: An Education Strategy. Sourcebook* (Washington, D.C.: U.S. Government Printing Office, 1991), p. 19.
60. Theodore R. Sizer, *Horace's Compromise: The Dilemma of the American High School* (Boston: Houghton Mifflin, 1984); Ernest L. Boyer, *High School: A Report on Secondary Education in America* (New York: Harper & Row, 1983); John I. Goodlad, *A Place Called School: Prospects for the Future* (New York: McGraw-Hill, 1984).
61. Theodore R. Sizer, *Horace's School: Redesigning the American High School* (Boston: Houghton Mifflin, 1992).
62. Ibid., p. 197.
63. Ibid.

# CHAPTER **8**

# Sociology of Education

Sociologists study people in groups. The discipline of sociology is valuable to teachers and other educators because it enables us to see patterns in human behavior, patterns we might otherwise overlook because so many individuals demand our attention in school. Without demeaning the importance of individuals in the least, sociology helps us realize that behavior reflects the positions people occupy in society.

In other words, we can better understand schooling if we think of it as more than just a steady stream of individuals pouring through an institution. We need to step back, consider the individuals as members of social groups, and sort out the patterns in their behavior.

As a teacher, I quickly learned that *social class, race, ethnicity,* and *gender* have a powerful effect on the process of education. I found, to be blunt, that even in the schools of a nation that prides itself on equality of opportunity, some students are more equal than others.

As pleasant as it would be to pretend that schools take in students from diverse social backgrounds and give them all the same opportunities to succeed, that simply does not happen. Students who are members of some social groups come to school with advantages, and schools are organized in ways that help them maintain their advantages. Other students arrive with two strikes against them, socially speaking, and schools often throw the third strike.

In this chapter's opening section, we will examine social class differences in families and peer groups, differences that affect how well students do in school. One way schools respond to the differences is by separating students into ability groups and tracks, a process that brands many working-class students as second-class citizens. The next section surveys race and ethnicity, focusing on African-, Hispanic-, Asian-, and Native American students. At the heart of the chapter is an analysis of desegregation and bilingual education, two strategies designed to increase educational opportunities in a multicultural nation. The concluding section on gender focuses on both girls and boys, but the emphasis is on how females are the second sex in school, just as they are in society.

As you read this chapter, keep in mind the demographic trends we have discussed in earlier chapters. Remember that one in five students comes from a family living in poverty. Remember that by the turn of the twenty-first century, more than one-third of the nation's students will be African-, Hispanic-, Asian-, or Native American. The public school students of four states—Hawaii, New Mexico, Mississippi, and California—are already "minority majority."[1]

Consider also that the "traditional" American family—a wage-earning father, a homemaker mother, and two or more schoolaged children—is now a rarity. Only 4 percent of U.S. households fit that profile, while the percentage of students living with one parent is increasing. One in four students now comes from a single-parent family, and almost half of America's students will live in a single-parent home before reaching their eighteenth birthday.[2]

The trend toward single-parent families illustrates how interwoven the factors of class, race, ethnicity, and gender are. African- and Hispanic-American students are far more likely than others to grow up in single-parent homes. Fifty-eight percent of black children and 30 percent of Hispanic children are now living with one parent, compared to 20 percent of white children. Furthermore, most single-parent households are headed by a woman, and female-headed households are twice as likely as male-headed households to be living in poverty. Thus 44 percent of black children, 38 percent of Hispanic children, and 15 percent of white children are growing up in poverty.[3]

Although I have organized this chapter into separate sections on class, race and ethnicity, and gender, life is not so easily categorized. As you read, you should constantly look for connections and relationships, for you will see them often in the classroom.

## SOCIAL CLASS

Many Americans believe the United States is relatively free of the rigid social stratification we often criticize in other nations, but our country, too, has social classes, a class structure that influences education more than we may care to admit. While we can take pride in our efforts to educate children from all socioeconomic backgrounds, we should be concerned that once the students get to school, their backgrounds seem to play such a powerful role in their success—or lack of it.

### The American Social Structure

Based on studies conducted since the 1920s, sociologists have determined that the United States has a five-tiered class structure. In *Society and Education* (1992), Daniel U. Levine and Robert J. Havighurst describe the current social structure as follows:

| | |
|---|---|
| upper class | 2 percent of the population—people who have substantial wealth that is usually inherited. |
| upper-middle class | 16 percent of the population, including professionals, executives, managers, and more successful small-business owners and farmers. |
| lower-middle class | 32 percent of the population, composed of white-collar workers (such as clerks, salespeople, and teachers), small-business owners and farmers, and better-paid skilled blue-collar workers. |
| upper-working class | 32 percent of the population, composed of skilled and semiskilled blue-collar workers (such as craftspeople and assembly-line workers). |
| lower-working class | 18 percent of the population, ranging from unskilled manual workers (the "working poor") to the chronically unemployed. |

Sociologists use such factors as income, occupation, education, and housing to place people on the social class hierarchy. The size of the classes and the rigidity of their boundaries vary considerably throughout the country. As a rule, the larger the community, the wider the extremes of poverty and wealth and the sharper the separation of classes.[4]

## Sorting and Selecting in School

For as long as sociologists have studied social class, they have been intrigued with its effects on education. George Counts, whom we met in the last chapter as a social reconstructionist, was one of the first researchers to document how schools sort and select students by their social backgrounds. In *The Selective Character of American Secondary Education* (1922), Counts showed that children from more privileged backgrounds were not only more likely to attend high school but also more likely to take the schools' most prestigious academic courses. In *Middletown* (1929), a detailed portrait of life in a medium-sized Midwestern city, Robert and Helen Lynd showed that while parents from all classes said they believed in the importance of formal education, students from higher-status families enjoyed school more and stayed in school longer.[5]

Research conducted throughout the nation added details to the picture. As we saw in chapters 6 and 7, educators have diversified the curriculum during the twentieth century, developing different programs in their quest to "meet the needs" of students from different socioeconomic backgrounds. This trend, relatively new when Counts and the Lynds undertook their studies, soon swept the country. Other sociologists documented the results of the trend: The schools became stratified by social class. In the influential study *Who Shall Be Educated* (1944), which involved research in the South, the Midwest, and New England, W. Lloyd Warner and his associates used the metaphor of a sorting machine to depict educational stratification:

The educational system may be thought of as an enormous, complicated machine for sorting and ticketing and routing children through life. Young children are fed in at one end to a moving belt which conveys them past all sorts of inspecting stations. One large group is almost immediately brushed off into a bin labeled "nonreaders," "first grade repeaters," or "opportunity class" where they stay for eight or ten years and are then released through a chute to the outside world to become "hewers of wood and drawers of water." The great body of children move ahead on the main belt, losing a few here and there who are "kept back" for repeated inspection.[6]

Warner concluded that although the machine provides upward mobility for a few working-class students, it "keep[s] down many people who try for higher places."[7]

A study that brought the picture into even clearer focus appeared in the post–World War II era. *Elmtown's Youth* (1949) by August B. Hollingshead became a classic because it highlighted a pattern that appeared again and again in later research. In Elmtown High, a small-town school in the Midwest, Hollingshead found a startling correspondence between the socioeconomic status of students and their academic program or track. As Table 8.1 shows, nearly two-thirds of the upper- and upper-middle-class students were enrolled in the college preparatory program, and the rest were in the general track. These higher-status students shunned the commercial (business/vocational) track. By contrast, more than a third of the working-class students were in the commercial program, and fewer than 10 percent were in the college prep track. The placement of the lower-middle-class students fell between these two extremes.[8]

While it might be comforting to dismiss this phenomenon as a relic from the past, we cannot. The percentages have changed, but the pattern remains the same. Based on recent studies, my estimates of the current situation are in Table 8.2. Comparing it to Elmtown High in the 1940s, notice that higher percentages of students from all social classes are in the college preparatory program, reflecting the increased popularity of higher education generally and the attempt

**TABLE 8.1**    Social class and tracking: Elmtown High School in the 1940s.

| | Percentage of Students in Track | | |
| Social Class | College Preparatory | General | Commercial |
| --- | --- | --- | --- |
| Upper and upper middle | 64 | 36 | 0 |
| Lower middle | 27 | 51 | 21 |
| Upper working | 9 | 58 | 33 |
| Lower working | 4 | 58 | 38 |

SOURCE:    Adapted from August B. Hollingshead, *Elmtown's Youth* (New York: Wiley, 1949), p. 462.

**TABLE 8.2**  Social class and tracking: American high schools today.

| | Percentage of Students in Track | | |
| --- | --- | --- | --- |
| Social Class | College Preparatory | General | Business/Vocational |
| Upper and upper middle | 80 | 20 | 0 |
| Lower middle | 50 | 35 | 15 |
| Upper working | 20 | 55 | 25 |
| Lower working | 10 | 50 | 40 |

SOURCE: Estimates based on Daniel U. Levine and Robert J. Havighurst, *Society and Education*, 8th ed. (Boston: Allyn & Bacon, 1992), pp. 39–44; James S. Coleman and Thomas Hoffer, *Public and Private High Schools: The Impact of Communities* (New York: Basic Books, 1987), pp. 41–50.

to open college doors to students from lower socioeconomic backgrounds. Notice, too, that the relationship between social class and academic placement is still strong. Upper- and middle-class students are still far more likely to be prepping for college, just as working-class students are more likely to be learning how to repair automobiles of rotate crops. The same pattern of stratification by social class appears in middle schools that practice tracking.

Other studies show that social class correlates with almost every conceivable outcome of formal education, including grades, test scores, and participation in extracurricular activities. The higher your social class, the more likely you are to graduate from high school and attend college. The lower your social class, the more likely you are to drop out of school.[9]

But why? Now comes the hard part, for it is much easier to describe something than to explain it. At the outset, we need to realize that although statistics allow us to make generalizations about group behavior, individuals within those groups may act quite differently. Some working-class students do well in school, just as some wealthy students do poorly. Furthermore, the fact that social class *correlates* with many outcomes of schooling does not necessarily mean that social class *causes* success or failure. Other factors may be responsible. In a nation committed to equal opportunity, however, the strong statistical relationship between social class and so much of what goes on in school should prompt educators to take the ''why'' question seriously.

## Families, Peer Groups, and Schools

Sociologists have traditionally explained the influence of social class on education by analyzing the role of families, peer groups, and the schools themselves. We will consider each of these institutions in turn.

Beyond the obvious fact that more affluent parents can give their children more of the things that money can buy—books, magazines, toys, trips, and so forth—social class affects family life in several important ways. Linguistic studies show that working-class families often raise their children with a language system significantly different from the one used in school. Everyone speaks a dialect, as linguists point out, but some working-class dialects are very different from the "official" dialect of the school. Furthermore, working-class parents are less likely than middle- and upper-class parents to carry on extended conversations with their children and less likely to answer their children's questions as if they were talking with other adults. Beyond these differences, more and more working-class students whose primary language is not English are enrolling in U.S. schools, as we will see later in this chapter.[10]

Regarding disciplinary practices, working-class families tend to stress obedience based on respect for authority—"You'll clean up your room because I'm your mother and I told you to"—while middle- and upper-class parents are more likely to encourage obedience by cajoling and reasoning with their children—"Please straighten your room so you can find things more easily next time." Corporal punishment occurs more frequently in working-class homes, where many parents believe a certain amount of physical discipline is a good thing on principle. Middle- and upper-class parents tend to use corporal punishment sparingly, in exceptional situations.[11]

We would be wrong to conclude that working-class parents love their children less—fortunately, love does not recognize social class boundaries—just as we would be mistaken to apply the generalizations about any social class to all its members. But we would be blind to conclude that working-class children, as a group, come to school well prepared for what they will encounter. Such children often see school as an unfamiliar game with strange players and odd rules.[12]

Thus sociologists speak of the mismatch between the world working-class children know at home and the world they discover at school. Some students adapt; many do not.

The working-class peer group may hinder the transition more than it helps. Here we must avoid stereotyping working-class students as rebels who reject school and all it represents and more privileged students as serious scholars with a deep respect for learning. Actually students from all social classes seem to care more about clothes, cars, sports, music, and friends than about the academic subjects they are taking. Friends are especially important—by adolescence, they are the number-one influence in students' lives.

Still, there are differences among the social classes. Simply put, middle- and upper-class students are usually more willing to play the game. Typically, they take the courses and make the grades necessary to keep their parents off their backs, participate in a few extracurricular activities, and qualify for admission to some sort of college. Over the last two decades, more of these students have drifted into the general track in order to earn better grades with less effort. Among their friends, attitudes toward teachers and academic subjects may be quite cynical, but there is peer pressure to keep enough of the rules to stay in the game.[13]

One of the first lessons I learned as a new teacher was that working-class students often feel peer pressure *not* to play the game. In schools where working-class students are accustomed to wearing the label of losers, stepping out of character and doing well can be embarrassing—an open invitation to peer ridicule.

Critical theorists (see chapter 7) say working-class students who conform to peer pressure and refuse to play the game are *resisting* schooling.[14]

## Gangs: Working-Class Resistance in the Extreme

The peer group most dreaded by adults, gangs capitalize on their outlaw image to glamorize attitudes and behaviors directly opposed to those the school sanctions. Gang members get points from their peers for doing drugs and having sex at school, vandalizing school property, and intimidating teachers and "straight" students. As part of their rejection of the larger society, gangs despise almost everything the school stands for.[15]

To counter gang influence, educators are trying strategies ranging from the "crackdown"—symbolized by Joe Clark, the baseball bat–wielding principal popularized in the film *Lean on Me*—to working with youth-service agencies such as the YMCA and YWCA, the Boy Scouts and Girl Scouts, and the Boys and Girls Clubs of America. Jesse Jackson's People United to Save Humanity (PUSH) is leading the antigang campaign in several large cities. These efforts sometimes succeed in pushing gangs out of individual schools, but what gangs embody in the extreme—working-class resistance to schooling and to other conventional socialization—is growing in the 1990s.[16]

I must emphasize that most working-class students are not gang members. Even though gangs are spreading beyond large urban areas to smaller cities and suburbs, most teachers face working-class resistance on a less organized basis, class by class and student by student.

As a new high school English teacher, I noticed that every time I gave one particular student a good grade, his friends gave him a hard time, so I tried to get around the situation by telling him his grades privately. This strategy worked fairly well for him, but it failed with most of his peers. By the end of the year, I was still trying to reach working-class students, but I had concluded that more than my classroom methods needed to change.

## Ability Grouping and Tracking

Of course, critical theorists say. Working-class students resist schooling because they see the very structure of schools working against their best interests. Like other students, they hear the constantly repeated message that success in school will lead to success in life. But working-class students are more likely than other students to scoff at the message. As they watch the educational sorting machine crank out winners and losers, they can see their chances of success slipping away—beginning at a very early age.

Ability grouping and tracking, key components of the sorting machine, must bear some of the responsibility for turning off working-class students. Ability grouping involves placing students of similar ability together for instruction in particular *subjects*—forming separate groups for fast, average, and slow readers, for instance. Although research on the academic effectiveness of ability grouping is mixed, with as much evidence unfavorable to the practice as favorable, many teachers believe some grouping is necessary, especially in schools with students whose academic skills vary considerably. How else, they ask, can a teacher do justice to 30 students reading on several different levels?[17]

One answer is that differences in academic ability are relatively small when children first enter school. The studies most favorable to ability grouping show it offers only slight advantages to students in the top groups—their achievement tends to be as high in ungrouped classrooms. The studies least favorable to ability grouping show it does significant harm to the achievement of the students in the bottom groups. Far from narrowing the academic differences children bring to kindergarten and the first grade, ability grouping appears to widen them.[18]

Jeannie Oakes, whose books *Keeping Track* (1985) and *Multiplying Inequalities* (1990) have focused new attention on the inequalities of ability grouping, has concluded that without ability grouping in the elementary grades, middle and high school teachers would have much easier jobs. Oakes and other researchers suggest a number of alternatives to ability grouping. In *cooperative learning,* one of the more popular alternatives, teachers form learning teams composed of students with different abilities, students work cooperatively rather than competitively, and teachers assign grades based on individual progress. Cooperative learning seems to be beneficial to students of all abilities, and it is especially helpful in keeping slower students from falling farther and farther behind.[19]

With ability grouping, by contrast, students grow apart academically as they grow older, and the conventional wisdom among educators is that by middle school or high school something more than ability grouping is not only desirable but essential. That something more is tracking, which involves placing students in different *programs,* often called college preparatory, general, and vocational. Some schools have developed *sub*programs to sort students out within the main three tracks: advanced-placement college prep, regular college prep; high general, low general; regular vocational, remedial vocational. As a result of tracking, some students take four years of math and science while others take only one or two. Some learn a foreign language, while others pass time in study hall. Some write essays, while others fill in worksheets.[20]

Not surprisingly, students who take a less demanding curriculum perform less well on standardized tests. Research conducted by the ACT Assessment Program shows that students who do not complete a core curriculum in high school (four years of English and at least three years each of mathematics, social studies, and science) score significantly lower on the ACT's college entrance examination than students who take the core.[21]

*Changing the Odds* (1990), a study conducted by the College Board, points to algebra and geometry, laboratory sciences, and foreign languages as "gatekeepers" for college. Students who take these subjects are more likely than others to attend college. Geometry seems to be the most critical gatekeeper. "Students who take geometry are approximately twice as likely to attend college as those who do not," the College Board reports. Among students who take geometry, those from low-income families are almost as likely to attend college as those from high-income families.[22]

To put things positively, research suggests students from lower socioeconomic backgrounds have a great deal to gain from getting out of lower tracks and into programs with higher standards and expectations. Put negatively, the best way for educators to ensure that working-class students will never have a serious chance at jobs requiring a college degree is to encourage or simply allow them to take the easy way out of middle and high school.

A walk through almost any tracked school will reveal what research confirms. Lower-track students receive an education that differs not just in the quantity and quality of academic courses but also in the *climate* of instruction. Lower-track students believe their teachers are less concerned with academic skills than with their willingness to take orders and follow directions. Students in lower-track classes are less likely than others to have friends who want to go to college. Perhaps most seriously, tracking lowers the self-esteem of students in the least prestigious programs. Well aware they are the outcasts of the school, lower-track students band together in peer groups that guard their losers' image as if it were a badge of honor. Here is the *self-fulfilling prophecy* at its worst: lower-track students living down to expectations.[23]

The College Board believes the situation can be different. According to *Changing the Odds,* helping students raise their aspirations can increase the probability they will attend college. Among students who expect to complete a bachelor's degree program, low-income students are almost as likely as high-income students to enroll in college. At every income level, the College Board concludes, "students who want to get a college degree, and know which courses will lead them toward that goal, go to college."[24]

## Creating a Culture of Detracking

Since the mid-1980s, the tide of academic opinion has been turning against ability grouping and tracking. After evaluating studies such as those we have just reviewed, groups as diverse as the Carnegie Corporation, the National Education Association, and the National Governor's Association have gone on record in favor of less grouping and tracking. Jeannie Oakes, collecting evidence on local schools where such reforms are under way, has found that a *"culture of detracking* is more important than the specific alternative or implementation strategy chosen." Still, creating that culture is "unsettling" and "extraordinarily difficult," Oakes reports.[25]

An international comparison helps explain why. In Japan, a nation whose educational accomplishments many Americans envy, the state schools practice no ability grouping and much less tracking than our public schools, yet Japanese students regularly outperform ours on achievement tests. "Yes, but the Japanese are a homogeneous people, and we are not," comes the reply. That statement overlooks the fact that Japan also has social classes, but it does make a point. Our nation's penchant for grouping and tracking seems to be more social than academic.[26]

Historically, Americans have rarely questioned a set of interlocking assumptions about academic success, social class, and jobs. Throughout the twentieth century, as working-class children have come to school in larger numbers and stayed there longer, educators have voiced the assumptions in a variety of ways to justify ability grouping and tracking. Stated bluntly, these are the assumptions:

1. Many children lack both the ability and the interest necessary to succeed in school.
2. These children come disproportionately from the lower social classes.
3. They are probably destined for jobs that involve working with their hands rather than their minds.
4. Therefore, they need little or no academic training beyond the 3Rs.[27]

These assumptions have withstood challenges from educational theorists of all persuasions—perennialists, essentialists, and progressives. Most of the school reforms of the 1980s and 1990s have the unmistakable ring of essentialism in their calls for more academic work for all students, but given the deeply ingrained assumption that many students are incapable of academic success, exactly what their work will consist of remains to be seen. Our challenge is to make schooling more than a reflection of children's social class backgrounds, more than an assumption about their future roles in the labor force.

## RACE AND ETHNICITY

### Defining a "Sense of Peoplehood" in a Multicultural Nation

Although some people use the words interchangeably, *race* and *ethnicity* are not synonymous. Race is a *physical* concept, based on skin color and other physical characteristics. Ethnicity is a *cultural* concept involving such factors as language, religion, and nationality. Anthropologists generally speak of three races: Caucasoid (white), Mongoloid (yellow), and Negroid (black). Throughout the world, cultural differences have divided each race into numerous ethnic groups.[28]

Many ethnic groups are subdivisions of a particular race, but others are not. People of the black race in the United States have developed a strong collective identity that has forged them into one ethnic group, African Americans. Other ethnic groups, conversely, include more than one race. Hispanic Americans, for instance, can be of any race.

Think of ethnicity as a "sense of peoplehood."[29] The members of an ethnic group have a shared identity based on a common history and a sense of common destiny. The members of the group often share a language, religion, and other cultural traditions, and they often have common geographical origins. In the United States, many ethnic groups identify themselves by the nation from which their ancestors came. Thus we have German Americans, Irish Americans, Chinese Americans, Swedish Americans, Italian Americans, Polish Americans, Vietnamese Americans, and a host of others. Native Americans, the people who inhabited

North America before Europeans and Africans came to the continent, constitute an ethnic group with as many as 170 tribal subdivisions.[30]

Other groups in the United States emphasize nongeographical factors as the basis of their ethnic identity. Jewish Americans stress the religion of Judaism, while Hispanic Americans are unified by the Spanish language. As these two groups illustrate, though, the members of a group may view their ethnicity in different ways. Many American Jews put less emphasis on religion than on shared historical experience and a sense of common destiny. The word *Hispanic* is too general for some Americans, who may prefer the more specific ethnic identification of such names as Mexican American, Puerto Rican, and Cuban American.

The strength of ethnic ties also varies from group to group and person to person. The sense of peoplehood is usually stronger within groups of lower socioeconomic status. As people climb the ladder of success, they tend to think of themselves less as members of an ethnic group and more as members of a social class. Ethnic identity may also be weaker in large groups with a long period of U.S. residence. Americans whose roots lie primarily in England outnumber German Americans (although barely so, according to census figures) to form the largest "ancestral group" in the nation. Yet English Americans—sometimes called white Anglo-Saxon Protestants, or WASPs, a name some of them do not appreciate—generally do not think of themselves as ethnic at all. Moreover, many Americans have such diverse ethnic backgrounds that they do not identify with any one group. They prefer to think of themselves as just Americans.[31]

Still, since the mid-1960s, the United States has experienced an upsurge of ethnic consciousness, and a new wave of immigration has increased the nation's ethnic and racial diversity. One-third of these new immigrants are from Asia, another third from Latin America, and the rest from Europe and elsewhere. In absolute numbers, the immigration now under way may soon surpass the immigration that occurred from 1870 to 1920, which historians regard as the greatest mass movement of people in history. Twenty-eight million people came to the United States in that half-century, but the more than 15 million who immigrated in the quarter-century from 1965 to 1990 arrived at an even faster pace.[32]

The demographic data in Table 8.3 suggest why racial and ethnic changes are such strong forces in American society and why educators are finally taking the need for multicultural education seriously. Notice how the percentage of public school students who are African, Hispanic, or Asian American is increasing during the 1990s, while the percentage of students who are white is decreasing. These trends are likely to continue well into the twenty-first century, so that by 2020, about 40 percent of all Americans and 50 percent of all public school students may be racial and ethnic minorities. Indeed, these changes may eventually redefine *minority* and *majority* in the United States.

## African-American Students

As we saw in chapter 6, African Americans have a unique history. Africans began arriving in the North American colonies as involuntary immigrants in the early 1600s. During 250 years of slavery, African labor built up the colonies that became the southern states, while African culture influenced the entire nation more deeply

**TABLE 8.3** Racial and ethnic distribution of U.S. population and public school enrollment, 1990 and 2000.

| Group | Percentage of U.S. Population | | Percentage of Public School Enrollment | |
|---|---|---|---|---|
| | *1990* | *2000* | *1990* | *2000* |
| White American* | 76 | 71 | 70 | 63 |
| African American* | 12 | 13 | 16 | 17 |
| Hispanic American | 9 | 12 | 10 | 15 |
| Asian American | 3 | 4 | 3 | 4 |
| Native American | 1 | 1 | 1 | 1 |

Note: Some columns total more than 100 due to rounding.
*Excludes persons of Hispanic origin
SOURCES: Estimates and projections based on U.S. Department of Commerce, Bureau of the Census, *Statistical Abstract of the United States, 1992* (Washington, D.C.: U.S. Government Printing Office, 1992), p. 17; U.S. Department of Education, National Center for Education Statistics, *The Condition of Education, 1992* (Washington, D.C.: U.S. Government Printing Office, 1992), p. 293; and Daniel U. Levine and Robert J. Havighurst, *Society and Education,* 8th ed. (Boston: Allyn & Bacon, 1992), chap. 10.

than most whites realized. After the Civil War, the promise of freedom and equality for African Americans proved to be false. In the South, where more than 90 percent of blacks lived, whites imposed a "new slavery" at the turn of the twentieth century, turning to legally sanctioned segregation in an effort to keep blacks subservient. African Americans created a separate society behind the wall of segregation, using education to advance themselves and resist white oppression.[33]

School desegregation, the subject of the next section, is one of the most significant issues in African-American history. Separate schools were clearly unequal, and black people looked to desegregation as the major strategy for equalizing educational opportunities. By winning the legal right to attend formerly all-white schools, moreover, modern civil rights leaders hoped to build up enough momentum to break down segregation in other walks of life. But the goals that seemed so clear and simple during the 1950s and 1960s turned cloudy and complex during the 1970s and 1980s. Today, the desirability of desegregation itself seems questionable to some African Americans.

One reason is that African Americans have not shared equally in the benefits of desegregation and other social policies. On the one hand, more than 40 percent of African Americans are now middle class. The average income of black families with two wage earners has climbed to 85 percent of what similar white families earn. On the other hand, the average income of all black families has fallen to 60 percent of that for all white families. As the gap between middle-class and working-class black families widens, young African-American males growing up poor face especially tough obstacles.[34]

Not surprisingly, the statistical indicators on African-American students are mixed. The gap in achievement test scores between blacks and whites continues to narrow, although it remains wide. The percentage of black 19- and 20-year-olds who are high school graduates has risen to 78, although it remains well below the white percentage of 87. And among high school graduates, only 14 percent of African Americans aged 25 to 29 have completed college, compared to 30 percent of whites of the same ages.[35]

## Hispanic-American Students

Hispanics are a large, diverse, rapidly growing group. Actually Hispanics are several groups, unified culturally by the Spanish language and often the Roman Catholic faith but historically distinct.[36]

Mexican Americans, about 60 percent of all Hispanics in the United States, have a long history in the Southwest. By the early 1600s, Spaniards had settled much of the land in the present states of California, New Mexico, Arizona, Colorado, and Texas. For 250 years, the Spanish language and Catholic faith were dominant in this large territory.

The U.S. victory in the Mexican–American War (1846–1848) officially established a different culture, English-speaking and Protestant. Public schools and Catholic schools stressed conformity to the English (now called Anglo) culture, but the goal was usually separation rather than assimilation. Heavy legal and illegal immigration from Mexico to the United States at the turn of the twentieth century, during World War II, and especially since the 1960s has produced a modern Mexican-American population that is heavily concentrated in the Southwest, highly urbanized, largely working-class, and increasingly segregated.

Puerto Rico became a U.S. territory at the end of the Spanish–American War in 1898 and a commonwealth in 1952. Excluding the population of the island itself, 13 percent of Hispanics in the United States are Puerto Ricans. The poorest of American Hispanics, many Puerto Ricans travel back and forth between the island and the mainland, their circular migrations tied to the availability of jobs. Puerto Ricans are also the most highly segregated Hispanics. Typically, their children attend highly segregated schools in New York and other central cities.

Cuban Americans are the most prosperous Hispanics in the United States. Most have come to this nation since Fidel Castro's rise to power in the late 1950s. Many professionals and businesspeople left the island during the 1960s and 1970s, later to be joined by much poorer refugees. Now 5 percent of American Hispanics, Cubans are heavily concentrated in the Miami–Dade County area of Florida.

Recent immigrants from Central and South America account for 12 percent of Hispanic Americans. Often overlooked in academic research on the nation's Hispanic population, these people are culturally and economically heterogeneous. Many are political refugees from such countries as El Salvador, Guatemala, Nicaragua, and Colombia, and many are settling in Los Angeles and New York City.

The statistical indicators on Hispanic-American students are less favorable than those on African-American students. The test score gap between Hispanics and whites has narrowed, but not as much as the gap between blacks and whites. Forty percent of Hispanic 19- and 20-year-olds have not received a high school diploma, an alarming statistic that has changed little since the mid-1970s. Among Hispanic 25- to 29-year-olds who have finished high school, only 16 percent have also graduated from college.[37]

Nine percent of Hispanic students come to school with limited proficiency in English. How to help these students is a controversial issue, as we will see later in this chapter. With Hispanics expected to replace Africans as the nation's largest minority group early in the next century, the strong Hispanic desire for bilingual education strikes some Americans as logical and pluralistic and others as dangerous and separatist.

## Asian-American Students

The Asian population in the United States is growing seven times as fast as the general population, almost doubling between 1980 and 1990. Filipinos are the largest Asian-American ethnic group, followed by Chinese, Vietnamese, Koreans, Japanese, Indians, Laotians, and more than 70 smaller groups. Asians are concentrated in urban areas within several states. Forty percent of Asian Americans live in California, where they represent 10 percent of the population, and another 30 percent live in New York, Illinois, Texas, and Hawaii.[38]

Asian Americans are so diverse that the "model minority" stereotype conceals as much as it reveals. In fact, some researchers describe the academic achievement of Asian students as an inverted bell curve with large numbers of high achievers and low achievers and relatively few students in the middle. Four family-related factors influence where individual students fall on the curve: socioeconomic status, length of U.S. residence, level of education before immigrating, and proficiency in English.

Filipino, Chinese, and Japanese students are often from families who have lived in the United States since the 1800s or early 1900s. Along with Koreans and Indians, these students are usually middle class. In fact, the educational and economic attainment of well-established Asian-American families is much higher than that of the general population. Unfortunately, the grandparents in some of these families can recall overt anti-Asian discrimination through the World War II era and more subtle discrimination since.

Vietnamese, Laotian, Cambodian, and other Southeast Asian students are usually from families who immigrated after 1975 to escape political repression. With the exception of professional families who fled Vietnam in 1975 and 1976, most of these families arrived in the United States poor, speaking little English. More than 15 percent of today's Southeast Asian students have limited proficiency in English, double the 7 percent rate for all Asian-American students.

Desegregation is not a major issue for Asian Americans. Although they were segregated by law in California early in this century, most Asian students have moved out of ethnic neighborhoods and into schools where whites are in the majority.

Bilingual education is a major issue. As we will see later, Asian Americans often disagree with Hispanics on what kind of education is best for students whose native language is not English.

The statistical indicators on Asian-American students are impressive. Although there is considerable variation among Asian ethnic groups, Asian students as a whole are almost as proficient at reading and more proficient at mathematics than white students. Asians are less likely to drop out of high school and more likely to complete college than students in any other major racial or ethnic group.[39]

## Native American Students

Descendants of the original Americans face educational problems unlike those of any other group. Alternately romanticized, denigrated, and ignored, Native Americans are perhaps the least understood of the groups discussed here.[40]

Deprived of most of their land and forced onto reservations during the nineteenth century, Native Americans encountered powerful forces of assimilation in schools operated by missionary societies, philanthropic groups, and the federal government's Bureau of Indian Affairs. White educators tried to eradicate the culture of hundreds of tribes by stressing U.S. patriotism, banning native languages, and teaching students allegedly "superior" ways of farming and housekeeping.

Even though these policies produced miserable results, they continued into the second half of the twentieth century. Much native culture disappeared, to be sure, but few Native Americans assimilated. As late as 1950, half were still living on reservations amid rampant poverty.

Native Americans began a struggle to control their own education during the 1960s and 1970s. Today reservation schools are centers of tribal culture. But three-fourths of Native Americans now live off the reservations, where economic opportunities are greater but opportunities to regain their culture are fewer.

Although the Native American population has grown rapidly since the 1950s, it still accounts for only 1 percent of the nation's total population and public school enrollment. Thus the dire problems Native Americans face do not attract the attention they deserve. Among the four minority groups we have profiled, Native Americans have the lowest test scores, the highest dropout rates, and the lowest college completion rates. Nine percent come to school with limited proficiency in English.[41]

## DESEGREGATION OR RESEGREGATION?

### Historical Perspective

When the U.S. Supreme Court issued its decision in *Brown v. Board of Education of Topeka* (1954), the court raised a question the nation is still struggling to answer: Can segregated schools ever be equal? Since 1954, Americans have discovered how complex the question is.

In the wake of *Plessy v. Ferguson* (1896), African Americans had no more than the rhetorical equality suggested by the words *separate but equal*. The rhetoric bore no resemblance to reality. Black schools were inferior to white schools, and it was impossible to pretend otherwise. There were obvious differences in such tangible factors as physical facilities, courses of study, pupil-teacher ratios, teacher salaries, and overall expenditures per student. These inequalities, although greatest in the South, existed throughout the nation. By the 1950s, some school boards were narrowing—but by no means completely closing—the gaps between black and white schools, hoping to avoid or at least postpone a Supreme Court mandate for desegregation.[42]

When that mandate finally came on May 17, 1954, the court used language so clear and direct even supporters of desegregation were startled. Can segregated schools ever be equal? The answer was a unanimous no. The justices cited social science evidence to support their conclusion that even when expenditures and other tangible factors are equal, segregated schools are psychologically damaging to African-American students. Thus the court declared that "separate educational facilities are inherently unequal"—an unequivocal answer.[43]

*Brown* represented such a direct confrontation with established educational practice that the court did not issue an enforcement decree for a full year. When it called for desegregation "with all deliberate speed" in 1955 and ordered the lower courts to supervise the process, opponents of desegregation seized on the word *deliberate* and proceeded to drag their feet.[44]

In the South, massive resistance blocked the way as governors vowed "segregation forever" and state legislatures stalled for time. Lengthy legal battles ensued. Battles were also fought out of court as riots and other violent acts often made it necessary for federal troops to escort African-American children into newly desegregated schools. Taking massive resistance to the extreme, Prince Edward County, Virginia, simply closed its public schools from 1959 through 1964 to avoid desegregation. Confrontations of the same kind accompanied the desegregation of colleges and universities.[45]

But the quest for desegregated education drew strength from the Reverend Martin Luther King, Jr., and the larger civil rights movement, constant legal pressure from the NAACP, and after 1960, all three branches of the federal government. The major breakthrough came with the passage and enforcement of the Civil Rights Act of 1964. Title VI of the act gave federal officials the power to cut off federal funds to school systems refusing to desegregate. Other federal legislation passed in the mid-1960s made school systems throughout the nation, especially in the South, increasingly dependent on federal funding. The Civil Rights Act, national in scope but admittedly aimed at the South, was a powerful weapon indeed.[46]

Federal pressure produced remarkable results—in some parts of the United States. Table 8.4 shows that public schools in the South, the *most* segregated in the nation for African Americans as late as 1968, had become the nation's *least* segregated only four years later. They remain so today.

Compare the trends in other regions—the greatest contrast is between the South and the Northeast. Notice that although northeastern public schools were the nation's *least* segregated for African Americans in 1968, they became *more* segregated, while southern schools were moving rapidly in the opposite direction. Given the slow but steady progress of desegregation in western, midwestern, and border states, today the Northeast has the nation's *most* segregated public schools.

**TABLE 8.4**   Segregation of African-American students by region, 1968–1988.

| | Percentage of Students in 90%–100% Minority Schools | | | | | |
|---|---|---|---|---|---|---|
| Region | 1968 | 1972 | 1976 | 1980 | 1984 | 1988 |
| South | 78 | 25 | 22 | 23 | 24 | 24 |
| Border | 60 | 55 | 43 | 37 | 37 | NA* |
| Northeast | 43 | 47 | 51 | 49 | 47 | 48 |
| Midwest | 58 | 57 | 51 | 44 | 44 | 42 |
| West | 51 | 43 | 36 | 34 | 29 | NA |
| U.S. Average | 64 | 39 | 36 | 33 | 33 | NA |

*NA = not available
SOURCES:   Gary Orfield, *Public School Desegregation in the United States, 1968–1980* (Washington, D.C.: Joint Center for Political Studies, 1983), p. 4; Gary Orfield and Franklin Monfort, *Are American Schools Resegregating in the Reagan Era?*, working paper no. 14 (Chicago: National School Desegregation Project, University of Chicago, 1987), pp. 313–314, 392; Peter Schmidt, "Study Shows a Rise in the Segregation of Hispanic Students," *Education Week* (January 15, 1992), pp. 1, 19.

## De Facto versus De Jure

In order to understand these trends, we must distinguish between two types of segregation: de jure and de facto. *De jure* means "by law." De jure segregation is the result of legislation, policy, or official action: a state law or local school board policy requiring black students and white students to attend separate schools, for instance, or a public official's statements supporting segregation. Because laws, policies, and officials mandated segregation in every southern state, the eyes of the nation were on the South after the *Brown* decision. But de jure school segregation also existed in the border states and in school districts scattered throughout every region of the nation—the one in Topeka, Kansas, the Brown family sued, for example. During the 1950s and 1960s, this kind of segregation was obvious and relatively easy to prove in court—it was a smoking gun.

Vestiges of de jure segregation remain today, but in guises more subtle and more difficult to document. De jure segregation may take the form of a principal who quietly discourages black students from requesting voluntary transfers to a predominantly white school or a school board that opens new schools with attendance zones that increase segregation within the district. In a precedent-setting 1987 decision involving Yonkers, New York, a federal court of appeals ruled that de jure segregation can even take the form of a city government that locates public housing projects in a way that promotes residential segregation.[47]

Most segregation in the United States today, however, is *de facto,* which means "in fact." De facto school segregation is largely the result of segregated neighborhoods. The "fact" is that most Americans still choose to live among people of their own race. Such segregation is sometimes called voluntary, which is an accurate description only to the degree people can choose housing without encountering racial discrimination—and can afford housing of their choice.

Although the line between de facto and de jure segregation can be fine, as the examples in the preceding paragraph suggest, the Supreme Court and lower courts have tried to distinguish between the two since *Brown.* In the early 1990s, the Supreme Court reviewed the progress of desegregation in Oklahoma City and the Atlanta suburb of DeKalb County, two school districts that had been under court order to reduce de jure segregation. In the Oklahoma City case, the court ruled that once school districts prove they are no longer practicing de jure desegregation, they can end mandatory busing—even if doing so leads to resegregation. In the DeKalb County case, the court affirmed that districts are not legally obligated to correct resegregation caused by racial transition in neighborhoods.[48]

The distinction between de facto and de jure helps explain why public schools in the Northeast are more segregated today than they were in the 1950s. This change reflects demographic trends in the large urban areas of the Northeast, where whites have been leaving the central cities for the suburbs since the end of World War II. Many urban neighborhoods that were once white are now African or Hispanic. In addition, many of the whites who live in northeastern central cities today send their children to private schools.[49]

The same demographic trends have changed the racial composition of urban school districts throughout the nation. In Chicago, Houston, and Los Angeles as well as New York, Philadelphia, and Boston, minority students are now in the majority. In fact, minorities outnumber whites in every one of the 25 largest school districts in the nation.[50]

Looking at public school segregation in the nation as a whole, we can see different racial and ethnic patterns. Most Asian-American students attend majority-white schools. The segregation of African students, although extreme in central cities, has nevertheless held fairly constant since the 1970s. For Hispanic students, segregation is both extreme and increasing. "We now have Hispanic ghettos and barrios where virtually all the students are Hispanic," warns Gary Orfield, a Harvard professor of education and social policy and a national authority on school desegregation. As the Hispanic population increases, so does the segregation of Hispanic students.[51]

## Academic, Social, and Economic
## Effects of Desegregation

Turning our attention to the effects of school desegregation, we face a controversial question: Does desegregation improve the academic achievement of minority students? How we answer the question depends on whose research we accept.

One problem is that some researchers have approached the question with their minds already made up, obviously looking for evidence to support their ideological biases. Another problem is that researchers have studied the academic effects of desegregation using so many different methodologies and research designs that it is difficult to compare studies and draw conclusions. Despite these problems, answers are emerging from more than three decades of research on the question.

The basic answer is yes. The academic achievement of minority students *usually* improves as a result of desegregation. (Almost all the research has focused on African-American students, though the few studies on Hispanic students show the same pattern.) Robert L. Crain, senior social scientist at the Rand Corporation and principal investigator at Johns Hopkins University's Center for the Social Organization of Schools, has narrowed the many studies on the question to 93, the best studies (in his judgment) in a large and very mixed body of research.

Crain and his associates have drawn several explanations from these studies for why desegregation usually, but not always, improves achievement. Desegregation produces the greatest academic benefits when it begins early, with young children. The most rapid gains in achievement occur in the early primary grades. Moreover, the achievement of African-American students is highest in schools that are predominantly white and middle class, but where blacks are at least 20 percent of the student body. Like many other researchers, Crain attributes the gains for African Americans less to the "whiteness" of desegregated schools than to the schools' middle-class standards. Middle-class schools usually have better teachers and more demanding programs, characteristics benefiting all students.[52]

Overall, Crain's research indicates that successful desegregation can "raise a student's achievement in the first grade by a fraction of a year; if that student held on to this advantage throughout school, however, he or she would be approximately one grade level higher than if he or she had been in a segregated school."[53] Since estimates of the aggregate gap between black and white achievement put the difference at one-half year when children enter school, widening to two and one-half years by high school graduation, the academic benefits of desegregation can be significant. Crain, along with other researchers, notes that desegregation does not benefit blacks at the expense of whites. The achievement of white students rarely decreases and sometimes increases.[54]

Although academic achievement usually takes center stage in discussions of the effects of desegregation, its long-term social and economic benefits may be even more important. There is mounting evidence that desegregated schools are helping to desegregate society. African-American students who graduate from desegregated schools are more likely to attend desegregated colleges and universities, live in desegregated neighborhoods, and hold jobs in desegregated work places. School desegregation also seems to improve the racial attitudes of both whites and blacks toward their neighbors and coworkers. Robert Crain and his associates, who have conducted some of the research supporting these findings, believe school desegregation can help reduce the economic distance between blacks and whites, a gap that may account for much racial prejudice.[55]

## Busing

Public opinion polls on school desegregation show Americans of virtually all racial and ethnic groups are overwhelmingly for it—in principle. Mention the word *busing,* though, and the groups split, with two of three African Americans, three of five Hispanics, but only one of three whites in favor of busing for desegregation.[56]

Even so, the most recent Harris Poll on busing reveals "one of the most dramatic turnarounds [of public opinion] in recent history." Forty-one percent of all the people polled supported busing for desegregation.[57]

Even more significant, according to pollster Louis Harris, is the fact that for the first time "a whole host of key segments of the American public now actually favor busing." Harris's survey found that people under 30, those most likely to have ridden buses to desegregated schools themselves, are also most likely to favor it. Sixty percent of those aged 18 to 24 and 51 percent of those aged 25 to 29 expressed support. Moving up the age brackets, support decreases, to a low of 26 percent among people 65 and older. Most significant, perhaps, is the finding that 71 percent of all families whose children have been bused for desegregation rate the experience as "very satisfactory."[58]

These positive findings may not erase the memories of the bitter controversies that erupted in the 1970s, when busing for desegregation became a volatile political issue. Academic researchers fanned the flames with studies showing a connection between busing and "white flight" from public school systems. Other researchers countered that busing has generated the most resentment in central cities, which whites were leaving long before busing became a desegregation strategy. Conceding that busing may accelerate the loss of whites from central city schools, these researchers pointed out that some whites return to the schools once a controversy over a new desegregation program subsides and that metropolitan plans involving city and suburban systems have produced less white flight than plans involving central city systems alone.[59]

What is the status of busing today? More than half of all students ride school buses every day, but only about 4 percent are bused solely for desegregation. Most ride just to get to school. Nor is the emotionally charged image of "crosstown busing" accurate in most cases. The average school bus ride is about 15 minutes each way, with no difference in average length between all busing and busing for desegregation. While metropolitan (city/suburban) plans obviously increase time and distance on the bus, the longest school but routes are not in metropolitan areas for desegregation but in rural areas for transportation. Many rural students ride the bus an hour or more each way, but the length of their rides rarely causes controversy.[60]

## Magnet Schools

What bothers Americans most about busing for desegregation may be its involuntary nature. Court orders from federal judges often trigger resentment. Americans dislike riding school buses past their neighborhood schools, although the concept of neighborhood differs greatly from cities to suburbs to rural areas.

Magnet schools are designed to overcome both objections. Sometimes referred to as schools so good, students volunteer to attend them, magnet schools offer special programs to attract students from throughout a school district. New York City's School of Performing Arts and the Bronx High School of Science are two well-known examples, although they were established long before the term *magnet school* came into vogue. Magnet schools started during the 1970s and 1980s usually have *voluntary* desegregation—an alternative to court-ordered busing—as their major goal.

In addition to regular academic programs, magnet schools offer specializations not available elsewhere in a school district. One school may specialize in communications and mass media, another in health professions, another in foreign languages, still another in commercial art. For more traditional students, back-to-basics magnet schools featuring strict discipline and dress codes have proved popular in some districts.

The consensus is that magnet schools can be a good supplementary desegregation strategy, but that by themselves they probably cannot make a significant statistical dent in big-city segregation. They do offer the attractive prospect of positive, voluntary desegregation. And as the idea of educational choice continues to gain acceptance, magnet schools are becoming a key component in the public school choice plans some districts and states are adopting (see chapter 11).[61]

A major disadvantage of magnet schools, though, is that they can increase segregation by social class even as they decrease segregation by race and ethnicity. In some school districts, magnet schools have filled up with middle-class students, leaving working-class students in neighborhood schools everyone regards as second-class.[62]

## Neo-*Plessy* Thinking?

The 1980s and 1990s have not been prime years for school desegregation. Even though public opinion polls show support for desegregation in principle, the political climate has been chilly. Are Americans ready to settle for an updated version of *Plessy v. Ferguson*?

Consider the record of the last three presidents. The Reagan administration sought the dismissal of desegregation cases in several hundred school districts throughout the nation, sending the clear message that multiracial and multiethnic classrooms are not a top educational priority. The Bush administration virtually ignored desegregation in elementary and secondary schools. President Clinton, while more attentive to minority needs than his two immediate predecessors, has shown little interest in desegregation as a way to improve schools.

Instead, during all three administrations, educators have turned to *effective schools research* to guide policy. Advocates of this research say it is time to pay less attention to the racial composition of schools and more attention to their academic quality. Defining effective schools as those in which minority and poor students make high scores on standardized tests, researchers have found that such schools tend to have the following characteristics: teachers with high standards, a principal with strong skills in instructional management, an orderly but not oppressive climate, a clear set of goals, strong emphasis on basic skills, a high percentage of time on task, frequent evaluation of student progress, and close ties between home and school. Segregated schools with these characteristics can be effective schools, many educators are saying.[63]

"Let's get 'separate but equal' right this time"—is this the unstated agenda of the effective school movement? Leaders of the movement say educators must stop dreaming and start facing reality. However much we would like students of different races and ethnic groups to attend school together, the harsh fact is that demographics and politics have left many students in segregated schools. We must educate these students as best we can. For some students, there may even be advantages to segregated schooling.

Although the arguments in the preceding paragraph strike me as neo-*Plessy* thinking, I am aware of demographic and political trends. If present trends continue, many minority students—particularly those concentrated in large urban school districts—will remain in segregated schools.

Metropolitan or cross-district desegregation plans involving the predominantly white suburbs that usually surround central cities have met great resistance. Based on the Supreme Court's decision in *Milliken v. Bradley* (1974), a Detroit case, lower courts have ordered cross-district desegregation only when they have found state or suburban school officials guilty of de jure segregation. Since the mid-1970s, the courts have left big-city school desegregation largely untouched.[64]

As we saw earlier in this chapter, Supreme Court decisions during the 1990s have made it easier for school districts to end mandatory busing. Instead of busing, the latest desegregation court orders call for magnet schools and instructional improvements in predominantly minority schools.

Critics of desegregation say its advocates paint an idealized picture of its benefits. To be sure, desegregation does not always occur under the conditions advocates would like. Tracking, for instance, can defeat the purposes of desegregation by creating vastly different programs and expectations for different students within the same school. If minorities go to a desegregated school only to be grouped together in the lower tracks, their academic gains are likely to be minimal. Unfortunately, this kind of resegregation occurs frequently as a second-generation desegregation problem. Enrollment statistics may show that a school is desegregated, though a walk through the halls may reveal almost every class-room is highly segregated.[65]

Under these circumstances, critics charge, desegregation may backfire by reinforcing stereotypes. Minorities may lose self-esteem and come to resent whites for dominating the academic side of schooling. Whites may feel superior and look down on minorities.[66]

## "Acting White"

Controversy surrounds the role of racial and ethnic identity in academic achievement. According to anthropologists Signithia Fordham and John Ogbu, black students face strong pressure *not* to do well in school because many African-American peer groups view academic success as "acting white." Blacks who study and make good grades are seen as "Oreos": like the cookie, black on the outside, white on the inside. With racial pride centered on contemporary African "rap" culture, acting white is the last thing black students want to do. Therefore, they "put the brakes on" their learning.[67]

The debates over Fordham and Ogbu's research show how closely race, class, and gender are intertwined. Some researchers argue that peer pressure against academic achievement is a phenomenon primarily of class rather than of race, that middle-class African Americans are far less likely than working-class ones to hold the attitude that "playing school is a white thing." Other researchers interject the influence of gender, claiming African-American males face more peer pressure than females to hold back in school.[68]

The influence of desegregation is just as controversial. Advocates say desegregation gives African-American students greater incentives to succeed by exposing them to a wider range of peers and role models. Critics say just the opposite is true. In desegregated schools, pressure on black students not to succeed is even stronger because white students and teachers often treat blacks as outsiders, rejecting them and their culture.[69]

## African Identity Schools

Looking for a way out of what they term a "desperate situation," some African Americans are founding private schools to help students build racial identity and self-esteem. While "public schools are agents of the social order," the director of the Council of Independent Black Institutions states, "African-centered independent schools are not limited in responsibility to reproduce the status quo in social and power relations." Most of the 300 such schools already open have an *Afrocentric curriculum* organized around the study of history from an African point of view.[70]

While the movement toward private schools is growing, other African Americans are looking to public schools for the same kind of alternative. The decision of school boards in Detroit, Milwaukee, and New York City to establish African identity schools made the national news and sparked national controversy in the early 1990s. What attracted the most attention was not the Afrocentric curriculum but the plans to admit male students only.[71]

As the mass media pointed out repeatedly, more African-American males are in jail than in college. They are disciplined, suspended, and expelled far more often than other students; they are overrepresented in remedial and special education classes and underrepresented in top ability groups and tracks. To some African-American educators, this situation cries out for public schools that provide black male role models, special programs to involve parents, and "cultural innoculation" against negative racial stereotypes.[72]

Legal challenges based on Title IX (see the discussion later in this chapter) have opened all the African identity public schools to students of both sexes. Some schools are operating parallel programs for males and females. Although the schools are also open to students of any race or ethnic group, their cultural goals and their location in segregated school districts virtually ensure them an all-black student body.[73]

Are African identity schools promoting resegregation? Not at all, their advocates say, pointing to the widespread segregation that already exists in public and private schools. Many African Americans are isolated in lower academic tracks and one-race schools that "condemn students to a lifetime of segregation by sending them out into the world unprepared, untrained, and marginally literate." Confronting this harsh reality, educators in African identity schools have resolved to turn segregation against itself by preparing "academically competent and self-confident individuals" who can thrive in a pluralistic society.[74]

Can segregated schools ever be equal? Although the U.S. Supreme Court answered with an unqualified no in 1954, African-American educator and activist W. E. B. DuBois expressed mixed feelings the following year. The *Brown* decision posed a "cruel dilemma" to African Americans, he stated. Acknowledging the promise of academic and social gains, DuBois nevertheless predicted cultural losses as racial identity and heritage slipped away. Now the question is whether African Americans can use segregation itself to fulfill the promise and restore the losses.[75]

## BILINGUAL EDUCATION

### Washing Culture Out, Ironing Culture In

It may strike you as incongruous that inside a single public school, you can walk down one hall and find teachers working hard to wash Spanish out of one group of students—often in classes stigmatized as remedial. Walk down another hall, and you can find teachers trying just as hard to iron Spanish into another group of students—usually in college prep classes.

Welcome to the ongoing controversy over bilingualism and bilingual education. In a nation where conservatives and liberals agree that more students should learn foreign languages in school, sharp differences of opinion arise over how to educate the 2 million students who are classified as limited English proficient (LEP). Representing about 5 percent of the total enrollment in public schools, LEP students find their education caught up in cultural conflicts over assimilation, pluralism, and separation.[76]

If we listen carefully to the debate over bilingual education, we may be able to hear the voices of ordinary people, of students and parents who live in homes where English is not the primary language. About 60 percent of these families are Hispanic, and most of the rest are Asian.[77]

Based on opinion polls of Hispanic Americans, bilingualism is not an artificial cause promoted by politicians and activists. It is the genuine desire of the vast majority of Hispanics. Seventy-four percent of Hispanics say their language goal is to be bilingual; 20 percent say their goal is fluency in Spanish only; 6 percent say their goal is fluency in English only. Thus the pressure Hispanics have brought to bear on educators for bilingual schooling reflects a strong preference for bicultural living.[78]

It is more difficult to generalize about Asian Americans. On the one hand, they are less likely to ask schools to help maintain their native languages. Well-established Asian families with a long residence in the United States, in fact, often hold assimilationist attitudes on language. Recently arrived families—Vietnamese, Cambodians, Laotians, and others—seem most concerned that their children learn English. On the other hand, many of the new immigrants are trying to maintain their native culture in their homes, community centers, and houses of worship, because evidence is mounting that their children's loss of native language is weakening the family structure. As we will see in a moment, different models of bilingual education can accommodate these different desires.[79]

These subtleties may be lost on Americans who see Asians as the model minority and Hispanics as a self-seeking minority. Some Americans react with alarm to the Hispanic call for pluralism in schools and society. To some, it seems that Hispanics are asking not for pluralism but for segregation.

Predictably, a backlash against bilingualism developed during the 1980s. California, where almost one-third of Hispanic Americans live and where more than half of all public school students are minorities, became the first state whose voters declared English its official language and the second state to amend its constitution accordingly. Other states have followed. More than 35 state legislatures have debated the official-language issue, and about 20 have passed an English-only law. Two political action groups known as U.S. English and English First are leading a campaign to make English the official language of the nation. The campaign is directed specifically against bilingual ballots and certain forms of bilingual education.[80]

As chapter 6 indicates, bilingual education in the United States has a long but little-known history. In recent times, bilingualism became a hot issue after Congress passed the Bilingual Education Act of 1968. Responding to the complaints of Mexican-American parents in Texas, Congress resolved that students whose primary language is not English need some form of special assistance in school.

The Supreme Court's decision in *Lau v. Nichols* (1974), which involved not Hispanics but Chinese in San Francisco, affirmed the principle that school districts must do *something* to help. The court prohibited the policy of *submersion,* which forces LEP students to sink or swim with no special assistance in their native language. Standard practice in public schools for immigrants at the turn of the century, submersion remains the unofficial standard in some school systems today, *Lau* notwithstanding.[81]

Although the Supreme Court left a great deal of leeway for educators to decide how to help LEP students, the other two branches of the federal government have favored particular approaches. Federal policy on bilingual education has changed as political winds have shifted in Washington, D.C.

## Models of Bilingual Education

Since the 1970s, with Congress and a succession of presidents trying to shape language policy, attention has focused on three models of bilingual education: structured immersion, transitional bilingual, and bilingual/bicultural maintenance. By its very nature, bilingual education involves instruction in two languages, but the models differ in the amount of emphasis each language receives.

In the *structured immersion* model, teachers who know English and are supposed to know the students' native language provide instruction. Although students are supposed to be able to ask questions in either language, teachers encourage them to use English, and teachers always speak in English. My use of *supposed to* reflects the severe shortage of certified bilingual teachers, especially those who know Asian languages.

In the *transitional bilingual* model, teachers instruct students in their native language in some subjects—social studies or science, for instance—to keep them from falling behind as they learn English. Designed to ease the transition from the native language into English, this model often features separate classes in *English as a Second Language* (ESL), in which students practice reading, writing, and speaking English. Some school districts claiming to use the transitional model actually use ESL alone, offering no instruction in the native language.

Although the structured immersion and transitional bilingual models employ different methods, they have the same goal: developing skills in English as quickly as possible, ideally during the early elementary grades. Under both models, bilingual education ends when the students reach a specified level of English proficiency. Asian Americans generally prefer these two models.

The third model, *bilingual/bicultural maintenance,* has a different goal: developing and increasing proficiency in both English *and* the other language. In every grade, students take some classes taught in their native language and some taught in English, ideally by teachers who are fluent in both. The curriculum highlights the students' ethnic culture in a program of multicultural education. It is this model of bilingual education that has drawn the most criticism from U.S. English and similar groups, even though the transitional model has been more widely used. Critics charge that bilingual/bicultural maintenance programs often produce students who speak two languages poorly, students who are unprepared to compete in an English-dominant culture. Defenders of bilingual/bicultural maintenance reply that many programs do work well, urging educators to acknowledge the bilingual or even Spanish-dominant subculture in which most Hispanic Americans live.

## Bilingual Politics and Academic Research

The controversy surrounding the choice of models intensified during the 1980s when the Reagan administration tried to change federal policy on bilingual education. Whereas the Ford and Carter administrations had encouraged school systems to use the transitional model, President Reagan resolved to give state and local officials more discretion, arguing that research did not favor one model over the others. Actually, Mr. Reagan knew that many state and local educators shared his preference for structured immersion, the model that is least expensive and most compatible with assimilation. But Congress balked at the change, and most federal money is still earmarked for transitional or maintenance instruction.[82]

What does the research on bilingual education say? Just as with desegregation, the answer depends on whose research we accept. Advocates of all three models can cite literature to support their positions, and the political controversy over the research has taken fascinating twists and turns.[83]

A 1986 study funded by President Reagan's Department of Education embarrassed the administration when it rated the maintenance model most effective in developing language skills—in English as well as the native language. The more instructional time the students spent in their native language, the better their skills in that language *and* in English. When the study focused just on proficiency in English, the transitional model still came in second and immersion last.[84]

A 1991 study funded by President Bush's Department of Education found all three models effective with Hispanic students, a conclusion all sides cheered.

The Bush administration used the study to second Mr. Reagan's call for more state and local discretion. Advocates of the transitional and maintenance models interpreted the study as additional evidence in favor of programs that pay respect to native languages.[85]

The National Association for Bilingual Education is looking to the future with optimism, expecting federal support for the transitional and maintenance models to continue under President Clinton. Within the association, disputes between Hispanics and Asians and quarrels among Asian ethnic groups have subsided, at least for now. The association is trying to become a unified political lobby with a pluralistic educational agenda.[86] All the members want more funding, though as the president of California's Asian bilingual education association explains, "What works for Chinese may not work for Hispanics."[87]

## GENDER

### Shortchanging Girls

Prospective teachers often seem less interested in discussing the influence of gender on the process of education than the influence of social class, race, and ethnicity. Younger female prospective teachers may react with amazement or even amusement to the suggestion that in the 1990s, male and female students receive different treatment in school. "No one ever put me down for being a girl. I took the courses I wanted to take and participated in whatever activities and sports I chose," one of my students said recently. Many male prospective teachers have the same attitude: "No, I don't think I had any advantages or disadvantages in school because of my sex."

If an older student brings up the discrimination she (or sometimes he) faced in school, the rest of the class smiles and sighs with relief, grateful things have changed so much. To many future teachers, unequal treatment based on sex is a thing of the past, a quaint relic from another age.

Unfortunately, it lives on. *How Schools Shortchange Girls* (1992), a report form the American Association of University Women, has received front-page media coverage for

> challeng[ing] the common assumption that girls and boys are treated equally in our public schools. . . . There is clear evidence that the educational system is not meeting girls' needs. Girls and boys enter school roughly equal in measured ability. On some measures of school readiness, girls are ahead of boys. Twelve years later, girls have fallen behind their male classmates in key areas such as high-level mathematics and measures of self-esteem.[88]

Calling attention to the silence about gender in the debate over school reform, *How Schools Shortchange Girls* urges educators to consider gender alongside class, race, and ethnicity. Two of the report's authors speak throughout the nation, and they never fail to startle audiences when they point out that "girls are the only group in our society that begins school ahead and ends up behind."[89]

So think again. Have things really changed? When researchers asked students in grades 3–12 to respond to the question "If you woke up tomorrow and discovered that you were a [boy/girl], how would your life be different?" the answers were surprisingly consistent. Students of both sexes readily admitted that boys have it better than girls. Boys do not have to worry much about their appearance, the students said, but girls must be concerned with attractiveness and neatness or risk rejection. Boys can participate in a wider range of activities and choose among more careers, the students continued. Girls have to watch their behavior more carefully—they have to be "nicer" than boys. The students were also aware that girls have to be more concerned with their safety. In short, students of both sexes saw few advantages to being female and few disadvantages to being male.[90]

## Gender-Role Socialization

When confronted with such studies, prospective teachers tend to place the blame on the home: "Students must pick up those attitudes from their parents. Teachers would never favor one sex over the other."

Of course, there is abundant evidence that many parents still raise boys and girls differently. Males begin life as the preferred sex. By a ratio of more than 2 to 1, both future mothers and future fathers express their preference for boys. Some studies show that mothers tend to be physically and emotionally closer to their daughters, expecting them to need more attention and nurturance. Fathers tend to be rougher and more physical with their sons, and boys receive more encouragement from both parents to be independent. While parents may tolerate girls who are tomboys, few will allow boys to be sissies. Fathers are especially harsh with sons who show traits and interests society stereotypes as feminine.[91]

Gender-role socialization takes place outside as well as inside the family. Although it is now acceptable (in some cases, even fashionable) for girls to play with hammers and trucks, many stores continue to advertise and display boys' toys and girls' toys. Doctors' kits and tool boxes are for one gender; nurses' kits and kitchen sets are for the other. The games children play vary by gender, with girls' games more likely to take place indoors and more likely to emphasize cooperation over competition. Peer groups, churches, the media—all play major roles in teaching children proper masculine and feminine behavior.[92]

Thus it is understandable that prospective teachers look outside the schools for the origins of gender-role socialization. But it is all too easy to overlook how schools reinforce stereotypes students have learned elsewhere.

## Gender Bias in Textbooks

Numerous studies conducted during the 1970s documented the gender bias in textbooks. One influential study of elementary school readers showed that the books featured two and one-half to three times as many males as females and portrayed males in almost six times as many occupational roles. In what some researchers have called "the cult of the apron," the books rarely showed women working outside the home, even though a few women were, of course, nurses, secretaries, or teachers. Studies of secondary school textbooks uncovered the same patterns. Social studies books rarely mentioned women; literature texts presented few selections by female authors; science texts downplayed the contributions of women; math books featured males more frequently than females in word problems; and so forth.[93]

After women's groups brought pressure to bear on publishers, the books began to change, but not as much as many educators think. A 1980s study of elementary school readers found that while the overall ratio of males to females has narrowed, it is still nearly 2 to 1. Compared to older textbooks, the books used today present more career options for both sexes, but males hold up to 80 percent of all the careers. Publishers have also modified secondary school texts, though often in cosmetic ways. Token females, like token racial and ethnic minorities, are now on prominent display, but males remain dominant.[94]

Such portrayals are unrealistic in a nation where females are 51 percent of the population and almost half the labor force. Nearly 60 percent of married women are employed outside the home, and more than 90 percent of women work outside the home at some time during their lives. While women are moving into managerial positions and into the professions of law, medicine, and dentistry, men are not showing the same interest in fields women have traditionally dominated: Ninety-nine percent of secretaries and 95 percent of registered nurses are still women. In fact, most women who work outside the home remain in pink-collar jobs that pay low salaries, which helps explain why the wages of fully employed women average only 72 percent those of men.[95]

Few textbooks reflect these realities, even though new stereotypes may be replacing old ones. The irony of the situation is that some conservative groups are now charging that textbooks have changed too much, to the point of promoting nontraditional and antifamily life-styles. Often the evidence is a book's favorable portrayal of a female auto mechanic, a male nurse, or another stereotype-breaking character. Feminists, citing the continuing gap between the overall percentages of males and females in textbooks and the continuing masculine dominance of occupational roles, counter that they have not changed enough.

Such disputes can become quite heated, for both sides recognize that textbooks and other instructional materials do indeed affect the way students view the world. Research on multicultural education shows that what children read in school can reinforce gender as well as class, racial, and ethnic biases. Conversely, more favorable portrayals of nondominant groups can transmit more favorable attitudes to students. When curriculum committees meet to review books and school boards meet to adopt books (see chapter 5), the stakes are high.[96]

## Unequal Treatment in the Classroom

In the survey we examined at the beginning of this section, the students agreed that, in general, people treat boys better than girls. The students pointed out one major exception, though. Both sexes believed girls receive better treatment in school. The consensus was that teachers like girls more and pick on boys more. The students therefore concluded that girls have the advantage. Research suggests that the students' perceptions are right while their conclusion is wrong.

Girls *do* behave in ways teachers like and reward. In the classroom, girls tend to be quieter and more cooperative than boys. Girls depend more on their teachers and identify more closely with them. Remember, 72 percent of all teachers and 88 percent of all elementary school teachers are female. Some researchers describe the typical classroom as a feminized environment in which girls feel comfortable and at ease.[97]

Boys react to the classroom differently. Trained in the home to be more active and independent, boys often rebel against the routine of silence, seat work, and conformity. Some rebel so strongly they refuse to learn; others channel their activity in ways that appear to give them the academic edge over girls. Empirical studies of classroom interaction show that boys quickly master the art of getting their teachers' attention. Boys are eight times as likely as girls to shout out answers, and teachers—male as well as female—usually play along and acknowledge the boys' participation. Strikingly, teachers are more likely to reprimand girls for calling out in class, often with a comment like "Please raise your hand if you want to answer." Overall, boys dominate classroom discussion by a ratio of 3 to 1 over girls.[98]

Thus teachers spend more of their time interacting with boys. The research also indicates that the quality of interaction differs, with boys more likely than girls to receive specific directions, praise, and criticism: "Draw the picture like this" as opposed to "Mm-hmm" or "Okay." Few teachers realize they teach this way, but videotapes of classes reveal the underlying patterns of interaction. Such behavior is slow to change precisely because it is unconscious and unintentional.[99]

## Title IX

Some things have changed, though, and we can credit some of the progress schools have made toward sex equity to Title IX of the Education Amendments of 1972. Title IX states:

> No person in the United States shall, on the basis of sex, be excluded from participation in, be denied the benefits of, or be subjected to discrimination under any educational program or activity receiving federal financial assistance.

Protecting both students and employees, Title IX has helped open up courses, activities, and jobs once officially or unofficially closed to one sex or the other. In part as a result of Title IX, boys now take homemaking and consumer courses and girls are enrolled in industrial arts and agriculture classes. Title IX has made a tremendous difference in athletic programs, putting the pressure on sometimes-reluctant schools to provide equal opportunities for female and male athletes. Title IX has helped female teachers move into administrative positions once controlled by the "good old boy" network.[100]

No legislation is a panacea. Although approximately one-third of the students in homemaking and consumer classes are now boys and one-fifth of the industrial arts and agriculture students are girls, boys still outnumber girls by about 9 to 1 in such technical subjects as electronics and auto repair. While more and more females are participating in school athletics, budgets are still tilted toward male sports. And despite the fact that more than half the teachers taking school administration courses at many universities are women, 72 percent of school principals and 95 percent of district superintendents are men.[101]

In some areas, though, females continue to make progress. Some of the most encouraging news is that girls are closing the gender gap in high school math and science courses. A few years ago, it was unusual to find girls in upper-level math classes. Today it appears that girls are about equally represented in math up through calculus, where boys still enroll at a rate more than 50 percent higher than girls. The gender gap in first-year science courses has virtually closed in biology and chemistry but not in physics. In second-year science courses, boys still outnumber girls, with the largest gap in physics.[102]

Nor are all the gaps closed in higher education, where males continue to dominate the quantitative and scientific majors. In engineering, to cite the field with the greatest disparity, approximately 85 percent of the students are still men—although in 1970, 99 percent were men. Even females with exceptionally strong backgrounds in high school math and science choose quantitative and scientific careers far less often than males. After narrowing in the 1970s and 1980s, this gap does not appear to be closing further.[103]

## Cognitive Differences between Females and Males

Changing enrollment patterns are focusing new attention on the controversy over cognitive differences between females and males. For years, psychologists and sociologists have debated whether girls as a group really have superior verbal skills and whether boys as a group are really better at mathematical and spatial tasks. As we summarize a complex body of research, the evidence suggests the following:

1. Sex-related cognitive differences that standardized tests can measure generally do not appear until adolescence.
2. When differences do appear, they are small. Although females do slightly better on many tests of verbal ability and males slightly better on many tests of mathematical and spatial ability, differences *within* each sex are much greater than differences *between* the sexes. There are greater differences in math ability among boys, for instance, than between boys as a group and girls as a group.
3. The proportion of the differences that seems to be due to biological as opposed to social factors is no more than 5 percent.[104]

Many researchers conclude that people make too much of the cognitive differences between males and females. Some students, parents, and even educators use gender as a convenient academic excuse: "Of course he doesn't like poetry—he's a boy." "I'm not very good at math and technical things—most girls aren't." The research literature simply does not support such sweeping statements.

To be sure, there is disagreement over how much influence heredity has on sex-related cognitive differences. On standardized tests in science, for example, the gap between boys and girls is not closing and may even be widening. Boys outscore girls in science at the elementary and especially the secondary levels. On standardized tests in mathematics, the gap is smaller and is narrowing. Indeed, there is no gender gap at all on many math tests administered in elementary school, but by the twelfth grade, boys outscore girls in almost every area of math.[105]

Some researchers question why such gaps remain when girls are increasing their high school coursework in science and math. Even among students with similar high school backgrounds in science and math, boys still have the edge on standardized tests. Genetics must be the explanation, these researchers conclude.[106]

Other researchers counter that girls still experience subtle but powerful social pressure *not* to do well in science or math. As children grow up, boys receive more encouragement than girls to investigate electronics and mechanics. Pointing to the divergence in boys' and girls' test scores during adolescence, these researchers argue that girls who excel in science and math threaten boys on a traditionally masculine turf. Girls who want to be popular with the opposite sex had better not be too threatening. Peers, parents, teachers, counselors, textbooks, and other influences may also subtly—often unintentionally—discourage girls from being truly competitive with boys in science and math.[107]

## Toward the Future: Feminism and Education

In conclusion, I want to place our discussion of gender within the context of three phases of feminism. In the first phase, which we can liken to assimilation, women pursue the goal of equality with men. Striving to prove themselves equal to men in the public sphere—in school, on the job, and elsewhere—women measure themselves against masculine standards. Girls want to prove they can do math as well as boys. Women want to show they can practice medicine as well as men. Given the years of discrimination and exclusion women have faced, these concerns of first-phase feminism are quite understandable.[108]

In the second phase, which is more pluralistic, women recognize their differences from men and try to use their special qualities to enhance society. Carol Gilligan's *In a Different Voice* (1982) helped popularize second-stage feminism. Gilligan concluded that women and men see life differently, women through a lens of care and interdependence and men through a lens of rights and independence. In seeking equality with men in the public sphere, women must be careful not to abandon the feminine qualities that are so important at home, in the private sphere.[109]

Gilligan, Jane Roland Martin, Mary F. Belenky, and other feminist scholars urge women to bring such qualities as cooperation and nurturance into schools, workplaces, and the rest of the public sphere, where masculine qualities have traditionally dominated. The goal of second-phase feminist school reform is not educating girls to boys' standards but rather redefining education for all students, so all can hear the feminine as well as the masculine voice. Beginning with history and literature, think how the entire curriculum could change if such a reform took place.[110]

Reform this fundamental is exactly what critical theorists advocate, and they urge feminists to move into a third phase, a critical phase, in which women see their struggle as part of the struggle of all oppressed people. Nel Noddings of Stanford University points out that "just as men have dominated, and still dominate, women, so the wealthy and better educated dominate the poor and less educated." The voices of excluded groups will never be heard in schools unless they work together and confront larger issues of power and status. Third-phase feminism, with its call for more attention to the connections among class, race, ethnicity, and gender, forms a fitting conclusion for this chapter.[111]

## ACTIVITIES

1. Interview people who have been denied educational opportunities because of their social class, race, ethnicity, or sex.
2. Talk with public school officials about how their schools comply with Title VI of the Civil Rights Act of 1964, Title IX of the Education Amendments of 1972, and current federal guidelines on bilingual education.
3. Conduct your own research on bias in elementary and secondary school textbooks. Locate examples of stereotypes based not only on gender but also on class, race, and ethnicity.
4. Stage a debate on some of the issues in this chapter. For additional evidence to support your arguments, see the Recommended Readings and Notes.

## RECOMMENDED READINGS

American Association of University Women. *The AAUW Report: How Schools Shortchange Girls. A Study of Major Findings on Girls and Education* (Washington, D.C: AAUW, 1992). A superb summary of the research, this report is helping people rediscover issues school reformers have swept under the rug.

Bennett, Kathleen P., and Margaret D. LeCompte. *How Schools Work: A Sociological Analysis of Education* (White Plains, NY: Longman, 1990). Bennett and LeCompte introduce the sociology of education with an emphasis on critical theory.

Levine, Daniel U., and Robert J. Havighurst. *Society and Education,* 8th ed. (Boston: Allyn & Bacon, 1992). Here is the standard textbook on the sociology of education, an encyclopedic guide to the literature.

Oakes, Jeannie. *Keeping Track: How Schools Structure Inequality* (New Haven: Yale University Press, 1985). Oakes presents a compelling case for reducing ability grouping and tracking.

## NOTES

1. U.S. Department of Education, National Center for Education Statistics, *The Condition of Education, 1992* (Washington, D.C.: U.S. Government Printing Office, 1992), p. 108; "Who You Will Teach," *Teacher Magazine* (April 1990): 39. See Table 8.3 for trends in race and ethnicity.

2. "Today's Numbers, Tomorrow's Nation," *Education Week* (May 14, 1986), p. 22; "Children of Single Parents," *Education Week* (August 5, 1992), p. 3; Harold Hodgkinson, "Reform versus Reality," *Phi Delta Kappan* 73 (September 1991): 11.

3. "Children of Single Parents," p. 3; U.S. Department of Education, *The Condition of Education*, p. 108.

4. Daniel U. Levine and Robert J. Havighurst, *Society and Education*, 8th ed. (Boston: Allyn & Bacon, 1992), pp. 6–13.

5. George S. Counts, *The Selective Character of American Secondary Education* (Chicago: University of Chicago Press, 1922); Robert S. Lynd and Helen Merrell Lynd, *Middletown: A Study in American Culture* (New York: Harcourt, Brace & World, 1929), chap. 13.

6. W. Lloyd Warner, Robert J. Havighurst, and Martin B. Loeb, *Who Shall Be Educated: The Challenge of Unequal Opportunity* (New York: Harper & Row, 1944), p. 50.

7. Ibid., p. xi.

8. August B. Hollingshead, *Elmtown's Youth: The Impact of Social Classes on Adolescents* (New York: Wiley, 1949), pp. 168–192, 462.

9. Levine and Havighurst, *Society and Education*, chap. 2.

10. Joseph W. Newman, "Socioeconomic Class and Education: In What Ways Does Class Affect the Educational Process?" in Joe L. Kincheloe and Shirley R. Steinberg, eds., *Thirteen Questions: Reframing Education's Conversation* (New York: Peter Lang, 1992), pp. 187–191; Sol Adler, *Poverty Children and Their Language: Implications for Teaching and Treating* (New York: Grune & Stratton, 1979); Catherine E. Snow, Clara Dubber, and Akke De Blauw, "Routines in Mother-Child Interaction," in Lynne Feagans and Dale Clark Farran, eds., *The Language of Children Reared in Poverty: Implications for Evaluation and Intervention* (New York: Academic Press, 1982).

11. Victor Gerkas, "The Influence of Social Class on Socialization," in Wesley R. Burr, Reuben Hill, F. Ivan Nye, and Ira L. Reiss, eds., *Contemporary Theories about the Family* (New York: Free Press, 1979).

12. Donald A. Hansen, "Family-School Articulations: The Effects of Interaction Rule Mismatch," *American Educational Research Journal* 23 (Winter 1986): 643–659.

13. See Kathleen P. Bennett and Margaret D. LeCompte's *How Schools Work: A Sociological Analysis of Education* (White Plains, NY: Longman, 1990), chap. 3. The classic study of peer groups in James S. Coleman's *The Adolescent Society* (New York: Free Press, 1961). More recent studies include Philip A. Cusick's *Inside High School: The Student's World* (New York: Holt, Rinehart & Winston, 1971) and Penelope Eckert's *Jocks and Burnouts: Social Categories and Identity in the High School* (New York: Teachers College Press, 1989).

14. For contrasting views of resistance, see Henry Giroux's *Theory of Resistance: A Pedagogy for the Opposition* (South Hadley, MA: Bergin and Garvey, 1983) and Paul Willis's *Learning to Labour: How Working Class Kids Get Working Class Jobs* (Westmead, England: Saxon House, 1979).

15. Terry M. Williams and William Kornblum, *Growing Up Poor* (New York: Free Press, 1985); Francis A. Ianni, *The Search for Structure: A Report on American Youth Today* (New York: Free Press, 1989).

16. Levine and Havighurst, *Society and Education,* pp. 166–171.
17. Robert E. Slavin evaluates the research in "Ability Grouping and Student Achievement in Elementary Schools: A Best-Evidence Synthesis," *Review of Educational Research* 57 (Fall 1987): 293–350; and in "Achievement Effects of Ability Grouping in Secondary Schools," *Review of Educational Research* 60 (Fall 1990): 471–507.
18. Jeannie Oakes, *Keeping Track: How Schools Structure Inequality* (New Haven: Yale University Press, 1985); Oakes, *Multiplying Inequalities: The Effects of Race, Social Class, and Tracking on Opportunities to Learn Mathematics and Science* (Santa Monica, CA: Rand Corp., 1990).
19. Ibid.; Robert E. Slavin, *Cooperative Learning: Theory, Research, and Practice* (Englewood Cliffs, NJ: Prentice-Hall, 1990).
20. Arthur G. Powell, Eleanor Farrar, and David K. Cohen, *The Shopping Mall High School: Winners and Losers in the Educational Marketplace* (Boston: Houghton Mifflin, 1985).
21. *ACT ISSUEgram* 6 (January 1986): 3–5.
22. Sol H. Pelavin and Michael Kane, *Changing the Odds: Factors Increasing Access to College* (New York: College Entrance Examination Board, 1990), p. 49.
23. Oakes, *Keeping Track.* Also see Penelope L. Peterson, Louise Cherry Wilkinson, and Maureen Hallinan, eds., *The Social Context of Instruction: Group Organization and Group Process* (Orlando, FL: Academic Press, 1984), chaps. 8–10.
24. Pelavin and Kane, *Changing the Odds,* p. 56.
25. Jeannie Oakes and Martin Lipton, "Detracking Schools: Early Lessons from the Field," *Phi Delta Kappan* 73 (February 1992): 449, 454. Emphasis in the original.
26. See U.S. Department of Education, *Japanese Education Today* (Washington, D.C.: U.S. Government Printing Office, 1987).
27. Among the studies analyzing such assumptions are Martin Carnoy and Henry M. Levin's *Schooling and Work in the Democratic State* (Stanford: Stanford University Press, 1985) and Michael W. Sedlak, Christopher W. Wheeler, Diana C. Pullin, and Philip A. Cusick's *Selling Students Short: Classroom Bargains and Academic Reform in the American High School* (New York: Teachers College Press, 1986).
28. Stephan Thernstrom, ed., *Harvard Encyclopedia of American Ethnic Groups* (Cambridge: Harvard University Press, 1980); Richard T. Shaefer, *Racial and Ethnic Groups,* 2d ed. (Boston: Little, Brown, 1984).
29. This definition is from Milton M. Gordon's classic study *Assimilation in American Life: The Role of Race, Religion, and National Origins* (New York: Oxford University Press, 1964).
30. James A. Banks, *Teaching Strategies for Ethnic Studies,* 5th ed. (Boston: Allyn & Bacon, 1991).
31. For an analysis of some of these issues as they relate to whites, see Richard Alba's *Ethnic Identity: The Transformation of White America* (New Haven: Yale University Press, 1990).
32. John B. Kellogg, "Forces of Change," *Phi Delta Kappan* 70 (November 1988): 199–204. For more information, see Nathan Glazer, ed., *Clamor at the Gates: The New American Immigration* (San Francisco: Institute for Contemporary Affairs, 1985); David Reimers, *Still the Golden Door: The Third World Comes to America* (New York: Columbia University Press, 1985).
33. James D. Anderson, *The Education of Blacks in the South, 1860–1935* (Chapel Hill: University of North Carolina Press, 1988).
34. Levine and Havighurst, *Society and Education,* pp. 351–355. See William Junius Wilson's *The Truly Disadvantaged: The Inner City, the Underclass, and Public*

*Policy* (Chicago: University of Chicago Press, 1987) and *The Declining Significance of Race: Blacks and Changing American Institutions* (Chicago: University of Chicago Press, 1978).

35. U.S. Department of Education, *The Condition of Education,* pp. 5–6, 58, 62.
36. This section is based on the Ford Foundation working paper *Hispanics: Challenges and Opportunities* (New York: Ford Foundation, 1984) and on Levine and Havighurst's *Society and Education,* pp. 365–372.
37. U.S. Department of Education, *The Condition of Education,* pp. 6–8, 58, 62.
38. Much of the information in this section is from Peter Schmidt's "After Slow Start, Asian-Americans Beginning to Exert Power on Education-Policy Issues," *Education Week* (February 27, 1991), pp. 1, 18–20.
39. Peter Schmidt, "Asian-Americans Said Top Achievers, but Strengths Vary among Subgroups," *Education Week* (February 27, 1991), pp. 18–19; Levine and Havighurst, *Society and Education,* pp. 359, 382–387.
40. Much of the material in this section is from William A. Gollnick's "The Reappearance of the Vanishing American," *The College Board Review* 155 (Spring 1990): 30–36; and U.S. Department of Commerce, Bureau of the Census, *We, the First Americans* (Washington, D.C.: U.S. Government Printing Office, 1988).
41. Levine and Havighurst, *Society and Education,* pp. 359, 387–395.
42. Richard Kluger, *Simple Justice: The History of Brown v. Board of Education and Black America's Struggle for Equality* (New York: Knopf, 1976).
43. The complete text of the *Brown* decision is reprinted in Kluger's *Simple Justice,* pp. 779–785.
44. Kluger, *Simple Justice,* chaps. 26–27.
45. Ibid., Laughlin McDonald, "The Legal Barriers Crumble," *Just Schools,* a special issue of *Southern Exposure* 7 (Summer 1979).
46. Gary Orfield, *The Reconstruction of Southern Education: The Schools and the 1964 Civil Rights Act* (New York: Wiley, 1969).
47. "Public Housing Policy Linked to School Segregation," *NOLPE Notes* 23 (August 1988): 1. Gary Orfield analyzes the relationship between housing segregation and school segregation in *Toward a Strategy for Urban Integration: Lessons in School and Housing Policy from Twelve Cities* (New York: Ford Foundation, 1981).
48. Liz Schevtchuk Armstrong, "High Court Eases Rules for Ending Integration Plans," *Education Week* (January 23, 1991), pp. 1, 27; Mark Walsh, "High Court Eases Federal Guidelines for Desegregation," *Education Week* (April 8, 1992), pp. 1, 26.
49. Orfield, *Public School Desegregation,* chap. 2.
50. "Who You Will Teach," p. 39.
51. Peter Schmidt, "Study Shows a Rise in the Segregation of Hispanic Students," *Education Week* (January 15, 1992), pp. 1, 19.
52. Rita E. Mahard and Robert L. Crain, "Research on Minority Achievement in Desegregated Schools," in Christine H. Rossell and Willis D. Hawley, eds., *The Consequences of School Desegregation* (Philadelphia: Temple University Press, 1983), pp. 103–125.
53. Ibid., p. 111.
54. See Levine and Havighurst's *Society and Education,* chap. 9.
55. Jomills Henry Braddock II, Robert L. Crain, and James M. McPartland, "A Long-Term View of School Desegregation: Some Recent Studies of Graduates as Adults," *Phi Delta Kappan* 66 (December 1984): 259–264.
56. William Snider, "Opposition to Busing Declines, Poll Finds," *Education Week* (January 21, 1987), p. 6.

57. Ibid.
58. Ibid.
59. For arguments that busing is responsible for substantial white flight, see James S. Coleman's "Liberty and Equality in School Desegregation," *Social Policy* 6 (January–February 1976): 9–13; and David J. Armor's "White Flight and the Future of School Desegregation," in Walter G. Stephan and Joe R. Feagin, eds., *School Desegregation: Past, Present, and Future* (New York: Plenum, 1980), chap. 9. For counter arguments, see Thomas F. Pettigrew and Robert L. Green's "School Desegregation in Large Cities: A Critique of the Coleman 'White Flight' Thesis," *Harvard Educational Review* 46 (February 1976): 1–53; and Rossell and Hawley's "Understanding White Flight and Doing Something about It," in Hawley, ed., *Effective School Desegregation* (Beverly Hills: Sage, 1981), pp. 157–184.
60. The statistics on percentages of students bused and the length of their rides have changed little since the publication of *Fulfilling the Letter and the Spirit of the Law* by the U.S. Commission on Civil Rights (Washington, D.C.: U.S. Government Printing Office, 1976). Gary Orfield discusses the stability of metropolitan busing in "Public School Desegregation" and in *Must We Bus? Segregated Schools and National Policy* (Washington, D.C.: Brookings Institution, 1978).
61. Nolan Estes, Daniel U. Levine, and D. R. Waldrip, eds., *Magnet Schools* (Austin, TX: Morgan, 1990); Mary Haywood Metz, *Different by Design: The Context and Character of Three Magnet Schools* (New York: Methuen/Routledge & Kegan Paul, 1986).
62. Levine and Havighurst, *Society and Education*, pp. 324–326.
63. See Wilbur B. Brookover's *Effective Secondary Schools* (Philadelphia: Research for Better Schools, 1981); Ronald R. Edmonds' "Programs of School Improvement: An Overview," *Educational Leadership* 40 (December 1982): 4–11; Michael Rutter, Barbara Maughan, Peter Mortimore, and Janet Ouston's *Fifteen Thousand Hours: Secondary Schools and Their Effects on Children* (Cambridge, MA: Harvard University Press, 1979).
64. Levine and Havighurst, *Society and Education*, pp. 304–310.
65. Peter West, " 'Tracking' Hampers Minorities' Access to Math, Science Careers, Study Finds," *Education Week* (September 26, 1990), p. 8; William Snider, "Study Examines Forces Affecting Racial Tracking," *Education Week* (November 11, 1987), pp. 1, 20.
66. Gerald J. Pine and Asa G. Hilliard III, "Rx for Racism: Imperatives for America's Schools," *Phi Delta Kappan* 71 (April 1990): 593–600.
67. Signithia Fordham and John U. Ogbu, "Black Students' School Success: Coping with the Burden of 'Acting White,' " *Urban Review* 18 (1986): 176–205.
68. Levine and Havighurst, *Society and Education*, pp. 353–357.
69. Ibid.
70. Mark Walsh, "Black Private Academies Are Held Up as Filling Void," *Education Week* (March 13, 1991), pp. 1, 28–29.
71. Carol Ascher, "School Programs for African-American Males . . . and Females," *Phi Delta Kappan* 73 (June 1992): 777–782. On the Afrocentric curriculum, see Molefi Kete Asante's "The Afrocentric Idea in Education," *Journal of Negro Education* 60 (Spring 1991): 170–180.
72. Ascher, "School Programs"; Jawanza Kunjufu, "Detroit's Male Academies: What the Real Issue Is," *Education Week* (November 20, 1991), p. 29.
73. Ascher, "School Programs."
74. Donald Leake and Brenda Leake, "African-American Immersion Schools in Milwaukee: A View from the Inside," *Phi Delta Kappan* 73 (June 1992): 783–785.

75. W. E. B. DuBois, "Two Hundred Years of Segregated Schools," in Philip S. Foner, ed., *W. E. B. DuBois Speaks: Speeches and Addresses, 1920–1963* (New York: Pathfinder Press, 1970), p. 283.

76. Peter Schmidt, "Shortage of Trained Bilingual Teachers Is Focus of both Concern and Attention," *Education Week* (February 12, 1992), p. 10.

77. Peter Schmidt, "Three Types of Bilingual Education Effective, E.D. Study Concludes," *Education Week* (February 20, 1991), pp. 1, 23.

78. "Hispanics Nurture Identity, Survey Shows," *Education Week* (September 19, 1984).

79. Schmidt, "After Slow Start."

80. "In California, Nation's First Minority Majority," *Education Week* (September 21, 1988), p. 3; Chris Pipho, "Elections and Efficiency," *Phi Delta Kappan* 70 (January 1989): 350.

81. James Crawford, *Bilingual Education: History, Politics, and Practice* (Trenton, NJ: Crane Publishing, 1989).

82. For contrasting treatments of the political history of bilingual education, see Coleman Brez Stein, Jr., *Sink or Swim: The Politics of Bilingual Education* (Westport, CT: Greenwood, 1986); Rosalie P. Porter, *Forked Tongue: The Politics of Bilingual Education* (New York: Basic Books, 1990).

83. Kenji Hakuta and Laurie J. Gould, "Synthesis of Research on Bilingual Education," *Educational Leadership* 44 (March 1987): 38–45.

84. James Crawford, "Immersion Method Is Faring Poorly in Bilingual Study," *Education Week* (April 23, 1986), pp. 1, 10.

85. Schmidt, "Three Types of Bilingual Education Effective."

86. "Bilingual Education," *Education Week* (February 12, 1992), p. 10.

87. Quoted in Schmidt, "After Slow Start," p. 20.

88. American Association of University Women, *The AAUW Report: How Schools Shortchange Girls. A Study of Major Findings on Girls and Education* (Washington, D.C.: AAUW, 1992), pp. v, 2.

89. Myra Sadker, David Sadker, and Lynette Long, "Gender and Educational Equality," in James A. Banks and Cherry A. McGee Banks, eds., *Multicultural Education: Issues and Perspectives,* 2d ed. (Boston: Allyn & Bacon, 1993), p. 119.

90. Carol Tavris with Alice R. Baumgartner, "How Would Your Life Be Different," *Redbook* (February 1983), pp. 92–95. Also see Michigan Department of Education, Office of Sex Equity in Education, *The Influence of Gender Role Socialization on Student Perceptions* (Lansing: Michigan Department of Education, 1990).

91. Levine and Havighurst, *Society and Education,* pp. 419–420. An excellent film that makes these points is *The Pinks and the Blues* (Paramus, NJ: Time-Life Video, n.d.).

92. Jeanne H. Ballatine, *The Sociology of Education: A Systematic Analysis* (Englewood Cliffs, NJ: Prentice-Hall, 1983), pp. 77–79, 81. See also Jean Stockard and M. M. Johnson's *Sex Roles: Sex Inequality and Sex Role Development* (Englewood Cliffs, NJ: Prentice-Hall, 1980).

93. Women on Words and Images, *Dick and Jane as Victims: Sex Stereotyping in Children's Readers* (Princeton, NJ: Women on Words and Images, 1975); U.S. Commission on Civil Rights, *Characters in Textbooks: A Review of the Literature* (Washington, D.C.: Commission on Civil Rights, 1980).

94. Gwyneth Britton and Margaret Lumpkin, "Basal Readers: Paltry Progress Pervades," *Interracial Books for Children Bulletin* 14 (1983); 4–7; Sadker, Sadker, and Long, "Gender and Educational Equality," p. 114.

95. U. S. Department of Commerce, *Statistical Abstract of the United States, 1992* (Washington, D.C.: U.S. Government Printing Office, 1992), pp. 16, 387, 392–394; Levine and Havighurst, *Society and Education,* pp. 412–414.

96. Kathryn Scott, "Effects of Sex-Fair Reading Materials on Pupils' Attitudes, Comprehension, and Interest," *American Educational Research Journal* 23 (Spring 1986): 105–116; Patricia Campbell and Jeana Wirtenberg, "How Books Influence Children: What the Research Shows," *Interracial Books for Children Bulletin* 11 (1980): 3–6.

97. Raphaela Best, *We've All Got Scars: What Boys and Girls Learn in Elementary Schools* (Bloomington: Indiana University Press, 1983); National Education Association, *Status of the American Public School Teacher, 1990–1991* (Washington, D.C.: NEA, 1992), p. 80.

98. Myra Sadker and David Sadker, "Sexism in the Schoolroom of the 1980s," *Psychology Today* (March 1985): 54–57.

99. Ibid.; Marlaine E. Lockheed with Susan S. Klein, "Sex Equity in Classroom Climate and Organization," in Klein, ed., *Handbook for Achieving Sex Equity through Education* (Baltimore: Johns Hopkins University Press, 1985), chap. 11.

100. Jeana Wirtenberg, Barbara Richardson, Susan Klein, and Veronica Thomas, "Sex Equity in American Education," *Educational Leadership* 38 (January 1981): 311–319.

101. Ibid.; Helen S. Farmer and Joan Seliger Sidney, "Sex Equity in Career and Vocational Education," in Klein, *Handbook for Achieving Sex Equity,* chap. 18; National Federation of State High School Associations, *1990–1991 Handbook* (Kansas City: NFSHSA, 1990), p. 73; American Association of School Administrators, *Women and Minorities in School Administration: Facts and Figures, 1989–1990* (Washington, D.C.: AASA, 1990).

102. AAUW, *How Schools Shortchange Girls,* pp. 26–28.

103. Ibid.; Elizabeth K. Stage, Nancy Kreinberg, Jacquelynne Eccles (Parsons), and Joanne Rossi Becker, "Increasing the Participation and Achievement of Girls and Women in Mathematics, Science, and Engineering," in Klein, *Handbook for Achieving Sex Equity,* chap. 13.

104. One of the best analyses of these complex issues is Julia A. Sherman's "Sex-Related Cognitive Differences: A Summary of Theory and Practice," *Integrateducation* 16 (January–February 1978): 40–42. See also Levine and Havighurst, *Society and Education,* pp. 417–419.

105. AAUW, *How Schools Shortchange Girls,* pp. 24–26.

106. See, for example, Camilla P. Benbow and Julian C. Stanley, "Differential Course-taking Hypothesis Revisited," *American Educational Research Journal* 20 (Winter 1983): 469–473.

107. AAUW, *How Schools Shortchange Girls,* pp. 28–32; Karl L. Alexander and Aaron M. Pallas, "Reply to Benbow and Stanley," *American Educational Research Journal* 20 (Winter 1983): 475–477.

108. Ned Noddings discusses phases similar to these in "Feminist Critiques in the Professions," in Courtney B. Cazden, ed., *Review of Research in Education,* vol. 16 (Washington, D.C.: American Educational Research Association, 1990), chap. 8.

109. Carol Gilligan, *In a Different Voice: Psychological Theory and Women's Development* (Cambridge, MA: Harvard University Press, 1982).

110. See Jane Roland Martin's *Reclaiming a Conversation* (New York: Yale University Press, 1985) and Mary Field Belenky, Blythe McVicker Clinchy, Nancy Rule Goldberg, and Fill Mattuck Tarrule's *Women's Ways of Knowing: The Development of Self, Voice, and Mind* (New York: Basic Books, 1988).

111. Noddings, "Feminist Critiques," p. 396.

# CHAPTER 9

# Politics of Education

If politics is the pursuit of power and influence, then the politics of education is the quest to control the schools. Sometimes the quest generates so much controversy the media play up a particular episode, and Americans who ordinarily take little interest in the schools stop and pay attention.

When teachers go on strike or federal judges issue desegregation orders, average citizens follow the news and take sides. "Those teachers [or those judges] have gone too far this time," one citizen complains. "What do they want—to run the schools?" "No, they don't want complete control," another replies, "but they are willing to use the power at their disposal. Look what the school board did to provoke the strike [or court order]. Somebody had to call the board's hand."

Controversies can make the front page of the newspaper, but usually the quest for control of the schools goes on barely noticed by most Americans. The quest becomes part of the political routine. A local school board listens to a parent's concerns about standardized testing. A state legislature debates the education budget. The U.S. Senate's Education Committee holds hearings on the effectiveness of the Chapter I compensatory education program. The results of these deliberations may be even more far reaching than the effects of a strike or a court order, yet few citizens—including few teachers—pay close attention. This chapter shows what they are missing.

I will organize our discussion of politics around the three levels of government in the United States: *local, state,* and *federal.* At each level, numerous groups compete for control. Major players in the politics of education include elected and appointed officials, ranging from school board members to legislators to judges; education bureaucrats who work in local school districts, state departments of education, and the U.S. Department of Education; teachers and teacher organizations; other education groups, from university teacher educators to parent-teacher organizations; business groups; labor unions; foundations; testing companies; textbook publishers; religious groups; and individual citizens.

This list is long but incomplete. The reason is that so many hands work the controls of American public education. No single level of government and no single group of people is completely in charge. Instead, power is shared, and the balance of power among the levels and the groups is constantly shifting. In order to untangle a fascinating web of political influences, we will begin at the local level, move to the state and then the federal level, and conclude the chapter with a discussion of educational finance.

## LOCAL POLITICS OF EDUCATION

### Regulations from Above, Pressure from Below

Most Americans believe public schools should be run from the grassroots up. "Local control of education" gets high marks in opinion polls, and most citizens give the public schools in their own community much better ratings than public schools in general. Localism in education, it seems, is an almost unquestioned good thing.[1]

As we saw in chapter 6, though, local control has been slipping away since the last century, and the trend has only accelerated since the 1970s. Local school board members, traditionally the voice of the public in public education, feel hemmed in by regulations from above and pressure from below. The regulations come from the federal and especially the state level. The pressure comes from parents, teachers, and other citizens who sense the loss of local control and demand a more direct voice in running the schools.[2]

One of the great political ironies of the 1980s is that former President Ronald Reagan, a strong advocate of decentralization and local control, helped governors and legislators centralize control over public education in the state capitals. When Mr. Reagan came to Washington, the states were already taking on greater financial responsibility for public education. While he was in office, the federal government handed off even more of the bills to the states. Under two very different successors, Presidents George Bush and Bill Clinton, the state school reforms inspired by the Reagan administration's report *A Nation at Risk* (1983) have continued to generate one regulation after another for local school boards to follow.[3]

Pressure from below is also reducing the control of local boards. Restructuring, choice, school-based management, and teacher empowerment—these education buzzwords of the late 1980s and 1990s, which you have heard throughout this book, are testimonies to the flow of power and influence away from board members and toward parents, teachers, and other local political actors. Power and influence are also slipping away from local superintendents, the chief administrators who once ran school districts while board members quietly nodded their approval.

## Local Boards and Local Superintendents

Operating in a climate of change, 97,000 board members and 15,000 super-intendents are still trying to govern the nation's 15,000 school districts. These districts are quite diverse, ranging from New York City with its 1 million students to Big Cabin, Oklahoma, with its 58 students. Most districts are small—54 percent enroll fewer than 1,000 students each—yet the largest 4 percent, with 10,000 to 1 million students each, educate almost half the students in the nation.[4]

Americans say they want local governments to become more involved with education, and, in some districts, the voters seem to be paying more attention to school board elections. Why, the candidates in some communities even run on the issues.

I say this with tongue in cheek because local board elections have traditionally been low-interest, no-issue events. Drive through a community just before a school board election and look for the candidates' signs. Read the local newspapers and see whether the candidates are addressing any issues. Unless a controversy happens to be raging, the candidates may not even bother to campaign. Candidates in about half the districts, in fact, neither take stands nor campaign, and voter turnout is notoriously low. In other districts, by contrast, the elections are issue oriented and hotly contested. Candidates stake out positions, and large numbers of voters go to the polls to express their preferences.[5]

School board elections vary because communities vary. The power structure of a community has a strong influence on the way it selects people to oversee the public schools. Political researchers have developed a number of models to classify community power structures. Most of the models place communities on a continuum—from *monolithic* to *pluralistic,* for instance—based on how widely political power is shared. Does a single group of community elites dominate local politics, or do several groups, elite as well as nonelite, compete for control?[6]

*Monolithic communities* in which one group calls the shots are often rural areas, small towns, or one-industry cities. In these communities, the group in control may appoint the school board. If the members are elected, incumbents usually run without opposition.

At the other end of the continuum, *pluralistic communities* have competitive, sometimes bitter, school board elections. In such communities, typically suburbs and diversified cities, candidates campaign on the issues. Although they may state their positions as simply as "against new taxes" or "for family values," the candidates speak a language the voters seem to understand.

Once elected to a local board, the members are responsible for establishing policies for the school district. Local boards make policy within the limits set by the state legislature and state board of education. The state prescribes the minimum course of study required for high school graduation, for instance, but the local board approves the courses that satisfy the requirements. The state sets the requirements for teacher certification, but the local board approves the hiring of teachers. The state sends down state and federal money, but the local board approves the local budget.

The concept of *policy approval* is important. Traditionally, local board members have relied on the advice of the superintendent of schools, whom they appoint as the district's chief administrator. The superintendent, along with other administrators in the central office and in the schools, is responsible for managing the system on a day-to-day basis. The superintendent recommends policies for the board's approval.

Since the early 1900s, as chapter 6 points out, superintendents and their staffs have done much more than manage and recommend. They have often run the show. Superintendents enjoyed the peak of their influence from the 1920s through the 1950s. Board members held the votes, though more often than not they rubber-stamped the superintendent's recommendations. Superintendents presented themselves as educational experts, the *real* professionals in the school system. Their graduate degrees in school administration and experience in the schools set them apart from everyone else—board members, teachers, parents, other citizens—or so they were able to claim.[7]

During the reign of superintendents and their staffs, school board meetings were typically open-and-shut affairs. The superintendent set the agenda, coached the board through the meeting, and answered questions. At the end, the superintendent thanked the board for approving every recommendation intact. Local board meetings were usually dull, respectable, and poorly attended.

## Reinventing Local Control: The Changing Politics of School Districts

There have always been exceptions to this idealized portrait, of course, and in more and more school districts the exceptions are becoming the rule. The comfortable world I just described may still exist in rural and small-town America, but even there board members are increasingly likely to come under fire, and superintendents are finding their judgment increasingly called into question. The superintendency, once a stable job in many districts, has become a revolving door.[8]

One reason is that teachers have changed. The American Federation of Teachers (AFT) has long advocated teacher power, and superintendents and school boards have had to handle the larger AFT locals with care. The National Education Association (NEA), once little more than a punch-and-cookies society at the local level, is now a formidable union with impressive strength at the grassroots level. Teacher power is a reality, a fact of political life.

Parents have also changed. There have always been a few parents who refused to take no for an answer, who were determined to challenge a textbook, test, or discipline policy. Since the 1960s, activist parents have become more numerous and more insistent, or so it seems to teachers, administrators, and board members. These parents act as if the schools belong to *them.*

*School-based management,* a reform strategy designed to shift more decision-making authority down to individual schools, has the potential to strengthen the voice of teachers, parents, and other citizens. In Rochester, New York, the district whose well-publicized experiments in restructuring we studied in chapter 4, teachers hold the majority of the seats on planning councils in each school. In

Chicago, another system receiving national attention, parents dominate the planning councils. Opinions vary, though, on how much power local boards are actually sharing. Even in Rochester and Chicago, some teachers and parents complain that school-based management is just another cosmetic reform.[9]

Most local school boards are jealously guarding the power and influence they have left. Assertive board members, long a fixture in large urban school districts, are now appearing in districts throughout the nation, particularly in the once-complacent suburbs.

Assertive members come to the board with their own agenda. Fed up with high taxes and wasteful spending, they may try to bring sound business principles to the school system. They may poke into detailed financial records other board members never knew existed. They may cross the line into management and invade the superintendent's turf. Assertive board members may try to reform the curriculum, in which case they will almost certainly lock horns with parents, teachers, administrators, and especially state officials. Or assertive members may be the only representatives of their race or ethnic group on the board, which may lead them to challenge such policies as standardized testing and ability grouping or to push for multicultural curriculum reform. Assertive local board members often grow frustrated when they find that other players in the politics of education, whether in the same community, the state capital, or Washington, can make it so difficult to reform the schools.[10]

School districts are struggling to adjust to the changing politics of the 1990s. A decade ago, Ronald Reagan articulated the conventional wisdom that greater local control exercised through local boards would help solve the nation's educational problems. Yet Mr. Reagan's policies transferred more control to the state level. Conservative educator Chester E. Finn, Jr., a former official in Reagan's Department of Education, now advocates "reinvent[ing] local control." Finn wants to abolish local boards and make individual schools directly accountable to the state—a marriage of school-based management and centralized control. Although few observers believe such a fundamental change will occur, at least not in the near future, the politics of the 1990s have local board members looking anxiously over their shoulders.[11]

## Local Board Members: Demographics and Representation

What kind of people serve on local school boards? Since Americans cling so strongly to their belief in local control, it seems reasonable to find out more about the board members who represent the people. In the nation as a whole, the average member is a college-educated white male, aged 41 to 50, with an annual income of $40,000 to $59,000. He is most likely to hold a professional or managerial position.[12]

Of course, people with other demographic characteristics also serve on local boards. About 35 percent of the members are women—a dramatic increase over 1978, when only 26 percent were women. Minorities hold approximately 5 percent of the seats on the boards. About 3 percent of the members are African

American, 1 to 2 percent are Hispanic, and smaller percentages are Asian and Native American. Female and minority representation, still increasing on many other governmental bodies, appears to have stabilized on local school boards.[13]

Discussing this profile, the students in my Introduction to Education classes often say local board members "look just like average politicians." Local board members *are* politicians. Under the broad definition of politics as the pursuit of power and influence, board members are directly involved in the quest for control of the schools—but so are numerous other people, including teachers and parents, whom we usually do not think of as politicians. Perhaps we should, because some of them are as involved as board members in the quest for control.

What my students have in mind, though, is the more traditional view of a politician as an office seeker or office holder. Ninety-two percent of local board members are elected to office, and almost all of them run in nonpartisan contests in which they do not declare their affiliation with a political party. The remaining 8 percent are appointed by a mayor, city council, county commission, or another governmental body.[14]

How well local school board members represent their constituents is a controversial issue. Demographically, they do not reflect the U.S. population. Females, who make up 51 percent of the population, are still underrepresented on local boards. African and Hispanic Americans, who together account for about 21 percent of the population and 25 percent of public school students, are *seriously* underrepresented. And unlike most board members, most Americans are not college educated, nor are most Americans professionals or managers.[15]

The elite makeup of local boards has been a sensitive issue since the rise of common schools, with underrepresented groups complaining that board members neglect their children's educational needs. Africans and Hispanics, other racial and ethnic groups, the poor—their complaints are well documented if not well heeded.

"Do you have to be one to represent one?" This blunt, provocative question, recently put to the board in my community, goes to the heart of the representation controversy.

From one point of view, the answer to the question is a definite yes. If a group has been the victim of long-standing discrimination, members of that group have developed insights into critical issues that other people, however sympathetic and well intended, simply lack. Black Americans understand segregation, for example, as white Americans never can. The very idea of an all-white school board drawing up a desegregation plan for a district that is one-half black! In a district with a substantial percentage of African-American students, black representation on the school board is not just desirable. From this point of view, it is essential. The same reasoning is often applied to Hispanic representation and less frequently to the representation of women, the poor, and other groups.

From another point of view, this kind of reasoning is dangerous. It smacks of quotas. If the courts can order changes in election procedures that virtually ensure the election of blacks to local school boards—as indeed the courts have— what will be next? A decision that, depending on a district's demographic makeup, a certain percentage of board members must be women, or working-class people, or people with no more than a high school education? Granted that board members and their constituents often come from different backgrounds, the representatives can make an extra effort to stand in other people's shoes. There is no single African, Hispanic, female, or working-class perspective. There are many. Besides, two-thirds of board members say they regard themselves as trustees who can act as their own judgment dictates rather than delegates who are obligated to do what their constituents want. Thus the idea of demographic representation seems wrongheaded to some Americans.[16]

## Local Board Elections: At Large or by Subdistricts?

Although it is doubtful that court decisions will ever go as far as the above paragraph suggests, legal challenges to election procedures could eventually increase the percentage of African and Hispanic Americans on local school boards. We saw in chapter 6 that many communities elect their board members *at large*. Every voter can cast a ballot for every position on the board. Candidates campaign throughout the entire school district, for they are supposed to represent the whole community rather than particular neighborhoods, wards, or subdistricts.

Many local systems that once elected board members from subdistricts switched to at-large elections in the early 1900s. Turn-of-the-century reformers argued that people with the reputation and resources necessary to mount a district-wide campaign had broader vision than people elected to represent individual subdistricts. Reformers referred to the board members that at-large elections produced—successful professionals and businesspeople by and large—as persons of "the better sort."[17]

Not only do at-large elections introduce a social class bias into school board politics, but in districts where whites compete with African and/or Hispanic-Americans for control of the schools, they also introduce a racial and ethnic bias. I am not exaggerating when I describe the elections as competitions for control. In most at-large elections, the voters polarize by race and ethnicity, with whites voting for whites, blacks for blacks, and Hispanics for Hispanics.

Apparently many Americans believe you *do* have to be one to represent one. Except in communities where blacks or Hispanics are in the majority, at-large elections virtually ensure that whites sweep every seat on the school board.[18]

The balance of political power is shifting, though, and the changes now under way are a fascinating case study in the politics of education. In *Bolden v. City of Mobile* (1980), a voting-rights case that originated in my Alabama community, the U.S. Supreme Court ruled against a group of African-American voters who challenged Mobile's at-large elections. According to the court, the plaintiffs failed to prove that the city had adopted and maintained at-large elections with a discriminatory *intent*. Two years later, in an amendment to the Voting Rights Act of 1965, Congress overrode the decision by stipulating that plaintiffs need only show the discriminatory *effect* of election procedures.[19]

Encouraged by this change, African and Hispanic-American voters have filed a series of lawsuits against at-large elections. Beginning in the Southeast, spreading to the Southwest, and now reaching the rest of the nation, the legal challenges may reverse the decline in minority representation on local school boards. In Mobile, the change from at-large to by-subdistrict procedures led to the election of two African Americans to a five-person board, mirroring almost exactly the racial composition of the community. With the end of at-large elections in several Illinois cities, blacks are serving on local school boards for the first time in the twentieth century. Hispanics have won similar court battles in the Southwest, and the potential for further change is great. In Texas, where Hispanics are aggressively filing election suits, about 80 percent of the school districts still elect their board members at large. Native Americans, the nation's oldest and poorest ethnic group, have won a decision ending at-large elections in Big Horn County, Montana.[20]

Even though the courts have allowed the scope of at-large election suits to broaden, from discrimination against Africans to discrimination against Hispanics and now Native Americans, the courts have acted cautiously. In every case, the burden has been on the racial or ethnic group to prove that at-large elections have kept members of the group out of office.

The courts have not allowed the scope to broaden to social class—to discrimination against poor people as a group—even though the evidence is clear that school districts switched to at-large elections in order to ensure the dominance of high-status board members. Could poor people argue that at-large elections continue to deny them seats on local boards? That is an intriguing question, certainly, but the courts have consistently refused to consider social class as a factor comparable to race and ethnicity in discrimination suits.[21]

Since the 1970s, the most striking demographic trend on local school boards has been toward more female members. The percentage of minorities may start to rise again in the 1990s, but given the current level, it has quite a distance to climb. The trend is certainly not toward poorer members. Only 2 percent have incomes below $20,000, and just 8 percent earn less than $30,000.[22]

Although the demographics of local school boards have changed somewhat in recent years, the conclusion George S. Counts reached in his pioneering study *The Social Composition of Boards of Education: A Study in the Social Control of Public Education* (1927) still rings true:

> The [typical] board shows a tendency to be narrowly selective. It is composed, for the most part, of college and university men who occupy favored positions in society. The dominant classes of our society dominate the board of education.[23]

## STATE POLITICS OF EDUCATION

A varied cast of characters takes the stage as our discussion turns to the state level. Although I will put the spotlight on elected and appointed officials—governors, legislators, state school superintendents, and state school board members—you should be aware that many other actors have important roles.

Lobbyists for groups ranging from teacher unions to the chamber of commerce compete for control of the schools. Insiders know that restaurants in the state capital are where the real political deals go down. Lobbyists invite legislators to dinner, remind them of campaign contributions, and ask them to take particular stands on key issues. The governor and his staff receive the same treatment, and so, to a lesser degree, do the state superintendent of schools, other top officials in the state department of education, and members of the state board of education.

Meetings of the state board, once sleepy affairs, have become lively and controversial. Parents, teachers, and other citizens ask for time to state their views on issues ranging from alleged obscenity in textbooks to certification tests for teachers. The courts also play a role in the politics of education, for various actors ask them to referee disputes with other actors. These examples suggest the large number of players and the wide range of issues involved in the state politics of education.[24]

## Legislatures, Governors, Boards, Superintendents, and Departments

Legally, education is a function of state government. The U.S. Constitution does not even mention education; it is a responsibility reserved to the states. Within each state, the ultimate responsibility for public education rests with the legislature.

Much of the legislature's power is financial, for it has the authority to levy taxes and appropriate money to the schools. The state government is often the major source of funding for public education. While the legislature is in session, attention naturally focuses on the education budget, which is often one-third to one-half of all the money the state spends. Legislators who serve on the education committee, finance committee, and other committees with direct influence on the schools play leading roles in the state politics of education.

During the 1980s, state legislatures stepped up their involvement in educational policy making. Pressing well beyond financial matters, legislators tackled issues ranging from high school graduation requirements to teacher education standards. Along with governors, they reasserted their control over the schools. Later in this section, we will focus on the emergence of governors and legislators as school reformers.

State legislatures cannot run the schools alone, though, and historically they have delegated some of their authority to other groups. In every state but Wisconsin, the legislature has created a state board of education to oversee the state school system. Within the limits established by the legislature, state boards of education carry out three major responsibilities:

1. Setting standards for elementary and secondary schools.
2. Setting standards for teacher education and certification.
3. Distributing state and federal funds to local school systems.

Although these duties may look dry on paper, they are anything but. Just ask board members who have voted on a "No Pass, No Play" policy for high school athletes how strongly people feel about that issue, or ask them how many people tried to sway their votes on teacher certification testing.

Demographically, state board members are an exaggerated version of local board members. To an even greater degree than their local counterparts, state board members are middle-aged white males who are college-educated and professional or managerial. In about two-thirds of the states, the governor appoints the members of the state board of education. In two states, the members serve *ex officio*—by virtue of their holding another state office. In the remaining states, voters elect the board. The issues of representation we analyzed at the local level also apply to the state level, and minority voters are now challenging at-large elections to state boards of education.[25]

State board members turn over the management and operation of the state school system to a superintendent and an administrative staff. The state superintendent is often an up-from-the-ranks educator with experience as a teacher, principal, and local superintendent. Many state superintendents still come up through the "good old boy" education network. More than 80 percent are white males—middle-aged fellows who have learned how to get along. In 15 states, voters elect the state superintendent. In the rest, the superintendent is appointed by the state board or the governor.[26]

Historically, state superintendents have played *the* leading roles in the state politics of education. Horace Mann's official title in Massachusetts was Secretary of the State Board of Education, but in fact he was America's first activist state superintendent. Following in Mann's footsteps, state superintendents have tended to overshadow state board members. Billing themselves, like local superintendents, as educational experts, they have used their influence to shape policy. Since the emergence of reform-minded governors and legislators during the 1980s, however, state superintendents have lost some of their power.

If the state board's chief administrator is the state superintendent, the board's administrative staff is the state department of education. Ranging from secretaries and clerks to experienced educators with doctoral degrees, state department personnel are the bureaucrats who conduct the daily business of the state school system. State departments have grown in size and importance—some of the larger ones employ more than 1,000 people. State department personnel do such things as conduct research, issue teaching certificates, draw up curriculum guides, supervise testing programs, and make accreditation studies of local schools. Since the early 1980s, the responsibilities of state departments for curriculum and testing have increased tremendously.[27]

## Excellence and Accountability:
## State Politicians Discover School Reform

With the release of *A Nation at Risk* (1983) and the flood of education reports that followed, state politicians found an issue they could run with. Who could be opposed to a slogan as positive as "excellence in education"? Governors, legislators, state school superintendents, and state board of education members scrambled to be first in line to make the schools excellent.

In other chapters we have discussed the results of state reform. Teacher salaries have increased, most dramatically in states that lagged behind the national average. Standards in teacher education and certification have risen in almost every state. Higher standards for students, which we will examine closely in the next chapter, have also resulted from state reform. Understandably, higher salaries and higher standards have required higher levels of state spending.[28]

*Excellence,* as defined by state reformers, has come to mean *more* of something: higher salaries, higher standards, higher spending. In one sense, this approach is exactly what the times call for. Consider the example of higher teacher salaries, which are long overdue. If salaries have increased substantially in the school district where you plan to teach, you should probably thank the state government first. In the states boasting the most impressive gains in teacher salaries, governors and legislators can rightfully take the lion's share of the credit. (And they do.) But before you write a letter or make a phone call to the state capital, realize that higher salaries are a two-edged sword.

Responding to pressure from business leaders, governors and legislators are insisting that teachers prove themselves worthy of better pay. Business leaders see education as an investment, and a sound investment pays dividends. Believing that better schools are the key to economic growth, such groups as the Committee for Economic Development and the Carnegie Forum on Education and the Economy are pressing for accountability. They want the states to show the payoff from education dollars—that higher teacher salaries, for instance, produce higher student achievement.[29]

Teachers, as we saw in chapter 2, have legitimate concerns about accountability. They are wary of merit pay plans that base teacher salaries on student test scores. Teachers are also doubtful that career ladders will help their occupation as much as they help state politicians. Tennessee teachers joke that their state's career ladder has done more for former Governor Lamar Alexander's career than it ever will for any teacher's. While Alexander moved up and became U.S. Secretary of Education in the Bush adminstration, teacher salaries in Tennessee stayed in the same place relative to other states.

The state drive to set higher standards for teachers and students is also a mixed blessing. On the one hand, higher standards—like higher salaries—are long overdue. As a teacher educator, I am embarrassed that the states have had to force colleges and universities to turn out teachers who are at least literate. But I confess that my colleagues and I did little to raise standards before the states stepped in. As a former high school teacher, I resent the state-mandated measurement-driven curriculum. But I remember too many students drifting through school, bored and unchallenged, taking the easiest courses in an easy curriculum.

I acknowledge the problems. Most Americans do. Now we need to take a critical look at the state reforms designed to solve the problems.

In the era just before *A Nation at Risk,* the major state response to educational problems was jumping on the back-to-basics bandwagon that was already rolling through local school districts. Minimum competency tests for students were the most visible result of this first wave of state reform. By 1979, 37 states had mandated them. Some states also raised the grade point averages and college entrance exam scores required for admission to teacher education programs. Although the states often copied one another, especially in adopting minimum competency tests, there was little coordination of efforts.[30]

Within the states, much of the leadership came from state boards and departments of education. State board members, traditionally among the least important state politicians, were finally beginning to stretch their muscles, as if waking up from a long nap. State departments of education, led by state superintendents, stayed busy putting new board policies into effect. In most states, educational reform had still not attracted the sustained attention of governors and state legislators.

The release of *A Nation at Risk* in 1983, followed by report after report on the schools, changed the situation. Suddenly almost every state politician wanted to be a school reformer. The result was a second wave of reform, a wave that moved across the states in a surprisingly uniform way. Almost every state raised high school graduation requirements, expanded minimum competency testing into an array of "student performance indicators," and developed new tests for teacher education and certification.

Governors provided much of the leadership for these second-wave reforms. After 1983, the mark of a politically astute governor was a task force on education and a series of reports with excellence and accountability as their themes. Such "education governors" as Lamar Alexander of Tennessee, Thomas Kean of New Jersey, Rudy Perpich of Minnesota, Richard Lamm of Colorado, and Bill Clinton of Arkansas made school reform the central goal of their administrations. For several governors, especially Clinton and Alexander, school reform became a state issue with a national payoff.[31]

Now state reformers are coordinating their efforts. Governors exchange ideas in meetings of the National Governors' Association and the Education Commission of the States. The National Association of State Boards of Education provides a similar forum for board members, and state school superintendents work together through the Council of Chief State School Officers. Legislators have their own caucuses on education. Across the nation, the result of all this activity has been an emphasis on higher standards—of a sort.[32]

## The Politics of More of the Same

Operating at a safe distance from the local schools—above the action, we might say—state reformers have a peculiar perspective on public education. They have a wealth of information at their disposal, and staff members can generate more at a moment's notice. In meeting after meeting, state officials pore over seemingly endless statistics: population, per capita income, school expenditures, dropout rates, test scores. These quantitative data give the officials a quantitative view of schools. They think in terms of measurable inputs and measurable outputs.

Thus the higher standards the states mandate are almost always quantitative rather than qualitative. They call for *more of the same* rather than something different. If one math course is good for high school students, the two courses are better, and three or four courses are best. If a literacy test for prospective teachers is good, then a literacy test and a teaching field test are better, and so on. State officials seem less concerned with the content of math courses than with the number of courses. They worry less about the content of teacher tests than the number of tests.[33]

It is not surprising, then, that classroom teachers, the people closest to the action, are not very enthusiastic about school reform. In *The Condition of Teaching* (1990), a national survey of more than 20,000 teachers, 44 percent reported their morale has worsened since the release of *A Nation at Risk*. Teachers object to the regulations and paperwork acompanying state reform. They feel bypassed—understandably so, since state reformers rarely consult them. Worse still, they feel less positive than they did in the late 1980s about the effects of school reform on student achievement. The percentage of teachers who believe their students' basic skills in reading, writing, and math have improved fell from 60 percent in 1987 to less than 50 percent in 1990.[34]

Are teachers being too pessimistic? People who think so should take a careful look at the "performance indicators" that state officials swear by. As we will see in chapter 10, the indicators are mixed. On the minimum competency tests and national achievement tests that states mandate as quality control measures, the scores are indeed up. But teachers explain the scores are up because they are teaching the tests—not because students are learning more. On the National Assessment of Educational Progress (NAEP), a battery of exams for which teachers do not rehearse their students—at least not yet—the test score trends of the 1980s were generally up in science and math but down in reading and writing. Scores on the SAT and ACT college entrance examinations rose during the early 1980s, peaked at mid-decade, and declined into the early 1990s.[35]

Some state officials say they realize that "real excellence cannot be imposed from a distance. Governors don't create excellent schools; communities—local school leaders, teachers, parents, and citizens—do."[36] These words come from Lamar Alexander, who as chair of the National Governors' Association spoke for Bill Clinton and the other education governors who wrote *Time for Results: The Governors' 1991 Report on Education*.[37] Acknowledging the complaints of teachers, the governors admitted state reform has spawned regulation after regulation. They proposed "some old-fashioned horse trading. We'll regulate less, if schools and school districts will produce better results . . . [and] be accountable for the results."[38]

## School Reform on Hold: State Politics in the 1990s

State regulation has decreased in the 1990s, but the change has less to do with the governors' nicely stated educational rationale than with good old-fashioned economics. Quite simply, the money is running out. Governors and legislators now find themselves in the uncomfortable position of having either to cut programs or raise taxes—or both—just to balance the budget. As the reforms of the 1980s meet the economy of the 1990s, the politics of more of the same are slowing down.[39]

Instead of bringing new reforms on line, governors and legislators in most states are trying to hold reforms in place. Teacher salaries, which increased more than 20 percent in real dollars during the 1980s, are rising more slowly in the 1990s than they have since the mid-1960s. Higher entrance requirements for teacher education programs and higher high school graduation requirements are still in place, but they seem unlikely to rise further. And state-mandated standardized testing, that favorite back-to-basics reform, is in fact thinning out after a decade of piling test atop test.[40]

The education governors of the 1990s—Tommy Thompson of Wisconsin, Roy Romer of Colorado, Zell Miller of Georgia, George Mickelson of South Dakota, and others—are emphasizing reforms designed to encourage change at the local level. School-based management and other varieties of restructuring are popular with these governors. But local school officials faced with laying off teachers and increasing class sizes are complaining that the money to make reform work is just not there.[41]

State school reform was on hold when former education governor Clinton moved to Washington. Governors and legislators looked to the Clinton administration for a sense of direction as well as economic relief.[42]

## FEDERAL POLITICS OF EDUCATION

### Federal Money and Federal Influence

When Dwight Eisenhower watched John Kennedy take the presidential oath of office in 1961, the federal government was providing about 4 percent of the money for the nation's public schools. By the time Lyndon Johnson turned over the executive branch to Richard Nixon in 1969, the federal share had risen to 8 percent. When Ronald Reagan took over from Jimmy Carter in 1981, the federal contribution to the pubic school budget stood at an all-time high of 9 percent. Leaving office in 1989, Mr. Reagan felt pleased he had been able to trim the federal portion back to the mid-1960s level of 6 percent. And in 1993, when George Bush handed over the reigns of power to Bill Clinton, the federal share remained at 6 percent.

These figures, along with others displayed in Table 9.1, provide a rough sketch of the federal government's involvement in education. Seeing such figures for the first time, many prospective teachers express surprise—not that the percentages show a long increase followed by an abrupt decrease, but that *all* the federal percentages are so small. Compared with state and local funding, federal funding for education has never been great. Yet the federal government has managed to wring a relatively large degree of control out of a relatively small amount of money.

We can explain this phenomenon in two ways. First, federal courts have exercised much of the control. Consider the example of school desegregation. Many legal scholars regard the U.S. Supreme Court's ruling in *Brown v. Board of Education* (1954) as the most far-reaching court decision of the twentieth

**TABLE 9.1**  School revenue contributed by federal, state, and local governments.

| School Year | Percentage of Revenue | | |
|---|---|---|---|
| | *Federal* | *State* | *Local* |
| 1919–1920 | 0.3 | 16.5 | 83.2 |
| 1929–1930 | 0.4 | 16.9 | 82.7 |
| 1939–1940 | 1.8 | 30.3 | 68.0 |
| 1949–1950 | 2.9 | 39.8 | 57.3 |
| 1959–1960 | 4.4 | 39.1 | 56.5 |
| 1969–1970 | 8.0 | 39.9 | 52.1 |
| 1979–1980 | 9.2 | 49.1 | 41.7 |
| 1981–1982 | 7.4 | 47.9 | 44.7 |
| 1983–1984 | 6.9 | 47.8 | 45.3 |
| 1985–1986 | 6.6 | 49.4 | 44.0 |
| 1987–1988 | 6.2 | 50.2 | 43.6 |
| 1989–1990 | 6.3 | 48.7 | 45.0 |
| 1991–1992 | 6.4 | 47.9 | 45.7 |

SOURCES:  Figures for 1919–1920 through 1969–1970 are from U.S. Department of Education, Center for Education Statistics, *Digest of Education Statistics, 1987* (Washington, D.C.: U.S. Government Printing Office, 1987), p. 107. Figures for 1979–1980 through 1985–1986 are from National Education Association, *Estimates of School Statistics, 1987–88* (Washington, D.C: NEA, 1988), p. 21. Figures for 1987–1988, 1989–1990, and 1991–1992, respectively, are from National Education Association, *Rankings of the States, 1988* (Washington, D.C.: NEA, 1988), pp. 42–44; *Rankings of the States, 1990* (Washington, D.C.: NEA, 1990), pp. 39–41; and *Rankings of the States, 1992* (Washington, D.C.: NEA, 1992), pp. 45–47.

century. It is true that the federal government has spent a great deal of money carrying out the mandates of *Brown* and subsequent school desegregation decisions, but state and local governments, businesses, and individual citizens have spent even more. One reason the federal government's control exceeds its funding, then, is that federal courts can order sweeping changes and transfer most of the costs of compliance to other levels of government and other people.

Second, the federal government has increased the impact of its education dollars by earmarking them for particular purposes and insisting that state and local school systems spend them according to federal guidelines. *Categorical aid* to education—money provided with strings attached—enables federal officials to maintain control over federal dollars, even after the money has passed through state boards and departments of education and into the hands of local school officials.

During the 1960s and 1970s, Congress justified categorical aid as an essential political safeguard. State and local school officials had consistently neglected the needs of poor, minority, disabled, and female students, the argument went, so how could these same officials be trusted to spend *general aid*—money provided with fewer restrictions—wisely and equitably? While there was more than a little congressional self-righteousness in the argument, there was also an abundance of factual support, as chapters 6 and 8 of this book indicate.

President Reagan tried to change the terms of the argument. Even if categorical aid had been necessary during the 1960s and 1970s, he stated, it had outlived its usefulness. The people closest to the schools deserve more control over federal aid. As the nation has matured, state and local officials have changed— they have become more sensitive to the needs of all students. Besides, Mr. Reagan added, the courts are there to protect students who encounter discrimination.

Congress was not convinced. Despite Ronald Reagan's efforts, the categorical approach remains the key to federal aid to education. Accepted as a given by both George Bush and Bill Clinton, categorical aid offers the federal government a way to focus and magnify the effects of its spending.

## The Cold War, the Poverty War, and Other Battles

Historians say America's elementary and secondary school students have marched off to war several times as the federal government has drafted them to fight a variety of enemies. Mixing school children into military metaphors may seem startling, but in this case the imagery is appropriate.

After the Soviet Union orbited the satellite Sputnik I in 1957 and added a threatening new dimension to the Cold War, Congress responded by passing the National Defense Education Act (NDEA) of 1958. Believing America's students could help win the war, Congress provided categorical aid to improve math, science, and foreign language instruction in the schools. Through the NDEA, the federal government hoped to gain a scientific, technological, and military advantage over the Soviet Union.[43]

During the 1960s, President Johnson declared a War on Poverty, and Congress sent students into action all along the front lines. The Economic Opportunity Act (EOA) of 1964 gave the nation Project Head Start, a program designed to help preschool children compensate for what was then called "cultural deprivation"— in plain English, the negative effects of being poor. Compensatory education became a key weapon in the poverty war, and it remains so today. When Congress passed the Elementary and Secondary Education Act (ESEA) of 1965, the federal government launched its major educational offensive in the poverty war. Congress aimed the act at students who were "disadvantaged," another euphemism for poor. Title I reading and math programs brought compensatory education into the elementary grades. Other titles (sections) of the original ESEA provided money for libraries and instructional materials, for example, and educational research. Initially funded at $1 billion, by 1981 ESEA had provided more than $30 billion in categorical aid to state and local school systems.[44]

The Civil Rights Act of 1964 became a major federal weapon against racial and ethnic discrimination, which Congress regarded as a major cause of poverty. As the federal government channeled more money into public education, it gained powerful leverage over state and local school systems, especially in the South, the nation's poorest region. Making federal dollars contingent on desegregation helped bring southern school systems into line, and the many victories along this front of the poverty war encouraged Congress.[45]

Poverty proved to be an elusive enemy. Congress broadened its attack by expanding the ESEA, adding the Education of Handicapped Children Act (Title VI) in 1966 and the Bilingual Education Act (Title VII) in 1968. By 1972, when

Congress was ready to mount a new educational offensive, a president with a different set of priorities sat in the White House. Richard Nixon had less enthusiasm than Lyndon Johnson for fighting a domestic war on poverty, and Mr. Nixon was preoccupied with the hot war in Vietnam.[46]

Although Congress shared his preoccupation, it found time to pass the Education Amendments of 1972, which included funds for a variety of categorical programs: desegregation assistance under the Emergency School Aid Act, ethnic studies under the Ethnic Heritage Act, and improved education for Native Americans under the Indian Education Act. The best known of the 1972 amendments is Title IX, which prohibits sex discrimination in all educational institutions—preschool, elementary, secondary, and postsecondary—that receive federal funds.[47]

By the 1970s, poverty was not the only or even the major enemy the federal government was fighting with education. Although the Vietnam War had made military metaphors unpopular, it was obvious the legislative and judicial branches of the federal government were still home to many "happy warriors" with educational campaigns in mind.

The mood of the public, though, was changing. The media played up the backlash against federal activism. The controversy over school desegregation moved outside the South as federal judges tried to untie the knot of de facto and de jure segregation (see chapter 8). Although desegregation proceeded uneventfully in many school systems, the media paired the words *busing* and *Boston* in the public consciousness. The association was not a pleasant one.[48]

Congress charged into battle on behalf of the disabled with Public Law 94–142 (1975), which affirmed the right of all children to receive an appropriate education at public expense. The media played up the exceptions rather than the rule: teacher complaints about having to draw up IEPs (Individualized Educational Programs) rather than new opportunities for disabled students, and the high cost of educating the most severely disabled rather than the ease with which schools accommodated the majority of exceptional children.[49]

The backlash intensified. Many citizens believed the federal government had gone too far. In the late 1970s, President Jimmy Carter became the symbol of all that was wrong. The first presidential candidate endorsed by the NEA, Mr. Carter stuck to the federal educational agenda of the 1960s and early 1970s, just when the word *liberal* was becoming a pejorative in U.S. politics. Federal spending on education reached new heights during the Carter administration, and at the president's insistence, Congress voted narrowly to establish a cabinet-level Department of Education. To head the new department, Carter chose Shirley Hufstedler, a federal judge, judicial activist, and feminist. As Ronald Reagan pointed out on the campaign trail, the symbolism could not have been more appropriate.

## Mr. Reagan Goes to Washington

Ronald Reagan made short work of Jimmy Carter in 1980 and shorter work of Walter Mondale four years later. Education was not the main issue in either campaign, but the differences between Reagan and his Democratic opponents on the federal role in education mirrored their basic differences. Reagan promised to get the federal government off people's backs; Carter and Mondale promised to use the federal government to solve people's problems. Americans went to the polls and made two clear choices.

More than any other president since Lyndon Johnson, Ronald Reagan put his mark on the politics of education. Reagan's New Federalism realigned the roles of all three levels of government. The control of public education shifted downward, as we have seen, with state governments gaining most from the transfer. The responsibility for paying for the schools also changed, as federal funding for education fell dramatically during Mr. Reagan's first term in office. By 1984, inflation-adjusted dollars, the federal government was spending 21 percent less on elementary and secondary education than it had in 1980.[50]

Political observers were astonished at the change that had come over Washington. Even among liberal Democrats in Congress, there seemed to be a consensus that state and local school systems needed to rely less on Washington and more on themselves. Reagan predicted that the New Federalism would encourage state and local governments to fill in the gaps left by federal withdrawal.[51]

Agreeing to give the New Federalism a trial, Congress passed the Education Consolidation and Improvement Act (ECIA) of 1981. Under the umbrella of the ECIA, the administration redesigned and renamed the Title I compensatory education program, the pride of the happy warriors of the 1960s and 1970s. Title I became Chapter I of the ECIA—and much more than the name changed. Simplified eligibility requirements and fewer regulations from the Department of Education gave state and local school officials more control, and several years of budget cuts reduced the number of children the program served by nearly 800,000. As classroom teachers saw it, the change from Title I to Chapter I meant three things: fewer federal regulations, fewer federal dollars, and fewer students in the program.[52]

During Mr. Reagan's second term, members of Congress from both political parties realized federal budget cuts had put local school districts with large numbers of "at-risk" students into dire straits. Big-city and rural districts with poor tax bases were simply unable to make up for lost federal funds. Congress reasserted its role in educational policy making, so federal education budgets began to grow again, although in constant dollars federal spending on elementary and secondary schools remained more than 20 percent below the 1980 level.[53]

In education, as in other areas, the president and Congress were locked in a test of strength. The Democratic majority that now controlled both houses was ready to take on Mr. Reagan.

Beyond the budget wars, the best examples of the confrontation were the running battles over the enforcement of civil rights laws and court decisions. Reagan's critics in Congress accused him of being soft on discrimination against women and minorities. The president replied that he was simply trying to make state and local officials more responsible for policing themselves. Congress was the clear victor in the battle over the enforcement of the Title IX ban against sex discrimination. This victory clarified the federal government's right to cut off *all* federal funds to an educational institution if *any* of its programs practice discrimination. The battle over the enforcement of court-ordered school desegregation ended in a draw during the Reagan presidency. In the early 1990s, though, the U.S. Supreme Court handed him a belated victory by making it easier for school districts to end judicial supervision of the desegregation process—and to end busing for racial balance (see chapter 8).[54]

## Educational Advocacy: *A Nation at Risk* and Bill Bennett

Looking back on the Reagan years, educators in the 1990s and beyond will probably attach less significance to reductions in federal spending and federal control than to the advocacy role that emerged almost accidentally with the success of *A Nation at Risk*. No one in the administration expected the report to become an overnight sensation, yet it did. No one expected the report to do more than the New Federalism to galvanize the states into action, yet it did. *A Nation at Risk* became the educational document of the decade.[55]

The president who had been highly critical of federal involvement in education became an avid practitioner of a certain kind of involvement: advocacy. Without spending much money and without exercising much direct control, the Reagan administration used exhortation and persuasion to advance its educational goals. The U.S. Department of Education, which Mr. Reagan came to Washington promising to close down, became instead a national platform for the advancement of a conservative educational agenda—a "bully pulpit," Secretary of Education William Bennett liked to call it, conjuring memories of Teddy Roosevelt.

Advocacy became a call to arms, as once again the federal government sent America's students into battle. *A Nation at Risk* drafted them to fight an international economic war against such friendly enemies as Japan, Korea, and West Germany. Educational historian Joel Spring has called this competition the "Sony War," for *A Nation at Risk* summons up images of a full-scale invasion of Sonys, Hyundais, and Telefunkens:

> Our nation is at risk. Our once unchallenged preeminence in commerce, industry, science, and technological innovation is being overtaken by competitors throughout the world. . . . If an unfriendly foreign power had attempted to impose on America the mediocre educational performance that exists today, we might well have viewed it as an act of war. As it stands, we have allowed this to happen to ourselves. We have even squandered the gains in student achievement made in the wake of the Sputnik challenge . . . . We have, in effect, been committing an act of unthinking, unilateral educational disarmament.[56]

"History in not kind to idlers," the report warned. "We live among determined, well-educated, and strongly motivated competitors."[57]

The result of this kind of advocacy, as we saw earlier in this chapter, was a new wave of school reform. Almost every state produced a report echoing the call to arms of *A Nation at Risk*. Make the schools excellent, or suffer the economic consequences. Then the states went into action, and some local school districts are still wondering what hit them. Although the Reagan administration was not completely satisfied with the way state reform proceeded—it trampled local control in its path—the energy *A Nation at Risk* unleashed was stunning. Gearing students up for economic competition became the educational mission of the decade.

Could advocacy of another cause unleash another tidal wave of reform? Mr. Reagan pondered this question in 1985 when William Bennett succeeded Terrel Bell as secretary of education. Bell deserved much of the credit for *A Nation at Risk,* but he lost favor within the administration because "movement conservatives" considered him too liberal. Bennett's appointment, though, delighted conservatives. Heading the Department of Education during most of Reagan's second term, Bennett quickly became the nation's most visible advocate of educational essentialism (see chapter 7) and educational choice among public *and* private schools (chapter 11). Although Bennett advocated these causes with great zeal, the role he found most satisfying was serving as point man for the Reagan administration's moral agenda.[58]

Adopting the Judeo-Christian ethic as his theme, Bennett used the Department of Education's bully pulpit to advocate hard work, organized school prayer, good old-fashioned discipline, and the "Just Say No" drug policy. Opposition to abortion fit easily into the theme, as did sexual abstinence as the best defense against AIDS. Bennett attacked the NEA and other "vested interests" in education with moral fervor, casting them as the villains in the drama of school reform. What made Bennett so attractive to some Americans and so irritating to others was his right-versus-wrong, friends-against-enemies approach to the politics of education.[59]

These are the Reagan administration's legacies to education: cutbacks in federal spending and control, *A Nation at Risk,* increases in state spending and control, and Bill Bennett. During the 1980s, they turned America's education conversation around, changing the emphasis from *equity* to *excellence,* from *access* to *ability,* from *needs* to *standards of performance.*[60]

## George Bush, National Goals, and America 2000

Although during the 1988 campaign George Bush promised "to be the education president . . . to lead a renaissance of quality in our schools," he was unable to talk the reforms he wanted into place. Never matching the results the Reagan administration obtained with its advocacy, the Bush administration at best encouraged a discussion of national education goals; at worst the Bush administration simply echoed conversations that were already going on.[61]

During his first two years in office, Mr. Bush faced sharp criticism for being all talk and no action. "I would give him a C-minus, maybe a D-plus," said A. Graham Down, president of the Council for Basic Education, late in 1990. "I mean, he hasn't really done much except talk, and talk is cheap." This widely quoted statement stung Mr. Bush, for it came from the president of a conservative education group that wanted to support what it thought Bush wanted to do.[62]

Bush's first secretary of education, Lauro Cavazos, was a holdover from the final months of the Reagan administration, where he had a hard act to follow: Bill Bennett. Early on in Bush's presidency, it became obvious that Cavazos was a poor advocate, yet he stayed in the bully pulpit for two years.

Nor did the president himself, with one major exception, provide strong educational leadership during the first half of his administration. He focused his attention instead on the looming war with Iraq.

The one major exception was the Education Summit Conference held jointly with the nation's governors in the fall of 1989. Basking in media attention, Bush and the governors agreed to establish national goals for education and to promote accountability, flexibility, and restructuring. All well and good, most observers said, but the joint statement issued at the summit amounted to little more than a public relations document, a glossary of buzzwords from late-1980s "excellence in education" reforms.

Then, in February 1990, the president and the governors announced the six national goals that would provide the framework for the Bush administration's subsequent efforts in education. By the year 2000:

1. All children in America will start school ready to learn.
2. The high school graduation rate will increase to at least 90 percent.
3. American students will leave grades four, eight, and twelve having demonstrated competency in challenging subject matter including English, mathematics, science, history, and geography. . . .
4. U.S. students will be first in the world in science and mathematics achievement.
5. Every adult American will be literate and will possess the knowledge and skills necessary to compete in a global economy and exercise the rights and responsibilities of citizenship.
6. Every school in America will be free of drugs and violence and will offer a disciplined environment conducive to learning.[63]

Already competing with George Bush for the media spotlight was the up-and-coming education governor from Arkansas who cohosted the summit conference. Bill Clinton, a former chair of the National Governors' Association, personally helped draft the six national goals, which he has carried over into his own administration.[64]

When I first discussed the six goals with the prospective teachers in my classes, their reactions were identical to those heard around the nation. The goals are nice, ambitious, and unrealistic, my students said. Great rhetoric—but don't expect great results. After the remaining months of 1990 passed without the announcement of a plan for reaching the goals, supporters as well as critics of Mr. Bush marked down low grades in education on their presidential report cards.[65]

The confirmation of Lamar Alexander as secretary of education in March 1991, midway through Bush's four-year term, set the stage for a more active approach to the politics of education. Alexander had been the very model of a conservative education governor in Tennessee. Preceding Clinton as chair of the National Governors' Association, Alexander won the respect of his peers in both parties. Here was an intelligent, well-informed politician, sophisticated yet down-home. Alexander would make the best secretary of education yet, many observers predicted.[66]

In April 1991, Bush and Alexander unveiled America 2000: An Education Strategy, the administration's road map to the six national goals. Largely the work of the new secretary, the strategy consisted of four major components:

1. Voluntary American Achievement Tests keyed to "world class standards" in the core academic subjects.
2. "Break-the-mold" New American Schools—innovative institutions funded by business in each of the 535 Congressional districts.
3. Greater flexibility for teachers in exchange for greater accountability.
4. Tax-supported educational choice among public and private schools.[67]

America 2000 put the emphasis on action at the state and especially the local level. Bush and Alexander offered recognition as an official "America 2000 Community" to groups of local people who would adopt the six national goals, develop a community strategy for reaching the goals, devise a "report card" for measuring the results, and prepare to create an experimental New American School. Trying to build grassroots support, Secretary Alexander traveled the country promoting America 2000.[68]

But who would pay the bills? Harking back to the New Federalism, Bush and Alexander called on state and local government and business to fund most of the program. Yet administration officials insisted that "America 2000 is not expected to raise state or local spending. . . . The answer does not lie in spending more money on old ways—but to redirect our resources and our energies to new approaches.[69]

Supporters and critics alike pointed out that *someone* would have to come up with the billions of dollars it would take to reach the six national goals. Helping the nation meet those goals, after all, is what America 2000 was supposed to do. Although George Bush's education budgets were more generous than Ronald Reagan's, they fell short of full funding, even for existing programs.[70]

Bush stated that fully funding the Head Start program, for example—which he had promised to do during the 1988 campaign—was essential to reaching the first goal: All children in America will start school ready to learn. Bush proposed and Congress passed major increases in the Head Start budget, but the program still came up $5 billion short of the money needed to serve all eligible children. Even after the increases, Head Start could accommodate fewer than 40 percent of those qualifing for the program. Other federal education programs were in the same straits.[71]

While Congress debated America 2000, President Bush's popularity soared with Operation Desert Storm in 1991 and plummeted with the troubled economy in 1992. On the eve of the election, little of America 2000 remained alive.

The New American Schools did survive the change of administration in 1993. These schools are funded through a nonprofit private development corporation rather than the federal government. Headed by Thomas Kean, the former education governor of New Jersey we met in chapter 1, the New American Schools Development Corporation is tapping business and industry to fund the prototype schools.[72] Yet the business executives on the corportion's governing board are finding it difficult to raise money for the program. Some business leaders are accusing the federal government of "shirking its responsibilities for improving the nation's schools by foisting them onto the private sector."[73]

And so the nation's education conversation continued as President Bush left office. The conversation remained focused on terms set by the Reagan administration during the 1980s—terms that were quite familiar to the former education govenor who was preparing to move into the White House.

## Bill Clinton: An Education Governor as President

Will the Clinton administration try to shift 1980s-style state school reform to the federal level? With one education governor as president and another, Dick Riley of South Carolina, as U.S. secretary of education, the answer seems clear.

Excellence and accountability, the twin hallmarks of state school reform, are highly visible in Clinton's educational agenda. Like Riley and other education governors, Clinton has faith in standards and assessments. Clinton helped install minimum competency tests and raise high school graduation requirements in Arkansas, one of the best examples in the nation of a state that went back to basics via standardized testing.[74]

To those who warned him, "Oh, you can't do that, you'll increase the dropout rate," Clinton likes to point out that the dropout rate in Arkansas actually decreased—it is now the lowest in the Southeast—while the percentage of students going on to college increased from 39 percent in 1981 to 52 percent in 1991. The essentialist in Clinton feels confident that these improvements occurred "because there were no more bored students in high school who couldn't read."[75]

Now President Clinton wants to move ahead with national standards and national assessments. As we will see in chapter 10, many teachers fear such reforms would produce a de facto national curriculum and lead to "teaching the tests" on a larger scale than ever. The two teacher unions are split on the issue of nationalizing public education, with the NEA expressing strong opposition and the AFT giving cautious support.[76]

Clinton justifies his position on standards and assessments by citing the example of Jaime Escalante, the Los Angeles teacher who gained national prominence after the film *Stand and Deliver* dramatized his success with low-income Hispanic students. Clinton reasons that just as Escalante used the College Board's Advanced Placement Test in calculus to motivate his students, other teachers can use national standards and national tests to get the best work from their students.[77]

Teachers know the real world of the classroom is considerably more complex than the Hollywood version in *Stand and Deliver*. At least Clinton does not argue that teachers can work miracles with limited resources if only they try as hard as Escalante. That, unfortunately, was the lesson Presidents Reagan and Bush seemed to have gotten from the movie. For Clinton, "the real lesson is that all children can learn." But he adds that we need to "make sure that all our children start out on a level playing field, because national standards can't be fair unless they do."[78]

This statement suggests President Clinton's willingness to spend more money on public education, which he certainly did as governor of Arkansas. It also shows his willingess to admit that "the poor and the minorities and the immigrants have too often been victims of the system." Clinton mentions Jonathan Kozol's best-seller *Savage Inequalities* (1991) as a major influence on his thinking (see chapter 7). Kozol's plea to reduce the stark differences between schools for middle-class white students and schools for lower-class minority students appeals to the progressive in Clinton. To make the playing field more level, Clinton proposes full funding for Head Start, increased funding for Chapter 1, and federal assistance to improve school safety.[79]

Another way to make the playing field more level, according to Clinton, is to give Americans "more leverage in the schools they attend." Under Governor Clinton, Arkansas became the second state in the nation to offer parents and students statewide choice among public schools. But Clinton opposes "giv[ing] people public money to take to private schools," a stand that presented one of the clearest contrasts to President Bush's education platform during the 1992 campaign.[80]

The NEA and AFT endorsed Clinton and contributed to his campaign. At the 1992 Democratic convention, almost 10 percent of the delegates and alternates were teacher unionists. President Bush tried to use Clinton's teacher endorsements against him, claiming "This NEA crowd is fighting any kind of change because they just like [the education system] the way it's been."[81]

Mr. Clinton and the NEA both disputed the claim, and in fact their relationship has been rocky at times. Under Clinton, Arkansas became the first state to mandate competency testing for currently employed teachers. Only two other states, Georgia and Texas, followed Arkansas' lead, because other governors and legislators concluded that forcing teachers to take a simple literacy test was not worth the trouble and expense of fighting the NEA. Governor Clinton, though, argued that the public would not support higher taxes without the teacher test as a guarantee of accountability.[82]

Several years of cold war broke out between Clinton and the Arkansas Education Association, the NEA's state affiliate. More than 1,400 teachers resigned, retired, or lost their jobs as a result of the test. Even NEA members who supported teacher testing came to resent what they perceived as streaks of stubborness and confrontation in Clinton.[83]

Arkansas teachers eventually warmed to the education governor whose reforms paid off in substantially higher teacher salaries and per-student spending—even if some of the most impressive increases came while Clinton was running for president. Worried that teachers in other states would remember only the well-publicized fight over teacher competency testing, the NEA blanketed its members with pro-Clinton flyers during the 1992 campaign.[84]

Clinton brings a track record of school reform to the presidency. The record is eclectic: essentialist and progressive, conservative and liberal. The president who admires Jaime Escalante for making poor and minority students work hard also praises Jonathan Kozol for insisting that hard work isn't enough. School funding also matters, Clinton realizes, and a more equitable distribution of resources ranks high on his agenda.

One of the challenges he faced as governor of Arkansas was helping the legislature reform the state's educational finance system after the courts declared it unconstitutional. President Clinton is now in a position to exercise national leadership on this issue. As the last section of this chapter points out, the state finance systems that cause the quality of public education to vary so much from one school district to the next are under attack in courts throughout the nation.

## EDUCATIONAL FINANCE

Where children live has a powerful effect on the quality of the public schools they attend. Real estate agents are well acquainted with the question "How good are the public schools?" because parents who have the resources to do so shop for homes with the quality of local education in mind. Although public schools differ in many ways, one of the most important variables is *per-pupil expenditure*—the amount of money spent per student. Think of per-pupil expenditure as a financial package put together by local school boards with money received from the local, state, and federal governments.[85]

Table 9.2 ranks the states by their average per-pupil expenditures. As you can see, the annual cost of educating the nation's "average" public school student is well over $5,000. Variations among the states are wide. In four states and the District of Columbia the average per-pupil expenditure is more than $8,000, while seven states spend less than half the amount.

Viewed another way, the differences are even more glaring. In *every classroom* of 25 students, New Jersey, Alaska, New York, Connecticut and the District of Columbia spend about $100,000 more *every year* than Oklahoma, Arkansas, Tennesse, Alabama, Idaho, Mississippi, and Utah. Per-pupil expenditures tend to be highest in the Northeast, followed by the Midwest, the West, and the Southeast—but notice the exceptions to this rule.

In the nation as a whole, average per-pupil expenditures have risen by about 33 percent, adjusted for inflation, since the early 1980s, with most of the increase coming from state reforms inspired by *A Nation at Risk.* To set the record straight, much but not all of the new money has gone into teachers' pockets. Their salaries, as you may recall from chapter 2, have risen by about 21 percent since the early 1980s. The rest of the 33 percent increase has gone to pay for other school reforms.[86]

## Local Property Taxes: Some Districts Are More Equal Than Others

Keep in mind that average state per-pupil expenditures, while useful in making comparisons among states, conceal variations *within* states. Per-pupil expenditures tend to be highest in suburban school districts, followed by urban, small-town, and rural districts. Travel around the country and you will almost always

**TABLE 9.2** Average per-pupil expenditures across the nation, 1991–1992.

| | | | | | |
|---|---|---|---|---|---|
| 1. New Jersey | $10,219 | | 27. Illinois | $5,248 |
| 2. Alaska | 9,248 | | 28. Kansas | 5,131 |
| 3. New York | 8,658 | | 29. Montana | 5,127 |
| 4. Connecticut | 8,299 | | 30. Iowa | 4,949 |
| 5. D. Columbia | 8,116 | | 31. Nevada | 4,910 |
| 6. Vermont | 6,992 | | 32. N. Carolina | 4,857 |
| 7. Pennsylvania | 6,980 | | 33. Arizona | 4,750 |
| 8. Rhode Island | 6,834 | | 34. Georgia | 4,720 |
| 9. Massachusetts | 6,323 | | 35. New Mexico | 4,692 |
| 10. Maryland | 6,273 | | 36. California | 4,686 |
| 11. Delaware | 6,080 | | 37. Nebraska | 4,676 |
| 12. Wisconsin | 5,972 | | 38. Texas | 4,651 |
| 13. Oregon | 5,972 | | 39. Kentucky | 4,616 |
| 14. Maine | 5,969 | | 40. S. Carolina | 4,537 |
| 15. Florida | 5,639 | | 41. Missouri | 4,534 |
| 16. Michigan | 5,630 | | 42. Louisiana | 4,378 |
| 17. Minnesota | 5,510 | | 43. S. Dakota | 4,255 |
| 18. New Hampshire | 5,500 | | 44. N. Dakota | 4,119 |
| 19. Virginia | 5,487 | | 45. Oklahoma | 3,939 |
| 20. Hawaii | 5,453 | | 46. Arkansas | 3,770 |
| 21. Ohio | 5,451 | | 47. Tennessee | 3,736 |
| 22. Indiana | 5,429 | | 48. Alabama | 3,675 |
| 23. W. Virginia | 5,415 | | 49. Idaho | 3,528 |
| 24. Wyoming | 5,333 | | 50. Mississippi | 3,344 |
| 25. Washington | 5,331 | | 51. Utah | 3,092 |
| 26. Colorado | 5,259 | | | |
| U.S. Average | $5,466 | | | |

Note: Figures show expenditures per pupil in average daily attendance.
SOURCE: National Education Association, *Rankings of the States, 1992* (Washington, D.C.: NEA, 1992). Reprinted by permission.

find the highest per-pupil expenditures in the suburbs of major cities. Why do the students who live in suburban Shawnee Mission, Kansas, for instance, have more money spent on their public education than students who live in nearby Kansas City, in small-town Mullinville, or on a farm out on the plains? The main reason is that suburban residents are able to raise more money for the schools through local property taxes.

As the major source of local revenue for public schools, local poperty taxes work to the advantage of wealthier communities and to the disadvantage of poorer communities. In some cases, suburbs with high *property values* can set their *tax rates* low and still rank at the top of the state in per-pupil spending.

Consider the example of two school districts of about the same size, located in the same state. One district serves an upper-middle-class suburb where homes have an average market value of $200,000. The other district serves a less affluent community—it could be a central city, small town, rural area, or working-class suburb—where the market value of property averages $50,000. To keep things straightforward, let's assume property is taxed at full market value in this state.[87]

The residents of the upper-middle-class suburb have set their school tax rate at $1 per $100 of property value. The average home in this suburb, therefore, brings in $2,000 for the local schools. With the average family paying school taxes of $2,000 each year, these citizens can truthfully say they are trying hard to support public education.

The residents of the less affluent community have set their tax rate twice as high—at $2 per $100 of assessed value—yet the average home in their community generates only $1,000 for the schools. These residents can say they are trying twice as hard, but their *effort*—a technical term in school finance that means exactly what it says—yields only half as much.

You can appreciate the significance of this example if you think again of school finance as a package. In the nation as a whole, local governments contribute 46 percent of the money that goes into the package, and almost all the local money comes from property taxes. As Table 9.1 indicates, local governments have historically shouldered most of the burden for paying for public education. But Table 9.1 also shows that state governments have assumed a progressively larger share of the burden throughout this century, motivated in part by the desire to make the quality of education more uniform within each state.

In 1920, when local governments were responsible for raising more than 80 percent of school revenue, the differences in per-pupil expenditures within states were staggering. The amount of wealth in a local community virtually dictated the amount of money spent on the local schools. As we saw in chapter 6, race and ethnicity also influenced expenditures, for it was standard practice to spend less on African- and Hispanic-American students. In the early twentieth century, then, it was not at all unusual for some districts to spend 5, 10, or 15 times more per student than other districts within the same state.

## State Funds: Reducing the Inequalities

Such gaps have narrowed but not completely closed as the states have increased their spending on public education. Most states have developed *equalization plans* that base the amount of state funding each district receives on such factors as local wealth, effort, and student characteristics (the percentage of poor, minority, and disabled students, for instance).

In our example of the upper-middle-class suburb and the less affluent community, a state equalization plan would bring per-pupil expenditures in the two districts closer together. The state department of education would send more state money to the poorer district, and that district would probably receive more federal aid as well, since it would be likely to have more students qualifying for categorical federal programs.[88]

Two major 1970s court decisions shaped the trend toward more state funding. In *Serrano v. Priest* (1971), the California Supreme Court considered the complaint of John Serrano, who lived with his family in the working-class suburb of Baldwin Park in Los Angeles. Baldwin Park's property tax rates were twice as high as those in wealthy Beverly Hills, but because of the vastly different property values, the Baldwin Park school district could spend only half as much per student. With class sizes increasing and textbooks in short supply, Serrano felt dissatisfied with the public schools his two children attended.[89]

The California Supreme Court ruled that the state's school finance system, heavily dependent on local property taxes, "invidiously discriminates against the poor because it makes the quality of a child's education a function of the wealth of his parents and his neighbors." The court ruled that the California system violated the right to equal protection of the laws guaranteed by both the state constitution and the Fourteenth Amendment to the U.S. Constitution. Obviously, said the court, the school laws of California were not protecting the rich and poor citizens equally; the laws were making public schools as unequal as the wealth of the communities where they were located.[90]

The *Serrano* case created a sensation in school finance, precipitating a flood of similar lawsuits in other states. When a case from Texas, *San Antonio Independent School District v. Rodriguez,* reached the U.S. Supreme Court in 1973, many observers predicted a ruling similar to *Serrano*—a national mandate to reform school finance. The cases were virtually identical: unequal per-pupil expenditures, reliance on local property taxes, even a lead plaintiff who was poor and Hispanic.

But the Supreme Court issued no such mandate in *Rodriguez*. Instead, it left the matter up to the states. In a 5-to-4 decision, the majority pointed out that the U.S. Constitution does not guarantee the right to an education. The Fourteenth Amendment, therefore, cannot protect citizens from state school finance laws that allow per-pupil expenditures to vary from one district to another. The court suggested, though, that inequitable state laws might well violate state constitutions.

*Rodriguez* shifted the action back to the state level, and in the years since the decision, more than half the nation's state legislatures have overhauled their school finance systems to make them less dependent on local revenue. After the California Supreme Court reaffirmed its earlier decision and reissued its call for reform in *Serrano II* (1976), the state share of the school budget went from less than 40 percent to almost 70 percent. Since the late 1970s, for the first time in U.S. history, the state share of the nation's total spending on education has been greater than the local share.[91]

But battles over school finance are still raging because local differences persist. Only Hawaii and the District of Columbia, where there are no local school districts, have uniform per-pupil expenditures. In every other state, a substantial gap in per-pupil expenditures exists between the wealthiest and poorest districts. In 1990–1991, the smallest gap was in Delaware, where the wealthiest district spent 1.4 times as much per student as the poorest district—$6,106 versus $4,324. The largest gap was in Texas, where per-pupil expenditures were 6.8 times greater in the wealthiest district than in the poorest—$14,514 versus $2,150.[92]

To those who argue that money cannot buy everything, the best reply is that money can buy *some* things. To be sure, educators cannot correlate spending with achievement and promise that more dollars will produce higher test scores. As we found in chapter 2, too many factors outside the school influence student achievement for educators to issue that kind of guarantee. What educators can state with confidence, though, is that educational programs and services do not come free. Only money can buy them.[93]

In the wealthiest districts in a given state, high school students have access to a curriculum that offers five or six foreign languages, math and science courses through advanced calculus and second-year physics, challenging courses in other core subjects, and pupil-teacher ratios of 20 or 25 to 1. The cost may run to $8,000 or more per student.

The poorest districts within a state offer their high school students a very different curriculum: one or two foreign languages, no calculus or physics, unexceptional courses in other subjects, and pupil-teacher ratios of 35 or 40 to 1. The price tag may be $3,000 or less per student.

People who believe money doesn't matter should tour schools as different as these. Reading Jonathan Kozol's *Savage Inequalities* may be the next best thing. With great sensitivity to the human consequences of funding disparities, Kozol provides convincing evidence that only money can buy the programs and services needed to make America's public schools more equal.

Access, needs, and equality—these issues, downplayed in America's education conversation during the 1980s, may become important once again during the 1990s. Nowhere is there greater potential for leveling the playing field (to borrow President Clinton's phrase) than in the educational finance suits working their way through the courts in more than half the states.

## Lawsuits, Reform, and the Economy: Educational Finance in the 1990s

"Entire Kentucky Education System Unconstitutional!" This headline in the September 1989 issue of *Phi Delta Kappan* captures the impact of the court decision that sent public education in Kentucky back to the drawing boards. A lawsuit filed against the state by a coalition of 66 poor school districts is yielding change more far reaching than the plaintiffs had ever hoped for. Kentucky is under court order to reform its public schools from the ground up, paying particular attention to narrowing the gap between wealthy districts and poor districts in the state school system.[94]

Notice my terminology: the *state school system.* Americans have traditionally thought of public education within a state as a number of local school districts rather than a single school system. Yet the U.S. Constitution, the Kentucky Constitution, and every other state constitution make public education a function of the state government. Accordingly, the Kentucky Supreme Court ruled that the responsibilities for establishing, maintaining, and funding public schools rest solely with the state legislature.

Moreover, the court ruled, the legislature must carry out its responsibilities equitably and adequately. The state school system must provide *equal* educational opportunities to all students, regardless of where they live or how much money their parents and neighbors have. The state school system must also provide an *adequate* education to all students, one that prepares them to lead productive lives.

Concluding that the legislature had failed in its responsibilities, the court declared Kentucky's entire school system unconstitutional in 1989 and told the legislature to reform it. A task force appointed by the legislature and governor recommended changes in curriculum, governance, and, of course, finance. Several years later, the new system is still taking shape.

Political and educational officials in Kentucky are trying to use the court decision as leverage for implementing the latest national reforms. The officials have visions, for instance, of an accountability system that will use student performance assessments (see chapter 10) to reward successful schools and penalize unsuccessful ones. Reformers want to put a computer in every classroom and link every school via an electronic network. Reformers look to an extensive staff development program to help teachers and administrators learn how to share power in school-based management. But the success of these reforms hinges on the success of the financial changes designed to ensure equity and adequacy.[95]

States undergoing court-ordered financial reforms—the list already includes West Virginia, Montana, Texas, and New Jersey as well as Kentucky—find themselves in a dilemma. If they "level up" by giving more state money to poor districts, state taxes must increase to generate the extra revenue. Political rebellion may break out. If they "level down" by taking state money away from wealthy districts, rich and powerful people cry "Robin Hood!" Political rebellion may break out. Jonathan Kozol sees the same motive behind both kinds of resistance: the desire of better-off parents to keep their children better off.[96]

Most states, like Kentucky, opt for leveling up, stating at the outset that the goal is narrowing rather than completely closing the spending gap. Poor districts are told that if they make the required local effort—that is, if they set their tax rates at a specified minimum level—the state will provide additional funding to move their spending closer to wealthy districts. Poor districts whose local tax rates exceed the required minimum are rewarded with still more state funding. Leveling up is less threatening than leveling down to residents of wealthy districts, for they know they can keep their children ahead in this game.

But leveling up is expensive. Kentucky is paying for its reform package with a one-cent increase in the state sales tax and a 1 percent hike in corporate taxes. Even with these increases, the economic downturn of the early 1990s forced the state to cut its education budget and scale back or eliminate key programs—a pattern that became all too common across the nation. Thus the condition of the economy and political resistance are setting the limits of equalization.[97]

Even so, equalization is well under way in the 1990s. Throughout the nation, state court decisions in educational finance cases are running heavily in favor of plaintiffs from poor school districts. The Kentucky decision remains the most far reaching, but plaintiffs in other states are hoping their courts will follow Kentucky's lead.[98]

Remember that just as per-pupil expenditures vary *within* states they also vary *between* states. Notice the vast differences in spending from state to state shown in Table 9.2. The principle of financial effort applies here, too. Poorer states often try harder than wealthier states to raise money for public education—that is, poorer states often spend a greater portion of their total resources on the schools. But their effort yields lower per-pupil expenditures.

If Congress, urged on by President Clinton, increases federal spending on education during the 1990s, talk of massive federal assistance to poorer states may revive. For years, the NEA has argued that the three levels of government should split evenly the total bill for public education, with each level paying about one-third. By varying the exact mix of local, state, and federal funding from district to district and state to state, one-third funding could make per-pupil expenditures relatively equal throughout the nation.

Before the Reagan and Bush administrations, talk of one-third funding was serious; during the 1980s and early 1990s, the possibility seemed remote. Given the federal deficit, the state of the national economy, and the strong tradition of state and local control, what are the odds that the federal government will increase its share of the public school budget from 6 percent to 33 percent? In the short run, there is no chance at all. In the long run, the odds are still not good, though the NEA is already talking with Congress about making one-third funding a target for the twenty-first century.

## ACTIVITIES

1. Attend a local school board meeting. Ask to interview several board members and the superintendent about local control, representation, and other issues discussed in this chapter.
2. Find out how state school reform has affected the schools in your state since the release of *A Nation at Risk*. Compare the views of teachers, administrators, elected or appointed school officials, and state legislators. Is "more of the same" a fair description of state reform?
3. Talk with two members of Congress, one Democrat and one Republican, about how the federal politics of education have changed since the Clinton administration has been in Washington.
4. Contact the department of education in your state for information on how widely per-pupil expenditures vary from district to district. If your state has an equalization program, find out how it operates.

## RECOMMENDED READINGS

Kozol, Jonathan. *Savage Inequalities: Children in America's Schools* (New York: Crown, 1991).
    Kozol makes a compelling case for financial equalization by studying the lives of students and teachers trapped in second and third-class schools.

National Commission on Excellence in Education. *A Nation at Risk: The Imperative for Educational Reform* (Washington, D.C.: U.S. Department of Education, 1983).
*The* educational document of the 1980s, this report continues to influence the reforms of the 1990s.

Pipho, Chris. "Stateline," monthly column in *Phi Delta Kappan.*
Focused on current developments in the state politics of education, this column also reflects federal and local influences.

Spring, Joel. *Conflict of Interests: The Politics of American Education,* 2d ed. (White Plains, NY: Longman, 1993).
Spring presents an especially good analysis of how the politics of education have changed during the 1980s and 1990s.

## NOTES

1. Alec M. Gallup and David L. Clark, "The 19th Annual Gallup Poll of the Public's Attitudes toward the Public Schools," *Phi Delta Kappan* 69 (September 1987): 18–19; Stanley M. Elam, Lowell C. Rose, and Alec M. Gallup, "The 24th Annual Gallup/Phi Delta Kappa Poll of the Public's Attitudes toward the Public Schools," *Phi Delta Kappan* 74 (September 1992): 44–45.
2. Robert Rothman, "Historians Cite 'Steady Erosion' in Local Control," *Education Week,* Special Report (April 29, 1992), pp. 4–5; Lynn Olson and Ann Bradley, "Boards of Contention," *Education Week,* Special Report (April 29, 1992). p. 2.
3. National Commission on Excellence in Education, *A Nation at Risk: The Imperative for Educational Reform* (Washington, D.C.: U.S. Department of Education, 1983).
4. Olson and Bradley, "Boards of Contention," p. 3.
5. Ibid., pp. 7, 9–10; Beatrice H. Cameron, Kenneth E. Underwood, and Jim C. Fortune, "Politics and Power: How You're Selected and Elected to Lead This Nation's Schools," *American School Board Journal* 175 (January 1988): 17–19.
6. Willis D. Hawley and Frederick M. Wirt, eds., *The Search for Community Power* (Englewood Cliffs, NJ: Prentice-Hall, 1968); Michael Y. Nunnery and Ralph B. Kimbrough, *Politics, Power, Polls, and School Elections* (Berkeley, CA: McCutchan, 1971); Donald McCarty and Charles Ramsey, *The School Managers: Power and Conflict in American Public Education* (Westport, CT: Greenwood Press, 1971).
7. David B. Tyack and Elizabeth Hansot, *Managers of Virtue: Public School Leadership in America, 1820–1980* (New York: Basic Books, 1982); L. Harmon Zeigler and M. Kent Jennings, *Governing American Schools: Political Interaction in Local School Districts* (North Scituate, MA: Duxbury, 1974); Raymond E. Callahan, *Education and the Cult of Efficiency: A Study of the Social Forces that Have Shaped the Administration of the Public Schools* (Chicago: University of Chicago Press, 1962).
8. Joel Spring, *Conflict of Interests: The Politics of American Education,* 2d ed. (White Plains, NY: Longman, 1993), chap. 8; Frederick M. Wirt and Michael W. Kirst, *Schools in Conflict: The Politics of Education,* 2d ed. (Berkeley, CA: McCutchan, 1989), chaps. 6–7; Arthur Blumberg with Phyllis Blumberg, *The School Superintendent: Living with Conflict* (New York: Teachers College Press, 1985), chaps. 5–6.
9. Spring, *Conflict of Interests,* chap 8; Lynn Olson, "Up for Discussion," *Education Week,* Special Report (April 29, 1992), pp. 24–25.
10. Blumberg, *The School Superintendent,* chaps. 5–6.

11. Chester E. Finn, Jr., "Reinventing Local Control," in Patricia F. First and Herbert J. Walberg, eds., *School Boards: Changing Local Control* (Berkeley, CA: McCutchan, 1992), chap. 2.

12. The *American School Board Journal* publishes a current demographic profile of local board members in every January issue. See Daniel M. Seaton, Kenneth E. Underwood, and Jim C. Fortune's "The Demographics of Board Service," *American School Board Journal* 179 (January 1992): 36–37; and Beatrice H. Cameron, Kenneth E. Underwood, and Jim C. Fortune's "It's Ten Years Later, and You've Hardly Changed at All," *American School Board Journal* 175 (January 1988): 20.

13. Ibid.

14. Cameron, Underwood, and Fortune, "Politics and Power," p. 18.

15. Ibid. See Table 8.3.

16. Cameron, Underwood, and Fortune, "Politics and Power," p. 19.

17. David B. Tyack, *The One Best System: A History of American Urban Education* (Cambridge, MA: Harvard University Press, 1974), part IV.

18. William Montague, "A Vote for Power," *Education Week* (December 9, 1987), pp. 1, 16–17.

19. Ibid., p. 16.

20. Ibid., p. 17.

21. Joseph W. Newman, "Socioeconomic Class and Education: In What Ways Does Class Affect the Educational Process?" in Joe L. Kincheloe and Shirley R. Steinberg, eds., *Thirteen Questions: Reframing Education's Conversation* (New York: Peter Lang, 1992), p. 185.

22. Seaton, Underwood, and Fortune, "The Demographics of Board Service," p. 37.

23. George S. Counts, *The Social Composition of Boards of Education: A Study in the Social Control of Public Education* (Chicago: University of Chicago Press, 1927), p. 81.

24. For overviews of state school politics, see Spring's *Conflict of Interests,* chap. 7, and Wirt and Kirst's *Schools in Conflict,* chaps. 9–10.

25. Dinah Wiley, *State Boards of Education* (Arlington, VA: National Associations of State Boards of Education, 1983), pp. 15–16; Council of Chief State School Officers, *Educational Governance in the States* (Washington, D.C.: U.S. Department of Education, 1983).

26. "Chief State School Officers," *Education Week* (March 20, 1991), p. 22.

27. Wiley, *State Boards of Education.*

28. Dennis P. Doyle and Terry W. Hartle, *Excellence in Education: The States Take Charge* (Washington, D.C.: American Enterprise Institute, 1985).

29. See, for example, the Committee for Economic Development's *Investing in Our Children: Business and the Public Schools* (Washington, D.C.: CED, 1985) and the Carnegie Forum on Education and the Economy's *A Nation Prepared: Teachers for the 21st Century* (New York: Carnegie Forum, 1986).

30. Dennis P. Doyle and Terry W. Hartle, "Leadership in Education: Governors, Legislators, and Teachers," *Phi Delta Kappan* 67 (September 1985): 22–24.

31. Ibid.

32. Spring, *Conflict of Interests,* chap. 7.

33. See Arthur E. Wise's *Legislated Learning: The Bureaucratization of the American Classroom* (Berkeley: University of California Press, 1979) and "The Two Conflicting Trends in School Reform: Legislated Learning Revisited," *Phi Delta Kappan* 69 (January 1988): 328–333. Michael W. Kirst discusses the quantitative mindset in "Sustaining the Momentum of State Education Reform: The Link between Assessment and Financial Support," *Phi Delta Kappan* 67 (January 1986): 341–345.

34. Carnegie Foundation for the Advancement of Teaching, *The Condition of Teaching: A State-by-State Analysis, 1990* (Lawrenceville, NJ: Princeton University Press, 1990), pp. 12, 37–44, 34.

35. U.S. Department of Education, National Center for Education Statistics, *Trends in Academic Progress* (Washington, D.C.: U.S. Government Printing Office, 1991), pp. 1–10.

36. Lamar Alexander, "*Time for Results*: An Overview," *Phi Delta Kappan* 68 (November 1986): 203.

37. National Governors' Association, *Time for Results: The Governors' 1991 Report on Education* (Washington, D.C.: NGA, 1986). Also see the National Governors' Association's *Results in Education: 1987* (Washington, D.C.: NGA, 1987).

38. Alexander, "Time for Results," pp. 202–203.

39. Karen Diegmueller, "No 'Conspicious Improvement' Expected in State Finances," *Education Week* (August 5, 1992), p. 29.

40. See Harris J. Sokolofff and Marvin Lazerson, "When Reform Meets Recession," *Education Week* (October 3, 1990), pp. 26–27.

41. Chris Pipho, "Becoming an Education Governor," *Phi Delta Kappan* 72 (May 1991): 656–657.

42. Lonnie Harp, "States' Fiscal Woes Put Education on the Defensive," *Education Week* (January 23, 1991), pp. 22, 24.

43. For contrasting accounts of the federal role since World War II, see Joel Spring's *The Sorting Machine Revisited: National Education Policy since 1945,* rev. ed. (White Plains, NY: Longman, 1989), and Diane Ravitch's *The Troubled Crusade: American Education, 1945–1980* (New York: Basic Books, 1983).

44. Lynn Olson, "Title I Turns 20: A Commemoration and Debate," *Education Week* (May 1, 1985), pp. 1, 12–13; U.S. Department of Education, Center for Education Statistics, *Digest of Education Statistics, 1982* (Washington, D.C.: U.S. Government Printing Office, 1982). p. 171.

45. Gary Orfield, *The Reconstruction of Southern Education: The Schools and the 1964 Civil Rights Act* (New York: Wiley, 1969).

46. Joel Spring, *American Education: An Introduction to Social and Political Aspects,* 5th ed. (White Plains, NY: Longman, 1991), chap. 8.

47. Ibid.

48. J. Anthony Lukas, *Common Ground: A Turbulent Decade in the Lives of Three American Families* (New York: Knopf, 1985).

49. Steven Carlson, " 'Appropriate' School Programs: Legal vs. Educational Approaches," *Exceptional Parent* 15 (September 1985): 23, 25–26, 28–30.

50. David L. Clark and Terry A. Astuto, "The Significance and Permanence of Changes in Federal Education Policy," *Educational Researcher* 15 (October 1986): 4–13; Dennis P. Doyle and Terry W. Hartle, "Ideology, Pragmatic Politics, and the Education Budget," in John C. Weicher, ed., *Maintaining the Safety Net: Income Redistribution Programs in the Reagan Administration* (Washington, D.C.: American Enterprise Institute for Public Policy Research, 1984), chap. 6.

51. Ibid.

52. Clark and Astuto, "The Significance and Permanence of Changes," pp. 5–6.; Olson, "Title I Turns 20," p. 12.

53. Julie A. Miller, "21.2 Billion Budget Boosts Major Programs," *Education Week* (February 24, 1988), pp. 1, 17–19; Deborah A. Verstegen and David L. Clark, "The Diminution of Federal Expenditures for Education during the Reagan Administration," *Phi Delta Kappan* 70 (October 1988): 134–138.

54. James Crawford, "Grove City Bill Nears First Senate Hurdle," *Education Week* (May 20, 1987), pp. 11–12; Julie A Miller, "Senate Panel Clears Grove City Measure," *Education Week* (May 27, 1987), p. 14.

55. Lynn Olson, "Inside 'A Nation at Risk,'" *Education Week* (April 27, 1988), pp. 1, 22, 23.

56. Joel Spring, "Education and the Sony War," *Phi Delta Kappan* 65 (April 1984): 534–537.

57. National Commission on Excellence in Education, *A Nation at Risk,* pp. 5, 7.

58. For autobiographical accounts of the two secretaries of education, see Terrel H. Bell's *The Thirteenth Man: A Reagan Cabinet Memoir* (New York: Free Press, 1988) and Wiliam J. Bennett's *The De-Valuing of America: The Fight for Our Culture and Our Children* (New York: Summit Books, 1992).

59. Clark and Astuto, "The Significance and Permanence of Changes," pp. 10–11.

60. Ibid.

61. Quoted in Lynn Olson and Julie A. Miller, "The 'Education President' at Midterm: Mismatch between Rhetoric, Results?" *Education Week* (January 9, 1991), p. 1.

62. Ibid.

63. U.S. Department of Education, *America 2000: An Education Strategy.* Sourcebook (Washington, D.C.: U.S. Department of Education, 1991), p. 19.

64. Bill Clinton, "The Clinton Plan for Excellence in Education," *Phi Delta Kappan* 74 (October 1992): 131, 134.

65. Lynn Olson, "Now Comes the Hard Part," *Teacher Magazine* (April 1990): 12–15.

66. Julie A. Miller, "Educators Hail Nomination of Alexander as Secretary," *Education Week* (January 9, 1991), pp. 1, 32–33; George R. Kaplan, "Lamar Alexander and the Politics of School Reform," *Phi Delta Kappan* 73 (June 1992): 753–756.

67. U.S. Department of Education, *America 2000,* pp. 21–32; George Bush, "A Revolution to Achieve Excellence in Education," *Phi Delta Kappan* 74 (October 1992), 130, 132–133.

68. U.S. Department of Education, *America 2000,* pp. 31–32.

69. Ibid., p. 39.

70. See the four evaluations of America 2000 in *Phi Delta Kappan* 73 (November 1991), especially Harold Howe II's essay "A Bumpy Ride on Four Trains," pp. 192–203.

71. Mark Pitsch, "President's 1993 Budget Will Include $600-Million Increase for Head Start," *Education Week* (January 29, 1992), pp. 1, 26–27.

72. Ibid.; Dennis P. Doyle, "New American Schools Development Corporation," *Phi Delta Kappan* 73 (November 1991): 187.

73. Jonathan Weisman, "Businesses Sign on to Bush Plan, but Many also Raising Concerns," *Education Week* (May 8, 1991), pp. 1, 23.

74. Julie A. Miller, "With a Long Track Record on Education, Campaigner Clinton Speaks with Authority," *Education Week* (February 5, 1992), pp. 1, 14–15.

75. Ibid., p. 15. The quotations are from Clinton, "The Clinton Plan," p. 138.

76. Julie A. Miller, "Behind 'Love' of Clinton, Unease over Policy," *Education Week* (August 5, 1992), pp. 1, 46.

77. Clinton, "The Clinton Plan," p. 135.

78. Ibid.

79. Ibid., p. 136; Jonathan Kozol, *Savage Inequalities: Children in America's Schools* (New York: Crown, 1991).

80. Clinton, "The Clinton Plan," p. 136.

81. Julie A. Miller, "Teacher Delegates Turn Out in Force to Hail Clinton's Record on Education," *Education Week* (August 5, 1992), p. 45.

82. Miller, "With a Long Track Record," p. 14.
83. Ibid.
84. See "Bill Clinton and Education: The Arkansas Story," a special issue of *NEA Now* (August 24, 1992); and "Meet Bill Clinton," *NEA Today* (Ocotober 1992), pp. 10–11.
85. The standard textbook on school finance is Roe L. Johns, Edgar L. Morphet, and Kern Alexander's *The Economics and Financing of Education,* 4th ed. (Englewood Cliffs, NJ: Prentice-Hall, 1983).
86. Bush, "A Revolution," p. 132; National Education Association, *Rankings of the States, 1992* (Washington, D.C.: NEA, 1992), p. 22.
87. In some states, local property taxes are based on an assessed value that is only a percentage of market value—often as low as 10 or 20 percent. These states usually have higher tax rates. For a discussion of these issues, see Michael W. Kirst's *Who Controls Our Schools? American Values in Conflict* (New York: Freeman, 1984), chap. 6.
88. Johns, Morphet, and Alexander, *The Economics and Financing of Education,* pp. 242–243.
89. Charles A. Tesconi, Jr., and Emanuel Hurwitz, Jr., *Education for Whom?: The Question of Equal Educational Opportunity* (New York: Dodd, Mead, 1974), pp. 50–65; Spring, *American Education,* chap. 10.
90. Spring, *American Education,* p. 260.
91. David L. Kirp and Donald N. Jensen, "The New Federalism Goes to Court," *Phi Delta Kappan* 65 (November 1983): 206–210; William Montague, "Education-Finance Formula Is Biased, Texas Court Rules," *Education Week* (May 6, 1987), pp. 1, 19.
92. Lonnie Harp, "School-Finance Suits Look beyond Money to Issues of Quality," *Education Week* (June 17, 1992), pp. 1, 28–29.
93. Newman, "Socioeconomic Class," pp. 194–195.
94. Chris Pipho, "Entire Kentucky Education System Unconstitutional!" *Phi Delta Kappan* 71 (September 1989): 6–7.
95. Robert Rothman, "Ambitious Student-Assessment System Advances," *Education Week* (May 8, 1991), p. 14; Peter West, "Panels Clear Plan to Supply and Link All Kentucky Classes with Computers," *Education Week* (May 13, 1992), p. 18; Chris Pipho, "Re-Forming Education in Kentucky," *Phi Delta Kappan* 71 (May 1990): 662–663; Pipho, "Shaking Up the System," *Phi Delta Kappan* 71 (June 1990): 750.
96. Harp, "School Finance Suits," p. 28; Anne C. Lewis, "Money Talks," *Phi Delta Kappan* 71 (March 1990): 500–501.
97. Pipho, "Re-Forming Education"; Lonnie Harp, "Kentucky Reforms Stay on Track in Legislative Session," *Education Week* (May 13, 1992), p. 18.
98. Chris Pipho, "School Reform: Critical Mass or Critical Mess?" *Phi Delta Kappan* 73 (December 1991): 270–271.

# PART III

# Issues for the 1990s

# CHAPTER 10

# Teachers and the Curriculum

*Autonomy*: the right of the members of an occupation to make their own decisions and use their own judgment. Nearing the end of this book, I want to call attention again to teacher autonomy—the hallmark of professionalism. As autonomy relates to teachers and the curriculum, it is the freedom teachers have to decide what and how to teach. Unfortunately, the prevailing curriculum trends of the last 20 years have reduced teacher autonomy, and this chapter explains how teaching and learning have changed as a result.

Trying to put this chapter in touch with the real world of the schools, I have applied our earlier discussion of philosophies and theories of education directly to the classroom. In chapter 7, we examined a wide range of alternatives in search of what ought to be. Here we are more concerned with what has been, what is, and what lies ahead as we move toward the twenty-first century. Thus our focus is on *essentialism,* the theory that has dominated American education since the mid-1970s. Call it what you will—back to basics, excellence in education, the new basics—essentialism has been in command, although *progressivism* is making a surprising comeback in the 1990s.

The chapter opens with a discussion of back to basics and testing, testing, testing. The repetition is intentional. It reflects the nature of the *measurement-driven curriculum.* We will pay special attention to the conflict between standardized testing and teacher autonomy.

Next, we will examine trends that may be leading toward a *national curriculum* shaped by *national standards* and monitored by *national assessments.* Some plans for national curriculum reform put teachers at the center of the process, while other plans relegate teachers to a marginal role.

What do Americans need to know? This question goes to the heart of the debate over curriculum reform. Our answer begins with a look at the "new basics" curriculum that has moved into place since the release of *A Nation at Risk* in

1983. We will see that this essentialist curriculum now faces a challenge from progressivism. Then we will study the complex concept of *literacy,* which underlies much of the controversy over the curriculum. The debate over different kinds of literacy, especially *cultural literacy,* reflects the divergent views Americans hold of what they need to know.

## BACK TO BASICS AND TESTING, TESTING, TESTING

In the mid-1970s, Americans were convinced public education was in deep trouble. The media gave the nation regular reports on problems in the schools: lax discipline, drug abuse, low standards, incompetent teachers. As proof positive the schools were in bad shape, many citizens pointed to declining scores on standardized tests, most often to the decline on the Scholastic Aptitude Test (SAT). Although it may be difficult to see from our perspective in the 1990s, an era in which standardized testing permeates schools at every level, a significant change occurred when the American public accepted standardized test scores as an important indicator of educational quality.

The president of the College Entrance Examination Board (CEEB) traces the use of the SAT as a quality indicator back to 1974, when "an alert education reporter noticed that the scores had dropped from the previous year. He asked for the figures for earlier years, and was thus able to take public note of the fact that since 1963 there has been a gradual, steady decline." Americans were fascinated. Right there in the numbers was scientific-looking documentation of a nationwide decline in the quality of education. And there, I contend, was a sign that back to basics and testing, testing, testing were just around the corner.[1]

### Outputs and Inputs

The alert reporter had picked up the nation's growing interest in judging schools by their outputs rather than their inputs. Since the release of *Equality of Educational Opportunity* (1966), popularly known as the Coleman Report, the *factory model* of schooling we discussed in chapter 2 had been making a comeback. Average citizens were starting to evaluate schools not by the resources going in but by the products coming out. According to the Coleman Report, there is little or no correlation between school inputs—facilities, programs, and teachers, the things money can buy—and school outputs, *if* the scores of students on standardized achievement tests are used as the outputs.[2]

But should test scores be used that way? Ordinary citizens who had never thought much about standardized testing were puzzled at first. Most parents had never even seen their children's test scores. What could a set of scores tell you that a graded homework assignment, a report card, or a talk with a teacher couldn't?

People who went to elementary and secondary school during the last 20 years may find it hard to believe, but in the not-too-distant past, Americans were just not curious about standardized test scores. In the first place, the complete standardized testing package typically consisted of only one or two IQ tests, several batteries of a nationally normed achievement test, and (for some students) a college-entrance examination. That, in most school systems, was the extent of standardized testing.[3]

In the second place, after teachers, counselors, and administrators reviewed the test scores, into the files they went. Case closed. Educators rarely released information on scores to students or parents, nor did the news media publish school-by-school, district-by-district, and state-by-state comparisons.

Before the 1970s, the question "How good are the local schools?" was usually a request for information on facilities, programs, and teachers. As the seventies wore on, however, the question became an invitation to discuss standardized test scores. Local school board members and administrators responded to *Equality of Educational Opportunity* as if James Coleman had insulted them to their faces. A frantic scramble to prove Coleman wrong ensued.

Trying to argue with Coleman on his own terms, dollars against test scores, local officials adopted the factory model as their own. Hoisting the banner of accountability, they set out to prove the schools could deliver scores for bucks. Citizens who had never paid attention to standardized testing had a bewildering array of nationally normed tests paraded before them: Stanford Achievement, Metropolitan Achievement, California Achievement, Comprehensive Basic Skills, Iowa Basic Skills.[4]

Without fully grasping the magnitude of the change, Americans were learning to think about schooling in a different way. Standardized test scores were becoming *the* measure of educational quality.

By the mid-1970s, with the economy turning sour and a tax revolt brewing, it was obvious that the factory model was not providing the evidence school officials needed to make public education look good. In most districts, scores on the national achievement tests were stagnant or declining. Then the media aggravated the situation by playing up the drop in SAT scores. By the time the CEEB and the Educational Testing Service (ETS) issued a report on the causes of the SAT decline, the average composite score had fallen from 980 in 1963 to 899 in 1977. The composite would fall 9 more points before bottoming out at 890 in 1980 and 1981.

"Why are SAT scores dropping?" people asked. But what they really wanted to know was "What's wrong with the schools?" By the late 1970s, the two questions had become synonymous.

## What's Wrong with the Schools?

The CEEB Report *On Further Examination: Report of the Advisory Panel on the Scholastic Aptitude Test Score Decline* (1977) contained several major conclusions, only one of which Americans wanted to hear. According to the CEEB, there were actually *two* declines: one before 1970 and one after. Moreover the declines had different causes.[5]

The major cause of the initial decline was a change in the pool of test takers. From 1963 to 1970, more students began taking the SAT—in particular, more poor and minority students who in earlier years would have been unable to attend college. Higher education opened its doors to these students, and the federal government eased the way by providing financial assistance. Thus the initial decline was not a sign the schools were in trouble. Americans paid little attention to this conclusion, however. People still cite the "unbroken seventeen-year decline in SAT scores" as evidence that something went wrong in the schools in the sixties, something that did not go right again until the eighties.[6]

Americans have also ignored repeated warnings from CEEB and ETS that college entrance exams are not valid indicators of the nation's "Gross Educational Product." More than a third of all graduating seniors take neither the SAT nor its rival, the ACT. College entrance exam scores tell us nothing about this forgotten third, nor do they provide information on the one-fourth of all 18-year-olds who drop out of school before graduation. In addition, CEEB and ETS say the SAT is an *aptitude test* measuring the potential for further academic work, not an *achievement test* measuring how much students have learned. Finally, CEEB and ETS caution against using college entrance exam scores to compare the states—as the U.S. Department of Education does with its annual "wall chart"—since the number and the socioeconomic background of the test takers varies so widely from state to state.[7]

What people do remember about *On Further Examination* is the conclusion that fit the conventional wisdom: One cause of the decline after 1970 was a "lowering of educational standards" in the schools. According to the report, teachers and administrators had responded to changing times and changing students by making concessions. Teachers and administrators were condoning high rates of student absenteeism. They were practicing grade inflation and social promotion. They were demanding less homework. They were allowing students to take the easy way out, and many students were doing just that, choosing the easiest courses and avoiding critical reading and careful writing. The report also pointed the finger of blame at society—at single-parent homes, television, social and political turmoil, and poorly motivated students—but what the media played up in the report, and what Americans remember, is that the schools had lowered their standards.[8]

*On Further Examination* carefully avoided making teachers the lone villains of the drama. The media and the general public were not so careful. In the late 1970s and early 1980s, the nation declared open season on teachers, engaging in round after round of "teacher bashing."

The assorted charges leveled against teachers were not so much false as misleading. For instance, the charge that teachers are to blame for poor student writing skills is accurate enough to graze the target, but it is nevertheless a cheap shot. Devoid of context, it ignores the social, political, and institutional influences on teaching and learning. How much writing do students do on their own, outside of school? Have the school board and the central office given teachers a decent writing curriculum to work with? And what about teaching load? As Theodore Sizer would later ask in *Horace's Compromise* (1984) and again in *Horace's School* (1992), how often can a high school teacher take home a stack of 120 to 175 compositions and do each of them justice? Factors like these limit what teachers can accomplish.[9]

But in the era before Sizer, John Goodlad, Ernest Boyer, and other progressives came to the defense of teachers, teacher bashers rarely pointed out such constraints. Quite the contrary, the message the public heard was that teachers had too few constraints. Given their weak intellectual ability, teachers had more autonomy than they deserved.

Thus a major goal of the back-to-basics movement of the late 1970s and early 1980s was telling teachers what and how to teach, then testing their students repeatedly to ensure teachers had followed orders. In chapter 7, I described the basics movement as a potent combination of essentialism and behaviorism. The desire to cut education down to the essentials led to an emphasis on reading, writing, and arithmetic at the elementary level and on English, social studies, science, and math at the secondary level. Using the tools of behavioral psychology, curriculum specialists reduced each of the 3Rs to a set of skills and the other subjects to a collection of facts and skills.

Because back to basics originated as a grassroots movement, it varied somewhat from one district to the next, but within each district the goal was standardization: getting a uniform curriculum into place. Supervisors distributed curriculum guides that told teachers, in far greater detail than ever before, what to teach and how to teach it. Standardized tests held teachers and students to the prescribed curriculum. The result, according to curriculum theorist Michael Apple, was the "deskilling" of the teaching force.[10]

To appreciate the significance of this change, consider the example of arithmetic. There are many skills involved in arithmetic and many methods of teaching children to add, subtract, multiply, and divide. Before the back-to-basics movement, teachers in most school districts had considerable freedom to decide which skills to emphasize and which methods to use. Teachers were able to vary their approach, in other words, based on their judgment and expertise.

Anarchy? Not at all. Autonomy. Within certain limits, teachers had individual autonomy. They could help students as they thought best. Their individual autonomy within the classroom allowed teachers to stake their tenuous claim to professionalism—or, more accurately, semiprofessionalism.

## The Measurement-Driven Curriculum

Remember the old saying among teachers: "When I close the classroom door, I'm in charge." Central offices have distributed curriculum guides for years, of course, and teachers have generally ignored them. But since the back-to-basics era, teachers have had to pay more attention to curriculum guides because standardized tests can now check up on teachers by checking on their students. To the degree a local system's curriculum reflects the content of standardized tests, teachers feel pressure to teach by the cookbook.

The *measurement-driven curriculum*—a curriculum in which tests shape teaching rather than the other way around—enables people outside the classroom to reach in and control instruction. I am not trying to make the process sound sinister. The advocates of measurement-driven instruction claim external control can be quite positive, a "catalyst to improve instruction." The evidence they cite is higher scores on standardized tests—on the tests for which teachers directly rehearse their students, that is.[11]

Teachers have become especially adept at rehearsing students for minimum competency tests, a breed of standardized tests developed during the back-to-basics era. These tests give school officials a way to monitor the work of teachers in every academic subject. Some minimum competency tests are system-wide final exams administered at the end of a semester or year; they determine a certain percentage of a student's grade in a course. Other minimum competency tests are checkpoint exams used to help decide whether a student should be promoted from one grade to the next. Still others are high school graduation exams covering a variety of basic skills students presumably will need to survive in society.[12]

Minimum competency tests, developed first at the local level, became a popular state reform in the years just before *A Nation at Risk*. Before the states took command of the excellence movement, they increased the momentum of back-to-basics by jumping on the minimum competency testing bandwagon. By 1980, 38 states required some form of minimum competency testing, and by 1990, 47 states were on the bandwagon.[13]

For all their popularity with school officials, minimum competency tests have come under sharp attack since they first appeared. Even the essentialist *A Nation at Risk* brushed them aside with the comment that they "fall short of what is needed, as the 'minimum' tends to become the 'maximum,' thus lowering educational standards for all." As we saw in chapter 7, minimum competency testing stresses lower-level rather than higher-level skills, which encourages teachers to emphasize rote learning rather than critical thinking.[14]

Beyond its value to school officials as a classroom monitor, minimum competency testing is a powerful political tool. When school officials were desperately seeking test scores—any test scores—that were rising rather than falling, they hit on minimum competency tests. Soon a newsworthy pattern appeared in district after district and state after state. As students and teachers got the knack of the tests, scores rose steadily and impressively. Within two or three years, passing rates climbed well above 90 percent and stayed there.[15]

Minimum competency tests bring the public good news. The schools are doing a better job, they announce. Almost everyone's child is minimally competent.

The other side of the coin is that some people's children do not pass the test. An analysis of minimum competency tests used as high school graduation examinations shows that the students who fail are disproportionately poor, minority, and disabled—the "at risk," as they are euphemistically called. Almost without exception, teachers and administrators can identify these students before the tests are ever given.[16]

So why have the tests? Because they symbolize a get-tough mentality. They reassure the public that the schools have standards. They provide an education box score that looks better than SAT scores, which fell from a 906 in 1987 to 896 in 1991—to their lowest point since the beginning of the school reforms inspired by *A Nation at Risk*. The verbal score of 422 in 1991 was the lowest ever recorded.

# The National Assessment of Educational Progress: A National Curriculum Driver?

Minimum competency test scores also look better than trends on the National Assessment of Educational Progress (NAEP), a battery of tests administered to a sample of 9-, 13-, and 17-year-olds at regular intervals since 1969. Educators generally regard the NAEP as the best of the education box scores because it taps a representative sample of the nation's students and because teachers feel no pressure to prepare their students for the test. Or, I should say, teachers *have felt* no pressure, but that may change, as we will find later in this chapter.

Interpreting trends in NAEP scores is like taking a Rorschach test. What people see in the numbers reveals their feeling about U.S. education, especially the public schools. Still, observers tend to agree that the most favorable NAEP trend of the past two decades is the significant improvement in the scores of African- and Hispanic-American students. The scores of white students have changed relatively little. Still, large gaps in performance remain between white students and minority students.[17]

Analyzing NAEP trends in more detail helps shed light on the effects of the back-to-basics movement. In reading, for instance, the subject generally regarded as the most basic of the basics, the scores of 9- and 13-year-olds improved during the 1970s, before the movement really took hold, and declined while the movement flourished during the 1980s. The reading scores of 17-year-olds showed a slight improvement over the two decades. On every NAEP reading test, all three age groups demonstrated greater mastery of lower-level skills than higher-level skills. Trends in writing scores are similar to those in reading.[18]

Different trends prevail in science, a subject that has not been viewed as basic enough to receive the attention paid to other core subjects. The scores of all three age groups fell during the 1970s and made a partial recovery during the 1980s. Even so, the science scores of 9- and 13-year-olds were no better in 1990 than they had been in 1969, and the scores of 17-year-olds were worse. The recovery that did occur during the 1980s was in lower-level skills. Proficiency in higher-level scientific skills remained poor for all three age groups. Trends in math scores are similar.[19]

The NAEP is the test to watch in the 1990s. During the second Reagan administration, Secretary of Education William Bennett and former Governor Lamar Alexander of Tennessee led a successful campaign to turn the NAEP, a high-quality but low-profile standardized test, into "The Nation's Report Card." The NAEP expanded to cover more students and more subjects and, for the first time, began reporting scores on a state-by-state basis. When Alexander became secretary of education under George Bush, he incorporated the NAEP into the administration's America 2000 proposal for a national system of educational standards and assessments. Congress rejected most of America 2000 but continued to expand the NAEP.[20]

As we will see when we discuss national standards and assessments, the NAEP is well on its way to becoming a high-stakes test. More than just a monitor of academic progress, the NAEP may soon be a test with life and career consequences for individual students—a national test driving a national curriculum.

## The Children of Lake Wobegon

Meanwhile, school officials who want to play up a good box score can brag about trends in the Stanford, Metropolitan, Iowa, and other nationally normed achievement tests we discussed earlier. Or can they?

John Cannell, a West Virginia physician, thought the news sounded a little too good when he heard that, in almost every local school district in his state, the scores of elementary students on the Comprehensive Test of Basic Skills were above the national norm. Because West Virginia, one of the nation's poorest states, ranks low on most other educational indicators, the doctor was surprised. Checking the data on several neighboring states, he found that their students, too, were above average. With surprise turning to suspicion, in 1987 Cannell conducted a survey of achievement testing across the nation. He discovered that state superintendents in every state boast that their students are above average.[21]

In other words, scoring above the norm *is* the norm. In all 32 of the states with statewide testing programs, elementary students scored above average; in the 18 states with locally selected tests, elementary students in the "vast majority" of the districts scored above average. Across the nation, Cannell estimates that about 90 percent of school districts and 70 percent of elementary students are above the national norm.[22]

These happy results suggest most Americans have moved to Lake Wobegon, Minnesota, Garrison Keillor's mythical radio community where "the women are strong, the men are handsome, and all the children are above average." Statistically, of course, the results don't add up. It is impossible for 70 percent of the students and 90 percent of the districts to be above average. Friends for Education, a group started by Dr. Cannell, has filed consumer fraud complaints against the four major publishers of nationally normed achievement tests.

The Lake Wobegon effect confirms what many teachers have been saying since the late 1970s: If the public wants higher scores, school officials will find a way to deliver them. As Cannell puts it, "The main purpose of the tests is looking good."[23]

In 1990, the CBS News program *60 Minutes* blew the whistle on the Lake Wobegon effect. A segment titled "Teacher Is a Cheater" focused on a South Carolina teacher who lost her job after admitting she gave her students the answers to a standardized test. She cheated; she acknowledged she was wrong. But instead of blaming the teacher, *60 Minutes* pointed the finger at her principal and her state superintendent of schools—indeed, at the entire education establishment—for putting pressure on teachers to teach tests and raise scores. Merit bonuses for teachers as well as grades, promotions, and graduation for students can ride on standardized test scores. The South Carolina teacher said she was only trying to keep "at risk" students from losing a game whose stakes are becoming very high.[24]

## Curriculum Alignment

Beyond outright cheating—which we hope is rare—how does the Lake Wobegon effect work? Because national achievement tests are renormed only once every few years, school systems have a chance to align their curriculum with the tests. What *align* means is that central office personnel change the curriculum to conform to the content of the tests, and teachers put emphasis on material they know the tests will cover. While the norms stay fixed for several years, the scores rise. More and more students become above average. The news about the schools sounds better and better.[25]

One of the most important curriculum debates of the 1990s is over teaching the test. Are there ethical and unethical ways to teach a test? Obviously, giving students answers to specific questions that will appear on a test is unethical. But what about showing students questions and answers that have appeared on earlier versions of the same test? And is it ethical to slant the entire curriculum toward the test to help students get better scores? Is it educationally sound? Students often take 10, 15, or more standardized tests each year, and teachers spend large amounts of time prepping their classes to look good. "Skill-'n'-drill," teachers call it.[26]

It is helpful to look back on similar debates in the early days of the back-to-basics movement. Critics warned that standardized tests would soon dictate the content of the curriculum. No, defenders of the movement replied. Educators design the curriculum, and testing companies can devise tests to measure whatever educators want. Score one point for the critics.

The critics also argued that there is more to any subject than any test can measure, but given the pressure to raise scores, teachers would narrow their instruction to just the items on the test. Not to worry, said back-to-basics advocates. Good teachers already cover what the test covers, and bad teachers need to start somewhere. Score a point for both sides.[27]

As curriculum alignment increases, even excellent teachers are feeling pressure to teach the test. Chris Pipho of the Education Commission of the States looks into the future of curriculum alignment:

> The advent of new, more powerful microcomputers now may be moving schools into yet another new era of accountability. . . . The selling point is higher test scores by aligning the instructional objectives with the goals and objectives of the state testing programs and other national normed tests. Test-item analyses and class, grade and school building status reports can be easily printed and instruction targeted to the weak areas. By cross-referencing objectives, teachers can locate the page in the textbook that can be used to help increase student test scores. . . . Principals and superintendents under the gun to look good on state test comparisons have in turn put teachers under the same kind of pressure.[28]

One superintendent whose district has aligned its curriculum to the tests says he is sold on the approach. His goal, cited by Pipho, is to "be able to track every student on a day-to-day basis, objective-by-objective.'' The superintendent will be also able to track every teacher, in just the same way.

## Pausing to Reconsider Testing, Testing, Testing

Standardized testing is time consuming and expensive. In states and districts that go in for testing in a big way, officials estimate that the process consumes a full month—more than 10 percent of the academic year. Time that could be used for other purposes slips away as teachers prepare students, administer tests, analyze results, and take remedial action.[29]

Testing is a multibillion-dollar industry in the United States. Since the beginning of America's latest back-to-basics movement, testing companies have tapped into the elementary and secondary school market as never before. Above and beyond fees paid to testing companies, a little-discussed expense of testing lies in personnel costs. Take the average teacher's salary of $34,148; multiply it by the percentage of time the teacher devotes to standardized testing; then multiply that number by 2,429,967, the number of teachers in the nation. If the average teacher spends only 5 percent of her or his time on standardized testing, the annual personnel costs amount to more than $4 billion.[30]

In the teacher-bashing era of the late 1970s and early 1980s, politicians, school officials, and the general public dismissed teacher complaints about excessive testing as sour grapes. Teachers who complained obviously had something to hide. Teachers who resisted were afraid of accountability, or so the rationalization went. But now the message teachers have been sending for years may be finally getting through. All but the most ardent advocates of behavioral essentialism are pausing to reconsider standardized testing.

Enough is enough, many state and local officials are saying, often citing time and money as reasons for cutting back on testing. Beyond these bottom-line considerations, the revival of educational progressivism (see chapter 7) and the push for teacher empowerment (see chapter 4) give officials other reasons to back off. Since the late 1980s, officials have been consolidating standardized testing programs and trying to reduce the overlap among different tests that measure the same skills. At the moment, informal autonomy seems to be flowing back toward teachers. For now, they are breathing a sigh of relief.

## NATIONAL STANDARDS PLUS NATIONAL ASSESSMENTS EQUALS NATIONAL CURRICULUM?

Teachers had better catch their breath while they can. As testing fever subsides at the state and local levels, it is rising at the national level. Controversy is swirling around the idea of nationalizing public education. Would national standards and national assessments produce a de facto national curriculum? How would a nationalized education system affect teaching and learning?

As we saw in chapter 9, decentralization has always been a hallmark of American education. But we also saw how local control has eroded as the federal government and state governments have asserted themselves. The reform movements of the 1980s and 1990s have made Americans more interested in comparing education across school districts and across states. Citizens want to see how their local schools rate. Opinion polls show about 70 percent of Americans in favor of "national achievement standards and goals," "standardized national testing programs," and a "standardized national curriculum."[31]

In one sense, we already have a national testing system. Across the United States, students bound for college take either the SAT or the ACT. Virtually all K–12 students take a nationally standardized test such as the California or the Iowa. Critics of this loose "system" argue that we have tried testing, testing, testing since the late 1970s, and the results are abysmal. Why would anyone propose more of the same to reform American education? Standardized testing is part of the problem, critics argue, not part of the solution.[32]

## The New Standards Project

Interestingly enough, some advocates of national assessment agree with the critics that existing tests are poor indicators of educational quality. The SAT and ACT, as we have seen, are simply not designed to provide box scores on American education. As for the nationally normed K–12 tests, they are an "absolutely terrible model of the kind of learning we want." Focused on isolated facts and lower-level skills, they "break [knowledge] into little bits so any nincompoop can fill in the bubbles."[33]

These harsh words about standardized tests come from Lauren Resnick, an educational psychologist at the University of Pittsburgh who is trying to develop a new system of national assessment. Along with Marc Tucker, the principal author of the Carnegie Forum's *A Nation Prepared* (1986), Resnick is codirecting the New Standards Project, an ambitious reform program that involves states and school districts enrolling nearly half the nation's students. Although Resnick shares the critics' disdain for existing tests, she nevertheless believes "there is zero political chance that this country, any time soon, will give up its current national testing system without having a replacement for it." Resnick and Tucker want to link the new assessment system they have in mind to new standards and a new curriculum.[34]

Resnick and Tucker argue that "national content standards" must be the first item on the reform agenda. Organizations such as the National Council of Teachers of Mathematics and the National Council of Teachers of English must take the lead in developing broad performance standards in each core subject. Once national standards are in place, classroom teachers must have the freedom to build a "thinking curriculum" that can help students meet the standards. "Teachers are the center," Tucker says. Only teachers can "change what happens in the classroom." Assessment experts can then devise a variety of ways to evaluate learning. A national system that is voluntary, teacher-based, and flexible, Tucker argues, can avoid the problems of the compulsory, teacher-proof, rigid reforms of the back-to-basics era.[35]

## Getting Reform Right

As attractive as the New Standards Project is from the standpoint of teacher autonomy, other proposals are attracting more attention in the political area. President Bush's America 2000 strategy, for instance, called for the development of "world class standards" in the five core subjects of English, math, science, history, and geography. Bush also proposed a voluntary system of American Achievement Tests, keyed to the new standards, to measure fourth-, eighth- and twelfth-grade students against national benchmarks. Hoping to see national tests in place by 1994, Bush suggested the "rapid deployment" of slightly modified tests from the NAEP. In other words, he wanted results—and fast.[36]

Congress gutted most of America 2000, including the American Achievement Tests, but the Democratic majority seemed just as impatient as Mr. Bush to bring some form of national testing on line. Ignoring the advice of educators that research and development should take the rest of the decade—or longer— Congress forged ahead and ordered an expanded version of the NAEP for 1994.

Many educators are worried that the NAEP may soon turn into *the* test for teachers to teach as a nationally aligned curriculum clicks into place in one district and one state after another. If the NAEP does create a de facto national curriculum, the test will serve as the ultimate example of top-down reform, hurriedly imposed without adequate consultation with teachers.[37]

America's teachers—and their students—deserve better. Setting national standards in each core subject should not be a quick-and-dirty process. The National Council of Teachers of Mathematics released the first set of national standards in 1989. Although many school districts are giving the standards good reviews, the math council already sees the need for revisions. Now the councils in the other core subjects must complete their standards and try them out with real students and real teachers in real classrooms. The process will take time.[38]

It will take even more time to reform the curriculum and design new assessments. The experience of Vermont, a state in the forefront of reform, illustrates the magnitude of the task. Elementary school teachers in Vermont are finding the new math standards quite challenging, for the standards emphasize problem solving and application instead of number drill and computation. In one school trying to implement the new standards, Vermont's state superintendent of schools watched as a teacher explained

> transformational geometry to 4th graders using only a square of paper. She and the students folded the paper, tore along the fold, and then talked about the shapes they created. . . . They put the shapes together, tried on the proper mathematical terms, stopped to write in their journals about what they had discovered, and then pushed on. A vision of mathematics as something one does, as a matter of problem-solving and communication, was what guided the enterprise. There were no worksheets and no textbooks. But I saw a lot of rigorous mathematics.[39]

Revising the curriculum and reshaping instruction cannot be accomplished overnight.

Assessment reform also takes time. Vermont's state superintendent says the new math curriculum "makes old-style, multiple-choice tests absurd." The superintendent is basically right, Resnick and Tucker admit, even though multiple-choice tests will almost certainly be one part of a national assessment system. The other parts, though, may not be pencil-and-paper tests at all. They may be performance assessments that evaluate what students know by giving them a chance to show what they can do.[40]

## Student Portfolios and Other Performance Assessments

*Performance assessment* involves "active application of knowledge and skill to problems, as much as possible drawn from the world outside the school."[41] Advocates describe performance assessment as more "authentic" then pencil-and-paper testing because it "elicit[s] the actual performances that we want students to be good at."[42]

Incorporated into a national assessment system, performance assessment could complement traditional testing. One day, for instance, a student could take a nationally standardized test of verbal and quantitative literacy. The next day, the student could participate in a national performance assessment that involves assembling a piece of equipment from written instructions and schematic diagrams.[43]

Other performance assessments focus on long-term work. *Portfolios,* which we examined as a teacher evaluation strategy in chapter 3, are also gaining acceptance as a way to evaluate students. A student's writing portfolio could contain representative materials collected over the course of a school year, including poems, short stories, and writing from subjects other than English. A math portfolio could include homework assignments, math applications in other subjects, and word problems the student writes about situations in the home or community. To highlight each portfolio, the student could select a "best piece" of work for the entire year.[44]

How is performance assessment working so far? After Vermont began a pilot program with portfolios in 1990–1991, teacher and student enthusiasm initially ran high. Soon, though, the old problems of time and money surfaced. Helping students assemble portfolios is time consuming, Vermont teachers have found, and evaluating portfolios takes still more time. The state superintendent's plan was for teachers to score their own students' writing portfolios and for 300 teacher volunteers to evaluate math portfolios statewide. When the superintendent asked the volunteers to serve without extra pay, however, only half the number he needed showed up.[45]

Time and money. Is America ready for performance assessment on a national scale? Keep in mind that Vermont is a small state. Imagine the logistics involved in a national system of performance assessment. Lauren Resnick estimates teachers would need up to eight weeks of paid professional leave each year to make such a system work properly. She adds that teachers in China and Japan already spend up to half their paid time "developing their lessons, developing their materials, and developing themselves."[46]

But this is America. Our nation lacks the political will to lighten high school teaching loads, Theodore Sizer points out, even though we know they make it impossible for teachers to do justice to their students. Can we expect the same nation to support reform that is even more expensive and even more fundamental? "It's all very well to change the writing assessment," Sizer states, "but it's something else to make it possible for teachers to teach writing properly. That costs money; that means changing the insides of schools; that's not happening."[47]

## The Promise and Peril of National Reform

Many advocates of national standards and assessments seem genuinely committed to changing the insides of schools, but they realize how much time and money will be needed. They also know the reforms they are promoting could turn into an "empty political promise with no resources to realize them"—a form of "national cruelty" to overworked teachers and unprepared students.[48]

What Americans may eventually get as their national test is an expanded NAEP. In the past, the NAEP has been administered to a sample of 9-, 13-, and 17-year-olds. If Congress extends its coverage to *all* students of those ages, the NAEP may never evolve beyond the multiple-choice format. A recent revision of the math test for 9-year-olds *did* break the multiple-choice mold—but it cost $150 per student to administer and score.[49]

If U.S. education continues to move toward national standards and national assessments, the national curriculum these reforms usher in may well amount to more basics and more testing—in short, to more of the same. And thus we return to a question we have asked throughout this book: How much time and money are Americans willing to invest to get reform right?

## WHAT DO AMERICANS NEED TO KNOW?

## Essentialists, Progressives, and the New Basics

In chapter 7, we studied the ongoing tug of war between the educational theories of essentialism and progressivism, a contest entering a new phase in the 1990s. Even though essentialists have done their best to discredit their rivals with the general public, progressives are gaining strength again. But it is still too early to declare a winner for the 1990s.

After the release of *A Nation at Risk* in 1983, talking about the Five New Basics was very in. Four years of English, three years of mathematics, three years of science, three years of social studies, one-half year of computer science—these new basics are essential for all high school students, the National Commission on Excellence in Education (NCEE) told Americans. The arts are also important, the commission stated, and college-bound students need at least one more basic, foreign languages.[50]

Essentialists have used the NCEE's recommendations as a yardstick to measure the success of curriculum reform. Looking back on curriculum trends since 1983, essentialists have mixed feelings about what the yardstick indicates. On the one hand, 42 states have raised their course work requirements for high school graduation. On the other hand, most states still fall short of NCEE recommendations. The average state's requirements are four years of English, two to three years of social studies, and only two years each of math and science. Only ten states require three years of math, and just four states require three years of science. Overall, a mere three states—Florida, Louisiana, and Pennsylvania—mandate the complete set of New Basics for all students.[51]

State legislators who love to talk about school reform have shown that their rhetoric and their wallets are in different places. In 1991, Alabama proudly became the first state to exceed the new basics by requiring four years of study in all four basic subjects. At the same time, though, the Alabama legislature postponed enforcing the requirements until the state could pay for them. The posture reflects the split between school reform and political reality in many other states. Nationwide, it would be an expensive proposition indeed to implement the recommendations of *A Nation at Risk.* Training and hiring the teachers needed to teach the additional math and science courses alone would carry a price tag of several billion dollars.[52]

Progressives fault the Reagan and Bush administration for talking up higher standards and passing down the bills to state and local taxpayers. The two administrations did little to increase the supply of teachers beyond encouraging state and local school systems to hire virtually anyone with a bachelor's degree in the arts and sciences (see chapter 1). Where is the kind of financial support the federal government provided through the National Defense Education Act of 1958, progressives ask?

According to the progressives, essentialists also emphasize quantity over quality. As we saw in chapter 9, excellence in education has often meant more of the same, especially for the least able students. One more year of worksheet science, another required course in skill-'n'-drill math—this is excellence? The quick fix isn't working, says perennialist Mortimer Adler, who joins the progressives in charging that the weakest students are still drinking dirty water.

William Bennett, one of Adler's favorite adversaries, recognizes the problems with more-of-the-same curriculum reform. Bennett designed the model essentialist curriculum of *James Madison High School* (1987) and *James Madison Elementary School* (1988) to offer something different: studies that are common to all and challenging to all. Bennett stipulates that all students must choose their three years of math from algebra I, plane and solid geometry, algebra II and trigonometry, statistics and precalculus, and calculus. The science curriculum requires students to select three courses from astronomy/geometry, biology, chemistry, and physics or principles of technology. In every area of the curriculum, Bennett outlines rigorous content.[53]

Yet school districts have hardly rushed to adopt the James Madison curriculum. One reason is that the curriculum is out of alignment with the standardized tests that essentialists themselves have put into place. An even more fundamental reason is that many educators simply do not believe every student can rise to meet high demands. As one teacher really told me, "Average and below-average kids just can't do what Bennett expects—at least not in schools as they are today.''

Bennett, Chester Finn, and other leading essentialists reply that kids will achieve if adults insist on achievement. If adults don't, kids won't. This answer sounds good in political forums, for it implies that respect for authority, hard work, and other traditional values can cure the ills of American education.[54]

Simplistic and deceptive, counter the progressives. Bennett and Finn still haven't learned their lessons. Even in their latest books—Bennett's *The De-Valuing of America* (1992) and Finn's *We Must Take Charge* (1991)—the two essentialists are not paying attention to the problems that keep teachers from reaching more students. Crowded classrooms, different learning styles, outmoded teaching methods—Bennett and Finn either ignore or minimize these problems. And when progressives propose their own solutions, essentialists reject them. Lower student-teacher ratios? Not cost effective, essentialists claim. Multicultural education? Academically weak and culturally divisive. Cooperative learning? Holds bright kids back. And so the arguments continue.[55]

## The Great Literacy Debate

The debate over what Americans need to know often degenerates into shouting matches over why Americans don't know enough and how to reform the schools to make them learn more. The issues are considerably more complex, and underlying all the arguments is the concept of *literacy*. Unfortunately, people often toss the concept around without bothering to define it.

*Basic (or rudimentary) literacy* is the ability to read and write a simple message. By that standard, between 85 and 99.5 percent of adult Americans are literate. Estimates of about 95 percent appear to be most accurate.[56]

Then there is *functional literacy,* the ability to read and write well enough to perform adequately in daily life. Because functional literacy is a highly subjective concept, estimates of the functional literacy of adult Americans vary widely—from a high of 97 percent to an astonishing low of 46 percent. The media have focused a great deal of attention on alarmist studies depicting a nation hobbled by a massive, increasing illiteracy problem.[57]

When we consider that about 25 percent of the nation's students drop out of school before high school graduation, perhaps even the gloomiest estimates of functional literacy should not shock us. Still, it is hard to believe that one of every two adults lacks the literacy skills necessary to cope with life.

*Literacy: Profiles of America's Young Adults* (1986), a study conducted for the NAEP, dismisses alarmist estimates of rampant functional illiteracy as ''scare figures.'' They may make sensational copy for the evening news, but they mislead the nation about the nature and extent of the problem. No, ''people are not walking around bumping into walls because they can't read,'' the director of the NAEP study reassures us.[58]

The study suggests Americans have an oversimplified view of literacy. It is not a single skill, something people either have or lack. Literacy is a continuum of many skills.

The ETS researchers who conducted the NAEP study identify three different kinds of literacy, each involving a number of skills: the *prose literacy* necessary for understanding and using information in narrative texts; the *document literacy* needed to understand and use graphic and tabular information; and the *quantitative literacy* necessary to do the arithmetic involved in balancing a checkbook, for example, or figuring a tip. For each kind of literacy, the researchers measured the performance of young adults on everyday tasks of varying difficulty.

The results are not surprising: the more complex the task, the poorer the performance. While almost 96 percent of young adults can locate a single item of information in a moderately long newspaper article, fewer than 9 percent can state the theme of a poem that uses an unfamiliar metaphor. More than 98 percent can find the expiration date on a driver's license, but only 10 to 30 percent can perform various tasks involving arrival and departure times on a bus schedule. While about 90 percent can add two figures on a bank deposit slip, fewer than 10 percent can use unit pricing to determine the best value at a grocery store.[59]

America is not on the verge of collapse, to be sure, but "the question is whether people with only moderate literacy skills have the flexibility to shift into new environments." Faced with the changing demands of a technological society, the schools must stop "shooting for the bottom line," the president of ETS concludes. "We need to work for higher levels of performance than typically is accounted for in state minimum-competency standards."[60]

## Is Literacy Slipping Away?

In the 1991 study *Literacy in the United States: Readers and Reading since 1880,* historian Carl F. Kaestle of the University of Wisconsin, Madison, puts the arguments over literacy into perspective. Kaestle and his research associates join the debate over "whether students today are performing better than their age- and grade-level counterparts of yesterday."[61]

As we saw earlier, one popular position in the debate is that U.S. education went astray in the late 1960s and 1970s. Advocates of this position claim students' reading skills steadily improved from the early 1900s through the mid-1960s but then went into a tailspin, only to recover somewhat when the schools went back to basics. People who hold this opinion regard the era before the 1960s as the golden age of American education. The evidence they cite usually consists of "then-and-now" studies, which involve "giving a group of students today the same test that was given to a comparable group of students years earlier," and trends in standardized test scores.[62]

After evaluating the evidence, Kaestle rejects the golden age view. Then-and-now studies are technically flawed and inconclusive, he states. Kaestle also issues warnings about interpreting trends in college entrance exams and other nationally standardized tests. After cautioning that "the data are sketchy and the trends are murky," Kaestle and his associates nevertheless venture the "educated guess" that "schoolchildren of the same age and socioeconomic status have been performing at similar levels throughout most of the twentieth century."[63]

Kaestle takes an especially close look at trends in standardized test scores from the 1960s to the present. The evidence simply does not support the popular view that "permissive schools" turned out poor readers during the late 1960s and 1970s, he maintains, nor that the back-to-basics movement improved reading skills by raising standards and restoring order to the schools.[64]

Kaestle also evaluates the evidence on functional literacy. A variety of studies suggest that between 20 to 30 percent of adult Americans have difficulty with the reading they do in everyday life. Moreover, there may be a mismatch between "school-reading skills" and "job-literacy skills." The school curriculum focuses mainly on prose literacy, and within that area on stories and poems. Reading in the workplace, by contrast, involves prose of a technical nature (memoranda and advertising copy, for instance) and requires document literacy skills as well.[65]

Finally, Kaestle looks at literacy differences among groups. Although the gender gap has virtually disappeared, differences associated with class, race, and ethnicity persist. "Even if schools today are performing about as well as they have in the past," he reminds us, "they have never excelled at educating minorities and the poor."[66] Despite the gains minorities have recently posted on the NAEP, Kaestle warns against complacency, because large literacy gaps remain. In another study, *The Subtle Danger* (1987), Kaestle and his colleagues caution that as minorities and the poor become a larger part of the school population and labor force during the 1990s, lagging literacy skills will prove costly "to the economy, to the national defense, and to the attainment of economic and social-justice goals."[67]

In the final analysis, we should not base our quest for higher levels of literacy on squiggles in test score curves or fears about economic competition. "The fundamental threat posed by America's literacy problems today is not that the Japanese will beat us at math tests and computer chips," Kaestle concludes, "but that democracy will wane in the twenty-first century." Faced with the demands lying ahead, an America that continues to reserve higher-level literacy skills for the privileged few cannot survive.[68]

## Cultural Literacy

My use of the word *continues* in the last sentence reflects Kaestle's belief that our nation has never done a good job of sharing higher-level literacy. Some Americans strongly disagree, blaming the schools for failing to do today what they once did so well: not only developing literacy skills but transmitting literate culture.

A well-matched pair of essentialist treatises published in 1987 set the tone for a new round in the literacy debate: *Cultural Literacy: What Every American Needs to Know* by E. D. Hirsch, Jr., and *What Do Our 17-Year-Olds Know? A Report on the First National Assessment of History and Literature* by Diane Ravitch and Chester Finn. That year also marked the appearance of Allan Bloom's *The Closing of the American Mind,* a perennialist critique of higher education. William Bennett drew heavily on these three books in his curriculum for the James Madison schools, and the books by Hirsch and Bloom were on the best-seller lists for weeks—a testimony to the continuing popularity of traditional theories of education.[69]

Taken together, these works advance the position that some knowledge is so valuable all Americans should possess it. There is indeed a common culture, and the schools are obligated to transmit it. *Cultural literacy,* according to its advocates, is familiarity with the knowledge educated people share. The newsworthy part of debate over cultural literacy is the claim that today's schools, unlike those in the past, are doing a woefully poor job of exposing students to the common culture.

When Hirsch, Ravitch, Finn, and Bloom first went public with the news that the schools are graduating one class of cultural illiterates after another, journalists stopped to listen. Since then, conservative newspaper columnists have had a field day criticizing the curriculum. James J. Kilpatrick has observed with characteristic bluntness that "the typical 11th-grader, culturally speaking, is an ignoramus." William F. Buckley, perhaps with tongue in cheek, has proposed to solve the problem by requiring students to pass "a common information IQ test" in order to get a driver's license.[70]

Such a test, says Buckley, could be based on the list of nearly 5,000 items "every American needs to know" in the back of Hirsch's book *Cultural Literacy.* Drawn up by Hirsch and his associates, the now-famous list is an attempt to define a cultural knowledge base for the nation and its schools. As a prospective teacher, you should read the list—and the entire book—for yourself. There are many obvious choices on the list: Shakespeare, nuclear energy, California. There are also some curious choices: Fanny Farmer, éminence grise, Marianas Trench.

Trying to validate the list, Hirsch sent a multiple-choice test based on some of the items to 600 lawyers, "on the assumption that lawyers are literate." Those who returned the test correctly identified an average of 92 out of 100 items. Since cultural literacy is, by definition, familiarity with the knowledge educated people share, Hirsch pronounced his list valid. Then, presumably he awarded a framed certificate of commendation to every lawyer who scored 92 or above.[71]

My little jest mirrors the more lighthearted criticism of *Cultural Literacy.* Including the list in the book was a stroke of marketing genius—it made large numbers of people buy the book—but it may have been an intellectual blunder. The list makes for great cocktail party conversation, and that is part of the problem. The message of the book gets lost in jokes about the list.

Veteran teacher Susan Ohanian, a frequent contributor to the popular education press, calls it a "loony list." Why does it include Babe Ruth and Ty Cobb but not Lou Gehrig or Hank Aaron? she wants to know. Why Gilbert and Sullivan but not Rodgers and Hammerstein? Why the "Rime of the Ancient Mariner" but not *Moby Dick*? Why the trombone but not the tuba?[72]

The list is arbitrary, not in the sense of capricious or whimsical (check your dictionary), but in the sense of discretionary and perhaps even dictatorial. Although Hirsch regards the list as "provisional" and not "definitive," he titles the list "What Literate Americans Know." These 5,000 items are among the things my educated colleagues and I know, he says, and look—some lawyers agree with us. Trying hard not to sound smug, Hirsch includes with every book a card readers can return to suggest items for addition or deletion.[73]

By his very tone, though, Hirsch sets the list up for a fall. And by its very nature, the list turns cultural literacy into a game of Trivial Pursuit.

Hirsch makes a stronger case for cultural literacy in the body of the book. "Facts and skills are inseparable," he says. Unless children become familiar with the traditional background information of literate culture, they will never be able to move from lower-level to higher-level academic skills. Content is not neutral. Only a curriculum that teaches reading skills in the context of literate culture can prepare young children to make sense of ever more complex reading.[74]

According to Hirsch, the content of worthwhile, significant reading *is* literate culture. The significant reading materials with which Americans can whet their minds are not stories about Dick and Jane and their successors; they are about Ulysses and the Cyclops, George Washington and Abraham Lincoln—and approximately 4,996 other subjects. Unless students acquire this stock of factual information, all the "decoding skills" in the world can take them only so far.

William Bennett echoes this argument in *The De-Valuing of America*. "Acquiring 'skills' should not come at the expense of acquiring knowledge," he insists. And, like Hirsch, Bennett believes changes in the curriculum have harmed students.[75]

Until the 1940s, Hirsch argues, the schools supplied literate culture to students from all socioeconomic backgrounds. Then, under the influence of John Dewey, William Heard Kilpatrick, and other progressive educators, teachers and administrators overthrew the traditional fact-based curriculum for a curriculum based on broad understandings and general skills.

The new curriculum, harmful to all students, has been disastrous to students from "illiterate homes." Acquiring cultural literacy neither at home nor at school, these students have suffered most from the curriculum revolution. Children from "literate homes" suffered less in the early stages of the revolution, but as these more fortunate students grew up and *their* children went to school and studied the new curriculum, the decline in literacy from one generation to the next became noticeable. By the 1960s and 1970s, the decline had become so obvious the nation could no longer ignore it.[76]

Diane Ravitch and Chester Finn tell much the same story in *What Do Our 17-Year-Olds Know?* The schools got off the track when they shirked their responsibility for transmitting a common culture, and now the nation is suffering the consequences.

To find out what 17-year-olds do know, Ravitch and Finn analyzed the first NAEP assessment of history and literature, which high school juniors took in 1986. In both history and literature, the students answered correctly only a few more than half the multiple-choice questions. Looking forward, perhaps, to the day when the NAEP may drive a national curriculum, Ravitch and Finn offered their own assessment of the situation: "If there were such a thing as a national report card for those studying American history and literature, then we would have to say that this nationally representative sample of eleventh grade students earns failing marks in both subjects."[77]

The media were fascinated. Reporters told the nation that one-third of the students could not place Columbus's landing on North America or the signing of the Declaration of Independence within the correct half century. Two-thirds could not do the same for the Civil War. Half the students were unable to identify the theme of "Julius Caesar" or "Macbeth." Two-thirds could not say what the novel *1984* is about—even though the test was administered in 1986. And so the results went.[78]

Like Hirsch, Ravitch and Finn recommend returning to a curriculum that gives every student in every grade a heavy dose of literate culture. "What is needed?" Ravitch and Finn ask. "In a word, more. More knowledge, more teaching, more study, more learning—more history, more geography, and more literature at all grade levels."[79]

Essentialists are staking out the high ground, positioning themselves as socially concerned advocates who want students from all backgrounds to have the very best curriculum the schools can offer. "Conservative curricular content is socially progressive," Hirsch claims.[80] Ravitch and Finn second the point, arguing that cultural literacy is essential for all students, not just those in honors classes. "We cannot settle for an education system that imparts 'passable' amounts of important knowledge to its more fortunate students while the majority learn less than the minimum required for successful participation in the society they are about to enter."[81]

## The Critics Respond: Multicultural Literacy and a Better Future

As the debate over cultural literacy unfolds, critics of essentialism are trying to be careful how they make their rebuttals. Virtually all the critics begin by saying they, too, are against tracking, that they, too, want the best curriculum for all.

But the best curriculum, some critics contend, is not the one cultural literacy advocates have in mind. Hirsch and his colleagues want schools to transmit *a* cultural heritage rooted in Great Britain and Western Europe. Some critics, by contrast, want schools to pass along *multiple* heritages, acquainting students not just with Anglo-European culture but with African, Asian, Middle Eastern, and other traditions as well. These critics call for *multi*cultural literacy.[82]

Other critics emphasize a different point: that the essentialists have misread both the past and the present. There never was a golden age of literacy skills or literate culture, these critics argue. There never was an era when the schools pushed all students to high levels of achievement.[83]

There *was* an era when only a small group of students entered high school and an even smaller group exited with a diploma. In 1900, just 10 percent of the eligible age group went to high school and only 6 percent graduated. In 1920, 31 percent started and 17 percent finished, and in 1940, the percentages were 73 and 51. These statistics are for all 14- to 17-year-olds. The attendance and graduation rates of poor and minority students were much lower.[84]

Throughout these years, moreover, complaints abounded that even those students fortunate enough to get through high school were not acquiring literate culture. As the chair of the education committee of the National Association of Manufacturers grumbled in 1927, "Over forty percent of [high school graduates] cannot accurately express themselves in the English language or cannot write in the mother tongue."[85]

Does this sound like the golden age Hirsch pines for, an age in which literacy was "effectively taught to disadvantaged children under a largely traditional curriculum"? Surely this is not the era essentialists want to recreate in the 1990s.[86]

Reanalysis of the NAEP data Ravitch and Finn used in *What Do Our 17-Year-Olds Know?* also makes nostalgia seem unjustified. When another researcher compared the answers of students from the 1930s through the 1960s to questions matching the content of the NAEP questions Ravitch and Finn selected, the researcher found similar performance across the years. Today's students "are not demonstrably different from students in their parents' or grandparents' generation in terms of their knowledge of American history."[87]

Putting together several different strands of criticism, we can see a consensus forming. Instead of looking back to a golden age past, the critics look forward to a better future in which, for the *first* time, America's schools help large numbers of students reach high levels of multicultural literacy. Quite a task!

## A Message for Essentialists: Take the Blame along with the Credit

Critics, whether they style themselves progressives or not, also agree that it is time to stop flogging the ghost of John Dewey. Essentialism dominated U.S. education from the mid-1950s through the mid-1960s, and since the mid-1970s it has been dominant again. Even if progressivism is making a comeback in the 1990s, the schools are hardly packed with disciples of Dewey and Kilpatrick. The critics' point is that essentialists must now accept the blame as well as the credit for a complete "generation" of students, the ones who entered kindergarten in the late 1970s and early 1980s and are graduating from high school in the 1990s.

These students are not the children of general skills, broad understandings, and learning by doing. They are the progeny of back to basics, excellence, and testing, testing, testing. These are the students whose knowledge of history and literature is shocking; these are the ones whose SAT scores declined from the late 1980s into the 1990s.

Don't blame Dewey, the critics say. Blame, most charitably, the gap between essentialism as it is and essentialism as it might be. If the essentialists want to hold Dewey and his disciples responsible for the distortions of progressivism in the schools, then the essentialists must accept the responsibility for the distortions of their theory.

Essentialists must realize that their fact-based curriculum is a perfect match for measurement-driven instruction. When they call for "more," what the students get is more of the same. Officers of the National Council of Teachers of English and the National Council for the Social Studies fear that the recommendations of Ravitch, Finn, Hirsch, and Bennett—despite their good intentions—will only produce more emphasis on standardized testing and more pressure to teach the test. With the expanding NAEP serving as The Nation's Report Card, a new era of curriculum alignment may be just around the corner.[88]

It does not reassure teachers when Chester Finn responds to their concerns about teaching the test with such comments as "That's a problem I'd like to see us encounter before we dismiss it''[89] and ''Teaching to the test is a grand thing to do so long as the test does a good job of probing the knowledge and skills one wants children to acquire.''[90] Finn's attitude strikes teachers as shockingly out of touch with what goes on in classrooms.

And thus this chapter on the curriculum comes full circle. It ends as it began, on a note of concern for teacher autonomy. The conflict between the mandated, monitored curriculum and the freedom to teach is one of the most pressing educational issues for the 1990s.

## ACTIVITIES

1. Interview teachers who have been teaching for at least 20 years on how the curriculum has changed while they have been in the classroom. Ask for their views on standardized testing, teacher autonomy, literacy, and other issues discussed in this chapter.
2. Talk with a public school system's curriculum specialist about the James Madison curriculum. Find out whether or not any students in the system already have such a curriculum, then ask how—and why—the curriculum for other students differs.
3. Invite professors who hold opposing views on literacy, especially cultural literacy, to have a debate or panel discussion in your class.

## RECOMMENDED READINGS

''By All Measures: The Debate over Standards and Assessments.'' A special section in *Education Week* (June 17, 1992), pp. S1–S20.
   This report is an excellent introduction to the debate over nationalizing public education.
Hirsch, E. D., Jr. *Cultural Literacy: What Every American Needs to Know* (Boston: Houghton Mifflin, 1987).
   Hirsch's bestseller popularized the concept of cultural literacy.
Kaestle, Carl F., with Helen Damon-Moore, Lawrence C. Stedman, Katherine Tinsley, and William Vance Trollinger, Jr. *Literacy in the United States: Readers and Reading since 1880* (New Haven, CT: Yale University Press, 1991).
   Kaestle and his associates lend an invaluable sense of historical perspective to the debate over literacy.
Ravitch, Diane, and Chester E. Finn, Jr. *What Do Our 17-Year-Olds Know? A Report on the First National Assessment of History and Literature* (New York: Harper & Row, 1987).
   Along with Hirsch's *Cultural Literacy* (above), this book advances the essentialist argument that today's students are not learning vital factual information.

## NOTES

1. George H. Hanford, ''Some Caveats on Comparing S.A.T. Scores,'' *Education Week* (October 8, 1986), p. 20.
2. James S. Coleman, Ernest Q. Campbell, Carol J. Hobson, James McPartland, Alexander M. Mood, Frederic D. Weinfeld, and Robert L. York, *Equality of Educational Opportunity* (Washington, D.C.: U.S. Government Printing Office, 1966).

3. For a history of educational testing, see Clinton I. Chase's "How We Got Where We Are," chap. 2 of *Measurement for Educational Evaluation* (Reading, MA: Addison-Wesley, 1978).

4. See George F. Madaus's "Test Scores as Administrative Mechanisms in Educational Policy," *Phi Delta Kappan* 66 (May 1985): 611–617.

5. College Entrance Examination Board, *On Further Examination: Report of the Advisory Panel on the Scholastic Aptitude Test Score Decline* (New York: CEEB, 1977), p. 3.

6. Ibid. For more analysis of changes in the pool of test takers, see Harold Howe II's "Let's Have Another SAT Score Decline," *Phi Delta Kappan* 66 (May 1985): 599–602.

7. College Entrance Examination Board, *On Further Examination,* p. 3; Hanford, "Some Caveats," p. 20.

8. College Entrance Examination Board, *On Further Examination,* p. 4. The quotation is from p. 31. For a critical discussion of the report, see Ira Shor's *Culture Wars: School and Society in the Conservative Restoration, 1969–1984* (Boston: Routledge & Kegan Paul, 1986), chap. 3.

9. Theodore R. Sizer, *Horace's Compromise: The Dilemma of the American High School* (Boston: Houghton Mifflin, 1984); Sizer, *Horace's School: Redesigning the American High School* (Boston: Houghton Mifflin, 1992). I discuss teacher bashing in chapter 3 of this text in the section titled "Nostalgia for a Golden Age of Teaching."

10. Michael W. Apple, *Education and Power* (Boston: Routledge & Kegan Paul, 1982).

11. W. James Popham, Keith L. Cruse, Stuart C. Rankin, Paul D. Sandifer, and Paul L. Williams, "Measurement-Driven Instruction: It's on the Road," *Phi Delta Kappan* 66 (May 1985): 628–634. For a pointed debate on these issues, see Popham's "The Merits of Measurement-Driven Instruction" and Gerald W. Bracey's "Measurement-Driven Instruction: Catchy Phrase, Dangerous Practice," *Phi Delta Kappan* 68 (May 1987): 679–682 and 683–686, respectively.

12. Richard M. Jaeger and Carol K. Tittle, eds., *Minimum Competency Achievement Testing: Motives, Models, Measures, and Consequences* (Berkeley, CA: McCutchan, 1980).

13. Richard J. Coley and Margaret E. Goertz, *Educational Standards in the 50 States* (Princeton, NJ: Educational Testing Service, 1990), pp. 3–4.

14. National Commission on Excellence in Education, *A Nation at Risk: The Imperative for Educational Reform* (Washington, D.C.: U.S. Department of Education, 1983), p. 20.

15. Peter W. Airasian, "The Consequences of High School Graduation Testing Programs," *NASSP Bulletin* 71 (February 1987): 54–67; Madaus, "Test Scores," pp. 614–617; Laura Hersch Salganik, "Why Testing Reforms Are So Popular and How They Are Changing Education," *Phi Delta Kappan* 66 (May 1985): 607–610.

16. Gene I. Maeroff, "Revealing What Is Already Known," *Education Week* (June 17, 1992), p. S16; Airasian, "The Consequences of High School Graduation Testing Programs," pp. 60–62.

17. U.S. Department of Education, National Center for Education Statistics, *Trends in Academic Progress* (Washington, D.C.: U.S. Government Printing Office, 1991), pp. 8–10.

18. Ibid., pp. 1–8.

19. Ibid.

20. U.S. Department of Education, National Center for Education Statistics, *National Assessment of Educational Progress* (Washington, D.C.: U.S. Department of Education, 1991).

21. John J. Cannell, *National Norm-Referenced Elementary Achievement Testing in America's Public Schools: How All Fifty States Are above the National Average* (Charleston, WV: Friends of Education, 1987).
22. Ibid.
23. Robert Rothman, "Normed Tests Skewed to Find Most Pupils 'Above Average,' a Disputed Study Finds," *Education Week* (December 9, 1987), p. 1.
24. CBS News, "Teacher Is a Cheater," *60 Minutes* (1990).
25. Lynn Olson, "Districts Turn to Nonprofit Group for Help in 'Realigning' Curricula to Parallel Tests," *Education Week* (October 28, 1987), pp. 1, 19.
26. Robert Rothman, "E.D. Will Prepare 'Consumer Guide' on Standardized Tests," *Education Week* (February 17, 1988), p. 16.
27. For early debates on these and other issues, see Jaeger and Tittle, eds., *Minimum Competency Achievement Testing.*
28. Chris Pipho, "Curriculum Alignment—The Latest Accountability Model," *Education Week* (October 28, 1987), p. 26. For an excellent analysis of the clash between curriculum alignment and teacher autonomy, see Arthur E. Wise's "The Two Conflicting Trends in School Reform: Legislated Learning Revisited," *Phi Delta Kappan* 69 (January 1988): 328–333.
29. Gregory R. Anrig, " 'A Very American Way': Everybody's Getting into the Act," *Education Week* (June 17, 1992), p. S8.
30. Allan Nairn and associates, *The Reign of ETS: The Corporation that Makes Up Minds* (Washington, D.C.: Ralph Nader Report on the Educational Testing Service, 1980).
31. Stanley M. Elam and Alec M. Gallup, "The 21st Annual Gallup Poll of the Public's Attitudes toward the Public Schools," *Phi Delta Kappan* 71 (September 1989): 44–45.
32. Monty Neill, "Assessment and the 'Educational Impact Statement,' " *Education Week* (September 23, 1992), p. 28; Elliot W. Eisner, "A Vulgar Oversimplification," *Education Week* (June 17, 1992), p. S14.
33. Lauren B. Resnick, "The 'Most Promising Way' of Getting the Education We Want," *Education Week* (June 17, 1992), p. S5.
34. Ibid., p. S6.
35. Marc S. Tucker, "A New 'Social Compact' for Mastery in Education," *Education Week* (June 17, 1992), pp. S3–S4.
36. U.S. Department of Education, *America 2000: An Education Strategy.* Sourcebook (Washington, D.C.: U.S. Government Printing Office, 1991), pp. 42, 47–48, 70–71.
37. Linda Darling-Hammond, "The Implications of Testing Policy for Quality and Equality," *Phi Delta Kappan* 73 (November 1991): 220–225; Lorrie A. Shepard, "Will National Tests Improve Student Learning?" *Phi Delta Kappan* 73 (November 1991): 232–238.
38. National Council of Teachers of Mathematics, *Curriculum and Evaluation Standards for School Mathematics* (Reston, VA: NCTM, 1989).
39. Richard P. Mills, "Widespread Teacher Involvement," *Education Week* (June 17, 1992), p. S13.
40. Ibid.
41. Ruth Mitchell, "Beyond the Verbal Confusion over 'Tests,' " *Education Week* (April 29, 1992), p. 36.
42. Shepard, "Will National Tests Improve Student Learning?" p. 235.
43. Tucker, "A New 'Social Compact.' "
44. Robert Rothman, "Large 'Faculty Meeting' Ushers in Pioneering Assessment in Vermont," *Education Week* (October 10, 1990), pp. 1, 18.

45. Robert Rothman, "Vermont Forced to Delay Goal of Expanding Assessment System," *Education Week* (May 20, 1992), pp. 1, 21.

46. Resnick, "The 'Most Promising Way,' " p. S6.

47. Quoted in "Creating System 'Becomes a Question of Judgment and Risk-Taking,' " *Education Week* (June 17, 1992), p. S9.

48. Mitchell, "Beyond the Verbal Confusion," p. 36.

49. Darling-Hammond, "The Implications of Testing Policy," p. 234; Shepard, "Will National Tests Improve Student Learning?" pp. 237–238.

50. National Commission on Excellence in Education, *A Nation at Risk,* pp. 24–27.

51. Coley and Goertz, *Educational Standards,* pp. 7, 28–29.

52. "Alabama Graduation Standards Would Be Toughest in Nation under Reform Measure," *Alabama School Journal* 108 (May 17, 1991): 1.

53. William J. Bennett, *James Madison High School: A Curriculum for American Students* (Washington, D.C.: U.S. Department of Education, 1987); Bennett, *James Madison Elementary School: A Curriculum for American Students* (Washington, D.C.: U.S. Department of Education, 1988).

54. Bennett, *James Madison High School,* p. 6; Chester E. Finn, Jr., *We Must Take Charge: Our Schools and Our Future* (New York: Free Press, 1991), chaps. 7, 15.

55. William J. Bennett, *The De-Valuing of America: The Fight for Our Culture and Our Children* (New York: Summit Books, 1992), pp. 86, 194–195; Finn, *We Must Take Charge,* pp. 80–81, 219–222.

56. Robb Deigh, "Curse It, Count It, Cure It: The Arithmetic of Illiteracy," *Insight* (September 29, 1986): 10–14.

57. Carl F. Kaestle with Helen Damon-Moore, Lawrence C. Stedman, Katherine Tinsley, and William Vance Trollinger, Jr., *Literacy in the United States: Readers and Reading since 1880* (New Haven, CT: Yale University Press, 1991), p. 94. For alarmist studies, see Paul Cooperman's *The Literacy Hoax: The Decline of Reading, Writing, and Learning in the Public Schools* (New York: William Morrow, 1978) and Jonathan Kozol's *Illiterate America* (Garden City, NY: Doubleday, 1985).

58. Irwin Kirsch and Ann Jungeblut, *Literacy: Profiles of America's Young Adults* (Princeton, NJ: Educational Testing Service, 1986). The quotations are from Lynn Olson's "New Study Raises Concerns about Adult Literacy," *Education Week* (October 1, 1986), pp. 1, 16.

59. Kirsch and Jungeblut, *Literacy,* pp. 14–22.

60. Olson, "New Study Raises Concerns," pp. 1, 16.

61. Kaestle et al., *Literacy in the United States,* p. 80.

62. Ibid.

63. Ibid., pp. 127, 89.

64. Ibid., chap. 4.

65. Ibid., pp. 128, 121–123.

66. Ibid., p. 128.

67. Richard L. Venezky, Carl F. Kaestle, and Andrew M. Sum, *The Subtle Danger: Reflections on the Literacy Abilities of America's Young Adults* (Princeton, NJ: Educational Testing Service, 1987), p. 33.

68. Kaestle et al., *Literacy in the United States,* p. 291.

69. E. D. Hirsch, Jr., *Cultural Literacy: What Every American Needs to Know* (Boston: Houghton Mifflin, 1987); Diane Ravitch and Chester E. Finn, Jr., *What Do Our 17-Year-Olds Know? A Report on the First National Assessment of History and Literature* (New York: Harper & Row, 1987); Allan Bloom, *The Closing of the American Mind* (New York: Simon & Schuster, 1987).

70. James J. Kilpatrick, "11th-Grade Ignoramuses," *Mobile Press-Register* (September 20, 1987), p. 10A; William F. Buckley, Jr., "A Real Driver's Test?" *Mobile Press* (June 10, 1987), p. 8A.

71. "Hirsch Defends Cultural-Literacy List," *Education Week* (April 15, 1987), p. 9.

72. Susan Ohanian, "Finding a 'Loony List' While Searching for Literacy," *Education Week* (May 6, 1987), pp. 21–22.

73. Hirsch, *Cultural Literacy,* p. 146.

74. Ibid., chap. 5. The quotation is on p. 133.

75. Bennett, *The De-Valuing of America,* p. 61.

76. Hirsch, *Cultural Literacy,* chap. 5. Hirsch elaborates on these views in "Restoring Cultural Literacy in the Early Grades," *Educational Leadership* 45 (December 1987–January 1988): 63–70.

77. Ravitch and Finn, *What Do Our 17-Year-Olds Know?,* p. 1.

78. Ibid., chap. 3.

79. Chester Finn and Diane Ravitch, "Survey Results: U.S. 17-Year-Olds Know Shockingly Little about History and Literature," *American School Board Journal* 174 (October 1987): 33.

80. E. D. Hirsch, Jr., "The Paradox of Traditional Literacy: Response to Tchudi," *Educational Leadership* 45 (December 1987–January 1988): 75.

81. Ravitch and Finn, *What Do Our 17-Year-Olds Know?,* p. 252.

82. See James A. Banks, "Approaches to Multicultural Curriculum Reform," in James A. Banks and Cherry A. McGee Banks, eds., *Multicultural Education: Issues and Perspectives* (Boston: Allyn & Bacon, 1993), chap. 10.

83. See Patricia Albjerg Graham's *S.O.S.: Sustain Our Schools* (New York: Hill & Wang, 1992), pp. 16–17; and Stephen Tchudi's "Slogans Indeed: A Reply to Hirsch," *Educational Leadership* 45 (December 1987–January 1988): 72–74. A book that airs arguments on all sides of the debate is *Cultural Literacy and the Idea of General Education,* part II of *The Eighty-Seventh Yearbook of the National Society for the Study of Education* (Chicago: NSSE, 1988).

84. U.S. Department of Education, National Center for Education Statistics, *Digest of Education Statistics, 1992* (Washington, D.C.: U.S. Government Printing Office, 1992), pp. 49, 67.

85. Quoted in Richard M. Jaeger, "World Class Standards, Choice and Privatization," *Phi Delta Kappan* 74 (October 1992): 124.

86. Hirsch, "Restoring Cultural Literacy," p. 66.

87. Dale Whittington, "What Have 17-Year-Olds Known in the Past?" *American Educational Research Journal* 28 (Winter 1991): 776.

88. Robert Rothman, "Teachers Dispute Studies' Counsel on Humanities," *Education Week* (September 16, 1987), p. 23.

89. Quoted in ibid.

90. Finn, *We Must Take Charge,* p. 162.

# CHAPTER 11

# Private Schools versus Public Schools

One of the liveliest educational issues for the 1990s is the heightening competition between private schools and public schools. *Competition* seems just the right word. Historically the advocates of both kinds of schools have been quick to argue the superiority of their particular brand of education, with the arguments always spirited and sometimes bitter.

This chapter concludes *America's Teachers* with a look at the ongoing debate. First, we will survey the three sectors of private elementary and secondary education—*Roman Catholic schools, other religious schools,* and *independent schools*—and examine a demographic profile of private schools and their students. Then we will focus on Catholic schools, the largest network of private schools in the United States, and fundamentalist Christian schools, the fastest-growing private schools of the last two decades. Catholic schools and fundamentalist schools, as different from each other as they are from public schools, illustrate the diversity of American private education. *Home schools,* which we will examine in the context of fundamentalist Christian education, provide further evidence of this diversity. This chapter closes with a discussion of *government regulation* and *educational choice,* controversial issues shaping the future of both private and public education.

Although the distinction between public and private education was hazy until the middle of the nineteenth century—many church schools, for instance, received public funds and were open to children of all faiths—the common school crusades drew a sharp line between *public* schools controlled by state and local school boards and *private* schools controlled by churches and individuals (see chapter 6). Since then, Americans have engaged in a running debate on the merits of private schools and public schools. Over the past few decades, as public education has struggled with more than its share of problems, the arguments have intensified.[1]

The debate has always been political in the sense that it reflects disagreements over who should control the education of young people: governments, churches, or individuals? Now the arguments have become more partisan than they have in years.

The Republican Party has positioned itself as an advocate of private schools, not necessarily in preference to public schools but certainly as an alternative for those dissatisfied with public schools. According to many Republicans, government should provide money to help people choose the school, public or private, they think best for their children.

The Democratic Party, casting itself during the 1992 election as the party of change, has been trying to defend public education without appearing to defend the status quo. Warming to the idea of choice but only among public schools, many Democrats contend government should work to improve public education rather than siphon off money to subsidize private education.

With academic researchers wading into the fray, two books have moved to the center of the controversy. In *Public and Private High Schools: The Impact of Communities* (1987), James S. Coleman and Thomas Hoffer argue that private schools, particularly Roman Catholic schools, are academically superior. In *Politics, Markets, and America's Schools* (1990), John E. Chubb and Terry M. Moe build a case for the least amount of government regulation and the greatest degree of educational choice. As we examine the debate over private schools and public schools, notice the impact these books are having on the educational politics of the 1990s. If substantial sums of public money begin flowing into schools now considered private, the very definitions of *public* and *private* will change, and the most fundamental realignment of American education since the era of common school reform will take place.[2]

## THREE SECTORS OF PRIVATE ELEMENTARY AND SECONDARY EDUCATION

Roman Catholics built this nation's largest system of private schools on their religious objections to common schools. The religious emphasis in Catholic education continues, but now Catholics are calling more attention than ever to the intellectual quality of their schools, touting them as academic alternatives to public schools. Despite losing enrollment since the 1960s, Catholic schools remain by far the largest sector of private education.

Other religious schools constitute the second-largest sector of private education. Throughout U.S. history, people of many faiths have felt the need to give their children an education grounded in religious doctrine. Fundamentalist Protestants, the most prominent recent example, complain the values they stress at home and in church clash with the values that dominate public education. Schools sponsored by people of other faiths—including Lutherans, Jews, Seventh-day Adventists, Episcopalians, and Calvinists—offer still other alternatives to public education.

Independent (also called nonsectarian) schools with no religious affiliation, the third and smallest sector of private education, meet the needs of Americans seeking academic and social alternatives to public education—people ranging from those who feel their children are languishing academically in public schools to those who want their children to be educated with other students from a similar socioeconomic background. In the 1990s, independent schools are holding their own in enrollment.

Roman Catholic schools, other religious schools, and independent schools keep the public-versus-private-school debate alive. Zealous debaters often get carried away with their arguments and appeal to emotion more than to intellect, for it is difficult to compare public schools and private schools objectively.

The diversity of both kinds of schools should make us wary of such sweeping statements as "Private schools are academically superior" and "Public schools offer better socialization." Beyond the value judgments imbedded in these claims (What constitutes academic quality? What kinds of socialization are desirable?), we must realize that a Catholic school in central city Chicago, for instance, may be quite different from a Catholic school in the suburbs of Atlanta. Social class, race, ethnicity, and gender—the sociological factors whose influence on public education we examined in chapter 8—also affect private education, although Catholics contend their schools minimize the negative effects of these factors better than public schools. We would discover even more diversity if we compared almost any Catholic school with almost any fundamentalist Christian school, and including independent schools would heighten the contrast even more.

Public schools, of course, vary at least as much. A suburban school in the Silicon Valley of California, a county school in rural Mississippi, and a magnet school in New York City would strike us as more different than similar, and these are only three of several hundred thousand public schools. In some communities, virtually all students attend public schools, while in other places public schools have become just what the common school reformers of the nineteenth century feared—schools that serve only the children of the poor. Thus we must take into account an incredible diversity when we generalize about public and private education.

## A PROFILE OF PRIVATE SCHOOLS AND THEIR STUDENTS

With these words of caution in mind, we can learn a great deal from a demographic profile of private education. The statistics offer surprises and challenge conventional wisdom.

Throughout the twentieth century, private schools have enrolled between 7 and 14 percent of the nation's elementary and secondary school students. Given the massive social changes of this century, what is most striking about enrollment trends is the stability they reveal. As a percentage of all K–12 students, the low point of private school enrollment (7 percent) came in 1920, when public schools were key players in the campaign to assimilate immigrant children. Private schools attracted their largest share of students (14 percent) in 1959, when many children and grandchildren of turn-of-the-century immigrants were choosing Roman Catholic schools for *their* children. Thus the peak for private schools came, ironically, at the end of the 1950s, a decade that now has a rosy nostalgic reputation for "good public schools."[3]

The trends since 1960 also show more stability than change, calling into question the popular belief that ever-increasing numbers of students have abandoned public schools for private schools. In fact, private school enrollment decreased during the social upheaval of the 1960s, falling to 10 percent by 1970 and remaining near that level throughout the 1970s. After rising to 13 percent in the mid-1980s, the proportion of students attending private schools fell again to 11 percent in the late 1980s. Since 1990, private school enrollment has held steady at 11 percent, where it is projected to stay into the next century.[4]

Private school supporters who talk about a mass exodus from public schools need to recheck their arithmetic, but so do public school advocates who speak of large numbers of students returning from private schools. On the other hand, national demographic data may not change the opinions of true believers in either private or public education, for people tend to generalize from their own experience in local schools.

The diversity of private education helps explain how different people can hold such different impressions of whether private school enrollment is increasing or decreasing. During the 1980s, private schools lost students in central cities, where they have traditionally been strongest, and gained students in suburbs and nonmetropolitan areas. These geographical trends signaled fundamental changes in the makeup of the private school population.

## New Patterns within the Three Sectors

Roman Catholic schools, which could claim more than 90 percent of private school enrollment during the 1950s and almost two-thirds as late as 1980, now enroll about 55 percent of private school students. The closing of Catholic schools that had served their urban parishes for many years is a highly visible reminder of the declining popularity of Catholic education. Many of the Irish, German, Italian, Polish, and other white ethnic families who were the backbone of Catholic schools have moved to the suburbs, and they no longer seem as committed to Catholic education.[5]

Other religious schools, by contrast, now enroll about 30 percent of all private school students, up from 21 percent in 1980. Their growth has been most dramatic in suburbs, small towns, and rural areas. The U.S. Department of Education classifies other religious schools in three groups: those affiliated with a fundamentalist Christian school association; those affiliated with a national denomination or another type of religious school association; and those with no affiliation. Each group accounts for about 10 percent of private school students, with fundamentalist Christian schools growing most rapidly.[6]

Independent private education encompasses a variety of institutions, which the Department of Education also classifies in three groups: regular academic schools, including the selective boarding and day schools that belong to the National Association of Independent Schools (NAIS); special education schools that serve disabled and other exceptional students; and special-emphasis schools, such as military, Montessori, art, and alternative schools. As a whole, the independent sector of private education enrolls about 15 percent of private school students, approximately the same percentage as in 1980. This flat pattern disguises a great deal of variation, though. The rising popularity of special education schools, for instance, contrasts with the modest growth of NAIS schools and the downward spiral of military academies.[7]

Soon the Department of Education may have to add a new classification of independent schools: for-profit schools. Chris Whittle, the media entrepreneur whose satellite network beams news and commercials into schools via "Channel One," plans to operate a chain of commercial private schools. Under the auspices of the Edison Project, Whittle would like to open 200 schools in the fall of 1995, hoping to expand his system to 1,000 schools serving 2 million students soon after the turn of the century.[8]

Like Channel One, the Edison Project is controversial. Can the profit motive, as Whittle claims, create the right incentives to provide high-quality education to "student populations similar to those in public schools—at costs like those of public schools"?[9] Or will watching the bottom line, as critics claim, force the Edison Project to compromise its educational quality, its plans to attract culturally diverse students through scholarships, or perhaps both?[10]

## Who Goes to Private School?

Many private educators, like Whittle, bristle at the charge of elitism. Many are eager to shatter the "wealthy white kid" stereotype. They point out that about 40 percent of the students in both public and private schools come from families with incomes between $15,000 and $34,999. The largest sector of private education, Roman Catholic, is proud of its socioeconomic diversity. Historically, Catholic educators have welcomed children from all social classes, often adjusting tuition to match family income. The fastest-growing private schools, fundamentalist Christian, appeal primarily to lower-middle-class and upper-working-class families. "Havens for the Rich" is a label that fits very few private schools, their advocates insist.[11]

Public school advocates, though, point out major differences between private school and public school enrollment at both ends of the economic ladder. At the lower end of the ladder, fewer than 12 percent of private school students come from families with incomes below $15,000, compared to 31 percent of public school students. At the upper end of the ladder, more than 20 percent of all private school students—and almost 40 percent of independent school students—come from families with incomes above $50,000, compared to only 11 percent of public school students.[12]

Racially and ethnically, private schools show much less diversity than public schools. Minority students make up less than 15 percent of the enrollment in private schools, compared to 30 percent in public schools. But few schools, private or public, are completely segregated by race or ethnicity. Only 12 percent of private schools and 9 percent of public schools enroll no minority students. Many of the self-avowed "segregation academies" established from the 1950s through the 1970s to give white students an alternative to desegregated public schools have closed.[13]

Another aspect of racial separation is the growing popularity of private schools established to give black students an alternative to public schools. Families who choose African-American academies often say public schools are only worsening a "desperate situation" for people of their race. As we saw in chapter 8, about 300 African-American academies have opened, and the debate continues over whether the voluntary separation they promote represents a step forward or a step backward.[14]

For the largest number of minority students who turn to private education, Roman Catholic schools are the alternative. Students from the white ethnic groups that have traditionally dominated Catholic education are being replaced by Hispanics, Africans, and Asians. These students, sometimes called the new urban poor, now represent 22 percent of the enrollment in Catholic schools, with Hispanics accounting for 10 percent, blacks for 9 percent, and Asians for 3 percent. More than half the blacks come from non-Catholic families who, like the families choosing African-American academies, believe public schools are miseducating their children. The changing racial and ethnic balance of Catholic schools is a major topic of discussion among Catholic educators, and it promises to add fuel to the 1990s debates about private schools and public schools.[15]

## ROMAN CATHOLIC SCHOOLS

### James Coleman and the Issue of Academic Achievement

The academic quality of Catholic schools versus public schools continues to be another key issue in the debates. James Coleman, a sociologist of education at the University of Chicago, has focused national attention on the issue with his widely discussed studies. In *Public and Private Schools* (1981) and *High School Achievement: Public, Catholic, and Private Schools Compared* (1982), Coleman and his research associates argued that the best high schools—those whose students have the highest levels of academic achievement—share a set of characteristics. Their students attend school more regularly, take more academic (as opposed to general and vocational) courses, and do more homework. High-performance schools have a more disciplined and orderly climate.[16]

These findings, which should hardly seem startling by now, are consistent with the research on effective schools we reviewed in chapter 8. What made Coleman's research so controversial was his insistence that private schools are more likely than public schools to have these characteristics and that, as a result, private schools are academically superior.

Predictably, these generalizations drew the fire of critics. Public school defenders charged Coleman's conclusions went well beyond his data. Since few of the private schools in his study were non-Catholic religious schools or independent schools, the critics claimed Coleman's findings were valid, at best, for comparing Catholic schools and public schools. But furthermore, the critics continued, Coleman had failed to control adequately for student socioeconomic background. They pointed out that private school parents have higher average incomes as well as higher average levels of education, suggesting that such factors—which sociologists have found to correlate with student achievement—account for the higher achievement Coleman attributed to private schools. The critics called attention to other studies showing no significant differences in achievement between private school public school students from the same socioeconomic background.[17]

During the 1980s, these arguments seesawed back and forth. Coleman admitted his conclusions about non-Catholic private schools were tentative, but he stuck to his guns on Catholic schools. The many reanalyses of Coleman's data have highlighted the difficulties of generalizing about private and public schools. If a consensus is forming at all, it is around the position that while Catholic schools do not offer academic advantages to *every* student, they do to *some* students: in particular, African Americans, Hispanic Americans, and other students whose parents are likely to have lower incomes and less education.[18]

Because these are the very students who often receive what philosopher Mortimer Adler calls "dirty water" in public schools, they have the most to gain from attending a Catholic school. On the other hand, affluent white students—those who fit the private school stereotype—are the students most likely to receive "wine" (or at least "clean water") in public schools. These students have the least to gain from attending a Catholic school. The ongoing debate over Coleman's research is standing much of the conventional wisdom about public and private schools on its head.

Coleman's study *Public and Private High Schools: The Impact of Communities* (1987) is providing more than enough grist for the debates of the 1990s. Reasserting most of his original claims, Coleman tries to reinforce them in several ways. In this study, he pays more attention to differences between Catholic schools and other private schools and includes more data on student socioeconomic background. He also examines *gains* in student achievement over a two-year period instead of measuring achievement at only one point, as he did in his earlier studies.[19]

Catholic educators are welcoming this research, but other private schoolers are finding a mixture of good and bad news. Looking at verbal and mathematical skills, Coleman contends that students in Catholic high schools and show higher gains in achievement than students of comparable socioeconomic status in public schools *and* most other private schools. The evidence on achievement gains in Catholic schools strengthens his earlier conclusion that the schools themselves, not just the socioeconomic background the students bring to the schools, play a major role in academic success. As before, Coleman claims the academic benefits of a Catholic education are greatest for African, Hispanic, and poor students. He also points out that dropout rates are much lower in Catholic schools than in public schools and most other private schools.[20]

The qualifying *most other* is necessary because the elite independent schools in Coleman's study, such institutions as Phillips Andover Academy, have exceptionally high academic achievement and very low dropout rates. Other non-Catholic private schools, though, are comparable to public schools in many respects, and in some cases non-Catholic private schools fare worse by comparison. Students in such schools have higher dropout rates and lower achievement gains in both science and math than comparable students in public schools.[21]

## Private School Superiority?

The academic debate Coleman touched off in the 1980s is feeding one of the hottest political debates of the 1990s. A key point of contention in the educational choice debate is the academic quality of private schools and public schools. Obviously, a convincing affirmative answer to the question of whether private schools are academically superior to public schools would strengthen the case for educational choice. With popular opinion clearly favoring choice in some form and with a few Democratic politicians joining the Republican call to extend choice to private schools, advocates of public education are stepping forward to attack what they call the "myth" of private school superiority.

We will listen to the debate over choice at the end of this chapter, but here it is important to understand the latest twist in the arguments over academic quality. Are differences in achievement between private and public school students *large enough* to justify the claim that private schools are superior? Clearly not, answers Albert Shanker, president of the AFT, who as usual is in the front ranks of public school advocates.

On some standardized tests, Shanker points out, the achievement differences are very small. On the 1990 National Assessment of Educational Progress (NAEP) math test for twelfth-graders, for instance, the average score of public school students was 295 on a 500-point scale, compared with 302 for Catholic school students and 301 for students in other private schools. Moreover, the gaps between the scores of public school students and private school students were smaller in the twelfth grade than in the lower grades. These narrowing gaps cast doubt on Coleman's claim that students make higher achievement gains in Roman Catholic schools than in public schools.[22]

"This is amazing," Shanker wrote in the *New York Times,* "because youngsters in private schools are a far more advantaged group, so they should be leaving public-school students behind in the dust."[23] Appearing before a Congressional committee considering educational choice, Shanker testified that other standardized tests show similar patterns: achievement differences that start small and in some cases get smaller as students move through the grades.[24]

But even small differences can be significant, Coleman replied. Advocates of private education like to remind their critics that private school students post higher average scores than public school students on almost all standardized tests, and on some tests the differences are larger than those Shanker cited. On the

NAEP's 1988 assessment of writing, for instance, twelfth-graders in private schools outscored those in public schools by an average of 15 points (237 to 252) on a 500-point scale. On this test, the gaps widened rather than narrowed from the lower grades through the upper grades. Furthermore, Roman Catholic educators argue that comparing test scores of twelfth-graders may underestimate the advantage of Catholic schools. By the senior year, more of the weakest students have dropped out of public schools than out of Catholic schools, which has the effect of inflating average test scores in public schools compared to Catholic schools.[25]

And so the arguments continue. How much of the difference in achievement between private and public school students is due to the characteristics of the schools themselves? How much is due to the socioeconomic backgrounds of the students? Statistical analysis may never yield conclusive answers to these questions. In the next section, we will see how Coleman, who has built his career on quantitative research, is reaching beyond the numbers to answer these questions.

## Functional Communities and Value Communities

In *Public and Private High Schools,* Coleman stresses the importance of communities. He contends that a *functional community* surrounds most Catholic and other religious schools. Although the students in these schools many not live in the same neighborhood, their "families attend the same religious services and know one another."[26] The support of the functional community helps families pass their values from one generation to the next.

Independent private schools and a few public schools are surrounded by a different kind of community, a *value community* composed of "people who share similar values about education and childrearing but who are not a functional community."[27] As the name suggests, this kind of community also aids in the intergenerational transmission of values.

Most public schools, by contrast, are grounded in *no* community. Public schools once drew students from rural areas, small towns, and ethnic neighborhoods that constituted functional communities. But no longer. Today's public school attendance zones rarely correspond to either functional or value communities. Thus, according to Coleman, most public schools have lost their base of community support.

## Human Capital and Social Capital

Coleman argues that of all schools, Catholic schools are the most effective at increasing *human capital,* which economists define as the skills and capabilities that make people productive. Some students come from families with relatively little human capital—their parents may be poorly educated and unemployed. Yet some families lacking in human capital may have an abundance of *social capital,* which "exists in the *relations* between persons."[28] Families with social capital are close; parents and children share warmth, trust, and support. Some families, of course, lack both human capital and social capital, while other families have both. Still other families have human capital but lack social capital. The parents may be well educated but spend no time with their children.

Coleman says social capital exists in communities as well as families. People who attend the same church and share the same religious values can sustain one another. Thus he argues that the functional community surrounding Catholic schools can supply social capital to students who lack it at home. Coleman points to the remarkable success of Catholic schools with students from single-parent families, families in which both parents work outside the home, and families who rarely talk about school. To a greater degree than any other kind of school, Catholic schools offer the support that can help such students succeed.

Coleman puts his case for Catholic education into the larger context of "two orientations to schooling." Public educators try to keep parents at arm's length, he says, while private educators try to keep parents inside a community. Public schools are agents of the larger society and the state, trying to help children transcend the limitations of their family background. Private schools are agents and extensions of families, trying to help one generation transmit its values to the next.

"These two orientations are not in fundamental conflict," Coleman writes, as long as the values of the family and the society are similar. But when the orientations clash, the families who feel the greatest sense of conflict turn to private schools, hoping to find there the values they miss in public schools. Coleman uses this analysis to explain the rise of several different types of private schools. He contends that the search for homogeneous values led Roman Catholics to start parochial schools before the Civil War, some whites to establish segregation academies in response to the *Brown* decision, and fundamentalist Protestants to open Christian schools after the mid-1960s.[29]

## FUNDAMENTALIST CHRISTIAN SCHOOLS

Coleman's concept of community is an appropriate point of departure for our discussion of fundamentalist Christian schools. Most parents who send their children to Christian schools are products of the public schools. But public education has changed, fundamentalists insist. Interpreting the Bible literally and approaching their faith evangelically, they believe today's public schools promote secular values that clash with Christian values. Roman Catholics left public schools because they were too Protestant. Now fundamentalists are leaving public schools because they are not Protestant enough. Fundamentalists are opening their own schools and incorporating them into a functional community that also encompasses home and church.[30]

Critics initially dismissed fundamentalist schools as just another variation on the segregation academy theme, and, to be sure, the early stirrings of the Christian school movement did coincide with the desegregation of public schools in the South. Without question, the desire to maintain racial homogeneity played a role in the founding of some fundamentalist schools.[31]

During the 1970s, though, critics began to notice that many Christian schools were enrolling both blacks and whites and the schools were growing in parts of the nation where desegregation was simply not an issue. The schools are separatist by their very nature, but it now appears the separation their supporters have in mind is not racial. Paraphrasing the New Testament, fundamentalists say they are "in the world but not of the world." They are trying to lead religious lives in the midst of a secular society.[32]

Separation and independence are hallmarks of fundamentalist Christian schools. They do not constitute a distinct system, as Catholic schools do, but rather 4,000 locally controlled alternatives to public education. Although Christian schools are becoming more receptive to outside visitors, they continue to resist government regulation. Some schools are controlled by a local congregation of a national denomination, such as the Baptist Church, Methodist Church, Church of Christ, or Assembly of God. Other schools are under the control of a non-denominational congregation or a local foundation. Despite their insistence on local autonomy, many are affiliated with a fundamentalist Christian school association, such as Accelerated Christian Education, Oral Roberts Evangelical Fellowship, or American Association of Christian Schools.[33]

## Inside Christian Schools

Focusing attention on obtaining salvation and preparing for life in the next world, virtually every subject in Christian schools is informed by fundamentalist doctrine. Young children learn to read from textbooks that highlight morality and are strongly reminiscent of the *McGuffey's Readers* that were a staple of nineteenth-century public schools. In some Christian schools, students use the *McGuffey's Readers* themselves. The fundamentalist approach to science stresses God's role as creator, based on a literal interpretation of the book of Genesis. History is the story of God's relationship with people on earth. Modern literature to which fundamentalists often object in public schools—*Of Mice and Men, Catcher in the Rye,* and *The Chocolate War*—is simply excluded from Christian schools. Such literary classics as "Romeo and Juliet" and "Macbeth" may be included but in expurgated editions.

Some Christian schools use a packaged, programmed curriculum that draws a great deal of criticism from nonfundamentalist educators. Produced by such companies as Accelerated Christian Education and A Beka Book Publications, the curriculum features workbooks and other materials designed to let students proceed at their own pace with little or no assistance. A student might take a year-long course in algebra, for instance, working independently in a room—sometimes in an individual cubicle—surrounded by other students taking different courses.[34]

The developers of these materials downplay the importance of interaction among teachers and students. Nor do the developers deem critical thinking important. Instead, according to the publishers of the Accelerated Christian Education package, the curriculum is intended for "programming the mind to enable the child to see life from God's point of view." Such materials allow churches with limited budgets to start their own schools inexpensively.[35]

Critics of fundamentalist education often generalize the use of Accelerated Christian Education and A Beka materials to all such schools. Certainly, from the perspective of any of the theories of education we examined in chapter 7, the programmed, memory-oriented, all-but-teacherless curriculum makes an easy target. Many of the better-established Christian schools, though, have never used programmed materials, and some of the newer ones are discarding them. Fundamentalist schools, like fundamentalist Christians themselves, are not all alike.[36]

A visitor to some of the schools might be surprised at how traditional—that is, essentialist—their approach to education is. Well-disciplined students, enthusiastic teachers, and a familiar core of basic subjects can evoke, on the surface, the atmosphere of suburban public schools of the late 1950s.

But hearing an English teacher open discussion of a short story by asking "How would Jesus react in that situation?" or seeing a science teacher present evolution as a discredited theory can be startling. If the visitor examines an application for a teaching position, such questions as "Do you sense that God has called you to be a Christian school teacher?" and "How much time do you spend alone with God, reading the Bible and praying?" make it impossible to miss the fundamentalist orientation.

## The Struggle against Secular Humanism

That orientation, fundamentalists insist, offers the best hope for helping their children escape from secularism. Fundamentalists want Christianity to permeate every aspect of their schools, for they are firmly convinced that secular humanism, which they regard as another religion, permeates public education and every other aspect of public life.

To fundamentalists, secular humanism is the belief that people are capable of charting their own course through life without divine assistance. In other words, human beings can set moral standards and make their own determination of right and wrong. So defined, secular humanism flies in the face of fundamentalist Christianity, which requires that people look to God for guidance and take their moral standards from the Bible. Fundamentalists argue that because secular humanism deals with ultimate concerns about life and reality, it is indeed a religion. Just as some people seek answers to ultimate questions in Christianity or Judaism, which are *theistic* religions centered on a deity, other people look to secular humanism, a *nontheistic* religion centered on human beings.[37]

Fundamentalists charge that since the 1960s, when the U.S. Supreme Court ruled organized prayer in public schools unconstitutional in the *Engel v. Vitale* (1962) and *Abington v. Schempp* (1963) decisions, public education has been drifting away from its Judeo-Christian moorings. The moral and social revolutions of the 1960s and 1970s brought "sex, drugs, and rock and roll" into the schools, forcing students to make moral decisions at earlier ages. Just when students needed guidance more than ever, public education abandoned the yes-and-no answers found in a fundamentalist reading of the Bible for a situational morality that encourages students to weigh the consequences of their actions and make their own decisions.

Fundamentalists also find objectionable the content of many public school textbooks. They claim some social studies texts, for instance, say too little about the role of the Judeo-Christian tradition in U.S. history. Some literature books contain nonjudgmental portrayals of immoral behavior. Textbooks used in a variety of subjects, they say, convey the message "Think for yourself" rather than "Trust in God."

The cumulative effect of public education on students is subtle but powerful, fundamentalists conclude. By persuading students they are in charge of their own destiny, public schools promote the religion of secular humanism. From the fundamentalist point of view, Christian schools teaching submission to God's will offer a clear alternative.

In order to understand the kind of education fundamentalists want to foster in Christian schools, we must understand the changes they are trying to make in the public schools. Turning to the judicial system during the 1980s in their quest to reform public education, they won major battles in the lower courts only to encounter setbacks on appeal.

The widely publicized case *Smith v. Board of School Commissioners of Mobile County* (1987) put secular humanism in the national spotlight. The case originated in Alabama, where a federal district court judge sided with more than 600 fundamentalist plaintiffs and not only declared secular humanism a religion but also banned 44 public school textbooks for promoting the religion. If the First Amendment means public schools cannot advance the theistic religions of Judaism and Christianity, the judge reasoned, then neither can public schools advance the nontheistic religion of humanism.[38]

A federal circuit court of appeals rejected most of the district judge's arguments. The appeals court found that while certain passages in the textbooks are consistent with the set of beliefs fundamentalists call secular humanism, other passages are consistent with the doctrines of Christianity, Judaism, and other theistic religions. "Mere consistency with religious tenets," the court of appeals wrote, "is insufficient to constitute unconstitutional advancement of religion." The court pointed out that the textbooks expose students to a variety of viewpoints and beliefs, some religious and some nonreligious. The overall "message" the textbooks convey is neither the endorsement nor rejection of any religion. Instead, the books represent "a governmental attempt to instill . . . such values as independent thought, tolerance of diverse views, self-respect, maturity, self-reliance, and logical decision-making."[39]

In *Mozert v. Hawkins County Public Schools* (1987), a case originating in Tennessee, another federal circuit court of appeals considered different issues but reached essentially the same conclusion. In this case, which like *Smith* made national headlines, a group of fundamentalist Christians complained that the content of their children's public school readers offended their religious beliefs. A federal district court judge ordered the school board to allow the students to "opt out" of their reading classes and learn to read apart from other students—in the library, the study hall, and the home.[40]

The circuit court of appeals overturned the district judge's decision, concluding that requiring students to read a particular set of books is not the same thing as forcing them to accept a particular set of religious beliefs. "Instead, the record in this case discloses an effort by the school board to offer a reading curriculum designed to acquaint students with a multitude of ideas and concepts, though not in proportions the plaintiffs would like."[41]

The issue is, in part, one of balance and emphasis, although some fundamentalists take a far more adamant stand. On certain matters they simply do not want their children to exercise independent thought. Certain questions, answered by the Bible, are not open to debate. Believing their main responsibility as parents is instilling in children the *one* correct outlook on the world, helping them "see life from God's point of view," some fundamentalists find the clash of ideas in the public schools unacceptable. Because the federal courts of appeal in both the *Smith* and the *Mozert* cases declined to decide what constitutes a religion for purposes of the First Amendment and whether secular humanism is in fact a religion, fundamentalists may take the issues to court again during the 1990s.[42]

Meanwhile, the growth of fundamentalist schools continues, albeit at a slower pace than during the last two decades. In the 1840s and 1850s, Roman Catholics became the first major defectors from the common school movement. By the year 2000, it may be clear whether fundamentalist Protestants are becoming the second.

## Home Schooling

A few Americans are defecting from all institutional schools, both public and private. *Home schoolers* want to keep schooling within the family circle. Parents who decide to teach their children at home join a small but enthusiastic movement that now accounts for about 1 percent of the combined enrollment in public and private education.[43]

Home schooling has grown in popularity and changed in character since the early 1970s, when it was a radical chic alternative appealing mostly to parents who wanted to give their children an unstructured education. From the 15,000 home-schooled children of the early 1970s, the movement has grown to between 300,000 and 500,000 students in the 1990s. Today home schooling is, above all else, a religious movement. Religious convictions, most often grounded in fundamentalist Christianity, are the major motivation for about 90 percent of home-schooling families. Like parents in fundamentalist Christian schools, home schoolers are trying to fortify their children against the negative influences of a secular society. Unlike Christian school parents, though, they believe the home provides the warmest, richest environment for education.[44]

Parents who choose home schooling have to enjoy spending time with their children. The mothers who do almost 90 percent of the teaching in home schools say they appreciate the emotional as well as the academic aspects of their work. According to these mothers, the closeness that develops among family members does not have to be interrupted when children reach five or six years of age and start school. Bonds can continue to grow if families can sit down together, open their books together, and work together on academic studies, just as they do on other tasks.[45]

Home-schooling parents are often criticized for depriving their children of peer contact and sheltering them from the real world. Well accustomed to answering these charges, parents say their children spend plenty of time with their peers, especially friends from church, after their lessons are done. Home schooling gives parents more control over peer groups, which is exactly what they want. To an even greater degree than parents in conservative Christian schools, home schoolers feel a sense of moral and religious *obligation* to protect their children from certain aspects of society. Sheltering children is essential, they argue, in an age of drugs, gangs, and AIDS.

Home-schooling parents also feel strongly about the academic side of their work. The student-teacher ratio is really low in a home school, they joke, making the more serious point that individual attention is one of the greatest assets of their brand of education. Many home-schooling families affiliate with a fundamentalist Christian association to gain access to its packaged, sometimes programmed, curriculum. The security of such a curriculum is reassuring to parents who are learning to teach as they go. Few home schoolers have completed a state-approved teacher education program, and as many as half hold no more than a high school diploma. Yet home-schooling parents claim their children outscore public school students on many standardized achievement tests.[46]

Visitors who enter home schools full of skepticism often leave with a sense of admiration for the human qualities they find there. It is refreshing to see families whose members function well together. Favorable, even glowing reports in *Time, Harper's, Good Housekeeping,* and other popular media are making a once-exotic alternative seem more acceptable to the U.S. public. The Republican Party's 1992 platform endorsed home schooling as a worthy alternative to public schooling.[47]

But controversies over academic standards surround home schooling. Warm feelings and religious convictions aside, should people who lack state teaching credentials be allowed to teach? How closely should government regulate home schools and other private schools? Church and state come into conflict as home-schooling parents and fundamentalist Christian educators continue to test the right of government to set and enforce educational standards.

## GOVERNMENT REGULATION OF PRIVATE SCHOOLS

Many citizens who strongly disapprove of any religious group's efforts to reshape public education in its own image feel just as strongly that churches and individuals should have the right to control their own private schools. But do they have the right?

State regulation of private education involves striking a balance between the right of a state to ensure all children an education meeting minimum standards and the right of parents to educate their children as they see fit. Balancing the scales on this issue is a delicate task, judges and politicians have found. As a result of determined pressure from fundamentalist Protestants during the 1980s and

1990s, the scales have tipped away from government rights and toward parent rights. *Deregulation* of private education is the order of the day.

Although school laws vary considerably from state to state, we can divide the states into two groups in their approach to regulating private schools. In the first group is the small and diminishing number of states—fewer than ten—that try to make all private schools meet the same standards as public schools. Catholic schools, other religious schools, independent schools, and public schools alike must comply with regulations covering everything from the school cafeteria to teacher education and certification to the curriculum.[48]

Most states, though, are in the second group. They require all private schools to meet health and safety standards, submit attendance reports, and (in some cases) present student standardized test scores, but these states exempt private religious schools from academic regulations governing teachers and the curriculum. The states in this group want some degree of control over private schools, but they try to avoid church-state entanglement over academic issues.[49]

Private schools react to government regulation in different ways. Catholic schools willingly meet the standards of the states in which they are located. Even in states in the second group that exempt them from academic regulations, Catholic educators voluntarily comply, boasting that their teachers and curriculum not only meet but exceed public school standards. Many other religious schools and most independent schools also comply with the regulations of states in groups one and two.[50]

The controversy over regulation centers on fundamentalist Christian educators and home schoolers, both of whom cite religious reasons for rejecting state standards, especially those applying to teachers and the curriculum. Bitter disputes and legal battles have broken out in states in the first group, for fundamentalists regard their schools as ministries of the church. They argue that just as churches are free to select preachers with whatever educational credentials the churches prefer, the choice of teachers should also be free from government interference. Churches should also have the freedom to determine the curriculum for their schools, since sensitive issues ranging from sexual morality to the origins of the universe are involved. Many home-schooling parents reject government regulation using variations of these same arguments.[51]

Educational officials in states in the first group reply that requiring private schools to meet minimum academic standards is not only reasonable but essential. Officials often raise the issue of professionalism (see chapter 4). Just as all states regulate the training and licensing of physicians to ensure quality medical care and protect society from quacks, states must also set standards for teacher education and certification. State officials point out that some teachers in fundamentalist schools do not even have college degrees, much less state teaching certificates. Few home schoolers, as we have seen, meet state standards for teachers. Would society tolerate such a situation in medicine—or in dentistry, law, or any of the established professions? Certainly not.[52]

According to school officials, state curriculum regulations are broad enough to accommodate religious diversity. State standards often require only that schools teach certain subjects, which leaves private schools a great deal of control over specific content. A course in biology, for instance, could stress creationism and reject evolution but still satisfy state standards. Thus state officials argue that religious educators and home schoolers should have no objections to meeting minimum curriculum standards.

Naturally the debate does not end there. Fundamentalist Christian educators and home-schooling families challenge state officials to prove that graduates of state-approved teacher education and certification programs are measurably better than other teachers. As we have seen, state officials are hard pressed to do that. Ultimately, fundamentalist educators and home schoolers rest their case on their belief that education is a religious endeavor that government has no right to regulate.

Until the 1980s, state legislatures took a variety of stands in trying to settle these disputes, and the courts also sent mixed signals. In *Kentucky State Board for Elementary and Secondary Education v. Rudasill* (1979), a lower court refused to allow the state to make religious schools comply with academic standards. The U.S. Supreme Court let the decision stand. In *State [of Nebraska] v. Faith Baptist Church* (1981), a lower court took the opposite position and approved the state's academic regulation of religious schools. The U.S. Supreme Court let this decision stand, too. In both cases, the Supreme Court said it found no justification in the U.S. Constitution for hearing arguments on the educational and religious issues involved, a position that left states and private schools with no clear guidelines.[53]

During 1980s and early 1990s, though, fundamentalists won major victories in courts and especially in state legislatures. More than half the legislatures revised their laws on private schools, and in the process many states moved from group one into group two. Requirements that private school teachers hold state teaching certificates have almost disappeared. Instead, most states now require private school teachers, particularly those without college degrees, to pass state competency tests. States have relaxed curriculum regulations and substituted mandates that private school students demonstrate their ability on standardized achievement tests.[54]

Fundamentalist Christian educators and home schoolers are lobbying to reduce these requirements still further. In the 1990s, private schools are operating in a climate of deregulation.[55]

## EDUCATIONAL CHOICE

### *Politics, Markets, and America's Schools*

Deregulation is at the core of this 1990 best-seller by John E. Chubb and Terry M. Moe, a book that is still shaping the debate over private schools and public schools. Chubb is a senior fellow at the Brookings Institution in Washington, D.C.; Moe is a professor of political science at Stanford University. Their arguments for less government regulation and more parent-student choice help explain the common motivation behind the many experiments in educational choice.

Chubb and Moe start with the same question James Coleman and others are asking—What makes some schools more effective than others?—but conduct a statistical analysis that leads to a different answer. Searching for the key organizational factor that enables some schools to maintain the orderly climate, high expectations, and other characteristics of effective schools, Chubb and Moe isolate the factor of *autonomy,* which they define as freedom from external, bureaucratic control. The more autonomy schools have, the better they can organize themselves for academic achievement. A major reason private schools are generally more effective than public schools is that private schools generally have more autonomy.[56]

Chubb and Moe stand back and look at large-scale institutional differences between private schools and public schools. Private schools, they point out, "are controlled by markets—indirectly and from the bottom up." Power flows upward from students and parents, the consumers of educational services, to the teachers and administrators who provide the services. With relatively few external restraints on autonomy, private schools allow providers and consumers to make the educational arrangements they think best.[57]

Public schools, by contrast, "are controlled by politics—directly and from the top down." Power flows downward from a wide array of external agents—including politicians, administrators, teacher unions, and voters—all vying to impose their values on the schools. This is democracy in action, to be sure, but Chubb and Moe believe it has negative effects on the schools. The bureaucratic organizational structure of public education, designed to ensure compliance with political authority, puts shackles on providers and consumers alike. People caught in the system are unable to make changes.[58]

Chubb and Moe have little hope for the educational reforms of the 1980s and 1990s. Most of these reforms are failing because they do not reduce political control and increase market control. They are failing because they are not fundamental enough.

Chubb and Moe place great faith, though, in one particular reform. Like true believers, they come right out and say, "Choice *is* a panacea."

Choice is a self-contained reform with its own rationale and justification. It has the capacity *all by itself* to bring about the kind of transformation that, for years, reformers have been trying to engineer in myriad other ways. The whole point of a thoroughgoing system of choice is to free the schools from these disabling constraints by sweeping away the old institutions and replacing them with new ones.

With a vision of "better schools through new institutions," Chubb and Moe look to choice as a "revolutionary reform that introduces a new system of public education."[59]

We certainly cannot fault Chubb and Moe for merely tinkering with the system. Listen to their proposal. They want each state to redefine the concept of "public school" with minimal criteria, such as the standards most states now use to approve private schools. Any group or organization meeting the criteria—including an existing private school—can apply to the state and receive a charter to operate a public school.[60]

Each chartered public school will have the autonomy to determine its own admission standards, tuition, governance structure, and methods of operation. The state will hold public schools accountable for adhering to procedural standards—for complying with nondiscrimination laws, for instance, and for continuing to meet the criteria for public schools—but not for student achievement or any other quality assessments. That kind of accountability will come "from below," from "parents and students who directly experience [the] services and are free to choose."[61]

Students can apply for admission to any public school in the state. Using a combination of federal, state, and local funds, the state will pay the schools for every student they accept. Payments or "scholarships," as Chubb and Moe call them, will be larger for some students—the disabled and at-risk, for instance—than for others.

Existing school districts can continue to operate public schools, but they must compete for students with newly chartered schools. Districts retaining their "governing apparatus" of board members, superintendents, central office staff, and so forth must support them entirely with scholarship revenue.

A Parent Information Center in each district will provide counseling and facilitate the process of admission. Every parent will be required to visit the center at least once. The admission process will guarantee each student a school and a "fair shot at getting into the school he or she wants most."[62]

Will this plan, as Chubb and Moe claim, give the entire nation a "fair shot" at fundamental educational reform? The answer depends on how well market control works. All advocates of choice believe schools become more responsive to students and parents when schools have to compete for survival in the open market. But even true believers realize markets have their weaknesses. In fact, Chubb and Moe briefly review some of the problems of market control before dismissing them as less significant than the problems of political control.

## The Critics Respond

Listen now as critics of choice join our discussion of education in the marketplace. One of the best summaries of criticism is *School Choice* (1992) by Ernest Boyer, president of the Carnegie Foundation for the Advancement of Teaching.[63]

"The unequal distribution of income in society may bias certain markets in favor of the rich and against the poor," Chubb and Moe admit. That's quite an admission, critics reply. Although advocates of choice like to talk about helping the students who need help the most, critics question how much choice will improve the education of the poor and minority and students who now attend the *worst* public schools. How many of the *best* schools participating in a choice program will welcome an influx of these students? Chubb and Moe trust market forces, triggered by the higher scholarships their plan provides, to make poor and minority students "attractive clients to all schools."[64]

Dollars cannot overcome prejudice so easily, critics retort, going on to fault the Chubb-Moe plan for allowing chartered public schools to set tuition and admission standards as high as the market will bear, just as private schools do today. Critics charge that throwing public schools into the open market will make them more segregated than they are now, by income as well as by race and ethnicity.

A related market problem Chubb and Moe acknowledge is that "consumers may be too poorly informed to make choices that are truly in their best interests."[65] Accurate enough, critics say, and they point to an even more basic problem. Even when people have information, they do not always act in their— or, more important, their *children's*—best interests. This is a side of human nature economists feel uncomfortable discussing. Can market forces transform parents who neglect their children today into parents who make thoughtful educational decisions tomorrow? The critics say no.

"Transportation costs may eliminate many options," Chubb and Moe also admit.[66] Critics expand this point into a more comprehensive geographical argument. In many rural school districts, vast distances separate the few public schools. There may well be no private schools. In districts with high square mileage and low population density, how many new schools will market forces generate? Even if chartered public schools somehow spring up, can we reasonably expect students to make a daily round trip of, say, 100 miles to reach schools of choice? In large urban school districts, students may have to take long and sometimes dangerous rides on public transportation to attend the schools of choice they want most. How far can we expect these students to travel? Out in the suburbs, where transportation problems are fewer, the quality of public education is higher—sometimes rivaling the many competing private schools, Chubb and Moe admit. Can choice significantly improve the suburban situation? Given these geographical constraints, choice may not prove to be a panacea after all.[67]

And so the arguments continue. The Chubb-Moe plan is the ultimate proposal for educational choice—radical, far reaching, and fundamental, just as its authors intended. Now we can use the arguments over this proposal, pro and con, to evaluate other choice plans, including several that have already moved off the drawing boards and into the experimental stage in the schools.

## Tuition Tax Credits and Vouchers

Until the late 1980s, *tuition tax credits,* tax breaks for parents who send their children to private schools, were the most often discussed proposal for educational choice. Actually, they are an old idea, dating back at least to the early 1900s. Ronald Reagan became the first president to support tuition tax credits when he proposed a plan that would have allowed a private school family to reduce its federal income tax obligation by up to $500. The full credit would have been available only to families whose annual incomes are below $40,000, and families with incomes above $50,000 would have been ineligible for any credit. A majority of the Democrats in Congress joined forces with a few Republicans to block tax credits during the Reagan administration, effectively stalling the movement at the federal level.[68]

Opponents have traditionally used a constitutional argument against tuition tax credits, charging that since about 85 percent of private school students attend religious schools, tuition tax credits would violate the First Amendment by giving government support to religion. Not true, supporters have said—the financial benefits would go to parents rather than churches. The U.S. Supreme Court has never ruled on these exact arguments, but the court's decision in *Mueller v. Allen* (1983) gave tax credit supporters a way to circumvent sensitive church-and-state issues.[69]

*Mueller* has given tax credits a new lease on life at the state level. The Supreme Court ruled that the Minnesota legislature acted constitutionally when it provided an income tax deduction for educational expenses, since the deduction is available to parents of private *and* public school students. Obviously, the legislature did not pass the tax break to aid religion, the court reasoned. The legislature only wanted to help all parents meet the rising costs of education.[70]

Most of the Minnesota plan's benefits do go to private school families, though, because they can deduct not only tuition but also other educational expenses—such as textbooks, supplies, and transportation. Public school families pay no tuition, of course, and their other school-related expenses are much lower. The *Mueller* decision, a legal breakthrough for tuition tax credits, has prompted several other state legislatures to consider what supporters now call "educational tax credits for public and private school families." So far, however, only Iowa has joined Minnesota in passing statewide tax credit legislation.[71]

*Educational vouchers* are another strategy for promoting choice. Widely discussed since the 1970s, vouchers are "tickets" the government issues to parents to cover all or part of their children's educational expenses. Details of voucher plans vary. Vouchers can come from any of the three levels of government. Depending on the plan, vouchers can be valid in one local school district, in several districts, throughout a state, or throughout the nation. Some voucher plans apply only to public schools, while others apply to public schools as well as participating private schools. A small number of businesses, foundations, and individual donors are also providing vouchers to give low-income families more educational options.[72]

President George Bush proposed two kinds of federal vouchers as part of his America 2000 education strategy. First, he resurrected President Reagan's proposal to give Chapter I assistance directly to poor families in the form of vouchers they could redeem at either public or private schools. Next, Bush proposed federally funded tuition vouchers to help poor families send their children to private schools. Just as with tuition tax credits during the Reagan administration, a majority of Democrats aligned themselves with a small number of Republicans in Congress to defeat vouchers at the federal level.[73]

Granted the differences of opinion within both parties, the congressional action on tax credits and vouchers highlights an important difference between Democrats and Republicans. When the parties drew up their platforms for the 1992 presidential campaign, the Democrats came out for choice among public schools, while the Republicans supported federal dollars to help parents choose among public *and* private schools. Bill Clinton, known as an education governor, signed one of the nation's first public school choice laws in Arkansas, but education president George Bush campaigned for public-private choice.[74]

Democrats believe government should work to make public schools good enough for any student to attend. Despite the *Mueller* decision, Democrats argue that sending tax dollars to private religious schools—even indirectly, through the pocketbooks of parents—violates the separation of church and state.

With President Clinton in the White House and Democrats controlling both houses of Congress, Republicans form the loyal opposition on the issue of choice. Inspired by Chubb and Moe and by former President Bush, Republicans continue to argue that the "definition of 'public school' . . . be broadened to include any school that serves the public and is held accountable by a public authority."[75] As former Secretary of Education Lamar Alexander opined, government aid to religious schools is "as American as apple pie."[76]

## Experiments with Choice

The time for choice has come. Opinion polls show that more than 60 percent of Americans support public school choice. Depending on how the question is worded, at least 30 percent say they want to include private schools as well. The experiments we will review to conclude *America's Teachers* vary considerably. Their results are mixed. But choice as a principle—choice in some form—seems here to stay.[77]

Public school choice, in fact, has been around for quite some time, only under different names. As we saw in chapter 8, many school districts trying to facilitate the process of desegregation have opened magnet schools with a variety of academic and vocational themes. Many districts have also developed majority-to-minority ("m-to-m") transfer policies allowing students who attend a school where their race or ethnic group is in the majority to transfer to a school where they will be in the minority.

A few public school districts have incorporated magnet schools and voluntary transfers into more comprehensive choice programs. The best-known and most ambitious of the older programs is in District No. 4, East Harlem, New York, where choice began in 1974. Consistently ranked at or near bottom among New York City school districts in student achievement, East Harlem out of desperation encouraged teachers to save the system by designing new schools around innovative themes. By giving teachers more autonomy at the very time most school districts were taking it away, District 4 turned every school into a magnet school with the freedom to pursue its own goals. Here was an early venture in restructuring through school-based management (see chapter 4) and parent-student choice.[78]

Chubb and Moe praise the East Harlem experiment as an example of how to turn around an urban school system that has failed its poor and minority consumers. Today District 4 ranks 22 among New York's 32 districts in student achievement. Students now choose among schools with such names as the Academy of Environmental Science, East Harlem Career Academy, José Feliciano Performing Arts School, and Isaac Newton School for Math and Science. Having survived a financial scandal in the late 1980s, East Harlem remains a model of public school choice within a local district.[79]

Minnesota has taken the idea of teacher involvement in choice to the state level. As the result of a law passed in 1991, certified teachers can apply to the state board of education for permission to operate *charter schools,* institutions supported by public funds but free from most public school regulations. Charter schools are supposed to offer parents and students alternatives unavailable in regular public schools. True believers in choice see Minnesota expanding the definition of *public school* in a way Chubb and Moe would approve; opponents fear the "privatization of public education." Both sides may be right. The Minnesota state board of education issued the first charter to an existing private Montessori school.[80]

Minnesota is the acknowledged leader in yet another aspect of state-mandated choice. Since the 1980s, Minnesota students have been able to transfer to public schools outside their home districts. Provided there is room in the receiving school and racial balance is not upset, state and local money "follows" students into their new districts. About 80 percent of Minnesota's school districts participate in the program.[81]

Taking their cues from Minnesota, about 15 states have passed some form of "open enrollment" legislation. Several states—including Arkansas, Idaho, Iowa, Massachusetts, Nebraska, and Utah—now offer students statewide choice among public schools. Ohio allows transfers between adjacent districts. Colorado requires districts to allow transfers within their own boundaries. Several other states simply encourage districts to experiment with choice.[82]

How are state-mandated public school choice plans faring? Advocates point to the growing number of transfers. In some states with choice laws, more than 5 percent of students have changed schools within their districts. No state, though, has more than 2 percent of its students attending public schools outside their districts.[83]

Objections to statewide public school choice usually stem from financial inequities. Consider the case of Massachusetts. As chapter 9 points out, differences in wealth from one district to another produce wide disparities in local spending on education. After the Massachusetts legislature passed a hastily conceived choice law in 1991, poor districts found themselves saddled with a financial burden. When a student transferred from a poorer to a wealthier district, the law required the poorer district to pay the difference between its own local contribution and the higher local contribution of the wealthier district. In 1992, the legislature was forced to cap payments at $5,000 per student and to provide partial reimbursements to districts losing students.[84]

Moreover, the major beneficiaries of the Massachusetts law are middle-class white families who were already, at their own expense, sending their children to out-of-district schools in more affluent areas. Critics charge that choice programs offer kickbacks and rebates to such families rather than new options to poor and minority families.[85]

Among the many choice ventures of the 1990s, the most closely watched is the Milwaukee program billed as the nation's first real experiment with private school choice. Milwaukee is trying out a voucher plan that allows low-income students to attend private schools at public expense. In 1990, the Wisconsin legislature approved the Milwaukee Parental Choice Program and agreed to pay independent private schools $2,500 per year for each participating student. Beginning with 260 students in the fall of 1990, the program now enrolls over 500. More than 95 percent are African or Hispanic American. All are from low-income families.[86]

The Milwaukee experiment bristles with media intrigue. The major advocate of the program in the state legislature was an African-American woman, a Jesse Jackson Democrat who rankled some members of her party by joining forces with Wisconsin's Republican governor. U.S. Secretary of Education Lamar Alexander wasted no time endorsing the program. Chubb and Moe also support it, while many in the "education establishment"—officials in state departments of education and teacher unions—are opposed. While the program was getting under way, the mayor of Milwaukee called for closing down the public school system. Parents voiced loud complaints about one of the private schools in the experiment, and midway through the first year the school withdrew and went out of business, leaving 150 students stranded. Such things play well in the media.[87]

Private school choice is receiving mixed reviews in Milwaukee. Parents in the program have become more involved in their children's education, and parents are generally more satisfied than they were with the city's public schools. On the other hand, test scores of students in the program have not risen significantly, and more than one-third of the students did not return to private schools after the first year.[88]

Whether choice will prove to be *the* educational reform of the 1990s remains to be seen. The trend toward choice in some form is unmistakable, but so far choice seems to be neither panacea nor poison. It may not cure every ill of public education, but neither is it likely to kill the patient.

As the debate over choice flows into the larger debate over private schools and public schools, it seems appropriate to reflect on America's educational traditions. I hope my feelings about public education have come through in this book. I am critical of the public schools, but for what it is worth, they have my support. At the same time, I understand why some people support private schools.

The activities I suggest below are intended to help you see the contrast between the traditions of public education and private education. Think about the different principles underlying the two traditions. How do you, as a prospective teacher, feel about the principles of public or *common* schooling? Have the principles worked well enough in practice to merit your support? Now ask the same kinds of questions about the three sectors of private education.

The more experience I have with American education, the longer and more complex my answers to such questions become—now they have filled the pages of this textbook. I hope this book helps you find your own answers. The ongoing debate over public schools and private schools brings *America's Teachers* to a fitting conclusion.

## ACTIVITIES

1. Visit one school in each of the three sectors of private education: Roman Catholic, other religious, and independent. Talk with the teachers and principal in each school about some of the issues discussed in this chapter: the demographics of the student body, the qualifications and credentials of the teachers, the content and academic standards of the curriculum, and state regulations that affect the school. Also ask the teachers and principal why (or if) they prefer to work in a private setting, touching on such things as working conditions, salaries, and intangible rewards.

2. During your visit to each school, request permission to talk with a group of students. Ask them, too, about some of the issues in this chapter, especially their reasons for attending a private rather than a public school.

3. Stage a debate in your college class on tuition tax credits, vouchers, and state regulation of private schools.

## RECOMMENDED READINGS

Carper, James C., and Thomas C. Hunt, eds. *Religious Schooling in America* (Birmingham, AL: Religious Education Press, 1984).
Carper and Hunt offer sympathetic, well-documented chapters on Roman Catholic, conservative Christian, Lutheran, Jewish, and a variety of other religious schools.

Chubb, John E., and Terry M. Moe. *Politics, Markets, and America's Schools* (Washington, D.C.: Brookings Institution, 1990).
This book is at the center of the debate over educational choice.

Coleman, James S., and Thomas Hoffer. *Public and Private High Schools: The Impact of Communities* (New York: Basic Books, 1987).
Coleman and Hoffer present the best single brief for the superiority of private schools, especially Roman Catholic schools.

Peshkin, Alan. *God's Choice: The Total World of a Fundamentalist Christian School* (Chicago: University of Chicago Press, 1986).
Peshkin wrote this book after spending a year observing in a fundamentalist Christian school.

## NOTES

1. For an account of how the line between public and private schools was drawn, see Robert L. Church and Michael W. Sedlak, *Education in the United States: An Interpretive History* (New York: Free Press, 1976), chaps. 2, 3, 6.
2. James S. Coleman and Thomas Hoffer: *Public and Private High Schools: The Impact of Communities* (New York: Basic Books, 1987); John E. Chubb and Terry M. Moe, *Politics, Markets, and America's Schools* (Washington, D.C.: Brookings Institution, 1990).
3. U.S. Department of Education, National Center for Education Statistics, *Digest of Education Statistics, 1991* (Washington, D.C.: U.S. Government Printing Office, 1991), pp. 68, 12.

4. Ibid.

5. Ibid.; U.S. Department of Education, Center for Education Statistics, *The Condition of Education, 1986 Edition* (Washington, D.C.: U.S. Government Printing Office, 1986), pp. 189–190; U.S. Department of Education, National Center for Education Statistics, *Diversity of Private Schools* (Washington, D.C.: USDE, 1991), pp. 1–2, 8–9.

6. Ibid.

7. Ibid.; "Private Schools," *Education Week* (October 9, 1991), p. 9. For a look at schools belonging to the National Association of Independent Schools, see Pearl Rock Kane's "What Is an Independent School?" *Teachers College Record* 92 (Spring 1991): 396–408.

8. *The Edison Project* (Knoxville, TN: The Edison Project, 1992).

9. Ibid., p. 3.

10. See, for example, Linda Darling-Hammond's "For-Profit Schooling: Where's the Public Good?" *Education Week* (October 7, 1992), p. 40.

11. U.S. Department of Education, National Center for Education Statistics, *Private Schools in the United States: A Statistical Profile, with Comparisons to Public Schools* (Washington, D.C.: U.S. Government Printing Office, 1991), pp. 3, 46.

12. Ibid., pp. 27, 46.

13. Ibid., pp. 26, 39–40; U.S. Department of Education, National Center for Education Statistics, *The Condition of Education, 1992* (Washington, D.C.: U.S. Government Printing Office, 1992), p. 104.

14. Mark Walsh, "Black Private Academies Are Held Up as Filling Void," *Education Week* (March 13, 1991), pp. 1, 28–29.

15. U.S. Department of Education, *Private Schools,* p. 26; Bruno V. Manno, "Stereotypes, Statistics, and Catholic Schools," *Education Week* (November 13, 1985), p. 22; Anne Pavuk, "Catholic Schools Continue Enrollment Slide," *Education Week* (April 22, 1987), p. 9.

16. James S. Coleman, Thomas Hoffer, and Sally Kilgore, *Public and Private Schools* (Washington, D.C.: National Center for Educational Statistics, 1981); Coleman, Hoffer, and Kilgore, *High School Achievement: Public, Catholic, and Private Schools Compared* (New York: Basic Books, 1982).

17. Several journals invited Coleman, his critics, and his defenders to take up these arguments at length in their pages: *Educational Researcher* 10 (August–September 1981); *Harvard Educational Review* 51 (November 1981); *Phi Delta Kappan* 63 (November 1981); and *Sociology of Education* 55 (April–July 1982).

18. See William Snider, "Poor, Wealthier Catholic High Schoolers Found Gaining at Same Rate in Studies," *Education Week* (March 5, 1986), pp. 1–11; Andrew M. Greeley, *Catholic High Schools and Minority Students* (New Brunswick, NJ: Transaction Books, 1982).

19. James S. Coleman and Thomas Hoffer, *Public and Private High Schools: The Impact of Communities* (New York: Basic Books, 1987).

20. Ibid., chaps. 3–5. Coleman's studies of private schools led him to conclusions different from those he reached in *Equality of Educational Opportunity* (Washington, D.C.: U.S. Government Printing Office, 1966), often called "The Coleman Report." There he stated that achievement is more influenced by the socioeconomic background of students than by the characteristics of the schools they attend.

21. Coleman and Hoffer, *Public and Private High Schools,* chaps. 3–5.

22. Robert Rothman, "Debate on Merits of Public, Private Schools Reignites," *Education Week* (September 18, 1991), pp. 1, 16.

23. Albert Shanker, "What's the *Real* Score?" *New York Times* (September 8, 1991), p. E7.

24. Rothman, "Debate on Merits of Public, Private Schools."
25. Ibid.
26. Coleman and Hoffer, *Public and Private High Schools,* p. 9.
27. Ibid., p. 10.
28. Ibid., p. 221; emphasis in the original.
29. Ibid., p. 4.
30. For an excellent case study of Christian education, see Alan Peshkin's *God's Choice: The Total World of a Fundamentalist Christian School* (Chicago: University of Chicago Press, 1986). Another fine account, sympathetic but evenhanded, is James C. Carper's "The Christian Day School," in Carper and Thomas C. Hunt, eds., *Religious Schooling in America* (Birmingham, AL: Religious Education Press, 1984), chap. 5. Also see Susan D. Rose's *Keeping Them Out of the Hands of Satan: Evangelical Schooling in America* (New York: Routledge, 1989).
31. David Nevin and Robert E. Bills, *The Schools that Fear Built: Segregationist Academies in the South* (Washington, D.C.: Acropolis Books, 1976).
32. Virginia D. Nordin and Turner L. Williams, "More than Segregation Academies: The Growing Protestant Fundamentalist Schools," *Phi Delta Kappan* 61 (February 1980): 391–394; William J. Reese, "Soldiers of Christ in the Army of God: The Christian School Movement in America," *Educational Theory* 35 (Spring 1985): 175–194.
33. U.S. Department of Education, *Diversity of Private Schools,* p. 2.
34. Berniece B. Seiferth, "A Critical Review of the New Christian Schools," *High School Journal* 68 (December 1984–January 1985): 70–74. See also Dan B. Fleming and Thomas C. Hunt's "The World as Seen by Students in Accelerated Christian Education Schools" and Ronald E. Johnson's "ACE Responds," *Phi Delta Kappan* 68 (March 1987): 518–521.
35. Quoted in Seiferth, "A Critical Review," p. 71.
36. Donald A. Erickson, "Choice and Private Schools: Dynamics of Supply and Demand," in Daniel C. Levy, ed., *Private Education: Studies in Choice and Public Policy* (New York: Oxford University Press, 1986), pp. 90–91.
37. Alan N. Grover, *Ohio's Trojan Horse: A Warning to Christian Schools Everywhere* (Greenville, SC: Bob Jones University Press, 1977). The very existence of secular humanism is highly controversial, with People for the American Way, the American Civil Liberties Union, and similar groups charging that the concept is a smoke screen, a catch-all for anything fundamentalists dislike.
38. Joseph W. Newman, "Organized Prayer and Secular Humanism in Mobile, Alabama's Public Schools," in Joe L. Kincheloe and William F. Pinar, eds., *Curriculum as Social Psychoanalysis: The Significance of Place* (Albany: State University of New York Press, 1991), pp. 45–74; Kenneth P. Nuger, "The Religion of Secular Humanism in Public Schools: *Smith v. Board of School Commissioners,*" *West's Education Law Reporter* 38 (June 25, 1987): 871–879.
39. Quoted in "Freedom of Religion," *School Law Reporter* 28 (December 1987): 2.
40. Kenneth P. Nuger, "Accommodating Religious Objections to State Reading Programs: *Mozert v. Hawkins County Public Schools,*" *West's Education Law Reporter* 36 (February 19, 1987): 255–265.
41. Quoted in "Textbook Religious Matters," *School Law Reporter* 28 (December 1987): 3. For discussions of both *Smith* and *Mozert,* see Kenneth P. Nuger's "Judicial Responses to Religious Challenges Concerning Humanistic Public Education: The Free Exercise and Establishment Debate Continues," *Alabama Law Review* 39 (Fall 1987): 73–101; and Perry A. Zirkel's "The Textbook Cases: Secularism on Appeal," *Phi Delta Kappan* 69 (December 1987): 308–310.

42. Eugene F. Provenzo discusses these and related issues in *Religious Fundamentalism and American Education: The Battle for the Public Schools* (Albany: State University of New York Press, 1990).

43. Mark Walsh, "Home-Schooled Pupils Fare Well on Tests, Survey of Parents Finds," *Education Week* (February 13, 1991), p. 9. For introductions to the movement, see Jane Van Galen and Mary Ann Pittman, eds., *Home Schooling: Political, Historical, and Pedagogical Perspectives* (Norwood, NJ: Ablex, 1990); and John Holt, *Teach Your Own: A New and Hopeful Path for Parents and Educators* (New York: Delta, 1982).

44. Ibid.; Patricia M. Lines, "An Overview of Home Instruction," *Phi Delta Kappan* 68 (March 1987): 510–517; Kirsten Goldberg, "Pressure Pays Off for Home-Schooling Families," *Education Week* (September 30, 1987), pp. 11–12.

45. Walsh, "Home-Schooled Pupils."

46. Lines, "An Overview"; Goldberg, "Pressure Pays Off."

47. Sam Allis, "Schooling Kids at Home," *Time* (October 22, 1990), p. 84; David Guterson, "When Schools Fail Children," *Harper's* (November 1990), pp. 58–64; Linda Winkelried-Dobson, "I Teacher My Kids at Home," *Good Housekeeping* (March 1990), p. 80; Jill Lawrence, "Republican, Democratic Platforms Are Miles Apart," *Mobile Press Register* (August 15, 1992), pp. 1A, 4A.

48. Patricia M. Lines, "State Regulation of Private Education," *Phi Delta Kappan* 63 (October 1982): 119–123; Phyllis L. Blaustein, "Public and Nonpublic Schools: Finding Ways to Work Together," *Phi Delta Kappan* 67 (January 1986): 368–372.

49. Ibid.

50. Ibid.

51. James C. Carper and Neal E. Devins give these arguments a favorable review in "Rendering unto Caesar: State Regulation of Christian Day Schools," *Journal of Thought* 20 (Winter 1985): 99–113.

52. Michael D. Baker takes the side of the state officials in "Regulation of Fundamentalist Christian Schools: Free Exercise of Religion v. the State's Interest in Quality Education," *Kentucky Law Journal* 67 (1978–1979): 415–429; Goldberg, "Pressure Pays Off," p. 11.

53. Ralph D. Mawdsley and Steven P. Permuth, "State Regulation of Religious Schools," *NOLPE School Law Journal* 11 (1983): 55–64.

54. Ibid.; Louis Fischer, David Schimmel, and Cynthia Kelly, *Teachers and the Law,* 3d ed. (White Plains, NY: Longman, 1991), pp. 344–347; Julia Woltman, "Home Schooling Doubles in North Dakota since Deregulation," *Education Week* (November 8, 1989), p. 15.

55. Robert Rothman, "Court Strikes South Carolina Testing Requirement for Home Schoolers," *Education Week* (January 9, 1992), pp. 31, 36.

56. Chubb and Moe, *Politics, Markets, and America's Schools,* chaps. 4–5.

57. Ibid., p. 183.

58. Ibid.

59. Ibid., p. 217.

60. Ibid., pp. 219–225.

61. Ibid., p. 225.

62. Ibid., p. 222.

63. Ernest L. Boyer, *School Choice* (Ewing, NJ: California/Princeton, 1992).

64. Chubb and Moe, *Politics, Markets, and America's Schools,* pp. 34, 220.

65. Ibid., p. 34.

66. Ibid.

67. Ibid., pp. 169, 183–184, 190–191. For an analysis of educational choice in several different geographical settings, see George Uhlig's "A Question of Choice," *Kappa Delta Pi Record* (Winter 1992): 42–45.
68. Mark K. Kutner, Joel D. Sherman, and Mary F. Williams, "Federal Policies for Private Schools," in Daniel C. Levy, ed., *Private Education,* chap. 2. For a discussion of the arguments on tuition tax credits, see Thomas M. James and Henry M. Levin, eds., *Public Dollars for Private Schools: The Case of Tuition Tax Credits* (Philadelphia: Temple University Press, 1983).
69. Martha M. McCarthy, "Tuition Tax Credits and the First Amendment," *Issues in Education* 1 (1983): 88–105.
70. Ibid.; Kirsten Goldberg, "Lawmakers Adopt Income-Tax Credits for Tuition in Iowa," *Education Week* (May 20, 1987), pp. 1, 18.
71. Ibid.
72. For the pioneering work on choice, see John E. Coons and Stephen B. Sugarman, *Education by Choice—The Case for Family Control* (Berkeley: University of California Press, 1978).
73. U.S. Department of Education, *America 2000: An Education Strategy.* Sourcebook (Washington, D.C.: U.S. Government Printing Office, 1991), pp. 21, 41, 49; Julie A. Miller, "Senate Rejects Private-School Choice Proposal," *Education Week* (January 29, 1992), pp. 1, 26–27.
74. Lawrence, "Republican, Democratic Platforms."
75. U.S. Department of Education, *America 2000,* p. 41.
76. Quoted in Richard N. Ostling, "A Revolution Hoping for a Miracle," *Time* (April 29, 1991), p. 53.
77. Stanley N. Elam, Lowell C. Rose, and Alec M. Gallup, "The 23rd Annual Gallup Poll of the Public's Attitudes toward the Public Schools," *Phi Delta Kappan* 73 (September 1991): 47–49; Lynn Olson, "Claims for Choice Exceed Evidence, Carnegie Reports," *Education Week* (October 28, 1992), pp. 1, 12.
78. Sy Fliegel, "Parental Choice in East Harlem Schools," in Joe Nathan, ed., *Public Schools by Choice* (St. Paul, MN: Institute for Learning and Teaching, 1989), pp. 95–112.
79. Chubb and Moe, *Politics, Markets, and America's Schools,* pp. 212–215; Olson, "Claims for Choice Exceed Evidence," p. 12.
80. Lynn Olson, " 'Supply Side' Reform or Voucher? Charter-School Concept Takes Hold," *Education Week* (January 15, 1992), pp. 1, 22.
81. Jessie Montano, "Choice Comes to Minnesota," in Nathan, ed., *Schools by Choice,* pp. 165–180.
82. Mark Walsh, "Three States See Dramatic Rise in Open-Enrollment Participation," *Education Week* (October 28, 1992), p. 12.
83. "Arizona Open Enrollment Continues to Grow, State Report Finds," *Education Week* (June 3, 1992), p. 2; "News in Brief," *Education Week* (April 25, 1990), p. 15.
84. Karen Diegmueller, "Massachusetts Education Panel Votes to Repeal Choice Law," *Education Week* (May 13, 1992), p. 17; Walsh, "Three States See Dramatic Rise."
85. Diegmueller, "Massachusetts Education Panel Votes," p. 17.
86. Mark Walsh, "Wisconsin Court Upholds State's Test of Vouchers," *Education Week* (March 11, 1992), pp. 1, 27.
87. Ibid.; Lynn Olson, "Proposals for Private-School Choice Reviving at All Levels of Government," *Education Week* (February 20, 1991), pp. 1, 10–11.
88. Lynn Olson, "Milwaukee Voucher Plan Found Not to 'Skim' Cream," *Education Week* (December 4, 1991), p. 12.

# Index

Ability grouping, 152–153, 163, 209, 215–218
*Abington School District v. Schempp* (1963), 326
Academic critics, 1950s, 185–187, 190, 191
Academic freedom, 121, 126, 129–131
Academies, 143–144, 146
Accountability, 27, 42–44, 52, 108–112, 129, 185, 190–191, 253, 258–262, 269–272, 278, 289, 295–296, 333
Addams, Jane, 154, 156–158
Adler, Mortimer J., 180–185, 192, 301, 321
Administrators
    career ladders and, 49–50
    collective bargaining and, 96–97
    effective schools and, 229
    gender, 93, 238
    "professional" quest, 164, 252
    progressivism and, 154, 162–163
    standardized testing and, 292, 294–295
    teacher autonomy and, 11, 108, 110–111
    teacher dissent and, 131–133
    teacher evaluation and, 40–42, 44–45, 47, 109, 111, 124, 164
    teacher organizations and, 93–94, 98, 110–112, 164
    teacher selection and, 8
Aesthetics, 176
Affirmative action, 92, 198
African Americans, 218–232. *See also* Desegregation; Race; Segregation; Students, minority
    African identity schools, 320
    demographic trends, 7, 16, 70–71, 79–80, 210, 320
    historical trends in education, 140, 143, 152–155, 158–162, 166–167
    local school board elections and, 253–256

    poverty, 201
    Roman Catholic schools and, 321
    single-parent families, 210
    student testing and, 163, 293
    teacher testing and, 78–80
    in teaching force, 70–71, 73, 78–80, 92, 133
AIDS (Acquired Immune Deficiency Syndome), 124, 126–128, 131, 268, 329
Alcohol, 3, 122
Alexander, Lamar, 18, 50, 190–191, 259–261, 269–270, 293, 336, 338
American Achievement Tests, 270, 298
American Association of Colleges for Teacher Education (AACTE), 80
American Association of University Women (AAUW), 235–236
American Bar Association (ABA), 103
American College Testing (ACT) Program, 69, 73, 79, 216, 261, 290, 297
American Federation of Labor-Congress of Industrial Organizations (AFL-CIO), 91–93
American Federation of Teachers (AFT), 89–102. *See also* Teacher organizations
    career ladders and, 51–52
    Carnegie Forum on Education and the Economy and, 39, 51–52, 109
    differences with National Education Association, 28, 40–44, 52, 107–109, 164–165, 271
    federal politics of education and, 100–101, 272
    merit pay and, 39–41, 44, 48, 52, 92, 108
    teacher autonomy and, 11, 12–13, 107
    teacher education and certification and, 19
    teacher employment and, 121–123
    teacher professionalism and, 90, 103, 109–113
*American High School Today, The* (Conant), 186

Americanization, 156
American Library Association (ALA), 131
American Medical Association (AMA), 78, 100, 103, 105–106, 113
American Teachers Association (ATA), 92
America 2000, 18, 185, 191, 202–203, 268, 270–271, 293, 298, 335
Anderson, James D., 155
*And Madly Teach* (Smith), 70, 186
Anglo-Americans, 155–156, 219, 221
Apple, Michael, 291
Aristotle, 177
Arkansas, educational reform in, 271–272, 337
Aronowitz, Stanley, 199–200, 202
Asian Americans, 218–220, 222–223. *See also* Race; Students, minority
  bilingual education and, 232–235
  demographic trends, 7, 210, 320
  historical trends in education, 155
  local school board elections and, 254
  segregation, 155, 226
Assessment centers, 46–47. *See also* Teacher evaluation
Assimilation, 152, 155–158, 162, 167, 223, 232, 240, 317
Association for School, College and University Staffing (ASCUS), 20–21
Athletics, 238–239, 258
Axiology, 176

Baby boom, bust, and boomlet, 13–17, 20
Back to basics, 11, 14, 63, 81, 106, 175, 198–199, 259–260, 262, 271, 287–296
Bagley, William C., 185–187, 190, 192
Barnard, Henry, 146–147
Behaviorism, 44–46, 187–189, 291, 296
Belenky, Mary F., 240–241
Bell, Terrel, 268
Bennett, William J., 19, 183–184, 189–192, 198, 200, 267–269, 293, 301–302, 304, 306
Bestor, Arthur, 186, 190, 192
Bilingual education, 158, 167, 209–210, 222, 232–235
Bilingual Education Act (1968), 233, 264
"Bill of Rights" of teachers (AFT), 108, 122
Bloom, Allan, 74, 190, 304–305
*Bolden v. City of Mobile* (1980), 255
Books, text and library
  banning of, 130–131, 327
  fundamentalist Christians and, 327–328
  gender roles in, 236–237
  selection of, 131, 165, 237, 252, 257
Boyer, Ernest, 202–203, 291, 333
Brownson, Orestes, 148–150
*Brown v. Board of Education of Topeka* (1954), 92, 167, 201, 223–225, 232, 262–263, 324
Bruner, Jerome, 46
Buckley, William F., 305
Bush, George, 18, 68, 101, 185, 189, 191, 198, 202–203, 229, 234–235, 250, 262–264, 268–272, 293, 298, 335–336
Busing, 226–228, 230, 265, 267

California Achievement Test, 289, 297
Cannell, John, 294
Canon, 200
*Cardinal Principles of Secondary Education* (Commission on the Reorganization of Secondary Education), 168, 194
Career ladders, 27–28, 35, 39, 47–53, 104, 110, 259
Carnegie Forum on Education and the Economy, 18, 27, 35, 39, 49, 51–53, 58, 64–66, 78, 92, 97, 104, 108, 110–111, 259, 297
Carnegie Foundation for the Advancement of Teaching, 11, 105, 202, 333
Carter, James G., 145–147, 265–266
Carter, Jimmy, 100, 262
Categorical aid, federal, 263–265
Cavazos, Lauro, 269
*Changing the Odds* (College Board), 216–217
Channel One, 319
Chapter I. *See* Elementary and Secondary Education Act (1965)
Charter schools, 332–334, 337. *See also* Educational choice
Chicago, educational reform in, 252–253
Child abuse and neglect, 123–126
*Child and the Curriculum, The* (Dewey), 193
Childs, John, 196
Chubb, John E., 316, 331–338
Civil Rights Act (1964), 224, 264
Civil rights movement, 162, 220, 224
Clark, Joe, 215
Clinton, Bill, 19, 101, 199, 201, 203, 229, 235, 250, 260–264, 269–273, 277, 279, 335–336
*Closing of the American Mind, The* (Bloom), 74, 190, 304
Coalition of American Public Employees (CAPE), 93
Coalition of Essential Schools, 204
"Code of Ethics for the Education Profession" (NEA), 108, 122
Coker, Homer, 44
Cold War, 264
Coleman, James, 288–289, 316, 320–324, 332
Coleman Report. *See Equality of Educational Opportunity*
Collective bargaining, 30, 35, 37–39, 51–52, 89–90, 93, 95–98, 101–102, 109–112, 120, 165
College Entrance Examination Board (CEEB), 216–217, 288–290
Colleges and universities. *See also* Teacher education and certification
  academic preparation for, 167, 187, 197, 212–214, 216–217, 232, 271
  academies and, 144
  African-American students, 159–162, 166, 221, 224, 227
  Asian-American students, 223
  Hispanic-American students, 221
  Native American students, 223
  perennialism and, 180
  SAT score decline, 261, 288–290, 292, 308
Commission on the Reorganization of Secondary Education, 168, 194

Committee for Economic Development, 259
Committee of Ten, 167–169
Common school reform, 141–152, 315
Compensatory education, 198, 249, 264, 266
Comprehensive Test of Basic Skills, 289, 294
Compulsory attendance laws, 151, 162
Computers and computer science, 76–77, 184, 188, 278, 295, 300. *See also* Technology
Conant, James B., 186–188
Concerned Educators against Forced Unionism, 96
*Condition of Teaching, The* (Carnegie Foundation for the Advancement of Teaching), 11, 261
*Connick v. Meyers* (1983), 132–133
Consolidation of schools, 166
Cooperative learning, 201, 216, 302
Cooperman, Saul, 20
Council for Basic Education, 186–187, 268
Council of Chief State School Officers, 260
Council of Independent Black Institutions, 231
Counts, George S., 196, 199, 211, 256
Courts, 119–134, 152, 158, 166–167, 225–226, 228–233, 249, 254–256, 262–263, 266–267, 273, 275–278, 326–331. *See also* specific court cases
Covello, Leonard, 157–158
Crain, Robert L., 227
Creationism, 331
Critical theory, 199–200, 202, 215, 241. *See also* Postmodernism
Cuban, Larry, 168–169, 194
Cuban Americans, 219, 221. *See also* Hispanic Americans
Cubberley, Ellwood P., 154–156, 158, 160–161
Cultural heritage, 74, 157–158, 177, 180–181, 185–186, 188–191, 218–223, 230–235. *See also* Cultural literacy
Cultural literacy, 190, 288, 304–308
*Cultural Literacy* (Hirsch), 74, 190, 304–308
Curriculum, 287–309. *See also* specific philosophies and theories of education
  Afrocentric, 231
  collective bargaining and, 106
  critical theory, postmodernism, and, 200
  diversified, 152–153, 156, 162, 168, 211. *See also* Ability Grouping; Tracking; Vocational education
  educational finance and, 277
  government regulation of private schools and, 329–331
  measurement-driven ("cookbook"), 30, 45, 81, 106, 131, 188, 259
  multicultural, 157–158, 234, 253, 307–308
  national standards and assessments for, 190, 204, 270–272

"Dare Progressive Education Be Progressive?" (Counts), 196
*Dare the School Build a New Social Order?* (Counts), 196
Darling-Hammond, Linda, 69, 76
Darwin, Charles, 177

*Death at an Early Age* (Kozol), 201
*Democracy in Education* (Dewey), 192–194
Democratic Party, 100–101, 148, 198, 265–266, 272, 298, 316, 322, 334–335, 338
Desegregation, 198, 209–210, 223–232, 262–263, 265, 267, 336. *See also* African Americans; Race; Segregation
*De-Valuing of America, The* (Bennett), 189–190, 302, 306
Dewey, John, 154, 156–157, 162, 168, 177–178, 191–199, 201, 204, 306, 308
*Diminished Mind, The* (Smith), 186
Disability
  of students, 69, 127, 166–167, 264–265, 275, 292
  of teachers, 122
Discipline, student
  academic freedom and, 131
  essentialists and, 186–187, 268
  in magnet schools, 229
  parents and, 214, 252
  in private schools, 320, 326
  problems in schools, 9, 14, 269, 288
  teacher education and, 62–63
  teacher incompetency and, 122
District schools, 142–143, 145–147, 150, 184
Down, A. Graham, 268
Dropouts. *See* Students, dropouts
Drugs, 3, 14, 122–123, 158, 198, 215, 268–269, 288, 326, 329
DuBois, W. E. B., 154, 159–162, 232

Economic Opportunity Act (1964), 264
Edison Project, 319
Educational choice, 110, 191, 229, 250, 268, 270, 272, 315–316, 322, 331–338
Educational Excellence Network, 190
Educational finance, 273–279
  educational choice and, 272, 316, 333–338
  equalization trends, 165, 201–202, 272–273
  federal politics and, 187, 224, 262–268, 270–273, 301
  local politics and, 16, 98, 111–112, 165–166, 251, 261–264, 266, 270
  state politics and, 16, 98, 165–166, 250–251, 257, 260–264, 266–268, 270
  in segregated schools, 158–159, 166, 201–202, 223–224, 272
  teacher dissent and, 132
  teacher organizations and, 100–101, 279
  teacher salaries and, 38–39, 259
Educational reform. *See* Back to basics; Common school reform; Curriculum; Educational choice; Educational finance; Excellence in education; Progressive school reform; specific states and cities; Teacher professionalism
  national standards and assessments, 270–271, 287, 293–294, 296–300
  restructuring, 11, 27–28, 48–53, 109–112, 250, 262, 269, 336
  school-based management, 110, 250, 252–253, 262, 278, 336

Educational reform (*continued*)
    student testing and, 259–262, 292–300
    teacher attitudes toward, 11, 30, 92, 203, 261
    teacher education and certification and, 58,
        63–82, 103–104, 259–260, 262
    teacher empowerment and, 11, 97, 107–113, 296
    teacher organizations and, 92, 109–113
    teacher salaries and, 17, 27–30, 47–53, 259, 262
    teacher testing and, 69–80, 259–261, 272
Educational Testing Service (ETS), 74, 76–78, 82,
    104, 289–290, 303
*Educational Wastelands* (Bestor), 186
Education of All Handicapped Children Act (1975),
    127, 165
Education Amendments (1972), 231, 238–239,
    265–267
*Education of Blacks in the South, The* (Anderson),
    155
Education Commission of the States, 260, 295
Education Consolidation and Improvement Act
    (1981), 266
Education of Handicapped Children Act (1966), 264
*Education and Liberty* (Conant), 186
Education Summit Conference, 269
Effective schools research, 229–230, 320, 332
Eisenhower, Dwight, 262
Elementary and Secondary Education Act (1965),
    264–265, 272, 335
Elementary schools. *See also* Curriculum
    ability grouping, 216
    academic standards, 185, 257, 269, 289, 291,
        294, 298, 301–302, 308
    historical development, 141–147, 151–152, 162,
        167, 264
    textbooks, 236–237
*Elmtown's Youth* (Hollingshead), 212
*Engel v. Vitale* (1962), 326
English as a Second Language (ESL), 233–234
English-only laws, 233
Epistemology, 176
*Equality of Educational Opportunity* (Coleman et
    al.), 288–289
Escalante, Jaime, 271–272
Essentialism, 183–192
    back to basics and, 81, 168, 198–199, 287, 291,
        296, 300–302
    Bennett, William, and, 268
    Clinton, Bill, and, 271–272
    cultural literacy and, 307–308
    as dominant educational theory, 81, 168, 218,
        287
    versus progressivism, 179–181, 197–200,
        202–203, 287, 300–302, 308–309
Ethics, 176
Ethnicity, 218–223. *See also* Students, minority
    bilingual education and, 158
    Civil Rights Act (1964) and, 264
    critical theory, postmodernism, and, 141, 199–200
    Education Amendments (1972) and, 265
    equal educational opportunities and, 152, 155,
        167, 209

    gender and, 210, 235, 241
    literacy skills and, 304
    of local and state school board members,
        253–256, 258
    private schools and, 143, 317–320, 333–334
    social class and, 210, 235, 241
    teacher expression and, 133
    test bias and, 74
Ethnic studies, 265. *See also* Multicultural education
Evolution, 326, 331
Excellence in education, 92, 168, 185, 187, 190,
    258–262, 267–269, 271, 287, 301
Exceptionality. *See* Disability; Students, disabled,
    gifted
Existentialism, 178–179, 198

Factory model of schooling, 43, 192, 288–289
Families. *See also* Parents
    Asian-American, 222
    child-rearing practices, 213–214
    gender-role socialization and, 236
    government intervention and, 202–203
    home schooling and, 315, 328–329
    human capital and social capital, 323–324
    single-parent, 210
    "traditional," 210
*Family Educational Rights and Privacy Act* (1974),
    127
Fass, Paula, 155
Federal politics of education, 249–250, 262–273. *See
    also* Alexander, Lamar; Bennett, William;
    Bush, George; Clinton, Bill; Courts;
    Educational finance; Reagan, Ronald
    bilingual education and, 233–235
    desegregation and, 224–226, 229–230
    educational choice and, 316, 334–336, 338
    higher education and, 290
    historical trends, 165–166, 274–276
    teacher organizations and, 97–100
    Title IX and, 238–239
Feminism. *See* Gender
Finkelstein, Barbara, 147
Finn, Chester E., Jr., 184, 189–191, 198, 253, 302,
    304–309
First Amendment, U.S. Constitution, 129, 132–133,
    328, 335
Fischer, Louis, 124
Five New Basics, 188, 287–288, 300–301
Fordham, Signithia, 230–231
Foreign languages, emphasis on, 188, 198, 232, 264,
    300
*Foundations of Method* (Kilpatrick), 194
Fourteenth Amendment, U.S. Constitution, 123, 276
Franklin, Benjamin, 143–144
Friends for Education, 294
Fundamentalist Christian schools, 315–319,
    324–331. *See also* Private schools
Futrell, Mary, 12, 52

Gangs, 215, 329
Geiger, Keith, 12, 52, 93

Gender, 235–241. *See also* Students, female; Students, male; Teachers, demographic characteristics; Teaching, as men's work; Teaching, as women's work
  critical theory, postmodernism, and, 141, 199–200
  dismissal of teachers and, 121
  educational reform and, 155
  equal educational opportunities and, 144, 151–152, 166–167, 210
  ethnicity and, 210, 235, 241
  literacy skills and, 304
  of local and state school board members, 253–256, 258
  private schools and, 317
  race and, 210, 230–231, 241
  single-parent families and, 210
  social class and, 210, 230–231, 241
  teacher organizations and, 93–94, 112, 164–165
  Title IX and, 265–267
General aid, federal, 263–264
German Americans, 144, 154, 158, 219
G.I. Bill (1944), 166
Gilligan, Carol, 240–241
Giroux, Henry A., 199–200, 202
*Goldberg v. Kelly* (1970), 123
Goodlad, John I., 80–82, 203, 291
Gore, Al, 101
*Governing the Young* (Finkelstein), 147
Graduate Record Examinations (GRE), 74
Graham, Patricia A., 79–80
Grambling State University, 80
Granville County, North Carolina, merit pay in, 47–48
Great books of Western civilization, 181–184

Havighurst, Robert J., 210–211
Head Start, 264, 270, 272
Hesburgh, Theodore, 60
*Higher Learning in America, The* (Hutchins), 180
Higher-level academic skills, 188–189, 292–293
*High School* (Boyer), 203
*High School Achievement* (Coleman et al.), 320
High schools. *See also* Curriculum
  academic standards, 185, 203–204, 216, 251, 257, 260, 269, 271, 289, 291–292, 300–302, 306–308, 320–322
  historical development, 144, 146, 151–152, 160, 162, 164, 167–168, 194, 211–212, 307–308
  textbooks, 236–237
Hirsch, E. D., Jr., 74, 184, 190–191, 198, 304–308
Hispanic Americans, 218–222. *See also* Ethnicity; Students, minority
  bilingual education and, 232–235
  demographic trends, 7, 16, 210, 320
  educational finance and, 275–276
  Escalante, Jaime and, 271
  local school board elections and, 253–256
  poverty, 210
  Roman Catholic schools and, 321
  segregation, 226

single-parent families, 210
student testing and, 293
teacher testing and, 79
in teaching force, 79
Historical interpretation, 140–142, 153–156
Hoffer, Thomas, 316
*Hoffman v. Board of Education of the City of New York* (1979), 129
Hollingshead, August B., 212
Holmes Group, 27, 35, 39, 51–53, 58, 60, 64–67, 73, 78, 97, 104
Home schooling, 315, 328–331. *See also* Private schools
*Horace's Compromise* (Sizer), 203, 290
*Horace's School* (Sizer), 203–204, 290
Houston, Texas, merit pay in, 48
*How Schools Shortchange Girls* (AAUW), 235–236
*How Teachers Taught* (Cuban), 168–169, 194
Hufstedler, Shirley, 265
Human capital, 323–324
Hunter, Madeline, 44
Hutchins, Robert M., 180–181, 192

Idealism, 176–180, 184, 192
IEP (Individualized Educational Program), 265
Immigration, 144–145, 150–151, 153–155, 219, 232, 317–318
Independent schools, 315, 317–319, 321–323, 330, 338. *See also* Private schools
*In a Different Voice* (Gilligan), 240
Industrial education. *See* Vocational education
Industrialization, 144–145, 153
*In Search of Excellence* (Peters), 201
Integration. *See* Desegregation
*Intellectual Freedom Manual* (ALA), 131
Iowa Test of Basic Skills, 289, 294, 297

Jackson, Jesse, 215, 338
James, William, 177
*James Madison Elementary School* (Bennett), 189, 301
*James Madison High School* (Bennett), 189, 301
Japan, 187, 217, 267, 299, 304
Jefferson, Thomas, 144, 186
Jewish Americans, 149, 219, 316
Johnson, Lyndon, 166, 262, 264–266
Judeo-Christian tradition, 189, 268, 326–327

Kaestle, Carl F., 303–304
*Kalamazoo* case (1874), 152
Kean, Thomas, 20, 260, 271
*Keeping Track* (Oakes), 216
Kelly, Cynthia, 124
Kennedy, John F., 262
*Kentucky State Board for Elementary and Secondary Education v. Rudasill* (1979), 331
Kentucky, educational reform in, 277–279
Kilpatrick, James J., 305
Kilpatrick, William Heard, 194–196, 306, 308
King, Rev. Martin Luther, Jr., 224
Kozol, Jonathan, 199–202, 272, 277–278

Laboratory School, University of Chicago, 191, 193
Lake Wobegon effect, 294–295
Lamm, Richard, 260
Language, diversity in, 143, 154, 156–157, 213–214, 218–219, 221–223. *See also* Bilingual education
Latin grammar schools, 142–143
*Lau v. Nichols* (1974), 233
Lawyers, compared to teachers, 12–13, 21–22, 33–35, 45, 73, 78, 90, 92, 97, 99, 102–105, 108, 129, 330
*Lean on Me,* 215
Levine, Daniel U., 210–211
Life adjustment education, 197
*Life in Schools* (McLaren), 200
Literacy, 7, 13, 71–73, 77, 142, 302–304
*Literacy: Profiles of America's Young Adults* (NAEP), 302–303
*Literacy in the United States* (Kaestle et al.), 303–304
Local boards of education, 249–256. *See also* Local politics of education
    academic freedom and, 129–131
    AIDS regulations, 126–128
    collective bargaining and, 30, 37–39, 95–98, 109–112, 120
    educational choice and, 333, 336–338
    merit pay and, 40–44, 111–112
    progressive era reforms, 163–164
    segregation and, 222–226
    teacher autonomy and, 11, 106, 108–109
    teacher employment and, 120–124
    teacher job market and, 19
    teacher organizations and, 30, 35–39, 95–102, 120
    teacher salaries and, 35–39
    teacher testing and, 72
Local politics of education, 141–151, 163–166, 249–256, 274–276. *See also* Educational finance
Lower-level academic skills, 188–189, 292–293
Lynd, Helen, 211
Lynd, Robert, 211
Lyon, Mary, 144

*McGuffey's Readers,* 325
McLaren, Peter, 199–200, 202
McWalters, Peter, 109, 111
Madison, James, 144
Magnet schools, 228–230, 336
Mann, Horace, 146–150, 153, 165–166, 258
Martin, Jane Roland, 240–241
Master of Arts in Teaching (MAT), 66
Mathematics
    emphasis on, 187–188, 198, 264, 269, 271, 300–301
    gender gap in, 235, 239–240
*Medical Education in the United States and Canada* (Flexner), 105–106
Medley, Donald M., 44
Melting pot, 155–156, 158

Mental discipline, 167–168
Merit pay, 27, 35, 39–53, 92, 108, 111–112, 164, 294. *See also* Teacher salaries
Metaphysics, 176
Metropolitan Achievement Test, 289, 294
Mexican-Americans, 155, 219, 221, 233. *See also* Hispanic Americans
Mickelson, George, 262
Middle schools, 110, 213, 216. *See also* Curriculum
*Middletown* (Lynd and Lynd), 211
Miller, Zell, 262
*Milliken v. Bradley* (1974), 230
Milwaukee, educational choice in, 337–338
Minnesota, educational choice in, 335, 337
Modernization, 144–147, 153–154
Moe, Terry M., 316, 331–338
Mondale, Walter, 100, 266
*Moral Dimensions of Teaching, The* (Goodlad), 81
Morality
    Bennett, William, and, 191, 268
    common school reform and, 141–142, 147–148
    educational philosophies and theories and, 178–181, 186–187, 198
    Goodlad, John, and, 81
    private schools and, 325–330
Morris, Van Cleve, 179
*Morrison v. State Board of Education* (1969), 122, 134
*Mozert v. Hawkins County Public Schools* (1987), 327–328
*Mueller v. Allen* (1983), 335–336
Multicultural education
    bilingual education and, 234
    cultural literacy and, 307–308
    historical development, 157, 167, 219
    opposition to, 158, 253, 302
    student biases and, 237
Multiculturalism, 7, 210, 218–223, 308

National Assessment of Educational Progress (NAEP), 190, 261, 293–294, 298, 300, 302–303, 306, 308, 322–323
National Association for the Advancement of Colored People (NAACP), 159, 162, 166, 224
National Association for Bilingual Education, 235
National Association of Independent Schools (NAIS), 318–319
National Association of State Boards of Education, 260
National Board for Professional Teaching Standards (NBPTS), 35, 47, 51–53, 65, 77–78, 82, 104–105, 107–108
National Center for Innovation in Education, 109
National Child Abuse Prevention and Treatment Act (1974), 125
National Commission on Excellence in Education (NCEE), 17, 188, 300
National Council for Accreditation of Teacher Education (NCATE), 67, 69, 75–76, 105
National Council for the Social Studies, 61, 308
National Council of Teachers of English, 297, 308

National Council of Teachers of Mathematics, 297–298

National Defense Education Act (1958), 166, 187, 264, 301

National Education Association (NEA), 89–102. *See also* Teacher organizations
ability grouping and tracking and, 217
career ladders and, 52
Carnegie Forum on Education and the Economy and, 52
curriculum studies, 167–169, 194
differences with American Federation of Teachers, 28, 40, 44, 52, 107–109, 164–165, 271
educational finance proposals, 279
federal politics of education, 100–101, 265, 268, 272, 279
merit pay and, 40–41, 44, 48, 52, 92
minority teacher studies, 80
teacher autonomy and, 12, 107–109
teacher education and certification and, 19
teacher employment and, 121–123
teacher job satisfaction survey, 8–9
teacher professionalism and, 90, 103, 112–113
teacher testing and, 74, 77

National education goals, 268–272

National Evaluation Systems (NES), 74

National Governors' Association, 217, 260–261, 269–270

National Right to Work Committee, 96

National Science Teachers Association, 61

National Teacher Examinations (NTE), 68, 73–77, 104

*Nation Prepared, A* (Carnegie Forum on Education and the Economy), 18, 51–53, 64–66, 111, 297

*Nation at Risk, A* (National Commission on Excellence in Education), 267–268
educational reform and, 17, 29–30, 48, 188–189, 203, 250, 258–261, 273, 300–301
essentialism and, 185, 188–189, 203, 300–301
minimum competency testing and, 188, 292
teacher education and, 17, 62, 69
teacher salaries and, 29–30, 259, 273

Native Americans, 218–220, 223. *See also* Students, minority
demographic trends, 7, 210
historical trends in education, 155, 265
local school board elections and, 254, 256

Nevada, professional standards board, 107–108

New American Schools, 270–271

New England model, district schools, 142

New Federalism, 266–267, 270

New Jersey, alternate route into teaching, 20, 67–68

New Standards Project, 297–298

Nixon, Richard, 262, 265

Noddings, Nel, 241

Normal schools, 57–58, 60, 146, 148, 162

North Carolina Teacher Performance Appraisal Instrument (TPAI), 44–45

Northwest Ordinances (1785, 1787), 142–143

Nurses, compared to teachers, 10, 34, 70, 102, 112

Oakes, Jeannie, 216–217

Ogbu, John, 230–231

Ohanian, Susan, 63, 305

"Old Deluder Satan Law," 142

*On Further Examination* (CEEB), 289–290

*Outside In* (Fass), 155

*Paideia Proposal, The* (Adler), 181–184

*Parducci v. Rutland* (1970), 130

Parents. *See also* Families
educational choice and, 191, 331–338
educational politics and, 250, 252–254, 257
educational reform and, 109–110, 112, 187, 191
effective schools and, 229
ethnicity and race and, 156–158, 231
student testing and, 288–289
teachers and, 9, 109–110, 112, 123, 155

Pedagogy, 41, 58, 128, 162, 199

Peer groups, 213–215, 217, 230–231, 236, 329

Perennialism, 179–185, 190, 192, 218, 301, 304

Performance assessment, 204, 278, 299

Perpich, Rudy, 260

Peters, Tom, 201

*Peter W. v. San Francisco Unified School District* (1976), 128–129

Physicians, compared to teachers, 10, 19, 22, 33–35, 45, 52, 64, 69, 73, 78, 90, 92, 99, 102–105, 108, 113, 128–129, 330

*Pickering v. Board of Education* (1968), 132

Pierce, Charles Sanders, 177

Pipho, Chris, 295–296

*Place Called School, A* (Goodlad), 203

*Places Where Teachers Are Taught* (Goodlad), 81

Plato, 176–177, 181

*Plessy v. Ferguson* (1896), 158, 167, 223, 229

Pluralism, 152, 156–158, 162, 167, 231–233, 240

Political Action Committees (PACs), 100

*Politics, Markets, and America's Schools* (Chubb and Moe), 316, 331–334

Portfolios
student, 204, 299. *See also* Performance assessment
teacher, 46–47, 52, 77–78, 111–112. *See also* Teacher evaluation

*Postmodern Education* (Aronowitz and Giroux), 200

Postmodernism, 141, 199–200. *See also* Critical theory

*Power and the Promise of School Reform* (Reese), 154–155

Pragmatism, 177–180, 192

Prayer in schools, 268, 326

Preschool education, 202, 269

Private schools, 315–338. *See also* Educational Choice; Fundamentalist Christian schools; Home schooling; Independent schools; Roman Catholic schools
African identity schools, 231–232
historical development, 142–143, 146, 150–152, 156, 158
perennialism and, 183
progressivism and, 195–196, 201

Private schools (*continued*)
  race and, 226, 231–232
  state regulation, 103
  teachers, 33, 103
Professional standards boards, 107–109, 112–113
Progressive education, 163, 184, 192, 195–198, 306
Progressive Education Association, 195
Progressive school reform, 152–163, 192, 196, 255
Progressivism, 162–163, 191–204
  *Cardinal Principles of Secondary Education* and,
    168–169
  Clinton, Bill and, 272
  Dewey, John and, 154, 192
  versus essentialism, 81, 180, 184–185, 218, 287,
    296, 300–302, 308–309
"Project Method, The" (Kilpatrick), 194
Protestantism, 144, 150, 219, 221, 316, 324,
  328–329
Psychology, 163, 179
Public Law 91–142. *See* Education of All
  Handicapped Children Act (1975)
*Public and Private High Schools* (Coleman et al.),
  316, 321–324
*Public and Private Schools* (Coleman et al.),
  320–321
Puerto Ricans, 219, 221. *See also* Hispanic Americans
Puritans, 142

*Quackery in the Public Schools* (Lynd), 70
Quayle, Dan, 101

Race, 218–223. *See also* African Americans; Asian
    Americans; Desegregation; Segregation;
    Students, minority; white
  Civil Rights Act (1964) and, 224, 264
  critical theory, postmodernism, and, 141, 199–200
  educational reform and, 111
  equal educational opportunities and, 166–167,
    209
  gender and, 210, 230–231, 235, 241
  ethnicity and, 218–219
  literacy skills and, 304
  of local and state school board members,
    253–256, 258
  private schools and, 231–232, 317–320, 333–338
  social class and, 210, 219, 230–231, 241
  teacher dismissal and, 121
  teacher expression and, 133
  teacher organizations and, 92
  test bias and, 74, 79–80
Ravitch, Diane, 184, 189–191, 198, 304–308
*Ready to Learn* (Boyer), 202–203
Reagan, Ronald, 18, 166, 189, 229, 234–235, 250,
  253, 262–268, 270–271, 334–335
Realism, 177–180, 184, 192
Reduction in force ("riffing"), 123
Reese, William J., 154–155
Rehabilitation Act (1973), 127
Religion
  Bennett, William, and, 189, 268
  common school reform and, 141–145, 147–151

educational philosophies and theories and,
    176–179, 198
  ethnicity and, 218–219, 221
  private schools and, 143, 150–151, 315–331,
    335–336
  teacher expression and, 133
  teacher tenure and, 121
*Report of the Committee of Ten on Secondary
  School Studies,* 167
Republicanism, early American, 144, 148
Republican Party, 101, 198, 316, 322, 329, 334–335,
  338
Resistance to schooling, 215
Resnick, Lauren, 297, 299
*The Restoration of Learning* (Bestor), 186
Restructuring. *See* Educational reform
Rochester, New York, educational reform in, 11,
  49–52, 97, 109–112
Roman Catholic schools, 143, 149–151, 155, 221,
  315–325, 328, 330. *See also* Private schools
Romer, Roy, 262
Rugg, Harold, 196–197
Rural schools
  African-American students, 158–159
  busing, 228
  community power structure, 251
  educational finance, 266, 273–275
  historical development, 142–146, 152
  National Education Association and, 91, 94
  private, 317–318, 334
  teachers, 7, 21, 91, 94, 121
Rush, Benjamin, 144

*San Antonio Independent School District v.
  Rodriguez* (1973), 276
Sartre, Jean Paul, 178–179
*Savage Inequalities* (Kozol), 201–202, 272, 277
Schimmel, David, 124
Scholastic Aptitude Test (SAT), 69, 73–74, 79, 261,
  288–290, 292, 297, 308
School-based management. *See* Educational reform
*School Choice* (Boyer), 333
*School and Society, The* (Dewey), 191
Science
  emphasis on, 187–188, 198, 264, 269, 300–301
  gender gap in, 239–240
Secular humanism, 198, 326–328
Segregation, 152, 155–156, 158–162, 166–167, 201,
  220–223, 232–233, 319–320, 324–325. *See
  also* African Americans; Desegregation; Race;
  Students, minority; white
*Selective Character of American Secondary
  Education, The* (Counts), 211
Self-fulfilling prophecy, 217
Separation. *See* Segregation
*Serrano II* (1976), 276
*Serrano v. Priest* (1971), 275–276
Sex. *See* Gender
Shanker, Albert, 12, 18, 39, 44, 52, 93, 95–96, 322
Shulman, Lee, 46–47, 77, 105, 111
Sixteenth-section lands, 143

Sizer, Theodore R., 203–204, 290–291, 300
Smith-Hughes Act (1917), 166
Smith, Mortimer, 186
*Smith v. Board of School Commissioners of Mobile County* (1987), 327–328
Soar, Robert S., 44
Social capital, 323–324
Social class, 210–218
 common school reform and, 142, 151–152
 critical theory, postmodernism, and, 141, 199–200
 educational finance and, 274–279
 equal educational opportunities and, 151–153, 209
 ethnicity and, 219, 241
 gender and, 210, 230–231, 235, 241
 literacy skills and, 304
 of local and state school board members, 253–256, 258
 magnet schools and, 229
 private schools and, 143, 317–323, 333–338
 race and, 219, 230–231, 241
 test bias and, 74
*Social Composition of Boards of Education, The* (Counts), 56
*Social Frontier, The*, 196
Social reconstructionism, 196–197, 199, 211
Social workers, compared to teachers, 10, 33–34, 70, 102, 112
*Society and Education* (Levine and Havighurst), 210–211
*Souls of Black Folk, The* (DuBois), 161–162
Soviet Union (USSR), 186–187, 264
Special education. *See* Disability, of students, of teachers; Students, disabled, gifted
Spring, Joel, 267
Sputnik I, 186, 188, 264, 267
*Stand and Deliver,* 271
Stanford Achievement Test, 289, 294
State boards of education, 251, 256–260. *See also* State politics of education
State departments of education, 251, 257–260
State governors, 202, 224, 256–262, 269, 271
State legislatures, 146–147, 224, 256–262, 277–278, 301, 331
*State [of Nebraska] v. Faith Baptist Church* (1981), 331
State politics of education, 249–250, 256–262. *See also* Educational finance
 educational reform and, 17, 29–30, 49–50, 63–64, 66–69, 107–109, 267–268
 historical trends, 141, 144–152, 162, 165–166, 274–276
 local school boards and, 95, 250–251
 private schools and, 329–338
 segregation and, 222–226
 teacher autonomy and, 29–30, 106–109
 teacher education and certification and, 18–20, 58, 63–69, 71–72, 107–109, 145–147, 251
 teacher job market and, 19–20
 teacher salaries and, 17, 29–30, 36

 teacher organizations and, 95–102, 107–109
 teacher tenure and, 121
 teacher testing and, 71–72, 75, 272
Students
 affluent, 141–143, 152, 182, 211–214, 319, 321. *See also* Social class
 "at-risk," 167, 266, 292, 294
 demographic trends, 7, 13–16, 210, 219–220, 317–320
 disabled, 69, 127, 166–167, 264–265, 275, 292, 319
 dropouts, 109, 151–152, 167–168, 213, 220–223, 269, 271, 290, 302, 307, 322–323
 female, 142, 144, 146, 151–152, 155. *See also* Gender
 gifted, 182, 186
 immigrant, 150–152, 155–158, 272, 317
 male, 142, 146, 151–152, 231. *See also* Gender
 middle-class, 82, 152, 201, 212–214, 272, 319, 337. *See also* Social class
 minority, 20, 69, 79, 92, 110, 183, 197, 201, 272, 275, 289–290, 292, 304, 307, 319–320, 333, 336–337. *See also* African Americans; Asian Americans; Hispanic Americans; Native Americans
 poor, 7, 20, 69, 92, 110, 147, 153, 183, 197, 201, 210, 216–217, 264–265, 272, 275, 289–290, 292, 304, 307, 317, 321, 333, 336–337. *See also* Social class
 right to privacy, 126–127
 single-parent, 210, 324
 upper-class, 152, 212–214. *See also* Social class
 white, 82, 143, 147, 151–152, 201, 220–223, 226, 319–320, 337. *See also* Race
 working-class, 152, 209, 212–215, 218, 319, 321. *See also* Social class
*Subtle Danger, The* (Venezky, Kaestle, and Sum), 304
Suburban schools
 community power structure, 251
 educational finance, 201–202, 273–275
 gangs, 215
 National Education Association and, 91
 in 1950s and 1960s, 187, 326
 private, 317–318, 334
 segregation, 201–202, 228
 teachers, 7, 21, 36, 91
Superintendents, 11, 250–253, 256–258, 294–296, 298–299

"Talented tenth," 159
Taxes and taxation. *See also* Educational finance
 district schools and, 142
 educational reform and, 146–147, 151, 261–262, 273–276, 278
 local property, 202, 273–276
 New Federalism and, 266
 state, 278
 teacher organizations and, 13, 101
Teacher education and certification
 enrollment, 17–18

Teacher education and certification (*continued*)
   historical development, 57–58, 145–147, 151, 162
   liberal education, 60–61, 74
   nontraditional programs, 18–19, 59, 63–69,
      80–81, 104
   *Paideia Proposal* and, 183
   private schools and, 329–331
   professional education, 60, 62–64, 67, 75–77
   regional certification, 21–22
   standards, 16–20, 59, 64, 69–82, 103–104,
      107–109, 112–113, 186–187, 257, 259, 262.
      *See also* National Board for Professional
      Teaching Standards; Professional standards
      boards; Teachers, academic ability, competency,
      literacy skills, minority; Teacher testing
   teaching field, 60–62, 64, 75, 77
Teacher evaluation, 27, 35, 40–47. *See also*
      Accountability; Merit pay; Teacher testing
   by administrators, 40–42, 44–45, 47, 109, 111,
      124, 164
   career ladders and, 49–50
   collective bargaining and, 111–112
   educational malpractice and, 128
   by peers, 49–50, 108–109, 111, 124
   by student test scores, 48, 52, 108, 111, 128
"Teacher Is a Cheater" (CBS), 294
Teacher organizations, 89–102. *See also* American
      Federation of Teachers; National Education
      Association
   educational choice and, 338
   educational politics and, 12, 30, 196, 252
   educational reform and, 92
   historical development, 164–165
   job market and, 13, 18, 19
   liability insurance and, 94, 125
   merit pay and, 35, 39–44, 48, 51–52, 92
   teacher salaries and, 30, 33, 35, 37–39, 89–90,
      92–93, 95–96, 112–113, 120
   teacher tenure and, 120–121, 165
Teacher professionalism, 10–11, 102–113. *See also*
      Teacher organizations
   collective bargaining and, 96–97
   teacher attitudes and, 33
   teacher education and certification and, 78, 330
   teacher evaluation and, 47, 50
   teacher job market and, 22
   measurement-driven curriculum and, 11, 287,
      291–292
   "unprofessional conduct," 121–122
Teachers
   academic ability, 3–4, 7–8, 57–60, 64, 69–73
   autonomy, 10–12, 30, 102, 105–113, 204, 287,
      290–291, 296, 309. *See also* Teacher
      professionalism
   burnouts, 3, 10–11, 109
   competency, 7–8, 57–59, 64, 69–73, 121–122,
      147, 288
   concern for students, 3–10, 217
   contracts, 49, 96–97, 109–112, 120
   demographic characteristics, 6–7, 12, 31–33,
      79–80, 93, 110, 146, 164, 238

   dismissal, 121–123, 165
   dissent, rights to, 131–133
   dropouts, 10–12
   due process, rights to, 123–124
   educational malpractice, 128–129
   employment, 120–124
   expression, rights of, 121–122, 129–134
   intervenor, 51, 110–112
   job market, 13–22
   job satisfaction, 8–13
   lead, 35, 47, 49, 51–52, 110–111
   liability, 124–129
   literacy skills, 7, 13, 71–73, 77
   mentor, 49, 51, 59, 68, 110
   minority, 7, 22, 32, 35, 59, 68, 70–74, 78–80
   "moonlighting," 5, 32
   negligence, 124–125, 128–129
   personal appearance, 133
   political involvement, 123, 133–134
   private life, 122, 134
   public attitudes toward, 4, 11
   recruitment, 8, 22, 30, 80–81
   self-esteem, 10–12
   sexual preference, 122, 134
   standards for students, 7, 147, 203, 217, 229,
      288–290
   turnover rate, 12, 16, 37–38
   working conditions, 8, 11–13, 19, 90, 92–93,
      95–96, 112–113, 203–204, 290–291, 302
Teachers College, Columbia University, 185, 190,
   194–196
*Teachers and the Law* (Fischer, Schimmel, and
      Kelly), 124
Teacher salaries, 27–53
   contracts and, 95–98, 110–112
   discrimination and, 167
   educational finance and, 259, 273
   equalization campaigns, 167
   job market and, 13, 16, 19
   job satisfaction and, 10–12
   motives for teaching and, 4
   professionalism and, 108, 112–113
   state politics of education and, 259, 262, 273
   teacher organizations and, 89–90, 92–93, 95–96,
      112–113
   teacher recruitment and, 8, 95, 147
   women's work and, 5
*Teachers for Our Nation's Schools* (Goodlad), 80–82
Teacher strikes, 89, 96, 98–99, 249
Teacher tenure, 36, 38–39, 49, 120–121, 130, 165
Teacher testing, 69–82. *See also* Teacher evaluation;
      Teachers, minority
   merit pay and, 40–43
   National Board for Professional Teaching
      Standards and, 104–105
   nontraditional teacher education programs and,
      67
   private schools and, 331
   teacher organizations and, 92, 272
   state politics of education and, 259–261, 272
Teach for America, 20

Teaching
  extrinsic rewards, 10–11. *See also* Teacher salaries
  intrinsic rewards, 3–7
  job advantages, 3–5
  as men's work, 5, 142. *See also* Gender
  motives for, 3–8
  social value, 3–4
  as women's work, 5–6, 33–34, 70–71, 112, 146, 164. *See also* Gender
Technology, 46–47, 77, 187, 202, 264, 278. *See also* Computers and computer science
Tennessee, career ladder in, 49–50
Testing, standardized, of students, 287–300. *See also* Curriculum, measurement-driven
  accountability and, 48, 52, 108, 111, 128, 188–189, 204, 277
  African-American students, 163, 220, 293
  Asian-Amerian students, 222–223
  educational malpractice and, 128–129
  educational philosophies and theories and, 184–185, 188–191, 202, 204
  effective schools and, 229
  excellence in education and, 258–261
  gender differences, 235, 239–240
  Hispanic-American students, 221, 293
  historical trends, 163
  minimum competency, 106, 185, 188, 259–261, 271, 303
  national system of, 189–191, 204, 270–271, 306, 308
  Native American students, 223
  social class differences, 163
  teacher autonomy and, 11, 81, 204, 308–309
  teacher organizations and, 92
Testing, standardized, of teachers. *See* Teacher testing
Texas, teacher education reform in, 66–67
Thompson, Tommy, 262
*Time for Results* (National Governors' Association), 261
Title I. *See* Elementary and Secondary Education Act (1965)
Title IX. *See* Education Amendments (1972)
*Tomorrow's Teachers* (Holmes Group), 51–53, 60, 64–66
Tracking, 152–153, 158, 181, 187, 209, 212–218, 230–231, 307
Tucker, Marc, 297, 299
Tuition tax credits, 334–336. *See also* Educational choice
Tyack, David, 164

*Up from Slavery* (Washington), 159
Urbanization, 144–145, 153
Urban schools
  American Federation of Teachers and, 11, 51–52, 91, 96–97, 109
  community power structure, 251

educational finance, 201–202, 266, 273–275
gangs, 215
historical development, 144–146, 150–152, 157–158, 163–165
private, 226, 317–318, 334
segregation, 166–167, 201–202, 226, 228–230
teachers, 7, 11, 21, 36, 51–52, 91, 96–97, 109, 121, 201
Urbanski, Adam, 109–112
U.S. Congress, 249, 263–267, 270. *See also* Federal politics of education
  educational choice and, 334–336
  National Defense Education Act (1958) and, 187
  national testing system and, 293–294, 298
  sixteenth-section lands and, 143
  teacher organizations and, 99–102, 279
  voting rights and, 255
U.S. Department of Education, 265, 267–269. *See also* Federal politics of education
  private school classifications, 318–319
  teacher supply and demand statistics, 18
  "wall chart" of state statistics, 290

Values
  clarification, 179, 198
  functional and value communities, 323
  human capital and social capital, 323
  religious versus secular, 198, 324, 326–329
  traditional, 186, 302
Vermont, curriculum reform in, 298–299
Vocational education
  African-American students, 159–161
  historical development, 152–153, 156, 158, 168, 194, 197, 212
  philosophies and theories of education and, 182, 184–185, 194, 197
  Title IX and, 238–239
  tracking, 163, 187, 212, 216–218, 320
Voting Rights Act (1965), 255
Vouchers, educational, 334–336, 338. *See also* Educational choice

Warner, W. Lloyd, 211–212
War on Poverty, 264–265
Washington, Booker T., 154, 159–162
Washington, George, 144
Webster, Noah, 144
*We Must Take Charge* (Finn), 190–191, 302
*What Do Our 17-Year-Olds Know?* (Ravitch and Finn), 190, 304, 306–308
Whig Party, 148, 166
Whittle, Chris, 319
*Who Shall Be Educated* (Warner and associates), 211–212
"Why Do These Kids Love School?" (PBS), 201
Willard, Emma, 144
Wise, Arthur, 69
Women. *See* Gender